£20

One Public

One Public

New York's Public Theater in the Era of Oskar Eustis

Kevin Landis

methuen | drama
LONDON • NEW YORK • OXFORD • NEW DELHI • SYDNEY

METHUEN DRAMA
Bloomsbury Publishing Plc
50 Bedford Square, London, WC1B 3DP, UK
1385 Broadway, New York, NY 10018, USA
29 Earlsfort Terrace, Dublin 2, Ireland

BLOOMSBURY, METHUEN DRAMA and the Methuen Drama logo are trademarks of Bloomsbury Publishing Plc

First published in Great Britain 2023

Copyright © Kevin Landis, 2023

Kevin Landis has asserted his right under the Copyright, Designs and Patents Act, 1988, to be identified as author of this work.

For legal purposes the Acknowledgments on p. ix constitute an extension of this copyright page.

Cover design and illustration by Rebecca Heselton

All rights reserved. No part of this publication may be reproduced or transmitted in any form or by any means, electronic or mechanical, including photocopying, recording, or any information storage or retrieval system, without prior permission in writing from the publishers.

Bloomsbury Publishing Plc does not have any control over, or responsibility for, any third-party websites referred to or in this book. All internet addresses given in this book were correct at the time of going to press. The author and publisher regret any inconvenience caused if addresses have changed or sites have ceased to exist, but can accept no responsibility for any such changes.

A catalogue record for this book is available from the British Library.

A catalog record for this book is available from the Library of Congress.

ISBN: HB: 978-1-3502-8346-6
ePDF: 978-1-3502-8348-0
eBook: 978-1-3502-8347-3

Typeset by Newgen KnowledgeWorks Pvt. Ltd., Chennai, India
Printed and bound in Great Britain

To find out more about our authors and books visit www.bloomsbury.com and sign up for our newsletters.

To my parents, for their loving support of me and their excitement about theater

CONTENTS

Acknowledgments ix

Introduction 1

1 One Public 11

The Park

2 Delacorte Summers 41

3 Under the Lights 63

Interlude: Kenny Leon and Beowulf Boritt 93

Lafayette

4 Four Twenty-Five 103

5 Coming Home 131

Interlude: Justin Vivian Bond and Bridget Everett 159

Broadway "Bound"

6 Building the Disco 169

7 Listen to Me 189

Interlude: Lin-Manuel Miranda 210

To the People

8 Courting Controversy 221

9 The American Neighborhood 245

Interlude: Kwame Kwei-Armah 269

Hope

10 Rebirth 279

Epilogue: Oskar Eustis 287

Notes and Sources 297
Index 305

ACKNOWLEDGMENTS

Writing a book about artists in the height of their artistic creation is a daunting task. One wishes to be as accurate as possible while also recognizing the vulnerability any artist feels in the exposure of themselves that their art demands. For that reason, I wish to thank the scores of people I have interviewed and consulted in the creation of this book. I do my best to capture the essence of your stories. Forgive me when you disagree.

Oskar Eustis allowed me access to The Public Theater knowing that I would write about him, and would do so as fairly as possible. That, too, is risky and vulnerable. The chance to build an archive of oral histories has been a professional highlight of my life and has afforded me the heady space to indulge in countless stories about American theater. My thanks to Oskar for this trust.

Many thanks to the extraordinary editing team at Bloomsbury/Methuen: Sophie Beardsworth, Ian Buck, Sam Nicholls and Dom O'Hanlon. To the people who probably do not even know how important they have been for me as I have tackled this work, I appreciate you: Kenneth Pickering, Andrew Kircher, Ciara Murphy, Max Shulman, Teresa Meadows, Mark Gordon, and Jessica Slaght. To my colleagues at the University of Colorado, Colorado Springs, and to my family, thank you for your patience.

One Public mostly comprises the interviews that I have done over several years, and from my own observations within the theater. I have decided not to footnote every interview quotation in the book, so as not to disrupt the flow of the story. All quotes not officially attributed in footnoted form come from interviews with me, and are listed at the end of the book. Where it feels that the date of the interview is important to its context, I indicate that in the text.

Introduction

On the wall in the offices of the Lafayette headquarters of The Public Theater in New York, there is a poster that reads, "Artists are a force for change, culture belongs to everyone, we are one public." Its placement, near the staircase that leads to the administrative offices, is a continual reminder to the staff of the goals of the company. Theater is not simply "razzle dazzle," to use the late founder Joseph Papp's words. It exists to transform and unite communities; the company was pointedly founded on political and social grounds. That it is famous for and survived turbulent times because of a mega hit called *A Chorus Line* is merely an ironic happenstance, albeit an utterly transformative happenstance. Several decades after that production, The Public regained international attention and acclaim for *Hamilton*, a phenom of a show that pointedly asserted that American history belonged to all ethnicities, all gender identities, to *everyone*. While several iconic productions define the history of the Theater (*Hair, A Chorus Line, The Pirates of Penzance, Bring in 'da Noise, Bring in 'da Funk, Caroline, or Change, Fun Home, Hamilton*), it is the everyday management choices and the myriad other productions and events that it sponsors that illuminate the ethos of the company.

This book explores the contemporary Public Theater, and outlines how the company, now known internationally for Broadway hits, tries to maintain the founding principles that are proudly displayed on the walls. The Public is often referred to as the American "de-facto national theater," and this study will examine that title and endeavor to uncover how national stories find a voice inside the doors of its Astor Place headquarters, on the Central Park stage, and, increasingly, in mobile productions that travel to underserved communities in New York and around the country. Through success, failures, and controversy, the stature of The Public grew over the past twenty years, alongside cultural and social shifts, political transitions, a hurricane, a pandemic, and a racial reckoning. At the center of *this* story is the current artistic director, Oskar Eustis. His presence as a statesman for inclusivity in American art now rivals that of the founder of the company in the eyes of many of The Public's supporters and enthusiasts. But the story is far more than just Eustis, and far more complex than a telling of the times of a larger-than-life leader. The promise of The Public Theater—the inclusivity, the access, the democracy, the leftist politics—makes for a complex stew of contradiction, where triumphs *and* missteps are all the more pronounced because of the lofty goals of the company.

The biggest challenge for The Public Theater is its name. It's a promise that holds the company to an incredibly high standard.

At the outset, a note on the development and creation of this book is perhaps apt. Over twenty years ago, Oskar Eustis was a professor of mine in the graduate theater program at Brown University. We remained close over time and several years ago I unofficially moved into the offices at the Lafayette Street headquarters as a "scholar in residence." On sabbatical from the University of Colorado, I was invited to be there, to use the place as a theater think tank of sorts and work on whatever projects I thought important to pursue. I noticed a lack of archival recording of the contemporary Public, and so decided to start interviewing some of the legions of artists who have made The Public a cultural touchstone in New York and indeed the entire country over Eustis's tenure. This has been blissful and fulfilling work as it has allowed me to learn from and record the stories of so many people who have had immeasurable impact on American cultural life. I continue the work to this day—identifying actors, designers, producers, and directors and inviting them to sit down with me over a cup of coffee and talk about their experiences at The Public Theater. These interviews have been collected for an oral history archive that will be, when I am finished with my writing, placed in a library and preserved.

I quickly realized that the collection was a rich documentation of Eustis's years as artistic director and that a synthesis of the interviews, combined with reflections from my years embedded in the company, could make for an important document about The Public. While there are a couple of superb books about Papp and his importance to the American theater, little yet has been written about Eustis's imprint on the company. As of this writing, he is entering his seventeenth year and is under contract for at least six more. It's a remarkable statement of trust that will see Eustis approach a tenure as consequential as that of Joe Papp.

Free for All: Joe Papp, The Public, and the Greatest Theater Story Ever Told, Kenneth Turan's oral history account of the Papp days, is perhaps the most well-known book regarding that history, and is expansive about the tenure of the founder and original producer of The Public and the New York Shakespeare Festival. *One Public* is the first book written about Oskar Eustis and the first to fully commit to exploring the methodologies of many of the various divisions of the company. It will likely not be the last, since Eustis and The Public are changing the face of the American theater in ways still being understood, unpacked, and critiqued.

While Turan effectively created a document of elegantly woven together interviews of Papp-era artists, the intention here is to use my observations within and without the company as a foundation of a narrative of the last twenty years of the theater. In that way, this book is an exploration of the archive that I have developed. I have been given access to the company and the artists affiliated with it, and while I rely heavily on the words of others, I do not shy away from allowing the story to flow with first-person accounting and personal assessment fueled by my close understanding of how things work at The Public. While most people have spoken to me on the record, others have chosen to speak to me on background. This has been especially true in the wake of the extraordinary tension, pain, and sadness brought to the fore by the racial reckoning at The Public and in American theater. I do my game best to create an accurate and lively story about how The Public operates, all the while being careful of the careers and reputations of those who make the company work. Through all, I remain a professor of theater, far away from the lights of Broadway, and thus hopefully may offer a perspective that goes beyond the inside access that I have had. Some of the most colorful interviews, stories, and casual conversations come from the myriad staff members, technicians, designers, and board members that I have intersected with. Their commentary makes up the backbone of the manuscript and the ideas that guide the story, even if I do not always quote them directly.

While Eustis does embody the contemporary Public, hackles inevitably rise from those who rightly want JoAnne Akalaitis and George C. Wolfe, the other two artistic directors, to have their due. They should, they have, and they will, both in the pages of this book and elsewhere. However, as I write this, I am keenly aware that there are many who validly worry that the tenures of those great artists (especially Wolfe, who ran the company for eleven years) are being ignored or pushed aside to tell an easier story—Oskar Eustis is the heir of the legendary Joseph Papp. In fact, in the summer of 2020, the sidelining of Wolfe's legacy was one point in a list of concerns brought by many members of the staff to the leadership. The implications are deep and complex, especially when noting that it is a woman and a man of color who have not yet had their tenures unpacked. It's The Public. This is a problem.

The conundrum of how to address these two giants of American theater history has obsessed me throughout the writing process. Akalaitis, who ran The Public for one fraught year after the death of Papp, is one of America's most celebrated theater creators. An artist of impeccable precision and the founder of the legendary and historic experimental theater company Mabou Mines, she continues to direct, teach, and influence art around the world. Wolfe remains at the height of his artistic acuity. A staple at the Tony Awards as a director and producer of the highest degree, he was responsible during his tenure for *Bring in 'da Noise, Bring in 'da Funk*, *Topdog/Underdog*, *Caroline, or Change*, and other plays that have a permanent place in the American canon. His commitment to giving voice to African American experience on the stage is rivaled only by the likes of artists such as August Wilson and Suzan-Lori Parks.

Wolfe and Akalaitis need books dedicated to their work and there is no question that they will be studied for years to come. Wolfe, especially, is so central to The Public story that it is fair to say that it cannot be near complete until his biography is written. Under his ten years of leadership, he showed a dedication to musical development, extraordinary commitment to diverse voices, and the ingenuity to create a cabaret club within the walls of the institution, all the while supporting new work alongside classic retellings of Shakespeare. That Wolfe is not fully considered in this study points to several realities. First, my intent is to look at the Theater of the past twenty years and contextualize it within the politics and social realities of the current time. Second, my long association with Eustis makes me far more capable and authoritative in assessing and describing his tenure. Finally, the national recognition of The Public, and its financial success (pre-Covid) over the past ten years, has been unparalleled in the history of the company, with the possible exception of its run between 1975 and 1985. The conceit here is that the values of the contemporary Public Theater, the *original* morals and guiding principles espoused by its founder, are acutely expressed through the programming of Oskar Eustis. They are also challenged in an era of extreme wealth inequality, division, and deep conversations about equity and inclusivity at the highest levels of American theater.

The events of 2020 and 2021 have allowed me to refocus my views on this theater, just as theater companies around the country have had to take a hard look at their missions and values. The basic tenets of theater as espoused by The Public—radical inclusivity, community building, a left-liberal ethic—were necessarily brought into stark relief in a year that saw deep political division, a racial reckoning through protests and calls for systemic change, and a pandemic that made sharing the same space and the same air an impossibility. And yet, the research that I have collected in my years interviewing many of the members of The Public's extended family, I have found, holds up to the scrutiny of the moment. The fundamental challenges that were exacerbated by the events of the past couple of years have been present for a long time and perhaps were simply coming to an inflection.

And so, this book has two clear goals. On the one hand, it looks at the years of Eustis's tenure and builds a narrative about how the company operates, using specific plays and interviews with the people who created at the theater over the past two decades. On the other, the study looks at the social, financial, and political challenges in American professional art creation, many that were highlighted by the events that began the third decade of the twenty-first century. The book assesses the promise of The

Public and the ways it is keeping up (or not) with those values. And in that, the book puts the microscope up to American theater writ large.

Chapter 1 introduces The Public Theater's history by offering glimpses into the founding principles of Joseph Papp and some of the stories of those early days—stories that are now legendary and deserve retellings. The framing of the contemporary Public comes in its history and through the words of Papp, Eustis, and some of the many well-known artists who have worked for the company over the decades.

"The Park," the first section of *One Public,* is devoted to Shakespeare, since he is the author upon which all things at The Public are built and linked to the founding and illustrious history of the company. The story unfolds with a look at the operation and legacy of Shakespeare in the Park through the creative process of some of the noteworthy productions during Eustis's tenure. For example, Meryl Streep's performance in *Mother Courage,* Diane Paulus's revival of *Hair,* Daniel Sullivan's acclaimed *The Merchant of Venice,* starring Al Pacino, and Eustis's 2017 polemic *Julius Caesar* are positioned as examples of the power of the Central Park in the redevelopment of classic work, and the ability of The Public to tie (or attempt to tie) its plays to the political and social structures of the moment.

The second section, "Lafayette," turns its attention toward the productions that develop at the downtown headquarters of The Public near Astor Place in the East Village. "Four Twenty-Five" more broadly explores how the seed of an idea is nurtured at the East Village headquarters and how it subsequently develops and evolves. Through interviews with production staff, the chapter uncovers the various avenues that new work development takes. Specifically, Eustis discusses his own creative process and outlines his methods of dramaturgy at the theater. Eustis is known as the most prominent dramaturg in America, and that process will be explored and considered by the many people who act as theatrical midwives of The Public.

"Coming Home" looks at the specifics of several of the plays that have had success in the theaters of 425 Lafayette. "The Gabriels," a cycle of three plays written by Richard Nelson, tracked the life of one family over the course of three nights during the 2016 election year. Nelson was given three opening nights and wrote his plays—*Hungry,* *What Did You Expect?*, and *Women of a Certain Age*—with a deadline of 3:00 p.m. on those evenings, assuring an electricity and "present-ness" that reflected an American national consciousness in relation to the tumultuous presidential election. After the theater shut down during the Covid-19 pandemic, it was Nelson who Eustis turned to, to help develop an entirely new type of Zoom-based theater to deal with the crisis.

Suzan-Lori Parks's 2019 *White Noise* is the subject of an extended discussion with the author and the production's director. Her position as a master writer chair underscores the dedicated relationship The Public has with development of new work from its inception. The play is contextualized alongside her other major success of the past decade, *Father Comes Home from the Wars*. Underscored, too, is The Public's commitment to stories about class stratification in the United States. Lynn Nottage's *Sweat* centered on the intersection of race, class, and the dissolution of the American dream in Reading, Pennsylvania. The focus on Nelson, Nottage, and Parks over many years places in context several of the passions and goals of Eustis's tenure.

One of the most compelling aspects of The Public story during the Eustis years has been the expansion of its programming—from the plays of the season, to 365 days' worth of productions at Joe's Pub (the cabaret club on the first floor), to artist talks and community conversations, to a Shakespeare educational division, to national and international initiatives focused on community building. The enormity of the output by 2019 was a strain on the entire operation but perhaps demonstrated how smaller, special artistic projects might be the saving grace of a theater bloated with content and, eventually, facing down existentially difficult times. Joe's Pub, in part because of the enormity of its programming, will be discussed relative to other parts of the company, not in its own section. It is important to note that, while fully part of The Public Theater family, the Pub operates in many ways independently and is run on a completely different schedule and process than anything else in the building. It will inevitably be the subject of an entire book at some point in the future.

The third part of the book, "Broadway 'Bound,'" looks at the delicate negotiations and the politics that are in play when transferring work from The Public to one of the forty-one Broadway houses. What makes a hip-hop musical about a treasury secretary (*Hamilton*), or an intimate look at a young lesbian growing up in 1980s Pennsylvania (*Fun Home*), or a play about a group of women living in the midst of the Liberian Civil War (*Eclipsed*) uptown Tony favorites, while a musical like *Here Lies Love*, a rock concert about Imelda Marcos by the inimitable David Byrne, has to settle for rave reviews and no broader uptown accolades? "Building the Disco" is a detailed exploration of the Byrne extravaganza at the LuEsther Hall with interviews from Byrne himself, as well as Eustis, director Alex Timbers, and production lead Ruthie Ann Miles.

"Listen to Me" focuses attention on *Fun Home*, one of the most transformative and important productions in The Public's history. It is here that one sees a full development of a show, through a glimmer in one artist's eye, through a laboratory process, and finally to a Broadway stage. *Hamilton* is used as a case study on the development of scenography, and its costume designer Paul Tazewell and set designer David Korins discuss the challenges of transfer vis-à-vis the technicalities of design. Through all, discussion revolves around the conundrum that The Public has faced since the premiere of *Hair* in 1967: How does commercial success affect and alter an image of inclusivity, social justice, and grassroots creation?

The final part of the book, "To the People," highlights what has been a through line of the story and what will inevitably be a focus of the future of the company and Eustis's career. "Courting Controversy" addresses The Public Theater's engagement with and connection to the furthering and deepening of social, racial, economic, and inclusive commitments within the art form, and confronting the almost continual strain and backlash that comes with that promise. The protests following the murder of George Floyd in 2020 ripped across America and further heightened The Public's ongoing conversation about inequity and its role in highlighting anti-racist policies and procedure, and shone a light on the flaws within the organization and New York theater writ large. The chapter focuses on the ways that the company faced crises over the tenure of Oskar Eustis, and a case study analysis of the controversial productions of Michael Friedman and Alex Timbers's *Bloody Bloody Andrew Jackson* and Dan Collins's *Southern Comfort* rounds out that inquiry.

In the wake of the transformational tidal shift of the Covid crisis and its effect on live performance, The Public now sees itself even more strongly as a community organizer. "The American Neighborhood" looks at those branches of often Shakespeare-inspired work that have developed in the past ten years. The Mobile Unit, modeled after the original Papp productions on the back of his flatbed truck, takes Shakespeare directly to "the people," performing fully mounted productions in shelters, churches, prisons, and community centers around New York City. Public Works, created by Lear deBessonet and now helmed by Laurie Woolery, directly partners with organizations throughout the five boroughs, providing classes and development workshops, all leading to an enormous pageant in Central Park at the end of the summer season.

These programs are the models of the future of theater and are already seeing adoption around the country and even from the National Theatre of London. The interest in expanding these offerings to make them the national face of The Public is described and challenged as it raises the complexities of an organization presenting itself as a beacon of "social good," which can easily, without great care, border on the culturally hegemonic. One is thus required to interrogate the "culture belongs to everyone" mantra by asking, "what culture?" "by whom?" and most critically, "for whom?" The perceived need for pageant style performance, Eustis believes, arises out of a specific type of social anxiety related to class inequality. Observations of the Mobile's *Summer of Joy!* and *Romeo and Juliet* and the recent summer pageants in Central Park, including the 2019 *Hercules* extravaganza, are used to understand the successes and failures of the various modes of Shakespeare producing. Further, the pandemic and its extraordinary effect on American theater will be looked at through the lens of social organization and the new digital platforms and technology-based "solutions" to outreach.

The idea of an "American National Theater" amid a capitalist/socialist dialectic rounds out the section on The Public's influence nationally and acts, too, as a coda for the book. "Rebirth" tracks The Public Theater's trajectory and reassessments of how theater is made in America. A study that began with a broad look at The Public, its history and leadership, to its roots in Shakespeare in New York and then to its commitment to new work, and finally to national influences, concludes with a last chapter that looks at possible ways forward during troubling times. The Covid pandemic and racial reckoning acted as litmus tests of sorts for a company often caught in the middle of its "to the people" ethos and the stark reality of uncertain economic forces. What will leadership in American theater look like in the near future and how has Eustis's career at The Public transformed the theater? While I cannot make solid predictions, this part hopefully will give us questions to ask and trends to watch.

What sort of a company can produce *Hamilton* and *Fun Home* in successive years, win back-to-back Pulitzers (*Hamilton* and *Sweat*), while running seven theaters and multiple programs, a cabaret club (Joe's Pub), a yearly festival of new work (Under the Radar), a mobile Shakespeare company that delivers plays to the five boroughs of New York (Mobile Unit), a community theater education and performance collaboration (Public Works), a talk series (Public Forum), a Broadway funneling wing (Public Theater Productions), and a Shakespeare think tank (Public Shakespeare Initiative) in addition to developing artists and engaging with university residencies? Oskar Eustis's Public, modeled after the one created by Papp, was an institution that was humming and, at times, bursting at the seams.

And then, for eighteen months, *it all went away*.

What are the founding principles that stay? What economic factors persist despite a changing social fabric? What happens next? The irony is that a company run on the socialist ideals of its founder and its current leader is now a corporation no matter how you look at it, where the artistic director is chastised for being perhaps too handsomely paid. And in the midst of that, the placement of "corporation" within the contemporary artistic world is now more complicated. Chay Yew, the former artistic director of Victory Gardens Theater in Chicago, a partner organization to The Public, perfectly reflects this conundrum:

> What Oskar did ... is to bring back some of the producorial muscle that Joe Papp may have had and amplified it with probably more of a—which is the irony for a socialist—a more capitalist bent on creating art. To ensure that the coffer is being replenished so that he can do the art that he needs to do at The Public Theater. So, in a very interesting sort of a way, Oskar is being entrepreneurial ... Oskar is Vietnam, Oskar is China. They are still communist. But he has found a way to say, "we can be capitalist too."

There is a book in Oskar Eustis's office that chronicles the National Theatre of London. When I first saw Daniel Rosenthal's 800-page epic, I assured myself and Eustis that I had no desire to create something similar. *The*

National Theatre Story is extraordinary, an exhaustive history of a cultural barrier-breaker. The Public Theater, in many ways, fits that mold in America, but my effort over the past several years and into the future is to capture the *spirit* of the company, and actually resist a definitive history. By the time these words are read, The Public will have produced scores more plays—some brilliant, others that miss the mark. The world will lurch through a pandemic, international conflict, new presidents, and cultural leaders. Together, the stories told over the following pages will ideally allow you to get a *sense*, through the words of the people I have chronicled in my oral history archive, of how the theater is operated and how ideas develop. To paint that picture, I have had to decide on several specific examples and productions in each part, which necessarily means I have left out many, many more that could easily go in any of the other versions of this book that continue to dance in my mind. Where possible, I have selected plays and cultural events that I have had the opportunity to witness firsthand, that moved me in some way. While I focus on directors, composers, playwrights, and producers, artists from across the organization and artistic practices are considered. As one must do when having to be artistically choosy, I try to be clear about my own biases, open minded about contradictory opinions, and honest about the fact that the future of theater is always-already uncertain. In fact, that is what makes it exciting; it both grows with and reflects its society.

I am indebted to the people of The Public Theater. When I sit in the offices at Lafayette, the staff knows that I write about their work and, therefore, their livelihoods. I am keenly aware of the need for artists to create without the fear of a "tell-all" book or gossipy article. That is never my intention in these pages, though I hope many of the anecdotes are lively, and often entertaining, peeks behind the scenes of American theater at the highest level. While it will be clear that I admire the company, Eustis et al. knew I was not intending to write a "palace biography." Where necessary, I point to places where the Theater falls short of its intended goals or loses step with its mission. On the other hand, it is important to write upfront: I admire The Public Theater, its mission, and its artistic director. I hope to encourage the reader, theater enthusiasts, theater practitioners, and theater scholars to examine a famed cultural institution to understand and perhaps apply the lessons gleaned.

Through all, in addition to being a scholar, I too am a lover of theater and approach this as an opportunity to illuminate the power of a unified artistic community in the creation of art and the edification and betterment of a society, with the power of one public.

1

One Public

FIGURE 1.1 *425 Lafayette. Courtesy Kevin Landis.*

One spring morning, several members of The Public Theater staff were invited to the large conference room on the second floor of the Astor Place headquarters of the famed New York City institution. The email came from the office of the artistic director, Oskar Eustis. It would be a quick meeting, but one that Eustis believed was immediately necessary. An article had recently appeared in a reputable theater publication that used Aristotle's *Poetics*, the fourth-century BC treatise on theater, as a foundation for a contemporary dramatic analysis. As a lover of dramatic theory, Eustis was concerned with what he read. It misinterpreted the theory, he believed, and he wanted to gather some of his staff to piece together why it bothered him so much. This sort of theoretical deconstruction is often done in academic circles, in college classes, and occasionally in the conference rooms of some theater companies. As a professor on sabbatical at The Public that year, I sat in on the meeting.

While the exact content of our beef that day is lost to my memory, the passions engaged around the table are not. It was electric. Eustis challenged his colleagues to assess the argumentation, to pull apart why and how the elegant Aristotelian theory was here rendered toothless, bland, and even incomprehensible. Opinions were free flowing, incredulity abounded, voices were raised, and some even stood up for the problematic reasoning, finding new ways to assess the author's intention. As I sat there, not only as visiting member of the company but also as a quiet theater anthropologist taking it in, I allowed my mind to contextualize the moment. Here we sat in a conference room in New York's East Village, at the headquarters of a theater company that at that time had three shows running on Broadway, several other plays preparing for openings, and myriad musical performances scheduled at the cabaret venue downstairs.[1] The artistic director, who even by that time was one of the biggest names in American theater, was overseeing a midday debate about an ancient Greek philosopher. I allowed myself to wonder, "What's the catch? Does this have any larger consequence?"

I did not, however, linger on that thought too long, since I knew Eustis well. I met him at Brown University twenty years before in a dramaturgy class, back when he was the artistic director of Trinity Repertory Company in Providence, Rhode Island. Not only did a conversation like this have consequence and relevance, but it was also of central importance to him. To engage in a "theater of ideas," as he puts it, is an important need for an arts organization such as The Public. In the theater press, Eustis is often referred to as the greatest dramaturg in America, a calling that he essentially reinvented during his time helping craft and hone Tony Kushner's epic *Angels in America* in the early 1990s. A dramaturg in the Eustis model is the right hand of the playwright and director, a literary eye who assesses the arc of the play, the character development, and the relevant research that

---

[1] *Hamilton, Fun Home,* and *Eclipsed* were all on Broadway at the time.

goes into delivering the work of art. Getting theater history and theory *right* is important to Eustis—he makes Aristotle, Plato, Brecht, and the others required reading in the many classes he teaches at New York University.

By the end of the meeting, as the lunch break had ended and passions had simmered down, we determined that Eustis would lead another mini class of sorts for the rest of the staff. A week later I received an email from Eustis's assistant. She told me that he wanted to know if I had a suggestion on a favorite translation of *The Poetics* and of Bertolt Brecht's *Short Organum for the Theatre*. The recommendations were to be sent to the entire staff in preparation for the upcoming meeting. Frantic, I fumbled through ideas in my mind, contacted some friends for suggestions, and sourced my library catalog. This was not what I expected when I came to The Public to help set up an oral history archive.

For the millions of theater enthusiasts who directly or indirectly know The Public Theater as the incubator of such works as *Hair, A Chorus Line, Bring in 'da Noise Bring in 'da Funk, Fun Home,* and *Hamilton*, the theater theory lesson in the conference room might seem an odd place to begin the story of the contemporary Public Theater and its now iconic artistic director. The commercial success that it has seen over the years, including sixty Tony Awards and a bevy of Drama Desk, Lortel, and Pulitzer Prizes, is an impressive façade for a company with humbler roots and dreams. Why have a debate about a deeply theoretical article in a building buzzing with activity, future plans, and general urgency? Because to not do so would run contrary to the philosophies of Joseph Papp, the theater's founder and one of the great artistic leaders of the twentieth century. He was an enthusiast, a ringmaster, a fighter, and perhaps *the* central fixture of New York theater producing for decades. Thirty years after his death, he continues to inspire adoration and also cast a shadow of influence on directors who have come after him. At the core of his beliefs was a social ethos that insisted on a theater that was at the center of democratic principles, a place of community unification, as well as a precinct of entertainment. Most of all, he wanted a theater that was made up of participants, performers, and audiences who represented the whole of their society, with no restrictions to access. In a recording created in 1988, Papp mused, "I never separated the theater from my origins, which were poor, and the need to reach people and make theater available."[2]

It is through this lens that I now see the debate in the conference room. Aristotle wrote of the theater that it reflects the community that watches the stories that it produces. He found that great drama affects a catharsis in the audience—an emotional and physical response that cleanses the senses, that allows the community to imagine and process personal and social challenges. Theater creators, thus, must understand the potential that their art has and the power that lies in their hands. Those values are at the heart

---

[2]Recording of Joseph Papp, August 25, 1988. Courtesy of Steven Cohen.

of the mission of The Public, and Eustis often reflects on the consequence on theatrical and social exchange. "It is no wonder," he often says, "that western democracy and theater were founded in the same decade and in the same city, Athens, Greece, 510–500 BC."

Two months after the "Aristotle meeting," at a glorious outdoor amphitheater in Central Park, a remarkable ceremony took place in the Delacorte Theater. It is a 2,000-seat playhouse near the Great Lawn that boasts the Frog Pond and the Belvedere Castle as a backdrop. Under those lights and in front of those seats, theater history over the past half-century has unfolded. Brought to life by people such as Sam Waterston, Cush Jumbo, Raúl Julia, James Earl Jones, Kevin Kline, Daniel Sullivan, and Diane Paulus, the Delacorte is the embodiment of American Shakespeare. It is there that Al Pacino dazzled audiences with his Shylock in a now legendary production of *The Merchant of Venice*. There that Meryl Streep toiled as the titular character in Bertolt Brecht's *Mother Courage*. On that stage, the great designer Ming Cho Lee erected some of the most memorable theater settings in New York's illustrious dramatic history. But on that particular night in mid-June, The Public Theater's *Public Forum* division hosted an immigration and naturalization ceremony. On the stage with Eustis was United States Secretary of Homeland Security Jeh Johnson, who administered the oath of American citizenship to forty individuals. The evening was punctuated by readings, songs, monologues—the stuff of theater, to be sure. But the climax was a naturalization ceremony.

The event could easily be read as exploitative, do-good-ism around something deeply personal; well-heeled theatergoers basking in the glow of something that felt morally right to them. In fact, it did feel awfully awkward. I attended and sat in those hollowed seats, uncomfortably watching soon-to-be American citizens take in elaborate song and dance, as they played a starring role in their own immigration saga. The experience takes on an even more problematic light, several years on, after an American presidency that crassly blended entertainment with consequential life events. Donald Trump was, in fact, roundly condemned several years later for overseeing an immigration ceremony in a video produced for his reelection bid.

To be fair, in the moment, the effort at the Delacorte seemed genuine, and those who created it did so out of deep belief in its righteousness. Indeed, one could see a company attending to its ideals of making the theater far more than simply the content of a two-hour play. It reflected a company that understood, even if occasionally inelegantly, that the Delacorte is magical, and that it can give extra symbolic weight to any event. Here was a theater company allowing social practice to merge with Shakespeare, to merge with song, to merge with a warm evening in Central Park. Aristotle, after all, wrote about theater being presented in an auditorium on the acropolis, a location that adjoined the agora, the place of gathering and community assembly. To be sure, those attending the immigration ceremony were Public Theater enthusiasts and it was likely not lost on many that the theater producing this evening was also responsible for the hit that was currently playing at the Richard Rogers Theater on Broadway, a musical that featured an immigrant from the Caribbean moving to the American colonies and helping found a nation; a musical written in the style of hip-hop and featuring a cast made up of actors of color. And not just incidentally, it was a gargantuan smash hit that was redefining what the theater could be in the twenty-first century and making The Public Theater tens of millions of dollars.

In these examples lies the great conundrum of the contemporary Public Theater: How can a company create art devoted to deep social justice and community building, and yet be sustained and made famous in large part due to deep pockets, elite venues, and huge spectacle?

It's a question that has been asked almost every day since the opening of *Hair* in 1967. It's the question that ties together all four of the artistic directors of The Public, their visions for the company, and also the struggles that they would have to face during their tenures.

That the company was founded on political and social grounds leads to a foundational question within these pages: How has Eustis taken those moral imperatives and adapted with contemporary times and ballooning economic pressures? Papp dealt with those conflicts and questions, too. The irony that The Public survived in its early years due to a major Broadway hit is rich. But even there, Papp saw the connection. "Even a show, which has been our greatest success and brought us the greatest amount of revenue and kept this theater alive, without which we probably would not have had a theater at this point, *A Chorus Line*, still fundamentally is making a social comment. It has to do with getting a job. I think part of its success is due so much to the strivings people have to get employment."[3]

For an audience leaving *A Chorus Line* humming "one, singular sensation" and wanting to take up dance lessons, the primary "takeaway" may not be the economic realities of being a struggling actor in 1970s America. But Papp always wanted to turn a conversation to social and economic justice. Eustis, too, rarely wavers in his public statements about a dogged need to tie all successes to the commitment of identifying and perpetuating a culture that belongs to everyone. Of his place relative to Papp and "artistic directing" more broadly, Eustis notes: "I believe that I am fortunate enough to have found an institution ... where what I believe and what I think the institution stands for are so tightly connected that most of the time I don't experience something as, 'This is me.' When I feel like I've done something really good I feel like *that's* The Public."

---

[3]Ibid.

The ideals and the conflicts and contradictions that they sometimes bring up are returned to again and again in conversations with the people who have made the company famous. Kevin Kline, an actor who was integral to the success of The Public in the 1980s before rising to film superstardom, recalls his friend Joe Papp's contribution to theater and the mantle that Eustis has picked up. "Oskar has been very steadfast, it seems to me, in continuing Joe's legacy, multi-racial, inclusive casting, modern plays, Shakespeare. ... This is multifarious, multifaceted, in the spirit that it's always been." From its inception, The Public was identified as a place where the New York community could come together. It is a theater that sees itself as that Greek agora, even if part of its mission includes favoring a nimble mobility—creating plays that move around New York City. While diversity is the goal, it has always had a history of broad-based activism, often with a deeply leftist political bent. Its founder was a socialist, after all. To punctuate his point about the theater's multifarious dedication to activism, Kline went on to reminisce about an incident that demonstrated Papp's devotion to the theater and social good:

> I got a call from Joe saying, "Hey, there's some squatters that they're trying to pull out of their housing. Can you come down? We're going to go protest this." I said, "What's the address? Okay." ... He was obviously very socially engaged in public issues, whether it's putting on the play of *The Normal Heart* or actually standing in front of the Helen Hayes Theater, in front of the bulldozers as they try to knock it down.

Steven Cohen, the associate producer of The Public and Papp's right hand, recalls the same incident from 1982 when the famed Helen Hayes theater was to be demolished (along with the Morosco, Bijou, Gaiety, and Astor Theaters) to make way for a large hotel. True to form, Papp was not going to let the theaters go without a public fight with the city—he would take a stand, and he would do it with some of the great artists in America:

> Joe was talking to about forty or fifty actors who all agreed to be arrested to protest the tearing down of the Helen Hayes and Morosco. ... Joe and I—and Gail [Gail Papp, his wife]—walked down the street. We walked to where the machines were going to tear down the theater. I went over to the commander of the police department for Midtown, and I said, "There's not going to be any problem here. Everyone's going to agree to be arrested. There'll be no display. Just tap them on their shoulder, and they'll just go into whatever vehicle you have. There'll be no problems." The commander said, "Great." Then Christopher Reeve came over to me. He said, "Steven, I can't get arrested." I said, "That's fine, Chris. No problem. This is all voluntary. Do you mind if I ask you why?" He said, "Superman cannot be arrested." "Christopher, you're absolutely right. You should go home. Thank you for coming here." So, he didn't get arrested.

That sort of activism is seen in the Eustis years (and with Wolfe and Akalaitis as well), albeit in more structured, theatrical ways: a naturalization ceremony, a Public-sponsored same-sex marriage on a Broadway stage, a controversial production of *Julius Caesar*, or any of the myriad town hall discussions on polemical topics. The Public continues to push and blur the line between entertainment precinct and political organization.

History Has Its Eyes

FIGURE 1.2 (a) *Founder Joseph Papp. Courtesy Ron Galella.* (b) *Artistic Director JoAnne Akalaitis. Courtesy Boston Globe.* (c) *Artistic Director George C. Wolfe. Courtesy Walter McBride.*

Well, they know it's for them because they bought the ticket with their time. They know it's for them because everything about it declares it's for them. It's free. It's public. That's why it's called The Public Theater.

—SAM WATERSTON

In Kenneth Turan's book *Free for All*, Joe Papp described the reason for the creation of The Public: "I wanted to bring Shakespeare to the people, that was the whole idea. I had to reach the thousands of people who lived and died in their neighborhoods."[4] To understand Papp, the organization, and the way it presents art to this day, it is necessary to understand the need to reach poor, non-white, and other underserved communities. That

---

[4] Quoted in Kenneth Turan and Joseph Papp, *Free for All: Joe Papp, The Public, and the Greatest Theater Story Ever Told* (New York: Knopf, 2009), p. 99.

drive—a drive his wife Gail Papp acknowledges was a matter of life and death for him—underscored much of the political tumult of the early years of The Public. The company began as roving productions, delivered by hardscrabble collections of dedicated theater makers to audiences often unfamiliar with Shakespeare. The stories of their first productions include harrowing tales of spectators yelling and throwing rocks at the inexperienced actors. Though creating superb theater was a goal of the perfectionist Papp, engagement was the key. The early work, by all accounts was deeply engaged.[5]

Papp, a young set hand at Columbia Broadcasting System (CBS), began what would become The Public Theater in 1954 with a singular focus on the creation of an American Shakespeare. His intent was to move around the five boroughs of New York with efficiency, to create a theater that looked and sounded like New Yorkers with an intended audience of people who could not get to the elite houses of Broadway. He was persistent in the face of financial and logistical odds, and that plucky idealism helped cement the "Shakespeare for all" mentality of the company.

If The Public now seems like a who's who of entertainment royalty—people like Streep, Kline, Parks, Ferguson, and Miranda—it obscures the compelling reality that many of those artists did not arrive at The Public as well-known figures. In those first years, the rough stages of Papp's New York Shakespeare Festival saw performances from George C. Scott, Colleen Dewhurst, James Earl Jones, and others. The history of The Public demonstrates a company that has consistently identified and nurtured the development of talent. Streep's professional stage career was secured through prescient casting choices at The Public when, soon after she arrived in New York, Papp cast her in 1975 in *Trelawny of the "Wells"* and, later, in *Measure for Measure* in Central Park. Kline, too, was a new acting student at Juilliard when he was tapped by Papp and his associate, Bernard Gersten, for the stages of The Public Theater. He recalls that first, important production in 1970:

> I get an audition and get cast in the ensemble understudying a few roles, and we're doing *The Wars of the Roses*. The three parts of *Henry VI* divided into two parts, and then *Richard III*. So, we're doing the tetralogy. Stuart Vaughan is the director. Donald Madden is playing Richard III and I'm carrying a spear and carrying a banner and carrying Charles Durning on a bier with twelve other guys. …
>
> I spent a summer doing that which was a great experience, especially because The Public needed money and we were going to have to close

---

[5]The history of Papp's Public Theater is told in the oral history by Kenneth Turan, *Free for All*, and Helen Epstein, *Joseph Papp: An American Life* (Boston: Da Capo Press, 1996). Turan's book is unrivaled for its in-depth investigation of the Papp years at The Public and I lean on Turan's and Epstein's superb work in my overview of the history of the theater.

the season early. We were doing these three evenings in rep, and Joe had the idea we were going to do a marathon. We're going to start at seven o'clock at night, go through the night, finish at 6:30 in the morning. The cast of *Hair* will come on stage and sing "Let the Sunshine In," and it was on the front page of every New York paper the next day and it was this huge event. And, of course, the money came in and the season went on.

A decade later, Kline starred in *The Pirates of Penzance* in Central Park and then on Broadway, to rave reviews ("Mr. Kline is in a class by himself," Frank Rich crooned).[6] He headlined *Hamlet* in 1986 at The Public, interspersing theater credits with his rising Hollywood stardom in films like *The Big Chill* (1983) and *A Fish Called Wanda* (1988). These star trajectories are not unusual, though it would not be quite right to suggest that The Public creates them. Rather, there seems to have been an uncanny ability within the artistic and casting directors to cultivate talent on the rise. Lin-Manuel Miranda, while already well known for his *In the Heights*, shot to superstardom because of The Public-produced *Hamilton*, a production that exemplifies The Public's mission-centric artistic development.

Though the association with high powered actors and producers is well established and seemingly inextricably linked, in the 1950s, The Public's mission and existence was in question almost constantly. The money troubles that Kline alluded to in the 1970s had followed the company from its inception through and into the Eustis years. But there was more at issue than simply cash flow; indeed, the personality and politics of the company's founder often challenged the future of the theater. In 1958, only a year after his production of *Romeo and Juliet*, Papp was ordered before the House Un-American Activities Committee on suspicion of subversive tactics, related to an earlier relationship with a California theater community that had been under investigation for communist ties. Papp was ready for the fight and publicly opined, "There are many problems in the theater: unemployment, the lack of permanent theaters where performers and technicians can learn their crafts, just to name two. It would be well for officials to concern themselves with this real problem and help to contribute to the cultural well-being of our people, rather than to destroy what little exists."[7] After the congressional hearing, he was promptly fired from his position at CBS.

The political witch hunts of the day created a backdrop for the birth of the Festival that was only elevated in theater lore by his much-publicized battle with Robert Moses, the colorful and imperial Commissioner of Parks. In 1959, as Papp was establishing his presence in the city parks, Moses insisted that the Shakespeare Festival charge an admission fee. The demand seemed

---

[6]Frank Rich, "Stage: *Pirates of Penzance* on Broadway," *New York Times*, January 9, 1981.
[7]Joseph Papp quoted in "Creation or Destruction," *The Village Voice*, vol. III, no. 35 (June 25, 1958).

largely arbitrary, perhaps simply a power play from a man convinced that Papp was a communist and hoping to find a way to destroy the fledgling company. To insist that the Festival have a fee, the thinking goes, Moses could eliminate the allure of Papp's creation and shut it down. The legal battles that followed pitted Papp against one of the highest-profile city politicians and his powerful team of deputies, creating a classic David and Goliath story. Papp eventually won, after an appeal that described Moses's argument as having "no rational basis," and the fracas cemented a degree of celebrity for the new company.[8]

The unfolding story of The Public and its eventual ethos and reputation, as with so many organizations, was built on these early existential brushes. But with the Moses hurdle cleared, the commissioner, in a complete reversal, proposed that the New York City Planning Commission build a permanent home in Central Park for the New York Shakespeare Festival. Within two years, the Delacorte Theater was constructed, and Free Shakespeare in the Park had a sense of permanence. It was an astoundingly quick rise, almost completely due to Papp's determination and bullying. The Delacorte itself was originally an anathema to Papp; his belief had always been to be mobile and not subject to the whims of the city government. But he reversed himself as well. The Delacorte was built and became, with perhaps the Oregon Shakespeare Festival, the headquarters of American Shakespeare—literally a physical destination, far beyond the original hopes and goals for a nimble mobile form.

The mobility that the company was founded upon did, in fact, fall away after the Delacorte became the central focus and after the current Public Theater headquarters was acquired in 1967. In addition to Shakespeare, Papp and his associates wanted to expand programming to include new American work. The old New York Public Library site in Astor Place, a grand building that was sold to the Hebrew Immigrant Aid Society, came available, and Papp and Gersten, seeing possibilities, negotiated a deal with the city, their sometimes nemesis. It was not an obvious choice; dreary, run down, and in the center of a terrible neighborhood, the library needed creative eyes to be seen as a theater. But in that—the roughness and impossibility—was the core of The Public's mission: Bring theater to the people, wherever they may be. Astor Place seemed right.

The very first production in the downtown theater was one of the greatest hits in the history of the company, and the production of Gerome Ragni and James Rado's *Hair* solidified the perception of Papp's extraordinary genius and astounding luck. A Shakespeare lover from the outset, the artistic director wasn't at all accustomed to the processes of seeking out, commissioning, and presenting original work. Meeting the writer of what became one of the great rock musicals of all time, on a train while returning from a teaching gig at Yale, while haphazard, perhaps highlights that there

---

[8]Turan, *Free for All*, p. 143.

is no agreed upon formula to cultivate and develop theater greatness. Early on, The Public established itself as a home to all and opened its doors to the idea that all were welcome to come in, to work, and experiment. Jeanine Tesori, the Tony Award-winning composer of The Public-produced *Fun Home*, expressed as much: "I think that if you have something to say, there is an invitation at The Public ... that building requires it. Even if they sell out every seat, it can't survive that way. It has to have something else. And I think it's interesting that it's built that way, on a system that's dependent upon other things ... it requires contribution and participation just like democracy. You have to be involved in it to make it work."

The new theater at Astor Place quickly became the year-round home of The Public, and the regulars at the Park became fixtures. Samuel Waterston, whose career has spanned stage and screen across seven decades, is still one of the most celebrated actors on the Delacorte, having performed there more than anyone else. Waterston recalls the 1967 Papp-directed bare bones production that featured Martin Sheen, while Waterston was working on Jakov Lind's *Ergo*:

> One of the things I remember to this day is sneaking in on a rehearsal of *Naked Hamlet*. It shocked all my expectations about what *Hamlet* ought to be. ... I was really an innocent, so *Naked Hamlet* was really hard for me to comprehend. ... Tom Aldridge painted himself white ... with a wallpaper glue applicator paint brush—great big 12-inch-wide paintbrush. He just sat on the stage and painted himself white. Again, these are experiences I'm telling you about through the eyes of a perfect innocent. ... Jack Hollander had a gigantic dildo taped to his leg—and Tom painted himself white. It's one of the funniest things I've ever seen.

Waterston's astonishment and innocence captured the essence of the new Public, a place that at once would audaciously produce fringy *Naked Hamlet* and *Ergo* and see massive popular success with *Hair*. With two theater venues already producing a divergent and eclectic array of programming, understanding exactly what The Public Theater was, and could be, was unclear. Papp was the consummate dreamer and big thinker, and while his successes were bold, there were many failures. His short takeover of drama at the Lincoln Center in the 1970s was one such example, a time when the company and its leader became overextended and eventually had to pull back. The Lincoln Center was not an ideal place of exploration and experimentation, and so the focus of the company was split. However, according to Waterston, the constant pushing was central to what made Papp: "It was obviously a take-it-or-leave-it attitude he had. The other side of saying he was taking big risks is that he was very interested in opening new ground. I think this is the central characteristic of the theater. It's what gives it its life. It's what gives it its right to be alive."

Steven Cohen would become Papp's assistant in the 1970s and 1980s, and recalls the methodology of expansion that both built the theater and imperiled it. There are few people who knew him in a professional context as well as Cohen.

> Joe's philosophy was when you're in trouble, expand. We were in trouble when I started at The Public in 1972. We were at like $1,900,000 in debt. Most theaters or most institutions would contract; Joe expanded by taking over Lincoln Center, realizing that having a bigger showcase—not necessarily a better showcase, but a bigger, more visible showcase—would attract more funding and a different kind of philanthropy. It worked, but at a certain point it got to be that we were losing so much money running those institutions that it became critical.
>
> Joe said the same thing to Mayor Beame when there was a financial crisis in the City of New York. At City Hall, the paint was crumbling on the outside. The place was in desperate need of a paint job. Joe said to the mayor, "Paint this place. Make it look like we're still a thriving city."

Cohen reflects Waterston's "take it or leave it" description and affirms the ongoing negotiation that The Public and its artistic directors have faced relative to commercial and social success. Indeed, if the blending of Shakespeare with new work, with cultural programming, concerts, and the like has long made The Public difficult to pin down, the punctuations in its history have been the major hits that found success at Astor Place or the Delacorte and then moved to Broadway. None is more exclamatory in the early years than the 1975 production of *A Chorus Line*. Marvin Hamlisch and Edward Kleban's little musical about dancers auditioning for a show was as simple as *Hair* was extravagant. Michael Bennett's indelible choreography cemented the production's popularity and when it transferred to Broadway, it was a hit. Running on Broadway longer than any other musical in history to that time, *A Chorus Line* garnered nine Tony Awards and became a cash cow for The Public Theater. It is now theater lore that the play was the singular reason that The Public Theater continued and survived the economic downturn of New York City in the 1970s. But it was bigger than that; the revenues actually sustained the theater well into the 1990s and even to the tenure of Eustis, long after Papp's death.

It is also taken for fact in theater circles that The Public rested on its financial laurels after the windfall of *A Chorus Line*. While difficult to gauge the veracity of the assumption, Patrick Willingham, the current executive director of The Public, is careful about putting that production and its success in perspective:

> I'll just say I think it's important because it's been pretty easy for a lot of people to look in the rear-view mirror with *A Chorus Line*. Was that

money wasted? Could they have done better? Well sure, of course. At the same time, Joe, Bernie, and team kept this organization vital, dynamic, and challenging and didn't destroy it in any way by the way they used the money that came in from *A Chorus Line*. ... There was no precedent for that level of success and that sort of money flowing into a not-for-profit organization.

While it is unquestionable that *A Chorus Line*'s profits sustained the company, it is also important to see how the success affected the programming. It is instructive, too, to compare its realities to the often false perceptions that surround *Hamilton*, the play that already is a historical barometer for the company. The Public did not consciously convert to a model of Broadway producing after *A Chorus Line* but rather continued to build new work in tandem with Shakespeare in the Park. By 1971, Papp, Gersten, and the philanthropist LuEsther Mertz had already taken a Park show to Broadway: *Two Gentlemen of Verona*, which was a proof of concept for *A Chorus Line* several years later. Before an era of commercial producers, *A Chorus Line* was the sole property of The Public Theater. One hundred percent of its revenue returned to the Public, and with the Broadway hit, touring companies, and regional productions that was a significant amount of money.

From a dollars and cents standpoint, though, it is nigh on impossible to compare *A Chorus Line* with what has become the other enormous hit in The Public's history. The $60 million company cannot possibly be sustained on one production anymore, even from *Hamilton*, a show that regularly earns millions on Broadway and now reaps revenue from tours and a Disney+ filmed version. While it does not return percentages to The Public that approach *A Chorus Line*, *Hamilton* pays back The Public about five percent of profit and one percent of adjusted growth, a healthy nest egg for the originating company (millions of dollars a year). Rather than operating off of the receipts, The Public carefully thinks of legacy in regard to the buffer that *Hamilton* provides. This foresight allowed the company to survive the first several months of the Covid crisis, without significant immediate layoffs and furloughs.[9]

Savings was not the priority with *A Chorus Line*, and after its success, Joe Papp and The Public were indeed able to operate through the 1980s and 1990s, churning out experiments, classics, and Broadway fare. Some of that money was invested into an endowment, but so much more went into ever-expanding programs. All the while, Papp fought and battled the

---

[9] Michael Paulson's and David Gelles's excellent overview of the success of *Hamilton* was accurate in 2016. Other estimates at its revenue implications are discussed in Chapter 8. With Covid closing theaters around the world, exact numbers fluctuate greatly. See Michael Paulson and David Gelles, "Hamilton Inc.: Path to a Billion Dollar Broadway Show," *New York Times*, June 8, 2016.

people around him to get what he wanted. Gordon Davis, who is the longest serving member of The Public's Board of Trustees, first met Papp in 1978 when Davis was elected the Commissioner of Parks, the job previously held by Moses. His initial reflection of Papp was vivid:

> He loved fighting with authority, and I was told when I got to be Parks Commissioner ... that there are three people who will come to you within your first month or two and propose something totally outrageous. One was Ron Delsener who did concerts in the Park. The other was Warner LeRoy who ran Tavern on the Green. The third was Joe Papp, and sure enough they all showed up; and Joe showed up with his architect, Giorgio Cavaglieri, to propose what he called a temporary structure over the Delacorte when in fact it had steel and concrete statues going 20 feet down into the ground. ... So, because I was the Parks Commissioner, inevitably I would get in a fight with Joe about something.

The Papp biographies by Turan and Epstein often relate that indefatigable style that defined the artistic director. But the sense of conflict and mischievous needling is ever present in the descriptions of Papp as well. Davis relates an early experience with Papp, when the newly appointed Parks Commissioner tested his new muscle by asking for tickets to the hottest show on Broadway:

> What better show for a young kid than *A Chorus Line*? It's all dancing. So, I asked Joe if he could arrange for tickets for my wife and we'll take our daughter. He said, "sure." So, we get to the Shubert Theater; and I look at the tickets and see the tickets are in the last row of the top balcony. They are the worst seats in the house. The worst seats. You're looking down the heads with binoculars. I have the worst seats in the house. So, I call him up the next day and said "how could you do this to me? It's not me. I mean I'm just a lowly Parks Commissioner who controls your life and the Park, but to a five-year-old daughter, how could you do this?" I couldn't help laughing because I said, "I've never met anybody who would do something low and this outrageous." And he said, "what are you talking about?" I said, "Joe, go fuck yourself." It was absolutely hysterical. I mean another person would be offended and outraged. My reaction was one of I couldn't believe he would do that ... but he did.

Following *A Chorus Line*, The Public Theater continued to produce hits and misses but there would be no success that could be compared to that production for the rest of Papp's life. Cohen's recollection that the "Papp way" was to expand when you are in trouble bears out when one considers the perhaps unusual marriage between The Public and Lincoln Center Theater. Papp was given control of drama productions from 1972 to 1977 in a partnership that could only be described as fraught. Understanding that Joe Papp was the most celebrated theater name in the country, placing him in charge of the storied house could have a logical reasoning. But Papp, like the institution that he created, had too much of a sense of *fight*, of antiestablishment determination for a partnership like that to succeed. He would quickly return to focus on new play development and Shakespeare at Lafayette and in the Park.

The theater produced some extraordinary successes in the years following *A Chorus Line*, including Ntozake Shange's choreo-poem *for colored girls who have considered suicide/when the rainbow is enuf* (1976), David Rabe's *Streamers* (1976), and the Kevin Kline-led *The Pirates of Penzance* (1980). *Pirates* was his star maker and an odd but not unusual Park production. Papp and Gersten created a theater that could accommodate summer fare beyond Shakespeare and the Wilfred Leach-directed version of the Gilbert and Sullivan musical was a success. After go-to actor Raúl Julia took on another gig, the role of the Pirate King was offered to Kline. He remembers thinking the project would be quick and easy, something he could take on before finding bigger fish to fry:

"Four weeks in the Park, how bad can that be?" And of course, it moves to Broadway and then we make a movie of it.

When the show became a big hit, I got to know Joe more and more and he was present and very helpful. In the middle of the run Joe said, "So when we finish this, you know, you have all the right attributes for Shakespeare, have you ever considered that?" I said, "Um, not only have I considered it …" Gilbert and Sullivan was not on my must-do list ever, this is a one-off. "I'm dying to do Shakespeare." He said, "Okay, well let's pick a part."

It was the beginning of a yearslong friendship between Kline and Papp. The actor recalls a tradition in the 1980s where, after every opening night in the Park, Papp would come backstage and ask Kline what they would do next. The loyalty was complete. Kline's agent, who also represented Raúl Julia and Stacy Keach, emphasized to the actor that he should always honor commitments to Papp. "Well, that's easy," Kline would reply. "If I'm going to play Henry V what could possibly be offered to me that's going to be [better]." Similarly, when John Travolta, one of the most famous actors on the planet at the time, called Papp to offer his services as the Pirate King for the film version of *Pirates*, the answer was simple: "We have our Pirate King." It was Kline.

The 1970s and 1980s saw the continued development of relationships between Papp's Public and other titans of American theater, from Elizabeth Swados (*Runaways*, 1978) to Larry Cramer (*The Normal Heart*, 1985) and Rupert Holmes (*The Mystery of Edwin Drood*, 1985). By 1990, Papp had built and helmed one of the most recognized cultural institutions in America for over thirty years. The tenure remains impressive, all the more given the continual output of new work that came from the Astor Place theater. But by 1990, Papp was slowing down, and dying of cancer.

Transitions

We have never followed the success course, even though we want to be successful, we hope to be successful. The theater has always managed to survive, one way or another, on the fact that it has certain ideals as an institution.

—JOSEPH PAPP[10]

The transition from Joe Papp to the contemporary leadership of The Public is a story rife with contradiction, scandal, and breathless retelling. So much so that it is difficult to tell comfortably and accurately what happened. As is the case in many theaters and cultural institutions, the move from the founding artistic director to the successor is one that can become existentially charged for a company. Papp knew this, and while it seems clear from several interviews with people who were there that no succession plan was solidly in place, Papp did speak about it at some length and expressed his concern about the company's future.

In August 1988, after his cancer diagnosis, Papp called Cohen into his office and asked him to bring a tape recorder and microphone. Knowing that the post-Papp days were approaching, he reflected on the pillars of the company and the ways that it could continue to exist. Plans swirled in his head, and he grasped at many possibilities, including a partnership with New York University, that never materialized. According to Kline, Cohen, and others, Papp told only a select few that he was dying. The recording, though, makes it clear that he knew his end was near and that the Festival needed some future planning:

> I'm putting this in the form of kind of a one-way discussion, so to speak, beginning my efforts to reconstruct the Festival based on my not being the leader of the Festival, is underway and has been underway for quite a while.
> ... We've won many prizes, as many prizes as any theater could hope to get in the long history we've had, which is over thirty years. So, consequently this theater has an imprimatur. A lot of it naturally is my particular philosophy, which has pervaded the theater, which is both social and artistic, the combination of the two.
> ... The board, at this moment, has good potential, and there's a lot of enthusiasm ... But with all of that there has not been the kind of leadership on the board where someone has come forward and really

---

[10]Recording of Joseph Papp, August 25, 1988. Courtesy of Steven Cohen.

taken the reigns to raise funds like John Lindsay has done at the Beaumont, at Lincoln Center. It needs that kind of push for us to get out of the kind of difficulty we're in now with the $3 million deficit. I don't think we'll ever get out of that kind of problem unless we have a very ambitious fundraising situation. However, I proposed—as I did to Jim Brigham last night—that one of the solutions is not to try to deal just with corporations.

Papp's concern about the budget and the leadership that would take the company out of its troubles is noteworthy. But the idea that the board did not have any leadership on the level of a Mayor Lindsay at the Beaumont largely ignored that *he*, Joe Papp, was that leader and that LuEsther Mertz *had* "taken the reigns" of The Public financing for years. But the end of his tenure was plagued with operational deficits, and those challenges continued under the leadership of JoAnne Akalaitis and George C. Wolfe. Willingham notes, "The focus wasn't on creating a reserve or an endowment from that money (*A Chorus Line*) that would throw off cash to stabilize the organization long term. It was really more about fulfilling the mission on a yearly basis. Joe did some amazing mission-focused activity during that period and, as we all know, dissolved the development department because he didn't think it was moral to fundraise when all of that money was coming in ... which is a wonderful *principle*." The Public Theater budget would not be tamed until Willingham's executive directorship, which began in 2011. He describes an organization that was in financial dire straits, with reserves nearly depleted. In 1990, Papp, too, was concerned and reflected it in his meanderings about the makeup of The Public Theater's board:

> I feel we should really be very careful who comes on the board now. Right now, I said we have five conservatives. The youngest people on the board are really of a conservative mode. People would think, "Isn't that strange?" ... I've been called a "flaming liberal" if not a communist. I for one encourage these people because I see past their party labels. I see good people. ... I'm in a funny position in one way because I'm trying to cultivate ... the right person to become the next leader of the Festival. It's not a question of ... this dictator wants to select his own kind of person. I'm not looking for that at all, any more than I look to select on the board only people who agree with me politically.
>
> I've been negotiating with a director who's one of the foremost directors in this country on the stage today. The young man—he's in his forties—he certainly is not like me. Fundamentally, he's an artistic person, a director. He makes his living as a director. As a director, he's an excellent organizer. I don't think he's ever operated a theater before, but he's had some experience in this. I invited him in to consider coming into the organization.

... If he accepts this position, he will become a leader of an institution. I can at least know that the choices of plays or the way they're done and the way he handles that will be on the highest artistic level. That to me is crucial because with all your social objectives without high quality work, it'll all come to no avail. You have to do it because the theater is our form of expression, and the skills with which we present our views is the key. Otherwise, you may as well read the newspapers or watch television or see a film. So, I'm hoping that this young man will accept the post.

The recordings are fascinating musings from a man facing death and the mystery surrounding the choice of a successor is ever present. In conversations with Cohen, and with others, the identity of the "young man in his forties" is foggy, but most likely is a reference to James Lapine, the Tony Award-winning director and librettist. Cohen remembers many names being bandied about, including Mike Nichols, who never wanted the job, and other famous stars who could continue to control the spotlight like Papp. Lapine was intrigued by the offer but decided not to take it. Kevin Kline also recalls that he was asked to take the reins, or at least help in the transition. Gail Papp, similarly, reflected that the decision was agonizing and unsettled for quite some time: "We talked a lot about it here at home. He didn't really go public with it. He tried to get various people interested in succeeding him. He talked to Meryl Streep about it. He talked to James Lapine. He talked to Jerry Zaks. He talked to several other people, outstanding directors. Nobody wanted the job." And why would they? By the end of his life, Joe Papp was esteemed, and his company, while legendary, had a fairly large yearly institutional deficit.[11] The great American carnival barker could never be replaced, and it seemed that he and everyone around him knew it. But Gail and Joe Papp had to come up with some plan, and eventually they did. Gail Papp recalls:

He tried to bring in somebody else and form what I call the troika version of the leadership of The Public. He proposed it to everybody who was involved. It was about seven people involved in this. And there was an explosion ... two out of the three people of the troika threatened to resign immediately.
 ... Okay. It'd be JoAnne. And it would be the associate producer at that time [Cohen] and then this third person who was Bob Marx, who was then I think at The Public Library, a very marvelous person.
 ... Joe thought that JoAnne was a marvelous artist. She had many qualities, including a societal viewpoint that he responded to, and they had a good relationship. Toward the end he did worry about whether

---

[11]Cohen notes that it's not entirely fair to say the company was not in good financial ways. Papp and Cohen *did* establish an endowment that offset the operating deficit.

she could lead the theater, but he never said so publicly, and the question remained unresolved in his lifetime.

Indeed, the Akalaitis-Cohen-Marx troika was rejected and Akalaitis rose to the top. In part, it seems that Papp's indifference to or skepticism about her leadership was caused by his own reluctance to accept the idea that a transition was inevitable. Helen Epstein writes that when Akalaitis was brought on board as Papp's artistic associate, she was not at all clear what she was being offered. Papp didn't reveal his cancer diagnosis to her, nor her role or salary at the organization. He was obviously not ready to transition power even as he was talking about it privately.[12]

Steven Cohen, similarly, is clear in his memory of the challenge of hiring a new leader and, in retrospect, why there was little chance that it would work out:

Landis: What was the consultation process? Was it just ultimately Joe's decision?

Cohen: It was his. The reality is the board at the time—would that board say "no" to Joe if he said, "this is the person I want to replace me?" I don't imagine that ever happening, that board saying "no." Now, what they were going to do after Joe passed away would be something else, but I don't think they would say no to him. I don't know if he consulted any of the board members, but our discussions—my discussion with him was just person after person—interviewing those people. The reality is JoAnne is the only one that said yes.

Akalaitis's one-year tenure—a time punctuated by infighting and, finally, her unceremonious firing—was, many agree, not the fault of the highly accomplished founder of the legendary Mabou Mines. From the outset, there were problems, many enumerated in a *New York Magazine* profile that recalled tabloids calling her an "abrasive ideologue" and quotes Akalaitis saying, "I'm bored by all the comparisons ... I never say to myself, 'What would Joe do?' Why would anyone hate me? It's not like *All about Eve*. I haven't stepped on someone's head to get what I wanted."[13] Cohen was appointed the managing director and Akalaitis's number two. He recalls the challenges she faced more succinctly: "Even the messiah would probably have a difficult time coming after Papp."[14] Indeed, New York theater critics were vicious to the new artistic director.

---

[12]Epstein, *Joe Papp*, p. 452.
[13]Phoebe Hoban, "Going Public: JoAnne Akalaitis Takes over for Papp," *New York Magazine*, October 28, 1991, p. 44.
[14]Ibid.

Gail Papp is careful to assert that the primary qualities in an artistic director are artistic vision coupled with a considered "social orientation." Akalaitis, she says, had it. Some of the producing choices, however, were met with resistance from The Public board. Her season was dark, morose; she produced the nineteenth-century Georg Büchner masterpiece *Woyzeck*, a fragmented play about a soldier descending into madness and murder, and the seventeenth-century John Ford bloodbath *'Tis Pity She's a Whore*. It is entirely unfair to claim that these and others were bad choices—they stand out as classics in the Western canon—but it is safe to bet that a resistant board and critics did not warm to Akalaitis's style. As is reflected in the *New York Magazine* article, most of the reasons seemed petty, gendered, and directly related to the comparisons that inevitably came. She couldn't raise money like Joe could. She couldn't maintain the Latino theater festival, a passion project of Joe Papp. She threw away Joe's favorite office plant (an actual complaint). None of the reasons seem compelling now, over thirty years later, and it is easy to suspect that The Public was not ready for a strong woman at the helm. After the highly patriarchal structure of Joe Papp, this seems entirely probable. This sense is backed by many I have spoken to. Gordon Davis described the board at the time as a "men's coffee klatch," a group of people who basically just found money for Joe. Gail Papp notes, finally, that the board of The Public did not really know how to function without Joe. Of Akalaitis, Oskar Eustis says, "Joe said once about JoAnne, the reason she was the right person to succeed him, she was a dyed-in-the-wool radical and nothing could change her, and that's true. It also made it hard for her to run the institution, but I think that aesthetic radicalism is something that, whenever we do it here, I feel like I am honoring JoAnne's memory."

After the board voted to end Akalaitis's tenure, the transition to George C. Wolfe was less complicated. In fact, one of the many possibilities that was floated during the original succession discussions was a quartet of famous directors: Akalaitis, Michael Greif, David Greenspan, and Wolfe. Wolfe wasn't available in the first go around, his career was on fire and was in the midst of staging *Jelly's Last Jam* and the mounting of *Angels in America* on Broadway. By 1993, though, Wolfe was ready to assume the head chair at The Public, requesting that it came with the title "Producer." Gordon Davis remembers, "It was that fast. It wasn't any debate. I doubt there was even a board vote of any kind. It just went to George. She was gone, and George was in; and the rest as they say is history."

Wolfe's leadership at The Public lasted a decade and as indicated before, deserves an entire book dedicated to its accomplishments. A company that prided itself on pushing traditional boundaries of diversity and inclusive casting, and being the most forward thinking and important theater organization in the country, now had one of the most prominent African American theater artists running the whole thing. Consistently, those who worked with and knew Wolfe during his Public Theater years describe a brilliant artist, but someone with a strong and unusual personality. Gail Papp says of her friend:

> I always liked George. I thought he was a terrific person. He had outstanding producer/director instincts and experience. Although he'd never run an institution—he had none of that kind of background—he certainly had the essential artistic ideas. And after he took charge of The Public Theater, the whole organization reflected his dedication to hiring people of color. It was very instructive. If you have someone like George heading an institution, he brings the people in because he knows where they live, and he's worked with them.
>
> For some reason I get along with complicated people. It was true when I was much younger, too. And George was a complicated person. At times obsessive, paranoid, difficult. But he also talked fluently and brilliantly, and he quipped constantly. He would go off on zany detours in conversation interrupted by bouts of hilarity, and I enjoyed that.

That Gail Papp highlights the fact that Wolfe "knows where they live" is important to a reading of the history of The Public. Just as Joe Papp insisted on a theater meant for people who live and die in the same neighborhood, and Eustis now focuses on ticket giveaways in all of the boroughs, The Public maintains an image of a theater intent on finding and cultivating its artists and audience where they live. One of Wolfe's great strengths came in his desire to broaden and build upon Papp's goals of an inclusive Public for all.

Wolfe quickly became the face of The Public, arriving on the job with a considerable amount of fame in the American theater. Kline, who was still very much involved with the theater, acting as an artistic associate, recalled being asked to oversee Shakespeare, his bailiwick, while Wolfe would focus on new play development. And yet,

> George is a very strong personality. There was never any contentiousness. I don't know how long I lasted as an associate producer. I said to Rosemary [Tichler], "Make it like an associate advisory something." I forget what my last title was because it was sort of like standby, the backup, auxiliary, ancillary commentator from afar, but emeritus.

Similarly, Steven Cohen was let go from the theater as managing director in 1994 and Wolfe ran the company solo. Wolfe served as the head of The Public Theater from 1993 to 2004 and oversaw more than one hundred productions including *Bring in 'da Noise, Bring in 'da Funk* (1995), Suzan-Lori Parks's *Topdog/Underdog* (2001), *Caroline, or Change* (2003), and so many others. He won a Tony Award for *Noise/Funk* as well as for directing Tony Kushner's *Angels in America: Millennium Approaches*. He oversaw the construction and founding of Joe's Pub, the cabaret club that is now a staple of The Public Theater. In one of the more intriguing side notes in contemporary American theater history, perhaps the most famous play of the last fifty years, Tony Kushner's *Angels in America*, was led by Wolfe after being commissioned at the Eureka Theater Company by Oskar Eustis and Tony Taccone. In selecting Wolfe to direct the Broadway production in lieu of his best friend, Kushner had a hand in propelling the careers of two titans of The Public Theater.

The focus on inclusiveness, artist-centric relations, and the public as a location for artists to grow and thrive is consistent from people discussing Wolfe's tenure, and something that Eustis would continue to develop. Like Akalaitis, Wolfe was an artist first and foremost. He spoke the language of artists and, especially, of musicians—some of his greatest successes came in his directing and producing musical theater. However, relations with the board during Wolfe's artistic directorship were not always easy, and there were even resignations in 2001, most prominently Larry Condon, chairman of the LuEsther Charitable Trust, who believed the company was not being run in a fiscally responsible manner. Gail Papp notes that there was a certain condescension in the way that people dealt with Wolfe, referring to him as a "crazy genius." He was—and is—indeed a genius, she says, and even her descriptions of him veer toward bemused astonishment: "Difficult, strange person," "Alarming hilarity." By the end, though, his frustrations with the board and his desire to get back to a "more purely artistic life," as he reported to the *New York Times*, convinced him to move on from his decade of artistic institutional leadership.[15] The announcement was something of a surprise to the theater community, but not to those who knew him well. Gail Papp remembers that Wolfe consulted with her during that time, needing a listening ear. Of one meeting she said, "It was a monologue of grievance, upset-ment, being driven mad with the familiar bouts of hilarity."

The departure of Wolfe ended a run that had reestablished The Public Theater as a cultural theater institution of note in America. The Public had endured difficult financial times during his tenure, including fairly substantial losses on Broadway and a massive economic downturn due to the attacks of September 11, 2001. By the time of his resignation in 2004, though, he and his team, including Executive Director Mara Manus, had rebuilt the financial viability of the company. It was operating on about a $12 million budget and had little debt. While Wolfe left the theater financially in a better place than when he started, it was, undoubtedly, his commitment to the founding philosophy of The Public that defined his career there. That, and his scrupulous commitment to diversity. The *New York Times* was the first to break the news of his resignation: "Mr. Wolfe has spent nearly a decade trying to build on

---

[15]Robin Pogrebin, "Wolfe Is Leaving Public Theater," *New York Times*, February 12, 2004.

the fierce commitment of the theater's founder, Joseph Papp, to new playwrights ... as the leading black stage director in the country and an openly gay man, he embodied The Public's determination to reach diverse artists and audiences."[16]

Enter Oskar Eustis

FIGURE 1.3 *The Public's fourth artistic director, Oskar Eustis. Courtesy Stephen Lovekin.*

Wolfe said of the next artistic director of The Public Theater, "It takes a profound passion that what you're doing is important ... if anybody has that, they can do the job."[17] In 2004, the board had a major decision on its hands and had two previous transitions to look at as examples. There was no appetite to reexperience the tumultuous transition of power of the early 1990s. Gail Papp recalls the needs that were clearly outlined by the board as the search began:

> Well, I think the utmost concerns of the members that were involved was someone who could run the institution and had some kind of proven ability to do that, in terms of their experience. In other words, nobody wanted to shoot from the hip again based on a person's directorial talents, necessarily. So, the agency went for people who had experience running theaters, which was a sensible thing to do. That was a route that Joe consciously avoided.

That avoidance of structure that was a hallmark of Joe Papp's tenure was not going to work for the contemporary Public Theater. By the end of Wolfe's time at the company, that $12 million budget, while not

---

[16]Ibid.
[17]Ibid.

enormous—especially compared to current numbers—made The Public a relatively large theater organization in New York City. While critically successful and newly financially stable, Wolfe's and Papp's years at the top were by no account financially consistent. Some of that came not only from artistic and managerial mistakes, but also from unavoidable crises (the 1970s economic downturn, the 9/11 attacks, etc.).[18] The board wanted executive leadership that could track a course of financial stability. Akalaitis was the only person who said "yes" in 1991 and Wolfe was the only one who was asked in 1993. Oskar Eustis, on the other hand, was hired after an exhaustive search conducted by a highly respected headhunter. And yet, it was the culmination of his lifelong dream, the place he wanted to end up all along:

> The Public was the mother ship; The Public was the most important theater of them all, so I felt that what I might be able to bring to the Theater was an ability to institutionalize, strengthen and make permanent, aspects of The Public's mission manifested in programs that would be strong enough that they would become permanent parts of what The Public did.

Eustis's tenure *has* been about strengthening the institution and the fundamental programs that made up Papp's mission that had necessarily retracted during the 1990s. He seemed to be the right person for the time. While he had been a director his entire adult life, the rap on him was that he wasn't a particularly strong director, something he doesn't deny. When he was hired in November 2004 (he officially began in January 2005), he came to the job with enormous experience and expectations as a leader, producer, manager, and glowing intellect—a charismatic one at that. His resume backed up that hope. As a teenager, he founded the Red Wing Theater Company with a friend of his. After travels in Europe, he returned to the United States where he served as a resident director and dramaturg and then artistic director at the Eureka Theater Company in San Francisco. He was the associate artistic director of the Mark Taper Forum in Los Angeles under the legendary Gordon Davidson before becoming the head of Trinity Repertory Company in Providence, Rhode Island, in 1994. While there, he helped form the Brown University/Trinity

---

[18] Broadly speaking, one might point to Papp's reluctance to build a robust institutional giving department or his takeover of Lincoln Center as clear missteps. Wolfe's Public lost millions on productions that didn't find their wings on Broadway, especially *The Wild Party* and *On the Town*. Those financial setbacks caused animosity and mistrust from some on the board. Eustis's Public has faced financial missteps and tumult, as well. *Bloody Bloody Andrew Jackson* made a loss on Broadway, and Hurricane Sandy and the Covid-19 crises have loomed large in the Eustis era for the strains they have put on the organization.

Rep consortium, a graduate level educational partnership in the arts. The Public hired him from Trinity.

His youth and upbringing hinted at the politically centered artist that he would become. He was born on July 31, 1958, to Warren Eustis and Doris Marquit. His father was a district attorney and his mother a professor of literature and women's studies. Both his stepmother, Nancy, and stepfather, Erwin, were also professors at the University of Minnesota. Erwin Marquit ran for governor of the state on the Communist ticket in 1974. To this day, Eustis carries around his mother's Communist Party membership card in his wallet. Politics and academia run thick and deep in Oskar Eustis's bloodlines.[19]

The charisma that he brought to those early directing and producing positions have been noted throughout his career. Tony Taccone, his partner at Eureka, commented, "If nothing else, Oskar is one of the bigger spirited human beings on the planet. His interest in political analysis, political theory, changing the world through art, was immediately apparent to me." His friend Chelsea Clinton, a longtime supporter of The Public Theater and of Shakespeare in the Park, recalls her first meeting with Eustis:

> I met Oskar for the first time at Shakespeare in the Park. I think my first impression of him was his hair. That's a terrible thing to say, isn't it?
>
> But it's just—it's honest. Kind of a copper mane, that lion-esque hair that was probably buffeted by the wind—or at least that is how it's romanticized in my memory. And just his dynamism and his clear passion for the theater, and his clear passion to convert those who may not yet be converted to why the theater remains such an important and integral part of not only how we think about the arts but how we think about culture and creativity and community more broadly.

That first impression of Eustis is common and echoed by many on his staff and other artistic leaders in the country. What Clinton first remembers is a sort of giganticness of the Eustis persona, a largeness that is mirrored by his own stature. He is a big man with a large, bright, toothy smile, an unruly goatee, and the ever-noticeable mane. Casual and formal at the same time, he often wears jeans, a puffy Patagonia vest with a formal blazer over the top. Or, at the park on a summer evening, he may be found in an impeccable seersucker suit with floppy bow tie. Often, he rides to work on a bicycle with a cigar clenched in his teeth. Several years ago, a holiday video card from the cast of *Hamilton* showed this image of Eustis, riding up to the steps of The Public Theater, hair buffeted by the wind,

---

[19]Rebecca Mead, "Stage Left: Oskar Eustis, The Public's Latest Radical," *The New Yorker*, March 15, 2010.

smoke billowing behind him as the actors sang "Here comes the general," from the musical number about George Washington. It's an easy laugh because it is so accurate. Oskar Eustis very quickly *became* The Public Theater.

Eustis would probably cringe at the Washington parallel because his inclination publicly is to talk about the Theater as larger than its leader—the sense that we are all one public, devoted to arts and its enormous power. Still, *impresario*, the word often associated with Papp, is now attached to Eustis. When he was hired, that sort of charismatic leadership was essential for a company that is sometimes called America's national theater. Even as arts leadership now is being challenged and reassessed, the role still seems to demand more than artistry; it needs a person that sees theater as an agent of social change, a location of cultural creation, and the willingness and ability to broadcast that message. Sam Waterston reflects:

> You have to find somebody whose sense of personal mission in their own life is parallel to the sense of mission that The Public has been committed to from the very beginning—cockiness, anti-authority, and a sense that the theater really has an important social and political purpose, that surely is its bottom line—that it must be entertaining and attention-getting, but that it has a meaning and purpose greater than that for the whole society. All these things have to be in the person in order for them to survive and for the institution to thrive.

From practice, and also deep authenticity, Eustis speaks about the mission of the company as if he is channeling Papp:

> The Public insisted within our field that we are all one art form, which is the way that formally we manifest the fact that here in this country, we are all one country. The democracy of the aesthetics, the egalitarianism and the aesthetics, is the artistic equivalent of the democracy of the country and of the politics.

Turan writes in the introduction of his tome on Joseph Papp: "Today, with no one since his death having come anywhere near his level of accomplishment, it's clearer than ever how singular his life's work has been."[20] In the mid-1990s, when Turan penned his book, this was certainly true. And still, his work is singular and remarkable. But today, Oskar Eustis has become the general, and thus accepts the adulation on the Tony Award stage as well as the condemnation that comes from the many choices made in the heat of the American theater spotlight.

---

[20] Turan, *Free for All*, p. 5.

Ghosts of the Past and Finding the Future

A curiosity of The Public Theater has always been its connection to social justice and structure, and the way it addresses those issues. As will be seen throughout, the company's relationship to leadership, with the exception of George C. Wolfe, is often white-centric. Even as those leaders and directors have publicly and vociferously committed to diversity in all of its forms, the fact is that so much of the artistic and directorial structure of the company from its inception has been skewed. This question of leadership and structure is something that Eustis, in recent years, has been forced to address and alter.

Gail Papp talks candidly about her late husband's aversion to considering structure. His roots and desires in the creation of art was to get Shakespeare into poor and often racially and economically diverse communities, even while protestors threw rocks or as city officials battled him. Eustis, too, talks at length about eliminating the financial, gendered, and racialized barriers to art at The Public, by bringing the people of the city and the country into his theaters, or by taking his theaters to them. He has refocused and reiterated the original program and brand of The Public, "Free Shakespeare in the Park," and notes that his goal is to make all of the tickets at Lafayette free of charge, too. These are tough philosophies to adhere to for a company that has produced phenomenal hits, Broadway productions where the ticket price might soar above $500, and a Shakespeare in the Park where patrons have to line up for hours while donors get a ticket in advance. It all does seem fairly inaccessible, through those lenses. How does The Public philosophy work for a company that must face the capitalist realities that come with enormous success, and perceived and real questions about accessibility?

People close to The Public Theater understand that, despite its plaudits and its renowned image that has arisen over its nearly seventy years, the institution tries to remain a family, as it was in Papp's time. In the last pages of Helen Epstein's book on Papp, she tells of the sorrowful days and months in the lead-up to the artistic director's death. Papp's son, Anthony, died of AIDS in June 1991, four months before his father. The outpouring of grief in the theater world that year was extraordinary, services attended by a veritable who's who of the arts and political community. In 2014, Oskar and Laurie Eustis's son, Jack, took his life, and the grief also resonated around the theater community. In a horrible parallel with Papp, Eustis, too, had to face the worst imaginable of all tragedies.

Unlike Papp, though, Eustis was at the height of his professional work when he lost his son and, though difficult to qualify, it is undoubtable that his work and his relationship to the theater has changed. In November 2014, *Fun Home* was months from its Broadway debut, *Hamilton* was two months from its Public Theater opening. A year and a half after Jack's death, as Eustis stood on the stage accepting the Tony for Best Musical for

Hamilton, it was impossible to not think about the extraordinary and awful journey he had been through.

In the years since, the output of The Public has been enormous, and there is no sign of Eustis slowing down. If anything, his personal tragedy paralleled a flourishing of the theater that he leads. In an interview with the *New York Times* in 2016, Eustis noted that the plays in his season now seem to have themes of loss: "Is it just suddenly I'm noticing that all of the plays that I'm trying to do have this quality, or have they been there, and I've just not seen it?"[21] Sam Waterston says, "He has not hidden the fact that it changed him. It has given him a kind of weight to things that might not have been there otherwise—that if he's doing the theater now, after that tragedy, it must be a very important thing to be doing. Nobody should trivialize it." It is difficult to see that there is a pattern in the output of The Public Theater, though it is true that its artistic stamp is now emblazoned with the initials "OE." In 2019, it was running at a furious pace and fully reacquainting itself with the mission. The following year the calculus would change.

---

[21]Michael Paulson, "*Hamilton* and Heartache: Living the Unimaginable," *New York Times*, October 13, 2016.

The Park

2
Delacorte Summers

FIGURE 2.1 *The Delacorte Theater. Courtesy Kevin Landis.*

Free Shakespeare in the Park, the foundation upon which The Public Theater is built, is, unsurprisingly, *in a park*. Self-evident, yes, but an important reminder. To double down on the obvious, the Park—Central Park in this case—is outdoors, under the stars, subject to the whim of the rain, the hail, the planes landing at LaGuardia Airport, the police helicopters, the sirens, the occasional protesters, and whatever else New York City has to throw at the Bard and those attempting to portray his stories. This scene—the bucolic chaos of performing in the elements—is as time tested as anything in the theater. From the Theater of Dionysus in ancient Athens, performed under the warm Greek sun, to Noh traditions in Japan, to Shakespeare's Globe on the South Bank of the Thames, a building open to the sky, so many of the foundations of theater revolve around the notion of a shared experience—an experience that is, often, in communion with nature.

From the early days of the New York Shakespeare Festival, being outdoors in the city was an expression of New York life at its finest. In the romantic version of events, hot, humid city days give way to soft evenings with croaking frogs, warbling birds, and the buzz of an expectant crowd that gathers near the Great Lawn to take in the words of the greatest playwright in the English language. In the beginning, under Joe Papp's direction and vociferous commitment to serve all corners of the city, the productions traveled around the boroughs. Papp thought that the model of reaching out to the city was essential to the soul of the work, even comparing it to Shakespeare's original company in the early seventeenth century.[1] Papp's idea was to get the words of Shakespeare into all corners of New York City, to place the work in conversation with the geographic and social nuances of the giant metropolis. "Get in and get out, fast," he said. He had no desire to build a structure that upon completion would fall under the auspices and control of the city government and the Commissioner of Parks.[2]

Papp eventually *did* recognize the benefits of a permanent home, especially with $250,000 in city funding dangled before him. By 1962, with the city support and a naming donation from Valerie and George Delacorte, that permanent home opened, just a few hundred yards east of the corner of 81st and Central Park West. Remarkably, the theater has not changed all that much in the intervening years, excepting some cosmetic updates and repairs. The venue at that opening production of *The Merchant of Venice* with George C. Scott and James Earl Jones looked about the same as for the 2010 version starring Al Pacino and Lily Rabe. The trees were bigger by 2010, and more skyscrapers and luxury condo spires loomed in the background,

---

[1] While Shakespeare's Lord Chamberlain's Men are associated with a permanent theater called the Globe, they did indeed perform at other locations, like the court at Blackfriars.
[2] Turan, *Free for All*, 152.

but the Delacorte was still fairly simple and decidedly plain for one of the most famous stages in the world: 2,000 seats in an amphitheater, green plastic folding theater chairs more akin to the Rose Bowl than Broadway, serpentine lines waiting for the small park restrooms, and lighting perched on massive booms, attached to what appear to be interstate highway signs. It still isn't glamorous. The dressing rooms are crammed under the bleachers, next to piles of technical supplies and broken-down scaffolding. Its tight quarters put movie stars next to spear carriers. For a program that prides its egalitarian bona fides, it all makes some sense at the Delacorte, and one could venture to say that the venue really shouldn't be all that advanced or luxe. It is outdoor theater. What it lacks in architectural innovation, it makes up for in its placement in, and intersection with, one of the most beautiful public spaces in the world.

Central Park and the people and creatures that populate it are, in many ways, the stars of the show, and that has remained the same over the decades. Examples come up continuously in writings and stories about the Festival. Legendary lighting designer Jennifer Tipton has worked in the amphitheater numerous times—from the 1977 Elizabeth Swados-conceived *Agamemnon* to the 2009 production of Euripides' *The Bacchae*—and points out that virtually the only thing that has changed over the years is the foliage: "In the early days, you could see the lake. There was a period of time when I didn't work there and then I went back to work, and I discovered that the trees had covered up the positions for the lights. Somehow, they hadn't told me about that." Tipton, Ming Cho Lee, Clint Ramos, Beowulf Boritt, David Rockwell, Rachel Hauck—famous artists all. But at the Delacorte, nature is the ultimate set designer.

Despite the most well-known lighting designer in the world being on the roster of Park artists, the reason for outdoor theater in the early days of the art form was actually directly related to light, but in an entirely elemental way. The sun was critical for the production of drama before the advent of electricity, and so the contemporary idea of an audience being plunged into darkness to witness an event taking place inside a frame in front of them was never really a consideration. We too often forget, then, that what we have lost in contemporary houses of theater is the ability to see the other theater goers, together with the actors, as part of the social and community event. The combination of electricity and indoor primacy in the theater is, in fact, very new. Nature and "outside-ness" helped make the theater what it was and is: a fulcrum for community engagement, much like a house of worship or a town square of old. It remains that way at the Delacorte and in other expressions of outdoor festivals across the country and the world. What was once the only way to present drama, in the elements and among neighbors, is now the source of magic and wide-eyed awe. A well-known *New York Times* review by Ben Brantley of *The Bacchae*, early in Oskar Eustis's tenure, captured the ineffable ecological charm that the Delacorte exudes:

> I saw a wonderful raccoon at the Delacorte Theater the other night. It appeared, as serene and silent as a rising moon, at the far edge of the open-air stage in Central Park where The Public presents its summer productions. Its face a shining-eyed mask, this creature froze for just a second to scrutinize the audience from the spotlight before being followed in unhurried procession into the darkness by two other raccoons.
>
> These reminders of the mysterious and often forgotten coexistence of the natural and urban worlds in New York City offered an appetite-whetting prologue to a play about the animal in humanity. I suppose I shouldn't admit that I kept thinking about those raccoons all through the 90 minutes of JoAnne Akalaitis' interpretation of *The Bacchae*.[3]

While Brantley's subsequent review was a withering critique of the production, that he started it with the study of the raccoons was what captured the attention. Brantley brought to the fore what may be the central beauty of America's central park: "the mysterious and often forgotten coexistence of the natural and urban worlds." The Public mantra, that culture belongs to everyone, is no more clearly reflected than in the Park and its leafy wildness, for it is there that the spirit of The Public is able to thrive. Tickets are free, distributed at lotteries around the city or to those who go to the Delacorte early in the morning and wait in line all day, again, in the blazing sun or through torrential downpours. The al fresco nature of the entire event, from start to finish, creates its energy. The contention here is that "park-ness," and the example that The Public has set with Free Shakespeare in the Park reflects an American addition to Shakespeare that is powerful and sometimes glossed over. There are certainly many global examples, but the contemporary expectation of a summer evening in a city park, taking in the words of Shakespeare, is American to the core, and the hub of that tradition is the Delacorte Theater.

And so, it is not the full story, as in Brantley's article, that the crossing of the natural and the urban is "often forgotten," for in theater worlds, that tie is utterly critical in the consumption and digestion of classic works of performance, even if we do not often think about it deliberately. It is in that intersection that the Delacorte stands out as perhaps one of the most powerful cultural locales in New York City and the United States. As a playful but oddly relevant example, the number of times that Public Theater actors, directors, and critics mention their run-ins with raccoons is too numerous to be ignored. It's so prevalent now that the furry scavengers are often used in the social media marketing of the festival; come for the raccoons, perhaps,

---

[3] Ben Brantley, "God vs. Man in an Open-Air Fight," *New York Times*, August 24, 2009.

stay for the Shakespeare? In fact, that popular *Bacchae* raccoon actually represents so much of the power of American summer Shakespeare. The creatures symbolically show, through their general disinterest in sword fighting and iambic pentameter, the fleeting nature of the theater and, if we are being philosophical, of humanity. A busy raccoon and her babies scurrying across the stage gives beautiful and accidental juxtaposition to Prospero's "We are such stuff as dreams are made on, and our little life is rounded with a sleep."[4]

In story after story, weather and park-dwelling critters are the focus of excited retellings and juicy anecdotes. Allison Janney, the Oscar award-winning star of film and television, had, and continues to have, a robust career on the New York boards. When asked about her one experience in Central Park, acting as Kate alongside Jay O. Sanders in Mel Shapiro's rendition of *The Taming of the Shrew* in 1999, she immediately remembers the elements—and yes, the raccoons:

> That goes in the category, "sounds better than it is." I am not someone who enjoys acting outdoors or fighting a raccoon to make my stage left entrance … or it's 99 degrees and humid and Mario Cantone and I would be doing rain dances under the stage and praying that we would be cancelled … I didn't take well to it. I appreciated it. I like going to the Delacorte Theater and *seeing* it.[5]

While Janney speaks of the experience with a good-natured nostalgia (all said with a smile) and continues to be a Public Theater fan, it is fair to say that the roughness is not ideal. But love it or hate it, everyone has a Park story wrapped up in the unusual conditions and the ability of that space to create magic, often inadvertently and in ways that become mythical and border on the artistically spiritual. Most discussions with Park actors start out with something akin to, "Oh let me tell you about the time when." What inevitably follows is a story about weather, wildlife, or comradery. Rarely does the conversation turn to the elegant phrasing or dramaturgical nuance of William Shakespeare. Perhaps it is because that part is a given.

Jay O. Sanders has performed in the Park on and off for forty-five years. In fact, Sanders is second only in Park prolific-ness to Sam Waterston. When recollecting on a Eustis-directed *Hamlet* in Central Park in 2008, he noted:

> There was one time where I would come down fully costumed and made up to play the Ghost. … I would show up and be pacing, just getting ready for my entrance, and the mists of Hell are starting to burn down there … and I'd look over, and there would be a mother and her four or

---

[4]From William Shakespeare, *The Tempest*, Act 4, Scene 1.
[5]Allison Janney interview with the author in UCCS Prologue Lecture Series, October 2016.

five baby raccoons, all sitting and looking at me like, "Who's this idiot?" You know? And I'd kind of plead with them: "You know, could you just take me seriously for a moment!?"

Sanders elaborated on the moment when Michael Stuhlbarg, as Hamlet, spoke to the eternal flame of his father: "There was at least one night ... where we had a crane take off right over his head, as though it was my spirit or something, before I arrived. You can't make this shit up." Jeanine Tesori, the Tony-winning composer and Public family member, composed the music for the Tony Kushner adaptation of Bertolt Brecht's *Mother Courage* directed by George C. Wolfe. She too, when asked about the beauty and magic of the Delacorte, quickly returns to the rightful residents of that theater: "And then at night it's beautiful ... and the raccoons line up and throw apples at you. I'm sure they're forming a union."

Shakespeare in the Park as a response *to* and an instigator *of* the connection between the human and natural world goes far beyond the tongue-in-cheek anecdotes about Central Park's famous fauna. Theater scholar Una Chaudhuri has even used the raccoons of the Delacorte and, primarily, Brantley's now famous friend, as a basis for an imagined community called Zoöpolis in a whimsical chapter of her book *The Stage Lives of Animals*. Chaudhuri considers the power and importance of what she calls *zooësis*, or the study of animals in art. Lest one scoff at the focusing on raccoons in the theater, the author is convincing that wildlife really is worth a consideration. Chaudhuri laments the responses she receives when she discusses animals in this way, "an incredulous giggle or dismissive snort."[6] It is, we now know, essential. It ties the contemporary theater to its ancestors, in eras and places in which storytelling, folklore, dancing, and theatrical performance spoke to the place in which it was happening, where the communion was being offered—where festivals began with the ritual slaughter of a goat or a prayer and salutation to the harvest and its bounty. That sort of consideration of nature, for sure, *is* too often forgotten.

Perhaps one of the finest love letters to the Park was furiously pounded out and posted on Facebook by Jesse Tyler Ferguson in the summer of 2013. The production of *The Comedy of Errors* was classic Park magic. Led by one of the most famous Public directors in the country, Daniel Sullivan, the comedy was a rollicking ninety-minute affair starring two popular summer performers, Ferguson and Hamish Linklater. In his post to his friends, Ferguson, through his genuine and heartfelt passion for the stage, captured the joy of a night in the Park. "An amazing night I will NEVER forget," he wrote:

---

[6] Una Chaudhuri, *The Stage Lives of Animals: Zoöesis and Performance* (New York: Routledge, 2017), p. 1.

About 30 minutes into our 90-minute show it began to rain. Nothing new for an actor doing outdoor theater. We continued for about 10 more minutes until it began to downpour. Buckets. At that point our stage manager, Cole, made an announcement to the audience over the sound system that we would hold until the storm passed. The audience cheered, encouraging us that they were willing to wait out the rain with us. After all, they waited all day for the free tickets that got them into the theater in the first place. ...

The rain only got worse. I began to realize it would be very unlikely for us to be able to continue. Our dancers would slip, the expensive sound equipment that we were wearing to amplify our voices would be ruined. Still, the audience stayed, only cheering harder when the rain increased.

Finally, the storm lightened, and Cole announced that we would begin again shortly which was met with applause and cheers from the audience AND the cast.

Then something beyond mother nature's control happened: the sound board fried and shut down. ... No mics to amplify. No speakers to play music for the dancers. Nothing. Stage Management was about to announce to the audience that we would have to unfortunately call the show.

Then Hamish and I had an idea.

Did George C. Scott have a body mic when he did *The Merchant of Venice* back in 1961 at this same theater? (Granted, he didn't have to worry about helicopters or private jets flying over the Delacorte Theater on their way to the Hamptons).

Let's finish the show wireless. Unplugged!

To my amazement Rebecca Sherman, our company manager took a deep breath and just said "Do it. It will be amazing."

What proceeded was one of the most magical hours of my life. ...

The brilliant De'Adre Aziza started where we left off, with her jazz influenced version of Sigh No More, the audience snapping along to keep the beat. ... During a moment that required a sound cue of a bell, I pointed at the church that was meant to be producing the sound and exclaimed "BONG! BONG!"... When Emily Bergl knocked a gun out of Tyler Caffall's hand the entire company, in unison yelled "BANG" and then produced the dying cat sound that was meant to follow. ...

The play ends with a quiet moment I share with my long-lost twin. The audience stayed completely still and silent to hear the final words of the play, laughing where the jokes were but then silencing immediately to hear the next lines. That's when I lost it. You never would have been able to tell because I was soaking wet, but I started to ugly cry.

I was so moved by this shared moment. It truly personified why I am fueled to put on silly costumes and wigs and pretend to be someone else in front of a collected group of strangers.

When we finally reached the end of the play the audience exploded into applause. We didn't bow though … all we could do was applaud right back to THEM.

From this day forward when I am asked why I want to act I will think upon last night.[7]

Ferguson received his Actors Equity card at The Public, and while he rose to television stardom in the intervening years, he credits the Delacorte as his home: "I love coming here because I feel free when I'm here. I feel artistically like I can do anything."[8]

The love for the theater, but more specifically this one particular stage, is reiterated by so many artists and attendees. Free Shakespeare in the Park is not, of course, just about the Park and its ecology and weather patterns. As self-evident as that is, so too are the other descriptors: "Shakespeare" and "Free." These three key elements have propelled the Festival to a peerless fame in the United States, and the way the productions are selected, produced, and received are uncovered in the following pages and in several examples.

John Douglas Thompson, another Park regular, reflects that it is the best summer job in America: "It's here in New York, it's outdoors, under the stars, with the elements. It's an event. It's rare that I've been involved in theater that transforms itself to be an event. … When you're doing it in the Park, it becomes this other New York event that transcends, almost beyond the play." Here is how it happens.

Taking The Public Uptown

John Douglas Thompson's assertion that the Park season is the best gig in the country is a bold statement for one of America's premiere Shakespeare actors, a man who regularly appears on Broadway and has no *need* to toil in the heat and sometimes unpleasant conditions. But his claim is not

---

[7] Jesse Tyler Ferguson, content provided to the author, July 15, 2016. Full article on the performance and Facebook story in *Hollywood Reporter*, https://www.hollywoodreporter.com/news/jesse-tyler-ferguson-performs-shakespeare-577342.

[8] Linklater, Ferguson's costar and friend, recalls the evening with equal passion. Of note he says, "Dan [Sullivan] was like, 'This is my valedictory. This is my swan song. I've been here for long enough.' And then we were sort of sitting in tech, and I was like, 'Do you really think Jesse Tyler Ferguson with a plate of pasta on his head wants to be your final statement?' And sure enough, next year he's doing *Lear*." Sullivan continues to be a staple director at The Public to this day. Chelsea Clinton is a longtime Shakespeare in the Park enthusiast and specifically remembers that famous production, "there are some for whom, I think, it is a particular gift to be able to animate Shakespeare's plays in that environment. Certainly … the quintessential person for me who does that is Jesse Tyler Ferguson."

isolated. Ruth Sternberg, the head of the technical side of all of The Public Theater's productions, describes the Delacorte as a sort of summer camp. On any given day at the Park during a production, in addition to actors and designers, she has 150–200 technicians working to pull off a show that will play almost every evening to about 1,800–2,000 patrons.

It is helpful to imagine and actually visualize the scope of what is done at the Delacorte. Any theater company that has performed a version of Shakespeare in the Park knows that the technical logistics of performing outdoors is complex and the labor grueling. For The Public, that means the construction of an infrastructure that will accommodate about 100,000 people annually at the cost of at least $1 million per production. Further, consider the numbers as they contrast to other theaters in New York and to The Public's "regular" season of offerings. The Public Theater performs in five venues at the headquarters at Lafayette Street, in addition to the cabaret club, Joe's Pub. The largest of those venues, the Newman Theater, seats 300 people. For context, the largest Broadway house, the Gershwin Theater, seats 1,933 patrons, and the smallest Broadway house, the Hayes, seats just under 600. In other words, the largest space at The Public is far smaller than the smallest Broadway house and the Delacorte is as large as the biggest theater on the Great White Way.

Practically speaking, on the busiest night at The Public downtown, there could be about 1,500 patrons entering and exiting the building. However, with show times staggered, there is almost never that many people at any given time, and it is rare that each of the five venues and the Pub are performing at the same time. In contrast, almost every night in the summer, 2,000 people flood into the 81st Street entrance of Central Park and gather for one production. Around 10:00 p.m., the B and C subway lines on the West Side of New York are packed with Delacorte patrons heading home. More people see Shakespeare in the Park than any other show in The Public season, by far.

From a logistical standpoint, this means that the Park season is the largest single undertaking of The Public Theater all year, and with that come a host of challenges that are hardly noticed by the patron who has been queued up to get a ticket. Included in the long list of considerations and expenditures are concessions, costumes, lighting, animals, insufficient toilets, and complex dramatic text that has to be understood under the inevitable helicopters hovering above. What one has is something akin to a major league sporting event, albeit produced by a not-for-profit theater and presented to people who received their tickets free of charge.

Since the theater is open to the elements, it has to fully shut down at the end of the season and the lights, the sound, the sets, and practically everything else dismantled and trucked back down to Lafayette Street or into various storage facilities around New York. Each summer, most of The Public operating team relocates to Central Park and joins the over-hired staff and crew members for the extended Delacorte "summer camp." And camp is rough. They create an experience that is technically advanced in a space that has no roof, no grid, no place to hang sound equipment. In many outdoor theaters, these necessities can be hung on booms behind the audience, but the sheer size of this amphitheater dictates that Sternberg's team create a web of aircraft cable over the audience to hang speakers so that the audience can hear the miked actors. Sternberg outlined some of the many other considerations:

> Then there are towers. There's a bridge. The folklore says it's a highway sign that somebody told Joe Papp he could go get and use. I don't know if that's true or not, but it *looks* like a highway sign frame. [It's] a lighting position down-center in the back of the house, above the audience and above the booth.
>
> ...
>
> Then there are six individual towers that have little baskets at the top. That's where the lights get hung. Sometimes we put up trusses in the upstage-right and upstage-left corners for additional lighting positions, so we can actually have some backlight. We also use a lot of ground lighting.
>
> ...
>
> It's all outdoors, and there's no real place to do it. Anytime anybody's going up on any one of those trusses or up any of the poles for the lighting positions, everybody's in climbing gear and harnesses. It's safety first, and you're outside. If we see lightning in the distance during a show at the Delacorte, the follow-spots come down out of their towers because they're basically sitting on lighting rods. We have alternate positions for them that are on the wooden booth, which is considerably lower—a terrible angle. It's too flat. Everybody hates it, but otherwise we won't see the actors. We have to do something, but we can't put them up in the air.
>
> ...
>
> Scenery: It's the only theater we have that has trap space. None of our theaters down here [Lafayette] have trap space unless we build up a deck. Then once again, it's outdoors. There's the elements. There are the raccoons. There are the turtles. The raccoons eat things you'd never want them to eat, including cables and insulation. It's their house; we're just visiting.

The trap space is a luxury and has allowed some of the most pleasurable technical moments in the Park. Each time it is employed, designers and technicians restructure it and decide on its mechanics and use (elevators, doors, stairs). In *Julius Caesar*, the titular Trump look-alike was lifted from under the stage, stark naked in a golden bathtub to the delight of the audience. In the 2009 production of *Twelfth Night*, the pit was simply a set of stairs, and Anne Hathaway's Viola walked up as she was coming ashore on the coast of Illyria. But that concession to technical advancement is one of very few at the Delacorte. In the off season, it is essentially a shell; once everything is carted away, the stage is protected with an enormous covering and the sheds that act as costume and office space are winterized. The Public staff begins opening up the Delacorte as early as February, when cold temperatures are still common, and pipes and toilets can freeze. By early November, when they are finally and fully out of the space, the conditions can be similarly intemperate.

Acting on the Delacorte stage is not a usual undertaking and requires a flexibility and tolerance for the conditions. While John Douglas Thompson says that there is nothing else like it in the country, he admits that there are major hurdles in performing such intricate language in an enormous outdoor space:

> We rehearse in a room which is very similar to all kinds of rehearsal rooms.[9] But the stage that you move to ... is very, very different. And so, there are some technical challenges. There are some physical challenges that all need to be dealt with: how you move, how you're going to speak the text and the language. How you're going to create tension and drama onstage—it's all different from a normal, indoor theater.
>
> ...
>
> It makes it so much more expansive, and you have to be so much *more*. It's asked of you as an actor to be your biggest self. We often talk about rising to the challenge of Shakespeare, rising to the challenge of these characters, but in addition to that, when you're working in the Delacorte Theater for Shakespeare in the Park, you have to also rise to another level in bringing a great feel of felicity with the language, and physicality with your body in expressing Shakespeare's [text] and moments.

Jay O. Sanders also identifies the Delacorte's challenges as a performance venue since it's nearly a three-quarter thrust with audience often seeing the back of an actor or the side of the face. Even with a good mic system, adjustments for clarity have to be made so it is understood from the back row who is actually speaking. Seasoned actors adjust and develop a technique for performing on that stage.

> I don't even think about, I just do. You stay still while someone is doing something. Once it's established that they're talking, movement happens, but it's like passing the baton to say "This person is on. Now that person is on." Even though, at the same time, you are playing

---

[9]Rehearsals generally take place in an ordinary indoor studio on 42nd Street and are moved to the Park a week or so before previews begin.

a scene together ... There is the technical inclusiveness of the back rows of the theater with your eyes, which, if you do that, the audience becomes connected to you. If you don't, they will never quite fully accept you.

And there are Park rules to contend with as well. The Public does not own its theater spaces; rather, it rents both the Delacorte and Lafayette theaters from the City of New York for $1 a year. One imagines that that arrangement must have both thrilled and disgusted Joe Papp—having desperately wanted a theater that connected to the beating heart of the city and yet at ambivalent odds with his relationship with the city government. While the setup is mutually beneficial, adding to the cultural cache of the city, The Public Theater is a tenant and, naturally, has to respect the rules. Trees may not be trimmed or altered. If foliage is affecting a show or the aesthetics of a designer, the production team may place an order with the city for removal. The wheels of bureaucracy churn. The midnight Park curfew means that shows in Central Park have to end on time; if they hold too long for inclement weather, they risk being closed down before they finish the play.[10]

Some restrictions relate to intrusion of wildlife, which is, as noted, a constant hindrance in the Park. In the summer of 2019, early in the run of Kenny Leon's celebrated *Much Ado About Nothing*, a duck nested in the realistic-looking foliage of the stage, a setting representing a wealthy suburban Atlanta landscape. As the mallard stood watch center stage, the mother laid three eggs. The production crew was amazed, touched, and yet incapable of doing anything but watch. When the mother was away, they carefully covered the eggs with Tupperware in hopes that they might be protected from scavengers. The birds generally avoided the stage during performance but returned every morning to their plastic home. From a theatrical standpoint, the eggs and the ducks became part of the set and part of the design. They were treated with deep respect and care, just like the massive birds' nests above the box office and inside some of the lighting hoods. Sadly, "duckling watch 2019" ended several days before closing when it was reported that the eggs disappeared overnight, no doubt with raccoon paw prints all over the crime scene. It had become a social media Shakespearian tragedy.

The Delacorte truly is summer camp.

---

[10]Shakespeare Scholar in Residence, James Shapiro, is often responsible for cutting the Shakespearian scripts. He says that in addition to making sure the story is clearly told, he edits with an eye toward the Central Park curfew and inevitable rain delays.

The People's Park

You meet the elements ... I think it's the most magical place in New York ... The freedom that you feel under that sky, inside this troubled ... broken world, you just think ... there is still possibility. There's still possibility that things can be fixed and solved. You just have to participate and join the conversation, and we have to come together.

—JEANINE TESORI

"Just when you're about to lose faith in humanity, you see Shakespeare in the Park."

FIGURE 2.2 *Courtesy Tom Toro.*

Tom Toro's sketch of the Delacorte Theater for *The New Yorker* beautifully captures the allure that has been described by so many of the participants of the over sixty-year-old institution. "Just when you're about to lose faith in humanity, you see Shakespeare in the Park." The words are, of course, spoken by two woodland friends, a bird and a squirrel, as the pair look down on a crowd taking in a play with the lights glowing on the actors and the grand Belvedere Castle in the distance. The set that Toro sketches in his ode to Shakespeare in the Park is clearly the John Conklin-designed playground of the 2009 *The Bacchae*. Theater enthusiasts will note that *The Bacchae* is an ancient Greek tragedy by Euripides from around 405 BC, not a Renaissance offering of William Shakespeare. For many actors, designers, and directors, The Public and specifically Free Shakespeare in the Park have come to represent something far bigger than theater and Shakespeare himself. It is relevant to keep in mind that several of the seminal summer productions during Eustis's tenure that are considered in these pages were *not* written by William Shakespeare (*Hair, Into the Woods, The Bacchae, Mother Courage*, etc.). Shakespeare scholar James Shapiro notes that in America, "Shakespeare" has culturally become a way to highlight so many other things, from American politics to gender identity and class tensions. As with any superb writing, that lasting cultural effect can and should be relevant everywhere and at any time, but the American obsession with putting Shakespeare in a park has elevated his status as *the* artist of the American town square. Even if the play is not by Shakespeare, his name is the draw. Shapiro concludes, "Under the rubric of Shakespeare you can start bringing in all kinds of work. Without 'Shakespeare' you're not going to get the funding that is necessary."

And under the rubric of Shakespeare, and under the summer skies in America's Central Park, anything seems possible. Indeed, Jeanine Tesori's choice of the phrase "freedom under the sky" in the midst of a "broken world" immediately speaks to the geopolitical importance of the position of the theater in American life. That sense was all the more palpable in 2021, when The Public reopened from the pandemic with a production of the Jocelyn Bioh adaptation of *Merry Wives*, directed by Associate Artistic Director Saheem Ali. Patrons filed in, Covid vaccinations in hand, masks on faces, ready to rejoin the world in that, the most communal of New York theater spaces. For a couple of hours, the brokenness of the world washed away, and the focus turned to a group of friends in Harlem, written by a Renaissance poet, adapted and acted by artists of color in contemporary America. While Shakespeare is the focus of 90 percent of the productions, the play, perhaps, is *not* the thing, to ape Shakespeare himself. Since its inception, the Delacorte Theater's power and prestige is rooted in community communion, nature, and politics.

In June 2016, as the race for the White House was taking shape and a billionaire developer from New York was the presumptive Republican nominee, donors, staff, and patrons of The Public Theater gathered at the Delacorte for the annual gala. The event is special each year, an evening performance centered around a theme and often led by an esteemed American director and starring some marquee names. In 2016, the gala was called *The United States of Shakespeare* and featured F. Murray Abraham, Bill Erwin, Phylicia Rashad, Kate Burton, and John Douglas Thompson, among many others. At the end of the event, Christine Baranski walked onstage with a heavily made-up Meryl Streep in full Donald Trump drag—a belly that protruded over her belt, a bright red tie that extended to her knees, orange face makeup, and her own hair coiffed and teased into the future American president's signature look. The two joined each other center stage and belted out "Brush Up Your Shakespeare" from the musical *Kiss Me Kate*. With Trump as new contextual frame, the Streep/Baranski showstopper playfully eviscerated the candidate. "If she says your behavior is heinous, kick her right in the Coriolanus!"

The silly rendition of the president is now a bit quaint; when Streep sauntered on to the stage, the idea that the New York billionaire would win was still somewhat far-fetched. But the Streep roast highlighted The Public Theater's commitment to stepping fully into the political debate. Again, this is not a surprise to theater lovers and historians, who know well the role of public performance venues in world history. Shakespeare wrote with his patrons, Queen Elizabeth and King James, clearly in mind, and Aristophanes' comedies often commented on the Peloponnesian Wars to create satires of politics and social mores. As a producing organization, The Public Theater has confronted urbanization, diplomacy, immigration, and a host of other social issues, and woven them into the fabric of the institution under the "rubric" of Shakespeare. This lens provides one of the best examples in the United States of how a company can incorporate the needs of a city and nation into the infrastructure of the actual theater. Of particular note recently is how the theater has been used as a political tool and how it has confronted its goals of accessibility and inclusivity, sometimes with finesse and other times with an unsure hand.

* * *

The sheer volume of patrons, combined with its location, gives the Delacorte a platform like no other theater in America. In 2019, as Oskar Eustis was contemplating a plan for a $150 million renovation of the Delacorte, he noted, "The Delacorte is the place where you can actually reach enough people that can tip the scales. You can actually have an impact on the city, and by extension, on the culture as a whole." As grandiose ideas were floated, including a roof that could make the theater in the Park viable practically all year long, he noted that at its core the importance of the theater was the "cleanness of its offer." If they could make changes that would increase the offerings into the shoulder season, there would be a possibility that they could expand their numbers from 100,000 patrons to almost 200,000. The figures are fairly staggering and represent the total size of entire cities that are producing their own Shakespeare in the Park experiences. Eustis included in his plans ways to consider how he could allow for five matinees a week that would host thousands of school children, an important demographic that is underrepresented at The Public. Such was the largeness of the thinking about expansion in 2019, but the world crisis that engulfed theater put a temporary end to the grandiosity of the redesign of the Delacorte, even as it demonstrated a very real need for outdoor theater. The new $77 million plan (~$41 million from the city), drawn up in partnership with the Central Park Conservancy and the New York Department of Parks and Recreation, now focuses on a revamp of the backstage spaces, accessibility, lighting improvements, and a revision of the exterior for a more elegant and crisp visual appeal.

The redesign of the Delacorte speaks volumes about the ethos of The Public vis-à-vis the position of a cultural institution within the frame of a major city and, especially, its leafy center. The raccoons and the ducks are fun, but what they represent is the value of the park to the cultural life of a city. Eustis is never a more articulate champion of The Public and its history and future than when he speaks about economics and access. It occupies him every day and he notes, more than anything, "free-ness" is the central part of that crisp and clear "offer." It is his intention to find a way to make all of the productions at The Public free for all, though the resources to make that a reality are not currently available. To Eustis, the trials and complexities of mounting the plays every summer in a city park aren't worth anything unless "worth" is redefined, not just at The Public, but at theaters across America. He sees it as his duty as the leader of the organization to guide that conversation. It starts at Central Park, the place where the city, at its best, can feel egalitarian and communal:

> The Park itself is an expression of the same values that the Shakespeare in the Park tries to express. The fact that New York lavishes so much attention on a place that produces no economic value, that isn't about selling anything, that is free for anybody to walk into and enjoy—the movement to have city parks is an expression of the same idea that there are collective goods that should reach everybody, that Free Shakespeare in the Park embodies.
>
> ...
>
> You're not just walking into a beautiful place when you're walking into Central Park. You're walking into a beautiful urban *idea* that the city is where everybody is equal, that the city should be open to everybody. That in this time when so much of our architectural money is being spent on essentially gated communities—we're building private reserves for the wealthy—that a reserve that is explicitly for everybody, that's explicitly not for the wealthy. ... It's not just beauty. It's the *idea* of who the beauty is there for and what the beauty means. To me, that's what's the constant between Central Park and The Public—it's just another expression of this idea that we're all in this together.

His description of Central Park is, as is his wont, full of idealism that sometimes underemphasizes the financial realities of societal stratification. Central Park *does* produce economic value; one need only look at the asking price of an entry-level condo on 5th Avenue, or even buy an overpriced hot dog at a Park kiosk, to see that. The idealism, though, flows freely with Eustis, even as his knowledge of those very same economic realities is as sharp as any expert. He often quotes Jane Jacobs's influential work *The Death and Life of Great American Cities*, which is still, sixty years after its publication, an influential treatise on the use and misuse of American cities. Her book frames ways that cities can build those "collective goods" that Eustis mentions. More specifically, Jacobs notes that well-designed parks must have "demand goods"—something of value "equivalent to impulse sales in merchandising vocabulary."[11] She uses Free Shakespeare in the Park as a primary example. Happening upon a performance in a public park, and stopping to enjoy it, constitutes an "impulse buy," in her terms. But the "buy" in this case is the expenditure of time and care, not money. This lines up with Eustis's hopes: "I don't agree that individual people need to pay money in order to value something, and that idea I think is very much a product of our market hysteria or market hegemony ... the idea that the marketplace measures the value of everything. It doesn't, and culture is one of those things that it shouldn't measure the value of." The people of New York City, he believes, have already made their contribution, in tax dollars and by lending this corner of their park to the theater. They should be able to come to their park and see a good play.

And yet, art must be paid for, and this Shakespeare is some of the most expensive in the country. When Jacobs wrote of someone happening upon a play in Central Park, she was writing about a group of theater enthusiasts on a tiny budget attempting to activate city spaces, not a major American theater company in a 2,000-seat bowl. Papp's original shows were produced on a shoestring, funded from year to year, while now The Public's summer outings are well supported with major foundation donors like the LuEsther Mertz Foundation, the Jerome L. Green Foundation, and the Ford Foundation, and sponsorships from Delta Air Lines, Bank of America, JetBlue, and the like. While those tickets *are* free for anyone who lines up or gets lucky at one of the lotteries across the city, for others who want to forgo the lines, there are tickets available at top dollar (actually considered a donation to The Public), and their expense helps underwrite the free seats. To keep the socialist experiment that it always has been humming along, a phalanx of institutional giving staff creates a web of fundraising and donating strategies. And the Park is the center of that campaign for the entirety of The Public organization.

Kristen Gongora, the director of institutional relationships at The Public, explains that the Delacorte is the best vehicle for The Public to engage with the corporate world, in large part because of its capacity. Corporations can

---

[11]Jane Jacobs, *The Death and Life of Great American Cities* (New York: Random House, [1961] 1989), p. 108.

buy blocks of seats for clients, have backstage tours, and host small parties. All of that corporate money to support a socialist enterprise is elegant in a very Pappian socialist/capitalist way: Resist the moneyed and powerful publicly, and yet gladly accept the dollars so that others may attend the theater for free. Of course, with corporate sponsorship and high-dollar grant funding come the political implications that always worried Papp—how to use the levers of government without being beholden to politicians and boards. That becomes particularly difficult when producing work with unambiguous political viewpoints. It is no wonder, then, that many American political leaders enthusiastically attend Public shows or, in some cases, have strong words in condemning them. From President Clinton and his family to President Trump and his, to the various mayors of New York and cabinet officials and dignitaries, The Public, and particularly Shakespeare in the Park, is an animating cultural force. For some, being associated with the organization provides an important glow to their political motivations.

It is perhaps partly because of that glow that Eustis's friend, the former United Nations ambassador Samantha Power, decided during her term to take other ambassadors and diplomats to plays at The Public and on Broadway—a sort of theater diplomacy. She discovered that Shakespeare in the Park exhibited an enormous amount of American soft power; it demonstrated democratic principles, egalitarian ethics, and urban beauty, as well as quality professional art. When I spoke with her in 2018, one evening, in particular, stood out in her mind:

> I guess a very moving memory for me is at the very end of *Cymbeline*—which I thought was incredibly well done and was very moved by myself—I was sitting in this row of ambassadors from all different parts of the world—from different parts of Africa, from Latin America—and the Russian ambassador and his wife were sitting right behind me [Vitaly Churkin].
>
> And you might ask, given what was going on with us and Russia, why was he one of the recipients of this precious ticket? The answer is because I believe our theater and culture is at least a very large portion of our soft power, and even when we are fighting with our adversaries, we have to find sources of agreement and commonality. So, it made perfect sense to me that at the time of the nadir, I thought, in our relationship, he and his wife would be the perfect recipients, right? To remember all that we have in common.
>
> They've just invaded Ukraine. They are doing terrible things in Syria. I don't yet know about the election interference that lies a couple years ahead. But the metaphorical, in that case, curtain goes down, and the first person in the entire theater to spring to his feet, to ensure that there was a standing ovation for this lustrous performance, was the Russian ambassador. And of course, the way it works with standing ovations is if one person in the center of the throng is the first mover, it can have a cascading effect.

So, to watch this—it was like the wave at Yankee Stadium—to watch this ripple inspired by the Russian ambassador, who, it turns out, had been a child actor himself so really knew what he was praising, I was just so struck. It was very moving to me that he was so overcome. I think he may have even had tears in his eyes when he was clapping with his wife. So, just a reminder of how theater can cross culture but also cross divisions. There is something so universalizing about the message.

The moment was instructive as well as idealistic for Power. She eventually started using Public Theater plays as a way to influence other ambassadors: "The subversiveness of it and the sort of cascading effect snuck up on me." She talks of her fascination, long before she became America's top diplomat, of seeing the queues near the Delacorte during her morning jogs. She recalled how egalitarian it all appeared—future audiences that looked unlike the patrons lining up to see a show on Broadway. She acknowledged optimism for the country in seeing the civic and cultural commitment to building a day in the Park around "waiting"—waiting to get a free ticket to see a Shakespeare play: "It rewards determination and not wealth or connections." She went on:

> I start from the premise that we are getting ever more divided and ever more convinced of the merits of our own convictions in our separate echo chambers. ... But at times of division, there are not that many forms of activity that can bring people together physically and bring people together spiritually or metaphorically. So, I think the narrative of theater ... like film, but in theater it's a more interactive experience, where you're much more aware of the people around you, in part because you get up in the middle of it, and you have to step over them to get in and out. But the lights are up at a certain point, and you have a sense of those around you and you're laughing and hearing each other laugh.
>
> ...
>
> Why wouldn't we, at a time when we are more and more divided and do fewer and fewer things together, render that as easy as possible to make as available as possible? ... Just as voting should now be easier than it's ever been before instead of harder, so, too, having experiences that are kind of countercultural, frankly, in their unifying potential and in their in-person, physical, convening potential—that should just be made easier.

In 2022, her words rang even more true and pressing, with debates about voting rights, a full-scale war in Ukraine, and partisan divides that felt insurmountable. The nostalgia of an imagined, unified America of old is deeply felt in the Delacorte, under the stars, with the sound of the warbling birds and even the roar of the 737 aircraft overhead. In fraught times, that egalitarian need and the familial aura of a Delacorte summer can feel even "countercultural," to use the ambassador's words. It is Rockwellian

America, for all the benefits and flaws that that nostalgia implies. Indeed, the modeling of Central Park and Free Shakespeare in the Park as an exemplar of American strength should not be accepted without deep interrogation and skepticism, just as one might openly wonder why a diplomat from an oppressive regime should skip the line while New Yorkers line up for hours in the heat and others are cut out from the equation entirely.

As Jacobs demonstrated, the Park cannot be separated from economics. While Eustis says that Central Park "produces no economic value, [it isn't] about selling anything ... free for anybody to walk into and enjoy," he certainly understands that that comment is firmly situated in the realm of lofty idealism. Central Park is a massive source of economic value to the city and exists also as a supreme example of something that sociologists might say illustrates a citizen's "cultural capital," aided, in fact, by the fame and success of institutions like Free Shakespeare in the Park. Indeed, in this way, the Bard is an elite endeavor at the beginning of the twenty-first century, and attending a show speaks about social mobility, access, and a rare treat for the privileged few. Increasingly, Central Park is "central" only to the wealthy who either call Manhattan home or are tourists who saved up for the experience of being in New York City. Even Samantha Power's allusion to *soft power* is an assertion rooted in stratification and a touch of elitism, for good or ill. The reality, sixty years on, is that this unifying experience now is located in the epicenter of wealth and privilege.

Under the still-egalitarian dreams and missions, the reality of "privilege" in the Park is not lost on Oskar Eustis and, thus, why he spends so much time thinking about the ways to shore up the social missions that may have eroded over the years. Recently, he has redoubled The Public's efforts to diversify audience access to get the plays back to the people and underserved neighborhoods of New York (and the broader country). Diversifying the Central Park effort is a challenging conundrum. It comes down to one basic problem: Why would someone living in the outer boroughs, sometimes working two jobs, have any incentive to take a train to Central Park and line up for a ticket that they may or may not receive? Now, lotteries take place each morning at various locations throughout the city and many of the tickets are distributed in this fashion.[12]

The intersection of economic and racial diversity has been a conversation swirling around Shakespeare in the Park since the beginning. While The Public has not been unimpeachable when it has come to diversity in the productions that are produced at the Delacorte, it is well documented that Joe Papp made a point of casting actors of color in the 1960s, 1970s, and 1980s, believing that the mission of his theater demanded it. Sam Waterston says of his friend Papp: "Really what Joe was saying was the color of a person's skin and their ethnicity don't matter. The big question

---

[12]Public Works and the Mobile Unit directly confront these challenges and are discussed in Chapter 9.

is, can they act? Can they occupy the part? So, if you say it's nontraditional casting, it's sort of like a smokescreen. What happens is—the challenge is, can you look at a person as a person? Then we're going to put people in front of you that, try as you might, you're not going to be able to look at them as anything else but a person. Then they're going to shed new light on the part." By casting Black and Hispanic actors, often with less formal experience than other, comprehensively "trained" counterparts from high-dollar graduate programs, Papp was in fact making a fairly important claim about the way American Shakespeare should be. What Lin-Manuel Miranda did decades later with *Hamilton*, perhaps even more powerfully and suddenly, effected much the same thing. Reevaluating how stories are told and who gets to tell those stories had to be the goal of The Public that Papp envisioned.

With all of that duly noted and reflected in cast lists, it is not unnoticed that if economic, gender, and race diversity are central facets of what the Delacorte and The Public are committed to, it is unfortunate that so many of the productions at the Park have been directed by white men, a fact that is actively being addressed at the company. In the coming chapters, I have selected to focus on a group of plays that demonstrate a certain amount of diversity in the director's chair. But perhaps an even larger discrepancy illuminates the racial and political stratification that is so difficult to alter, even as The Public and other theaters try hard to change decades-old norms. The audience, in fact, is *the* essential factor when assessing the various mantras of The Public: *Culture belongs to everyone, one public, free for all*. Simply, the demographic makeup of the audience does not look like New York City as a whole. Neither is it geographically representative. The Borough of Manhattan is home to about 1.7 million New Yorkers and is nearly 60 percent white. For context, New York City has a population of about 8.8 million people and is nearly 42 percent white.[13] In short, it is no surprise that in a festival that takes place in the middle of the wealthiest and whitest neighborhood in New York City, the audience does not represent the whole city. Neither is it geographically representative of Manhattan—a disproportionate amount of audience come from the ritzy Upper West Side and Chelsea. But need it be this way, or is there a model that will help moderate the discrepancy? One only needs to go to the Classic Theater of Harlem's Shakespeare productions two miles away in Marcus Garvey Park to see vast differences in audience composition. The question of access, then, is not entirely related to geography and distance of commute, but rather a *feeling* of openness and connection for all New Yorkers (or lack thereof). Addressing this is clearly a work in progress, made all the more urgent in 2020 when Eustis faced enormous pressure from his staff to recommit to inclusivity and diversity. Hiring high-profile artists of color in leading

---

[13]Consolidated from the 2020 data of the US Census Bureau.

positions, such as new Associate Artistic Director Saheem Ali, has been a first step in acknowledging that the commitment to diversity was perhaps not as deep as reflected in the company's lofty ethos and historical precedents.

In discussions with Eustis now, there is no question that he recognizes these unmistakable challenges, especially as they awkwardly run contrary to The Public's mission. In the summer of 2020 he said, "For all the progressiveness of The Public Theater, the hierarchy has just been astonishing. I mean from Joe Papp to JoAnne Akalaitis to George Wolfe to me, this is an organization that has always had the leader, who everything else seems to circle around. And I'm trying to start changing that ... it's part of a serious attempt to look at getting more voices into positions of authority."

The effort to diversify and create offerings that show off New York City, while also welcoming New York City to Central Park, is a lasting influence that Eustis wants for his tenure: break down economic barriers, break down audience homogeneity, break down political elitism. Ticket distribution sites in New York have grown from five to forty-five in the course of a couple of years and The Public has implemented daily giveaways online. The numbers *are* shifting. While national attendance at professional theater hovers around 80 percent white, the Delacorte is now at around 65 percent. That is still merely representative of the demographic of Manhattan, not the city of New York as a whole, but the trend lines are clearly moving, albeit very slowly.

One only need look at the choice of plays, the ticket distributions, and staffing decisions to see the renewed focus on diversity and inclusion. And it extends beyond race and gender, with offerings that directly confront income inequality, class, and political ideology. In 2016, Janet McTeer starred in a Phyllida Lloyd-directed all-female version of *Taming of the Shrew*. The 2019 production of Kenny Leon's *Much Ado About Nothing*, the 2021 Jocelyn Bioh adaptation of *Merry Wives* set in Harlem, and the 2022 revisioning of *Richard III* with Danai Gurira as the titular King consciously chose to center the stories around Black communities, with cast and design teams consisting primarily of people of color. Leon's conception and development of *Much Ado* is the focus of the "Interlude" at the end of this section.

* * *

Central Park, for all the symbolic idealistic weight that it carries, is not the same place as when Colleen Dewhurst trod the boards at the Delacorte, or when Joe Papp loaded up the flatbed for trips around the five boroughs. Reaching the people, in the place where they live and die, is now far more complicated. And yet, when it starts to work—when ticket lotteries affect a diversification in the audience, when The Public hosts pageants starring citizens of New York, when casts begin to look like the people of the city— it's hard not to wax idealistic and hopeful. On those soft, warm evenings, one can muse, as in Toro's *New Yorker* cartoon, "Just when you're about to lose faith in humanity, you see Shakespeare in the Park."

3
Under the Lights

FIGURE 3.1 *Post-show* Hair. *Courtesy Bryan Bedder.*

Oskar Eustis began his job as the artistic director of The Public Theater in 2005, as the new millennium was gaining speed and developing its identity. Already, war and terrorism were defining global concerns, and the attacks of 9/11 were fresh in the minds of New Yorkers. George W. Bush had just been inaugurated to his second term in office. In August, Hurricane Katrina would devastate New Orleans and the Gulf Coast and erode any confidence in the reelected president. In those first years of the tenure of Oskar Eustis at The Public, great changes in the geopolitical order were shaping up. America would remain in what appeared to be an endless quagmire in Iraq, terror threats intensified, while the financial collapse of Lehman Brothers and other major American banks defined an era of monetary unease and growing global recession. In November 2008, the United States elected the first African American president; the subsequent years saw smartphone use explode, and Facebook, Twitter, and other social media platforms became the primary means of distribution of information and misinformation. While gun violence intensified, cannabis was legalized in many states, as was same-sex marriage, and the age of Obama ushered in hope and a more progressive vision of the future. Just as quickly, the pendulum swung back with the election of Donald Trump, the rise of populist and antidemocratic regimes around the globe, nuclear proliferation, fear of immigration, and renewed social tensions fueled by political bipolarity. In 2020, as a new decade officially began, a pandemic swept across the globe and altered the way every living human being would consider social engagement and community. This, combined with the menace of misinformation fueled by profligate lies about the veracity of the 2020 presidential election in the United States, broadly eroded confidence in institutions.

Eustis is not a political leader in a traditional sense, but the bully pulpit he can wield as head of one of the most prominent cultural institutions in the United States should not be underestimated. At the very least, the years in which Eustis has had the opportunity to run The Public have been extraordinary, and he has made the spirit of the times his artistic muse by supporting the best artists in the country to comment on and add to societal debate. In that way, the deeply political and opinionated Eustis was perhaps the perfect person for the job: first a producer and intellect, and perhaps only secondarily an artist. He used the tumult and instability of the times as any great artistic leader would—that is to, as Hamlet tells us, "Hold as 'twere the mirror up to nature: to show virtue her feature, scorn her own image, and the very age and body of the time his form and pressure."[1]

Shakespeare in the Park—in Central Park—is an ideal location to show the world her image, her form, and pressure. And just as the world, and America's place in it, has altered and undergone drastic change, The Public has reflected those changes and those disruptions under the lights in Central Park. But William Shakespeare only wrote about thirty-eight plays—give or

---

[1] From William Shakespeare, *Hamlet*, Act 3, Scene 2.

take a couple, depending on who you ask. While the summer offerings are often augmented with other artists, capturing the global zeitgeist of any era is a lot to ask of a singular Renaissance poet. And yet that is exactly what is asked of him every year.

Since the 1970s, with the exception of a few lean years, The Public has presented at least two shows per summer season, each running approximately four weeks. The plays are not designed for review and public critique; they are free, ephemeral, and necessarily have a closing date. They are there, ostensibly, to serve the immediate audience, their needs and the realities of the world at the moment.[2] So that rehearsals can continue and so that a production will never be "complete" and ready for review, the plays run in previews for three weeks, have a premiere, and then officially run for about one week. It's brief, quick, over and done, in a flash—and often a flash with great attention paid. The model has been the same for some time and Eustis has continued the tradition of highlighting some of the best actors, designers, and directors in America to produce in the Park. While Papp's early Public helped establish the careers of many well-known stage and film actors, including George C. Scott, Olympia Dukakis, Sam Waterston, Colleen Dewhurst, and Jerry Stiller, Oskar Eustis can attract known performers with greater ease now that the venue has such a bright spotlight trained on it. Actors *want* to perform there. In the Eustis years, the Delacorte has remained a draw for some of the most sought-out actors in America, including Danielle Brooks, Phylicia Rashad, Annette Benning, John Lithgow, Janet McTeer, Oliver Platt, Al Pacino, Meryl Streep, Anne Hathaway, and Audra McDonald.

While to *just* focus on those famous names misses the point of the Park, anyone assessing the plays that are performed there often and necessarily recall stories that involve movie stars or natural calamities, or both. "Remember the time that Meryl toiled in the heat during rehearsals for *Mother Courage*?" But the Delacorte hardly needs a star to propel attendance—the theater is always packed and generally the show becomes a culturally relevant event. Focusing on a star under the stars at the Delacorte should not be ignored, either, for again there is something obviously powerful in the intersection of the famous and the everyday. It is there that so many of the juiciest and most evocative stories originate, and once the audience is packed in, Eustis's goals for the theater can take off. Political proselytizing? No. But Shakespeare in the Park plays have clear intentions, and those intentions, despite the iambic pentameter and long, confusing character lists, are fairly easy to suss out.

In Eustis's time as artistic director, he has produced scores of major productions and events at the Delacorte Theater, from Shakespeare to the

---

[2]There are exceptions, of course. While The Public, and especially its Shakespeare in the Park offerings, aren't really aiming toward Broadway premieres and life beyond their relatively brief runs, the post-*Hamilton* era is challenging that not-for-profit model. This will be addressed throughout.

Greeks, and Brecht to Sondheim. Any thought of a democratic model in which a board of advisors adjudicate the possibilities of a summer of classical work is mistaken. While those involved in regional theater understand this top-driven selection as *de rigueur*, it's worthy of note that the summer productions in the central park of America's largest city—plays that often attract broad attention from tourists, enthusiasts, critics, academics, and politicians—are chosen by Eustis alone. He acknowledges, of course, that he consults with staff and gathers the opinions of those artists and producers he trusts the most, but the decision is his.[3]

Of those decisions and of those productions, several stand out as having captured attention far beyond the Park and New York City. *Mother Courage and Her Children*, *Hair*, *The Merchant of Venice*, and *Julius Caesar* each tapped into a cultural and social moment that allowed them to exist in a broader national conversation. Some of that came from the use of a celebrity drawing in crowds and media attention. But more accurately, the plays produced a stir that intersected art with the spirit of the era—the zeitgeist—by using the location of Central Park as a town square, to highlight a star, appeal to nostalgia, and always to make a social or political statement. The following narratives uncover some of the ways that these particular theatrical markers were achieved.

Mother Courage and Her Children

In 2006, during Eustis's first full season of producing, he chose a marquee performance of Brecht's *Mother Courage* starring Meryl Streep, Austin Pendleton, and Kevin Kline. The play was to be directed by the former artistic director, George C. Wolfe, with music by Jeanine Tesori and an adaptation by Eustis's best friend, the Pulitzer and Tony winner Tony Kushner. With a lineup that remarkable, as star-studded as anything in the history of The Public, *Mother Courage* is a fine example of The Public using star power to propel the summer season and to illuminate classic work and contemporary politics.

While the staging of *Mother Courage*, a non-Shakespearian play, was the central focus of the summer of 2006, Eustis was not turning his back on the Bard in his first full season—the summer also featured the Moisés Kaufman-directed *Macbeth* in the Delacorte. It was *Mother Courage*, though, that was clearly the perfect play for the new artistic director and, with its socialist overtones and staunch anti-war bent, for The Public Theater as a whole.[4] The

---

[3]As noted before, this is starting to change, as more senior artistic staff are brought into the decision-making process.
[4]To be clear, *Mother Courage* was neither Eustis's first production at The Public, nor entirely his idea. His first show was *Two Gentlemen of Verona* in the summer of 2005 and Rinne Groff's *Ruby Sunrise* at Lafayette that fall. *Mother Courage* was quite clearly the first marquee event of his tenure as head of The Public.

play, which is set during the Thirty Years War, was part of a series of Brecht's epic works that confronted the rise of fascism in Europe through the eyes of a woman using her children to help sell wares at wartime. A frank look at war profiteering and the horrors involved in the intersection of capitalism and conflict, the play was particularly apt in 2006, as America was in the midst of what many worried was an unending battle and occupation of Iraq and war in Afghanistan.

The play combined some famously mercurial people in its development and production. Eustis brought in Wolfe to direct, a year after his departure from the artistic director's chair, making the play, according to Eustis, something he could not really produce himself. When George was in the room, he assumed the role of alpha. The relationship with Wolfe is currently not strong and has been punctuated with hurt feelings over the years, especially when Eustis made the decision in 2008 to pull the plug on the Wolfe-directed production of John Guare's *A Free Man of Color*, citing financial considerations. But that was still several years in the future when Eustis hired Wolfe to direct *Mother Courage*. Even so, he says, he tried to stay "hands off" to allow the former artistic director to run the show and manage the stars.

Add to that mix Tony Kushner, arguably the most famous playwright in the United States at that time, and you had a trio of men with large egos and complicated histories. It is somewhat astounding that the production worked at *all*. Kushner's most famous play, *Angels in America*, was originally commissioned and produced by Eustis and Tony Taccone at Eureka Theater, and then codirected by the duo at the Mark Taper Forum in Los Angeles in November 1992, when they were all in their thirties. When it moved to Broadway, Eustis was replaced by Wolfe as director because Kushner wanted a "different sense of theatricality," according to the *Los Angeles Times*. He thought that Wolfe would have "a more elegant flow as opposed to a more rambunctious feeling. ... There's a level of polish in George's work that is not important to Oskar."[5]

It was a painful slight for Eustis. *Angels in America*, in both of its parts, became an international success, immediately joined the canon as one of the important scripts in American theater history, and hauled in seven Tony Awards, including one for Wolfe for direction.[6] Eustis said, "I spent about a year, very angry, very distanced from him. The way we put the friendship back together is really through Tony's unbelievably consistent generosity and refusal to let go of me."[7] Similarly, Taccone recalled, "I think it took us a

---

[5] Tony Kushner quoted in Don Shirley, "Angels Director Calls Split 'Amicable,'" *Los Angeles Times*, December 20, 1992.
[6] The Marianne Elliott-directed revival of *Angels* in 2018 won three more Tonys, best play and acting awards for Andrew Garfield and Nathan Lane.
[7] Oskar Eustis quoted in Boris Kachka, "What Oskar Eustis Has Learned from 30 Years of Friendship with Tony Kushner," *New York Magazine*, October 24, 2017.

while to feel like we could trust each other again, but it happened."[8] Eustis remains best friends with Kushner and has, as is said, let bygones be bygones. Tense relations between Wolfe and Eustis have eased recently, but due to their delicate relationship over the years, his presence at The Public is minimal.

In the summer of 2006, the man who would become one of the most powerful theater artistic directors in America largely stayed on the sidelines of *Mother Courage*. The play in Central Park was helmed by Wolfe and was driven by the star power of Streep, Kushner, Tesori, and Kline. Eustis says, "I was a young producer at The Public and George was the previous artistic director, and it became very hard for me to produce George. It was not an easy process and I'm sorry about that because I think the show wasn't as successful as it would have been had I been able to fully exert myself as a producer, but I had to take more of a back seat than I do now." Many reviews concurred about the play's success, noting that Streep was extraordinary while the overall effect, according to the *New York Times*, was "a production in search of a tone."[9]

Eustis was not, by any stretch, completely absent from the production—his involvement in the play's selection, casting, and dramaturgy was long in the making. Kushner, too, had been thinking about the *Mother Courage* for a while and recalls beginning the conversations with Streep several years before when he, Streep, and Mike Nichols were filming the HBO version of *Angels in America*:

> The first table reads of *Angels in America*, when Mike was making the movie, were the first time I'd spent any time with Meryl. We read through the first episode, then we took a coffee break. Meryl came up and asked me a couple of questions. We started chatting, and then I said, "Okay, I've waited so long to ask you this question. Can I just ask it now, even though we've really just met?" She said, "Anything." I said "You have to do *Mother Courage*. It's my favorite play. It's a part you have to play." Meryl said "You know, it's funny. A lot of people have said that to me." I said "If you do it, I'll translate it for you."

Eustis was involved in those early conversations, which centered around the creation of a new translation, and remembers casually discussing it on the *Angels* set in Rome. Shortly after he was named the new artistic director, Eustis, with Kushner, took Streep to the famed New York eatery the Union

---

[8] For full historical context: Taccone and Eustis were co-artistic directors at the Eureka Theater Company in San Francisco in the late 1980s. After seeing Kushner's *Bright Room Called Day*, they commissioned *Angels in America*, which they expected to be a ninety-minute comedy. When it turned into a seven-hour epic about AIDS and Reagan-era America, Eustis recalls thinking that it was too big for Eureka. Soon, he was headhunted away to the Mark Taper Forum to become its dramaturg and Taccone left to helm Berkeley Rep. *Angels* played at the Taper, Eureka, the Cottesloe in London, and then on Broadway.

[9] Ben Brantley, "Mother, Courage, Grief and Song," *New York Times*, August 22, 2006.

Square Café and offered her the role. They collectively decided on Wolfe to direct and Tesori to compose.

Kushner admits that his translation took a long time and the script expanded into epic length, as is his habit: "*Courage* is one of the biggest roles for a woman in the canon, and I was late with the adaptation and then I did tons of rewrites; I was asking her [Streep] to memorize and re-memorize a ridiculous amount. She was mad at me." Eustis and Kushner worked extensively with the Brecht estate, particularly Barbara Brecht-Schall, the tough-as-nails daughter of Brecht and Helene Weigel (the originator of the role of Mother Courage). Brecht-Schall was happy that Eustis, Kushner, and The Public wanted to do the play but was concerned with some of the script adaptations. Kushner recalled:

> When I sent the first draft of it in, she said, "Why are there all these obscenities? Why is the F-word being used so much?" I said, "Do you want it to sound like people in the middle of a war that they were born into and are going to die in, or do you want it to sound like some academic translation? The obscenities help give the dialogue some of the electricity of your father's original language. You're going to have to tolerate occasional swearing. He mostly opted for the scatological, but it's not a clean thing."
>
> I had actually done a production of *Mother Courage* that I directed with undergraduates of the University of New Hampshire, right when I was starting to work on *Angels* in the late '80s. We did it with the Dessau score, and it's so unpleasant, the prepared piano, the drum, and the flute, that you eventually can't wait for the songs to stop. It sort of hurts your ears. I sent that to her, and she said, "I get it." She really did. Oskar was great about handling the estate and making sure there wasn't going to be a problem—getting rid of the Dessau score. I had to talk Barbara Brecht-Schall into it. She was nervous about letting it go. I said, "The play is not dated at all. The score is great, but it sounds like mid-century modernist music."

The play eventually received the blessing of Brecht-Schall and the estate, and The Public set about to fill out the cast. Christopher Walken came to Kushner's mind to perform as the Cook, after the author had seen him and Raúl Julia in a Joe Dowling-directed *Othello* years before. He was impressed by the American-ness of Walken's portrayal of Iago and describes him as a genius actor. As is often the case with The Public, and especially productions in the Delacorte, there is an unwritten, yet persistent, need passed down from Papp to create distinct "American theater." Defining exactly what that means is a tough task. Kushner helps with his description of the actor being authentically himself: "Walken doesn't do accents. He was there being Chris Walken, but it was terrifying." He would be perfect as the gritty cook in *Mother Courage*.

But all did not pan out with Walken. Kushner wrote several drafts of *Mother Courage* and Walken, who was working on a film at the time, had only read and memorized the first one. When rehearsals began, the actor was unsure if he wanted to commit to the project and all of the re-memorization. After much back and forth and some false starts with the actor, Walken decided to drop out. Kushner recalls, "Somewhere in the middle of all that, as I remember, Meryl quietly left the room, and at the end of the day, Kevin Kline was playing the cook." Kline confirms the behind-the-scenes negotiations, with Streep as the go-between. He had run into Streep at the annual Public gala, and she said to him, "Chris doesn't look happy. Are you doing anything this summer?" Kline confirmed that he was free. A couple of days later he received a call around midday. It was Streep.

"What are you doing this afternoon?"

"I give up. Am I the Cook?" Kline asked.

"Yes," she replied.

The show was not a particularly happy experience for Kline. "Taking over a role that someone has already started—It's like the train has left the station. I'm just jumping on a moving train, and you just try to fit in."

The production's success was completely dominated by the force and power of Meryl Streep and George C. Wolfe. Kline recalls that Streep starts at 110 percent and "goes up from there." And Wolfe insisted on an aggressive and rough dramaturgical and performance style that reflected Kushner's description to Brecht-Schall and the intent of the playwright. That grit was to happen even if it didn't seem to quite fit. Kline notes, "I remember once Meryl [said], 'Can you throw me up against the wagon and throttle me?' and I said, 'Yeah; I *could*.' But I'm just saying, 'But the chicken was overcooked,' or whatever it was. 'Is that [throttling] the *thing* here?' " The answer was "yes" because the production drove on that sort of fire and hyperbolic extremism. It corresponds to the Brechtian Epic Theater standards, which demand a disjointed melding of tragic circumstances with crass comedy and rough music hall tunes, a theater in which an audience can dispassionately watch and critically assess as if in Brecht's *smoking theater*, taking in a boxing match with a favorite cigar; detached, analytical.[10]

Streep was the boxer, and she dominated onstage and off, as evidenced by her acting as a de facto casting director in recruiting Kline. She worked closely with Tesori and Kushner on the script and score. Kushner gave the script, piece by piece, to Eustis, who speaks German and could interpret some of the original language better than Kushner. But the two relied on Streep, too, to assist in the development of many of the moments. Kushner remembers that there was a joke in the first scene when Mother Courage talks to the recruiting officer and sergeant about her children. The sergeant wonders aloud why her kids have different last names, and Kushner had inserted what he reflects as an "unfunny" joke explaining the children's

---

[10]Bertolt Brecht, *Brecht on Theater: The Development of an Aesthetic*, trans. John Willett (New York: Hill and Wang, 1992), p. 8.

multiple fathers. Streep drew him aside: "Can you come up with something a little funnier? I think this should be a laugh line. This isn't great."

Kushner: "All week long I thought of different versions of the joke, but it only got more and more baroque. I couldn't find it. Then Meryl found it, she literally made this up on the spot: 'Well, what do you expect? There are four points to the compass, and I've been pricked in every direction.' That's why she's Meryl Streep."

Some of the uniqueness of *Mother Courage* was in the ways it represented a collaboration of high-powered American theater professionals and how, for the most part, they all worked smoothly to create the unified whole. Tesori, too, composed music specifically for the production that reflected the spirit of the original Berliner Ensemble. But she did it in collaboration. "I loved working with Meryl. Our first rehearsal there were no words so we just sang at the piano so I could really understand the colors of her voice and talked a lot about the theater of war and the music of war and the placement of war in terms of how music has—what its job has traditionally and historically been."

Ruth Sternberg, who came with Oskar Eustis to The Public when he relocated from Trinity Repertory Company in Rhode Island, still counts *Mother Courage* as one of the most important productions of the Eustis years and affirms Streep's deep involvement at every level. The wagon that Mother Courage tows across the stage is *the* iconic set piece of any production of the play and it was important that Streep felt absolutely comfortable with it. A designer was hired to build the cart in conjunction with Streep. Sternberg says: "We hired him for the duration of rehearsals and tech, so that it could be built to however she wanted it. It's the way she [Courage] set up her life. The more she found out about the character, the more it would inform what the cart had to be."

The designer and Streep worked closely, assuring that every detail of the design conformed to the needs of the director and the actor. Nothing is haphazard, even in the Park, and that sort of detail applies to all actors and set pieces, not just world-renowned movie stars and big, iconic designs. Sternberg recalls an unusual and complex set piece that had to be developed during *Mother Courage*: "George wanted a jeep to drive onstage to deliver one of Mother Courage's dead sons on the hood. It's illegal to have a combustion engine on stage in a theater in Central Park. Who knew?" So, they gutted a Jeep and wrapped the frame around a golf cart. But even there, problems arose. "Even if you go with the electric version, you have to guarantee—you have to figure out physically how to make sure the golf cart won't drive into the audience and kill people." They had to develop a mechanism by which the golf cart could be stopped if the person operating the vehicle somehow died with his foot on the "gas."

A Jeep, a bespoke cart, pyrotechnics, American acting and writing royalty, a new artistic director, and a legendary former artistic director—*Mother*

Courage had all of the elements to capture the national attention. While reviews and retrospective musings from Kline, Eustis, and numerous critics concede that the production had many flaws—its length and its bombast, to name a couple—few doubted the power that the performance had over the audience and the place that it still has in the history of Public Theater productions. That legendary status was compounded and solidified with the 2008 release of the John Walter documentary *Theater of War* that chronicled the creation of the production. Through all, one consistency reigns: Meryl Streep owned the Delacorte stage. Oskar Eustis reflects:

> Meryl is an icon because she represents not only everything that's best about The Public, she represents everything that's best about the arts. Which is: she is not a great artist, she is *the greatest* artist. She's the greatest actor of our time and she's demonstrated that over and over again.
>
> ... The memory that I have, and I'll never forget, is the "Solomon Song" that comes when Kevin and Meryl are in war-blasted Europe. Wolves are roaming the streets and villages, so many people have died, and they're singing for their supper ... and there was a snow effect. But the wind was blowing in such a way that it didn't come out [right]. It blew up stage and then the wind blew it back on stage so it seemed to come from nowhere, and sitting in the audience you could feel—this is August—"Oh fuck, it's snowing *now*," and there was this moment when we really thought it was.

Streep powered through and the affect created yet another of those indelible "Park Moments." The audience was thrilled, and Eustis remembers the most heartwarming ovation he has ever heard in his life in the theater. It recalls Jessie Tyler Ferguson's retelling of the squall that passed through *The Comedy of Errors*—audience and actor communion, a shared sense of space, emotion, and even perseverance. And that, Eustis says, is the Meryl Streep way:

> A director tip: if you want to know the key to having a happy cast who never complains about anything, put Meryl Streep in full costume, pulling the wagon around on the turntable in tech, in 100 degrees heat in the Park without complaining for a second, and I promise you nobody else got to complain about anything. Perfect professionalism.

Hair

Over the decades, several Central Park shows have gone on to a life beyond the Delacorte. In fact, there are two during Eustis's time that have the distinction of actually transferring directly from the summer season to Broadway, an unusual path that speaks to the immediate impact of the

Park. The first, in 2007–8, is more unusually distinct, as it captured the ineffable sense of Americana, as city parks sometimes can, combined with a nostalgic return to one of the most critical productions in the history of The Public Theater. *Hair* was the very first play that opened the Lafayette theater in 1967, the musical that Papp almost haphazardly programmed into his season because he needed something, *anything*, to open with. Written by Gerome Ragni and James Rado and composed by Galt MacDermot, *Hair* quickly became a touchstone of the antiwar movements of the 1960s and 1970s and remains one of the top three notable productions of The Public Theater's history[11]. At the height of the conflict in Vietnam, the musical about a young American drafted to go to war—lamenting and celebrating and *living* with his "tribe" of friends—captured the attention of the nation, for its infectious songs ("Age of Aquarius," "Good Morning Starshine," "Let the Sunshine In"), aggressive politics, and famous clothing-optional act-ender. When Oskar Eustis landed at The Public, the fortieth anniversary of *Hair* was just two years away.

Soon after he arrived in New York in 2005, Eustis set about meeting various artists that he wanted to engage at the Theater. Diane Paulus was a young director in New York who had gained some attention for *The Donkey Show*, her adaptation of *A Midsummer Night's Dream* that combined rock music and classic text in a disco-like mélange. She had been connected in some way to The Public since she was a child, as her father, Lawrence Paulus, televised several of the Shakespeare in the Park Productions for CBS. But she herself had never worked for The Public when she was invited to meet with Eustis at Lafayette. "People are telling me I should know who you are," Eustis told her. They talked in his office about her theatrical aesthetic and she was eventually asked to direct a staged reading at Joe's Pub with the East Village Opera Company, a group that focused on taking classics of opera and refashioning them as pop anthems. It was a style similar to her immersive *The Donkey Show*, which had become a cult classic. The Pub version of Shakespeare's *Troilus and Cressida* was followed by an offer that would alter the trajectory of Paulus's career.

In 2007, on the occasion of the anniversary of *Hair*, Eustis was planning a revival concert of the musical at the Delacorte in Central Park, and asked Paulus to direct.[12] She describes being beside herself with joy, having grown up with *Hair* and knowing all of the lyrics by heart. She was given nine days to direct the production for the Delacorte stage. True to form, the resources of The Public were made available, and she enlisted the help of Rado and MacDermot in the development and casting of the revival concert.

---

[11]While healthy debate could easily go on for ages, it is here assumed that the three most well-known musical events in the history of The Public are *Hair*, *Chorus Line*, and *Hamilton*. "But what about *Pirates of Penzance*, *Noise*, *Funk*, *Caroline*, *Fun Home*?" Debate away.

[12]The 1967 version of *Hair* performed in the Anspacher Theater at Lafayette. As the first play *not* to be staged in a park, its revival at the Delacorte was a fitting reversal.

Karole Armitage was brought in to do choreography that would focus on improvisation and natural movements. In line with the original Park methodology, it would be quick—with a short, intense rehearsal—socially engaged, and gone almost before people noticed that it was up.

A caveat is perhaps necessary. While this modus operandi of a lack of permanence in the Park is embedded in its operational modes and history (remember Papp never wanted a permanent structure), it is actually rarely like this in actuality. The theater skirts an odd balance between being the ephemeral and rough summer camp, and yet often featuring entirely overproduced spectacles. It's in a park, unavailable for reviews until the last moment, consciously for the people of New York, and not intentionally preparing for a life beyond the Park. On the other hand, movie stars show up, budgets are enormous, and as was the case with a production of *Hercules* in 2019 (seemingly incongruous with the stated values of Public Works, the division that produced it), they actually partner with major corporations (Disney in that case). Sometimes the productions clearly do have future ambitions that can hardly allow the plays to be categorized as *ephemeral*.

But in 2007, *Hair* would be a celebratory concert version—up quickly, over quickly. Paulus and MacDermot cast a production that included amateurs and professionals alike. *Hair*, she believed, had to evolve and fit the times, and yet the spirit of 1967 must also shine in. Paulus reflects:

> *Hair* is the kind of piece that is defined by being larger than just a piece of theater. That's the deal with *Hair*. It's just like *Hamilton* today is defined by the fact that it's not just theater. It's our history, it's our culture, it's a revolution. So, I knew that my job as the director was to harness energy around that interest and that drive to make that alive ... and we did several things. We worked very intensely on creating what was our concert script. And Jim [Rado] was right there with me showing me every version of *Hair* he's written since '67, and he's written many. So, we were looking at, I don't know, ten different scripts and versions from the original Public, to the one on Broadway, to the revisions he's made since, because as Jim says, "*Hair* never stops, *Hair* keeps growing." ... The concert format gave us license to really go in and create a version that was lean and mean.

The artistic team was firm in the belief that *Hair* needed to be new and current, not a dusty revival from a bygone era. Paulus continuously reasserted that *Hair*'s success as both the concert and its subsequent restaging the following year was due to the moment in time; a play that, like in 1967, captured a topical expression of hope and a person's ability, through activism, to make change.

The weeklong concert that closed the Delacorte summer season in September 2007 starred Jonathan Groff and Patina Miller and was a popular hit; the Delacorte was buzzing at capacity every evening. The concert was such a crowd-pleasing triumph that Eustis quickly decided that Paulus's vision would be given a full production the following summer on the stage in Central Park. As Paulus recalls, it was then that the full weight of the musical and its commentary on American culture hit her cast:

> So, it's a year later, 2008, and we re-met as a company. So many of those cast members were crying because they were saying, "I can't do this. I can't be a hippie. I'm not an activist. How can I do justice?" You know, it was one thing to throw yourself off a cliff at a concert, but now with this onus of "We're doing it, we're doing it for real." So many of these young people in this cast just said, "I don't know how to do this, I'm not going to be authentic, I'm not as committed to our country and the protests of what we believe in as the hippies were in their day. So how can I do this?"
>
> And what I witnessed was over the course of the rehearsal for that production and our journey to Broadway and our run on Broadway, it made those actors activists. And Jimmy used to always say that everybody that did *Hair*, it changed their life. And I think for everyone in this company, it changed how they thought about what it meant to be alive today, what it meant to be an artist and how your political beliefs, your values, your aspirations for social justice could be expressed through your work as an artist.

According to Paulus, *Hair* reminds us that there are no rules, that human beings are able to recreate their world, and that those themes always have resonance. In the rehearsal process, MacDermot reminisced that during the original production several members of the audience joined the actors on the stage as the tribe danced and sang "Let the Sunshine In," the symbol of the individual to join the collective and effect change.

"Oh my god, we have to do that," Paulus exclaimed.

She formally inserted the idea into her production, encouraging the actors to facilitate audience engagement in the final number. On the first night, even after the team had practiced inviting the audience to dance, no one was exactly sure what would happen. A rehearsal room was one thing, the filled 1,800-seat Delacorte was quite another. One hundred people, followed by two hundred, followed by three hundred, took to the stage and started jumping up and down on the deck, swinging and swaying to the climactic song. As the audience danced onto the stage, at the back of the theater Ruth Sternberg's eyes widened in horror. Eustis turned to her, beaming, and said, "Isn't this wonderful?" "No!" she yelled.

Somehow, no one bothered to tell The Public Theater's head of technical operations that hundreds of New Yorkers would be dancing on her stage and jumping up and down, potentially multiplying their weight by twenty times. Strindberg recalls, "I asked him later, 'Did we know that people were going to dance on the stage?' He said, 'Yeah, they always do that.'" Sternberg left the theater, made some phone calls, and by the next morning had engineers at the Delacorte reinforcing the stage with I-beams.

While rolled out with the potential for disastrous mishap, Paulus now realizes that this moment exemplifies what *Hair* has become in the American consciousness, and what her production was able to highlight. Here, in this moment of celebration, an audience could join together and create a *happening*, a moment of community, communion, and connection that, though controlled, felt organic and even spontaneous. There could be no better place than in the middle of Central Park in New York City, and that is how the Park and its identity as a gathering place changed and deepened a decades-old musical. It infused the production with a revived sense of community, a present-ness that wasn't only about Vietnam and the 1960s, but also about love, compassion, and social awareness that any era needed to connect with. Rooted in 1967, the Paulus/Eustis *Hair* became entirely 2007.

The production transferred to Broadway the following year, was nominated for eight Tony Awards, and eventually won Best Revival of a Musical. Even on Broadway, the audience participation was fully incorporated into the production, and at the Tony Awards the actors filled the theater, grinding and dancing with the stars filling Radio City Music Hall. When the show went out on a national tour, the tech rider insisted that actors could come off of the stage, stand on chairs, and dance with patrons. Paulus notes, "That's what the production is, it breaks the fourth wall. It says, 'You are here.' And if we're not doing that, we're not doing the show." The fourth wall was further broken when, in July 2011, the Broadway producers joined Eustis and announced that gay couples who had recently won the right to legally marry would do so at the end of the production, on the stage and, of course, joined by the dancing and cheering audience.

The Park discoveries remained a part of the Broadway production and its impact is felt on the revival and subsequent re-revivals of *Hair*. It was there that *Hair* was boldly reconceived, and it had a lasting effect. In the *New York Times*' fawning review, the power of nature flooded in: "Even the very visible onstage band, under a tie-dyed canopy, feels as if it had sprouted there, like so many musical mushrooms."[13] With *Hair*, and that final moment of celebration—when audience joins with performer on a stage on a summer evening—the power of the outdoor stage could not have been more vibrant and alive. What Brantley would refer to as a "hormonal vitality" was born out of a need to recreate a classic American musical, slowly over the course of two years—to reconceive how the spirit of 1967 could come alive on the eve of the election of Barack Obama. At the very end of my extended interview with Diane Paulus, the director offered a coda to her reminisces of her production. "Can I offer one more anecdote?" she asked:

---

[13] Ben Brantley, "Let the Sun Shine In, and the Shadows," *New York Times*, September 14, 2008.

I'll never forget this night when we were doing it at the Delacorte, when the dance party had ended, and there was this man sitting on the stairs. And he was a businessman, in probably his early sixties, late fifties, and he had the three-piece suit on, and he had his glasses in his hands. And he was crying and shaking. And Kacie Sheik went up to him, who was playing Jeanie, and some ushers came around, and they were congregating around this gentleman saying, "Are you okay? Can we help you?" You know, maybe he was sick. And he staggered to his feet, and he said, "No, no, no, I'm all right. I was just—I was in Vietnam, and I'm having a memory right now. I suffered in the field with grenades blowing off all around me. And yet: I got my hands, I got my hair, I got my teeth, I got my body, I got my—" And he started saying the lines of "I Got Life," and it was like he was having a flashback, you know, and he was so visibly re-experiencing kind of the trauma of being in Vietnam, but asserting his self in this moment using the words of "I Got Life."

The Merchant of Venice

Hair's transfer from the Park to Broadway is not the only example of that trajectory during Eustis's years at The Public. But it is well to remember that that is rarely the goal of a Delacorte production, nor is it the yardstick by which to measure success.[14] While Daniel Sullivan's 2010 *The Merchant of Venice*, starring Al Pacino, did, in fact, perform in the Park and on Broadway, it was in the production's Park recreation of a classic script (like *Hair* and *Mother Courage* before) that *Merchant* affirmed its place among the most important productions in Central Park in Eustis's tenure. Sullivan took a script often thought to be difficult, if not impossible, to appropriately produce in twenty-first-century America and revitalized it, making the antisemitic tropes and cringeworthy insults powerfully evocative for their horror and reflection of contemporary society.

When Oskar Eustis turned to Sullivan to helm *Merchant* in the 2010 summer season, the director was already one of the most successful and celebrated theater artists in America. He had run the Seattle Repertory Company, was an instructor at the University of Chicago, and had been nominated for six Tony Awards, including a win for his 2001 direction of David Auburn's *Proof*.[15] The 2010 season at the Delacorte would pair *The Merchant of Venice* with a version of *The Winter's Tale* directed by another legendary director, Michael Greif. It was the first time that The Public would

---

[14] While the allure of Broadway transfers is impossible to avoid at the moment, that doesn't seem to be the case for plays presented at the Delacorte. This complex dance, between the ethos of a not-for-profit theater and the lights of Broadway, will be examined in Chapters 6 and 7.
[15] Since 2010, Sullivan has been nominated for another two Tony Awards: The 2017 revival of *Little Foxes* and the Broadway transfer of *Merchant*.

present two productions in rep, meaning that the shows would rotate over the course of two months and share a common ensemble cast.

Following the line that Shakespeare in the Park is a summer camp, Hamish Linklater, who was in both casts, remembers the joy and anxiety of even the simple things—dressing room assignments and a specific call from the stage manager before the start of rehearsals:

> "Hamish, I'm thinking—Al has to have a dressing room mate, because nobody gets solo dressing rooms at the Delacorte, so we were thinking of asking you if you would want to." I was like, "Fuck, no. I'm not going to ruin my whole summer being terrified of Al Pacino in a dressing room." And I hung up, and I was like can you believe this? And all these actor boys from Long Island were like, "You're a fucking idiot. You got to do that! You got to do that!" So, I called back, "I would love to do it. I would love to be Al's dressing room mate."
>
> So, when we had the *Merchant* nights, I would be with Al in the dressing room, with no air-conditioning on because he was cold all the time, and him just eating blueberries and almonds saying, "I don't know how I am gonna do it, kid. I don't know how I'm gonna get out there." And on the *Winter's Tale* nights I had Ruben Santiago Hudson, who would come in, blast the air-conditioning because he was coming straight from a basketball game with his son, and him going, "I had a great day. I had a fantastic day. I cannot wait to get out there. I'm gonna tear it up. You should have seen my kid." I would just try to get dressed and get out of there fast, but both of them would just talk my ear off until "places," and then we'd go out. That was really sweet.

Hearing the stories of the plays in Central Park, one is continuously reminded of the intersections of different worlds. On the one hand, the "one public" universality of human connections, of movie stars and ensemble members, of free tickets and torrential downpours; on the other hand, the Park plays assiduously attempting to tell essential stories and tie back to deep political beliefs that are grounded in a liberal and even socialist foundation.

In 2010, Eustis was committed to presenting *Merchant* because he believed that it was past time to revisit the very first production presented at the Delacorte, and because the political and cultural zeitgeist was perfectly aligned for the script. In 1962, Papp inaugurated the new theater with *Merchant*, codirected by Gladys Vaughan and starring James Earl Jones and George C. Scott.[16] It was an audacious kickoff performance and stirred up significant controversy. *Merchant* tells the tale of Bassanio, who attempts to court the heiress Portia, but needs money to establish himself as a suitor. He goes to his friend Antonio to secure a loan of 3,000 ducats.

---

[16] It was followed the second summer by *The Winter's Tale*, making the 2010 pairing particularly elegant.

Antonio, short on cash, turns to Shylock, a Jewish money lender, to cover the bond.

That is the general setup of *The Merchant of Venice*, a tale of love, wooing, and, importantly for Eustis, financial dealing and the destructive power of money. But the treatment of Shylock has, over the centuries, become the focus of the play. Because Shakespeare's England was fundamentally antisemitic, the character and response to him from other characters were written in a way that felt deeply uncomfortable in contemporary America. Shylock is shown to be unreasonable and bloodthirsty when he insists on a brutal punishment (a pound of flesh) for Antonio after he is unable to repay the debt. In court, the beautiful Portia, disguised as a man, successfully argues the case for Antonio and, through crafty persuasion, convinces the judge that Shylock, being an "alien" (Jew) and having threatened the life of a Christian, must forfeit all of his money and his life. The humiliated Shylock is spared by the Duke, but only on the condition that he converts to Christianity.

The play is one of Shakespeare's finest, packed with some of his strongest poetry and most evocative characters. It is, however, one of his most problematic works, and continues to be debated in academic circles and by almost all audiences who see its staging. When Papp presented his rendition in June 1962, the first performance was cut short due to rain—but not before the crowd and critics had the time to recognize the importance of the evening. The *New York Daily News* exclaimed the following day that the rain "could not dampen Joseph Papp's triumph over adversity and adversaries."[17] And the adversity was certainly extreme, and the criticism pointed. The Board of Rabbis in New York had strenuously objected to its staging in a messy confrontation with Papp that ultimately persuaded Papp himself to publicly acknowledge his Judaism, something he had kept mostly under wraps.

That *The Merchant of Venice* wasn't touched by The Public for fifty years is not then much of a surprise. But in 2010, the political and social climate seemed right to Eustis, Sullivan, and the producing team. With the collapse of Lehman Brothers and the subsequent Wall Street bailout and US recession, Eustis saw the opportunity to restage the play with greed and leverage as the principal images. In selecting Sullivan to direct, Eustis knew the potential of producing a nuanced re-visioning of the controversial classic.

Sullivan started with casting vision, knowing that he wanted film star Al Pacino to play Shylock and a young actress named Lily Rabe to portray Portia:

---

[17]John Chapman, "New Shakespeare Plant Shines in Rainy Debut," *New York Daily News*, June 21, 1962. Reprinted at https://www.nydailynews.com/entertainment/theater-arts/shakespeare-park-rainy-debut-1962-article-1.2674665.

Al called me and asked me if he could get involved ... I had only thought of Lily for the role because I thought she was absolutely perfect for it, although she had never done Shakespeare before. But I knew her, and I knew that she would take to it. So, they were the first two and everything sort of fell into place behind that.

Rabe remembers a call from an agent inquiring about her interest in the part of Portia: "Oh, I have an offer to audition?" she wondered. "No," said the casting director, "You're the person he wants to play the part."

It is again not lost, nor should it be ignored, that The Public Theater time and again returns to a model in the Park that includes at least one or two megawatt acting royalty. At first blush, there may be something distressing with it, as it seems to feel contrary to the socialist universality of the program. Jordan Thaler, one of the long-serving casting directors, perhaps better than anyone puts to rest this incongruity: "The reason why people like stars in the Park ... it kind of blows my mind that someone thinking they've come to see Denzel Washington, or they've come to see Al Pacino, that the first play they're *ever* going to see is *The Merchant of Venice*. It's kind of just mind-blowing, that the first time that they may ever see live theater is going to be Shakespeare." The other reason, as is made clear often, is that The Public selects stars with deep connections to the theater and whose stage chops are unimpeachable. Pacino had spent some time working on the role of Shylock before signing on to the Sullivan production. He had performed the role in a film version in 2004.

Even with known actors, the play presents significant challenges and danger, since antisemitism is inescapable in the script. Any contemporary performance necessarily has to determine how to handle the final act, and a now-tragic play that ends with happiness and joviality. In text, the play is technically a comedy since the central love story is resolved and the young lovers are married. The fact that the resolution comes at the expense and humiliation of Shylock makes the celebratory last act extremely difficult to accomplish. The solution, in some ways, is obvious; the final moments have to have a power that is devoid of that celebration and levity. But how to do that? In fact, it's there, it's written in. By all accounts, Sullivan handled that delicate balance in the Park with finesse. He notes of the fifth act:

What has happened to Shylock has affected the people in the play to the degree that they can't carry on a healthy relationship. And that, I think, is what happens in the last act of *Merchant of Venice*. ... What began as a kind of a gambit turns into a serious act of disloyalty, as far as Portia is concerned, and we end the play not knowing whether Bassanio really loves her to begin with, and wondering will this relationship hold—the very serious question as to whether or not this relationship is built on the kind of trust that doesn't actually exist. And Shakespeare himself doesn't resolve it, so it gives you all kinds of permission to determine just the degree of irresolution that's there at the end.

In the Sullivan version, the baptism of Shylock happened on the stage: Pacino removed his yarmulke and was violently held under the water of an onstage pool that was the baptismal font. The "irresolution" that followed was haunting—the young lovers sat next to that font which, by the fifth act, could aptly be described as a reflecting pool, and were clearly distraught and grappling with what they had done to Shylock. The double visioning of the stage deftly focused the disturbing antisemitism of the play. Shylock is in no way a hero; Sullivan describes him as a "dignified victim" at best, but his bloodlust can hardly be ignored as it is central to the script. But in a performance of *Merchant* in Central Park, getting the nuance right required dexterity.

It was helped by the fact that the director and producer spent time focusing on the core of the script and the fact that the central story is not really about Shylock. Sullivan notes that Shylock represents the consequences of an abused heart. With recession and deep financial abuse hitting America, it was centrally important to show the misuse of power and the destruction wrought by financial greed, across all of the characters. This is where Central Park itself reenters the assessment of the success of the production. A play reconceived as an indictment on corporate greed in twenty-first-century America was made all the more effective set in the center of that moral morass, with the skyscraping condos of the super wealthy looming behind the timeless natural beauty of the Park. But Sullivan noted that he never wished to approach anything as universal as Shakespeare with blatant topical references, and indeed this performance was likely so successful because it was set in an era that could be viewed as somewhat Victorian, and not at all obviously modern. He notes, however, one clear nod to contemporary financial geopolitics:

> The only thing I did do was start it in the Stock Exchange ... and that had less to do with trying to connect with what was happening in the world today. ... I wanted to see, at the beginning of the play, Bassanio lose all his money. I wanted to see the event where he was so anxious to make money that he put his money down on some ridiculous stock that went belly up in front of us. So, he approached Antonio, and the need wasn't for her. The need was for the money.

Therein lay the key to the final act. Pacino's nuanced pain and the horror that he had been through was powerfully and violently resolved by the end of Act Four. What was left was the destructive realization from the lovers that they could not go on in any healthy relationship. The dependence on wealth was not centered in Shylock, but rather in them, and the "irresolution" in the Sullivan *Merchant* focused on the necessity of any audience member to look at the deep levels of their own culpability in the crisis that was befalling America and, indeed, the Western world.

Julius Caesar

That overt demand for self-reflection is no stranger in the theater, in fact it is at the core of the power of the form. Even the casual theatergoer can quote Shakespeare from *Hamlet* and insist that the theater holds a mirror to nature. Perhaps the most overtly political production staged at the Delacorte in the tenure of Oskar Eustis, which boldly raised the mirror in front of the audience, was a retelling that he directed in the summer of 2017. *Julius Caesar* at the Delacorte Theater in Central Park was immediately historic. For a week, the play accomplished something that is rare in theater; it garnered national news headlines, breathless discussion on morning talk programs, marketing campaigns, and feisty and often aggressive social media eruptions. For millions of Americans and most theater enthusiasts, Eustis's staging became the most talked about piece of theater since *Hamilton*. Why? The short answer was that Eustis imagined the charismatic Caesar as a Donald Trump look-alike and his wife, Calpurnia, a tall blond with a Slavic accent. A golden bathtub rose from underneath the Delacorte stage, Marc Antony wore a stars and stripes tracksuit, and Casca uttered the decidedly non-Shakespearian line: "But there's no heed to be taken of them / If Caesar had stabbed their mothers on Fifth Avenue, they would have done no less."[18] The choices, in Eustis's own words, were about "as subtle as a flying mallet." Indeed, when Trump/Caesar was stabbed to death in a bloody melee on the floor of the senate, 44 BC was 2017. For some Americans, hearing of this—gleaned only from reports on the conservative Breitbart News and grainy videos on Fox News—was an occasion for outrage.

Of course, the reason *Julius Caesar* became such a lightning rod in American theater and politics is a more nuanced story, and perhaps a story that reveals something about how live performance critique is situated within the context of a Trumpian America. I had had the opportunity to watch the rehearsals, the tech process, and several performances of *Caesar*. I anticipated that Eustis's return to directing, especially with a concept as blunt as this, might be a moment of theater history. After seeing an early rehearsal, it was clear that Eustis wasn't *implying* Trump; he was actually hitting us over the head with that flying mallet. This was going to get some attention, especially in Central Park, in the shadow of Trump Tower.

Eustis sat down for several interviews over the course of the development of the show: once during technical rehearsal, once on closing night, and one month after run. The conversations reveal many remarkable and

---

[18] Eustis notes that this line was the only piece of text that he altered in the script.

amusing moments of foresight and blindness, but also paint a picture of the process of producing at The Public and at the Delacorte. During technical rehearsals, Eustis made a prediction that his play may cause a tweet from the president: "That indeed is the goal of this entire endeavor, to provoke a tweet. What could be more noble a goal?" he joked. Two weeks later, in the wake of the shooting of Representative Steve Scalise, the president's son, Donald Trump Jr., put *Julius Caesar* in the spotlight with, yes, a tweet: "I wonder how much of this 'art' is funded by taxpayers? Serious question, when does 'art' become political speech & does that change things?" In part as a response to the tweet and the increasing controversy, Delta Air Lines pulled its sponsorship of Shakespeare in the Park and Bank of America and the National Endowment for the Arts balked at being part of marketing campaigns.

James Shapiro wrote a focusing article in the *New York Times* in the wake of the controversy. Of the corporate back-outs, he wrote: "In doing so, they have proved more sensitive than even Queen Elizabeth I. 'I am Richard II, know ye not that?' she famously remarked around 1601. Yet the queen pointedly refused to pull her support for Shakespeare's company, which continued to perform at court, or even for that play, though *Richard II* had been staged on the eve of an uprising against her near the end of her reign."[19]

Within the organization and inside theater communities, conversations swirled about the degree to which theater practitioners, professors, and the "liberal elite" were merely talking to themselves. In our interviews, Eustis noted and identified the obvious fact that most audiences are surely in the corner with The Public. While he accepted that fact, in the final interview he recognized that he may have missed some bigger opportunities. In the age of social media and with the powerful bullhorn of The Public adding national attention, *seeing* the play is actually only one mode of engagement with Shakespeare in the Park. Just as *Hamilton* reaches far more communities than have actually seen (or can afford to see) the production, *Julius Caesar* became famous for the response on social media, far more than for the live performances.

While *Merchant* provides an excellent example of a production in the Park that subtly approached American and world politics, *Caesar* was intended to play a heavy and loaded hand. Five days before the first preview, sitting in the empty Delacorte amphitheater on a blazing hot afternoon, Eustis mused about his blunt choices:

> It *is* a response to Trump; and the thing I've been struggling with is that there are definitely topical references in the show that don't need to be there that are more overt than any I've ever done in a show's production, and more than they would have to be. And I keep waiting for me not

---

[19]James Shapiro, "A Trumpian Caesar? Shakespeare Would Approve," *New York Times*, June 13, 2017.

to like them, but I keep liking them. ... I want this to feel like it's rapid-response theater of what's happening to our country; and so, the fact that it actually feels that way so far does not provoke any feelings of "my God! We're dumbing it down or we're simplifying it."

Certainly, never have I felt we're making inappropriate analogies because the analogies feel like they're absolutely rooted. It's a very powerful, popular, charismatic, narcissistic leader; and the one that was in Rome 2,000 years ago is not that different from the one who is sitting in the White House right now. So, that comparison has never felt forced to me as I've gone through the rehearsal prep.

Caesar is ripe for any epoch in world history because the rise against him—a man desperate to be a king—through assassination is ultimately an utterly misguided failure. One is left ambivalent about the message in the best of all ways; one witnesses all sides and is allowed to see how things *can* unfold. Eustis: "You have a group of people, relatively high-minded, who strike Caesar on March 15, 44 BC in an attempt to preserve democracy, and democracy is wiped from the face of the Earth for 2,000 years. So, they fail completely ... this is a warning parable about what happens when they try to save democracy by undemocratic means."

In that way, any director is tempted and largely duty bound to make contemporary cultural allusions to current politics when staging *Julius Caesar*. Shakespeare scholars can and do analyze and deconstruct the goals of the author and, in this case, the relative success of the Eustis production. Since there have been numerous articles that analyze this production, the concern here is to look at how the platform of The Public in Central Park affected the trajectory of the reporting on the production, and the plain fact that the controversy caught The Public off guard. How did he *not* see that a Trump look-alike being stabbed in the middle of New York wouldn't be deeply controversial? As with so much in the arts, intended audience matters. That same month, Americans saw the destruction of the career of comedian Kathy Griffin after she posed with the decapitated likeness of the president. When asked how much he hoped that *Caesar* would cause a stir, Eustis was candid about the types of audience who would witness it:

I don't fool myself about our audience. I think the majority of our audience is very much in a political corner that I'm comfortable with, that despises Trump. So, it's not like we're doing this into the teeth of a slate of Trump supporters, which means on some level we're preaching to the choir; but as I have said before, all preachers preach to the choir. That's what they do. There's no church on Earth in which Muslims wander in and are converted to Christianity by the preacher, just as there's no political forum on Earth that people who are completely opposed walk in and get converted. Preaching to the choir is a powerful and important tool for creating a sense of solidarity and commonality among a group

FIGURE 3.2 Julius Caesar, *2017. Courtesy Joan Marcus.*

of people with a shared belief system; and I don't mind doing that. If the primary effect of this show is to raise a red flag for a bunch of progressive New Yorkers that the threat of dictatorship is real and that we need to really think about it, I'm happy with that. I'll take that.

As is the case with all Shakespeare in the Park productions, the play continued to be developed and rehearsed after the opening previews, accounting for audience reaction and natural development of the work. The actors actually do continue to rehearse and rework scenes throughout the preview period, and that summer it was not uncommon for the *Caesar* cast and crew to be rehearsing for hours under the hot sun before welcoming a preview audience at 8:00 p.m.

Since reviewers technically may not review a New York show until it opens, details of the shows aren't widely public until it is about to close. In that way, the response to *Julius Caesar* did not come immediately; rather, the controversy grew and only hit its climax on the final weekend of the run, after leaks made it into the press. While the production was rife with allusions to Trump, the inflammatory image was of the conspirators tackling Caesar, stabbing him to death, and then bathing in his blood, as is textually accurate. It was this that became the focus of the outrage from the political Right.

Laura Sheaffer, a staffer at the Christian conservative media outlet Salem Media, first described her experience at the production on June 6 to Joe

Piscopo on his conservative radio show (almost two weeks into the run). In it, she described her shock about the production and its disrespect of the Office of the Presidency. The interview eventually raised the alarm at other conservative outlets, including Breitbart News, and then at Fox specifically, only one week before closing. Fox's reporting, in turn, attracted the attention of Trump Jr., and the Delta and Bank of America statements came shortly thereafter. The pulling of support hardly hurt The Public Theater; what was lost from corporate support was easily surpassed within a week by a flurry of donations to the company. The attention, though, created consistent protest for the last week of the production, and, on a few occasions, disruptions of the actual performances, including one protestor who rushed to the stage. Eustis and his family received death threats.

I phoned Eustis on the closing night and asked generally how he felt: he was exhausted, exhilarated, and still a bit surprised. Speaking of the solidarity and comradery that the Delacorte facilitates, he related, "Friday night a protestor got on stage. When we got the protestor off stage Buzz [Cohen, stage manager] said, 'actors can we take it from "freedom, liberty."'" The audience gave a standing ovation at that moment for the company. That was exhilarating."

But those moments were not without conflicted counter feelings. When Eustis stopped by the dressing room, several actors were crying, deeply affected by the powerful symbolism that was broken by a protective, albeit invisible, boundary being crossed. Increased security was brought in for the final week of performance. Eustis said, "This doesn't feel like fun and games, doesn't feel like … you know, look, we stirred up the hornets' nest. It feels kind of scary and deeply tiring." Eustis admitted to being surprised by the type of reaction that the production received, noting that the content of his show—what actually happened on the stage—wasn't questioned all that strongly. The backlash that occurred was based on the radio interview and amateur videos and still photographs that were "smuggled" out of the theater and played on Fox News and other conservative outlets. He noted, "So, in other words, all of the objections are to the optics of seeing a Trump lookalike stabbed to death on stage." This sort of know-nothing-ness did have larger, national ramifications. Shakespeare festivals around the country received threatening emails and condemnation because people read in the news about Shakespeare in the Park and didn't understand or distinguish the difference between a production in, say, Massachusetts, and the famous festival in Central Park.

One such organization was Shakespeare and Company in Lenox, Massachusetts. Allyn Burrows, the artistic director, later explained that because it owns the URL "shakespeare.org," the company was an easy target for ill-informed people to rail against Shakespeare. Of the response, Burrows commented:

> It was pretty powerfully vituperative … over the weekend we had gotten a slew of voicemails, overnight, 4 am, 5 am, of real vitriol … pouring over

the bow ... "we hope that ISIS finds you and kills you all." "We hope your whole family dies from the worst disease possible." And then the emails started coming in ... people hell bent on pissing on us.

According to Burrows, Shakespeare and Company responded not by distancing itself from The Public, but by explaining the plot and the morals of *Caesar* to angry callers: "Let's not tell them that it wasn't us ... we stand shoulder to shoulder with the theater's right to freedom of speech."

Eustis expressed disgust at the conservative media response and genuine concern for the other theater companies that were being targeted. The Public could handle it, but could other, smaller theaters make it through the odd Shakespeare backlash of 2017? Eustis's frustration that final night bubbled to the surface in our conversation:

> On Friday night, the assassination happened and then the protestor jumped on stage and claimed we were normalizing violence against the Right ... as if the protestor hadn't watched what just was in front of him, and that's the disappointing part. It's not the fact that this protestor was upset, that is not about my show. It's about a distorted lying version of my show, and I probably shouldn't have been surprised because that's what the Right does, and the Alt-Right particularly.
>
> One more rant and then I'm done: As we know, there's been lots of indignant tweeting from Laura Ingraham and others saying how would the Left respond if this was Obama. Well, we know how the Left would respond because Rob Melrose did that in 2012 in his production of *Julius Caesar*. It played at the Guthrie, and it played across the country, and there was no response because we actually watched the show and responded to the show. We didn't have any media machine using images from the show to stir up what is, you know, not a real debate. In that way, I feel like the show has exposed a fault line in the country; but in terms of actual discussions with the Right, it's not a real discussion.

The social media maelstrom aside, *Caesar* did encourage some sophisticated editorials, articles, and testimonials from the likes of scholars like Shapiro, Stephen Greenblatt, and others. But is the general public reading theater scholars as they assess the productions that are happening in America's park? Some do, for sure, but it's often reviews and social media that draw attention, which is why The Public was particularly upset with the national paper of record, the *New York Times*. Driven by its need to engage with "art as news," to meet the moment of "outrage as product" the *Times* broke with tradition and released a review of *Caesar* before opening night. Eustis commented:

> For our New York shows, we started letting the critics in several days before opening with the understanding that all reviews of any kind are

embargoed until opening night so that in this particular case, for example, the *Times* critic Jesse Greene came on Wednesday. The opening night was the following Monday. The normal procedure which has been followed for as long as anybody can remember is that then the *Times* would publish in their Tuesday edition. So, it would come up late Monday night. The *Times* called on Friday and told us that they were going to break the embargo.

I give them credit: they called, we talked, and I ended up talking to the deputy cultural editor, and they said that because this show had become news that they felt that it was now part of the news cycle and not the art cycle, and they wanted to run it as soon as possible as their contribution to the news cycle. ...

I got into a pretty ferocious fight, and what I kept saying is if you think this is news, I'll give you an exclusive interview. Come down and do a news article about it, but this is not news. This is a review of my show. They posted it Friday at 4:00 p.m. and it ran in the Saturday paper—that meant about half of the major reviewers hadn't seen the show when the *Times'* review ran; and so, reviewers were seeing the show after having read a review of the show from the *Times,* which is just a terrible precedent.

Eustis was later quoted in a separate article in the *New York Times*, issuing the paper a blistering critique. He was impressed that they actually printed what he had said:

I don't want to criticize anybody except the *New York Times*. The fact that you guys broke the decades-long precedent on embargoing reviews, in response to what Breitbart had done—because that's what you did, because Breitbart ran a story, other people picked it up, and you broke your arrangement with us. That's a perfect example of how we are allowing the right-wing hate machine to change our relationships to each other, and that is bad. You and I, and the *New York Times* and I, will recover from it, but still, I think it's not what we should be doing.[20]

Further, the controversy highlighted the difficult relationship between theater companies and corporate sponsors. Never did Eustis criticize corporations for their choice of dropping their support of the theater. They had a bottom line to tend to. Eustis only said, "That dialogue, I feel, is really happening and the clarification about the issue of the sponsorships withdrawing support, and that means, in terms of freedom of expression. I think that conversation has been welcome and necessary and really good." The debate is not a new one. Joseph Papp, near the end of his life and with his theater company struggling to find solvency, said to Steven Cohen, "one of the solutions is not to try to deal just with corporations. Corporations are unpredictable. Some

---

[20]Eustis quoted in Michael Pailson, "Julius Caesar and the Politics of Theater," *New York Times,* June 13, 2017.

are okay. Some we're able to deal with. Others are very demanding, and you don't know what they're going to do next year."[21]

The conversations that the play gave rise to captivated the theater world for a few weeks in June 2017. But at the time, the genuine focus at The Public was the safety of the performers and staff. Many actors spoke publicly about the controversy; Corey Stoll, who played Brutus, wrote of the experience in an extended blog for the online platform Vulture.[22] I spoke with John Douglas Thompson, who played Cassius, a week after the play closed and he reflected on the feelings from the stage:

> You're trying to reconcile two separate realities: the reality of what you are doing with the play, and this new reality that interrupted that reality ... they're not reconcilable. So, you don't know if you need to take your mind out of the play to deal with this new reality or stay in the reality of the play. Those were the first moments. You're almost like in some level of shock. On some basic level, a moderate level of shock, because you don't really know what's happening. And then the thought comes in, certainly for me personally, as I watched these people, I started to look at their hands.
>
> Did they have a weapon? What could I read about their intention, and their level of aggression? How I would need to protect myself in the next few seconds if something was going to happen. These are all things racing through your mind, you know, every second. It's very tense.
>
> ...
>
> And then, you start to realize, wow—you start to almost want to blow a kiss to Shakespeare and say "my god, this is what your play [did]—this is your play, whether you intended it or not, and I've got to believe on some level, maybe you did—you knew in future generations that this play would have deeper and deeper, impactful meaning for some—would create controversy for others." And here we are as actors, living in this moment.
>
> ...
>
> You really can't figure it out at the time that it's happening. It's only later, when you decompress, either after the event, after the show is over, after the run is complete, when you decompress and you start to think about these events and say, "oh my god. How amazing was that, on one level. And how fearful it was on the other."

In the weeks following the production, The Public Theater convened conversations with staff about their feelings and experiences under the media spotlight. There were anecdotes from box office officials who shared

---

[21]Recording of Joseph Papp, August 25, 1988. Courtesy of Steven Cohen.
[22]http://www.vulture.com/2017/06/what-it-was-like-to-star-in-the-trump-themed-julius-caesar.html.

stories of angry and aggressive callers, to ushers who described their fear of being at the Delacorte in the final weekend. Eustis listened to the feelings of his staff; concerns, perhaps, from some that the organization did not do enough to protect its own. There was anger, to be sure. But others expressed feelings of solidarity and spoke at length about the liabilities of a democratic institution facing the democratic realities of free speech and protest.

After all was done, Eustis was mainly proud of the way he and his team dealt with the crisis, with a few exceptions: "I think we made a mistake in that we, for a few days, we held our fire, did not respond, just issued a pretty bland statement and assumed that it would die down. ... I think we were using an outmoded media head. We're using a head where stories are dictated by what's in the papers, that stories are driven by actual concrete events, and that wasn't what was happening here. The story was being driven by social media and by outrage and by the right-wing hate machine."[23] James Shapiro concurs, and in his recent book *Shakespeare in a Divided America* he writes that The Public, like political candidates in 2016, "badly underestimated" the power of new media to mobilize the far Right.[24]

Central Park, with its ability to act as an American town square, is what made *Caesar* one of the most controversial productions in the company's history. But if the Park is the town square, myriad questions arise about the choices that are produced there, and this may be at the crux of the issue with *Caesar*. Certainly, the anger was misplaced and driven by a know-nothing media culture. But contextually, was The Public not demonstrating that theater is for the liberal elites, the "choir" that Eustis admits preaching to? When pressed, Eustis always contends that his theater is for all political stripes and colors. He often quotes his colleague Jason Duchin, the head of the Bronx-based community building organization DreamYard. These sorts of programs must "lean into the read," tour shows to various parts of the country, and demonstrate that they are not simply creating art for themselves but are offering it to the nation and its varying political and social beliefs. That is the only way for a company that fancies itself a national theater. Eustis often says now that the red and blue divide in America is something

---

[23]"Our production of JULIUS CAESAR in no way advocated violence towards anyone. Shakespeare's play, and our production, made the opposite point: those who attempt to defend democracy by undemocratic means pay a terrible price and destroy the very thing they are fighting to save. For over 400 years, Shakespeare's play has told this story and we were proud to have told it again in Central Park. The Public Theater stands completely behind our production of JULIUS CAESAR. We understand and respect the right of our sponsors and supporters to allocate their funding in line with their own values. We recognize that our interpretation of the play provoked heated discussion; audiences, sponsors, and supporters have expressed varying viewpoints and opinions. Such discussion is exactly the goal of our civically engaged theater; this discourse is the basis of a healthy democracy." https://publictheater.org/A-NOTE-ABOUT-JULIUS-CAESAR/.

[24]James Shapiro, *Shakespeare in a Divided America* (New York: Penguin, 2020), p. 218.

that the theater must take some responsibility for. Of conservative America, he says:

> We've turned our backs on them. Just as the education system doesn't reach them, just as the economy doesn't reach them, just as the major media outlets don't reach them, the culture doesn't reach them. We've essentially let them stew in their own juices. And instead of saying that, we say, "No, we actually have to try and pioneer ways to demonstrate to you our values simply by showing up and giving our work to you." I think that would be a pretty significant thing to do.

This methodology would soon be attempted in the mobile production of Lynn Nottage's *Sweat* that toured to "Red America." The Park, though, provides a fundamentally different set of circumstances and unavoidable challenges, specifically its position, geographically and socially, in American life. Shakespeare in the Park is a national tradition in a way that it isn't in other parts of the world. I asked Shapiro about the American fascination with putting a British playwright in American parks, a tradition that has even seen the construction of replicas of the Globe theater:

> There's a recognition across party lines that Shakespeare is *something*, it's one of the last places of common ground in America, where those across the political spectrum can be exchange ideas, agree to disagree, and that is, I think, a function of our democracy in a way. ... We no longer have Vermont town hall meetings. Shakespeare, especially summer productions, functions in that way.

In essence, we see the universal in Shakespeare, and in that the possibility of democratic values, especially in times when those values are strained. What *Caesar* illuminated was that the town hall in Central Park had the ability to be nationalized through new technologies. But once it was nationalized, it was abundantly clear how divisive the discourse could become and how people distant from New York City might reflect on what they saw as a "liberal elite" maligning a president. Therein lay realities of art existing in the immediacy of the social media dominated culture, and the challenge of being seen by some as a national theater in such a varied and divided country. It also harkens to Papp's reluctance to involve corporations. Delta Air Lines and other corporate sponsors wanted no part of a "town hall" that grew to a national conversation that was starkly divisive and in conflict. Of course, that is antithetical to the dialectic that both theater and democracy espouse—conflict and debate is what a town hall purposely invites.

Theater in the age of outrage may have, for better and worse, attracted a kind of attention that both elevates the form and degenerates some of its efficacy as a "same space/same time" interpersonal connector. The appreciation of the social mediatized realities, while obvious and deeply influenced by President Trump and his methodology, was a slower realization at The Public, according to Eustis (and Shapiro). But on deeper inspection, The Public and Eustis did not really *miss* the opportunity that *Caesar* provided the company to exist and even bask in the social media spotlight. On the official opening night (mere days before closing night), Eustis took the stage and gave an impassioned preshow speech about the power of the stage and, especially, of Shakespeare's stage, to hold the "mirror up to nature." The speech is easily found on YouTube and referenced in many articles—and that is partly by design. Before he started, the artistic director asked the audience to record his comments, knowing that his play now existed far beyond the confines of the Delacorte.[25] *Julius Caesar*, then, reflects what certainly is a growing understanding in theater, a reality perhaps pushed along by President Trump himself: a nationalization, and even globalization, of artistic response—fury over the product, fueled solely by conversation in cyberspace and around tables in news studios.

The contemporary reality of immediacy and the hurricanes of social media is hardly surprising or unique. *Dear Evan Hansen*, the 2017 Tony Award-winning musical, has as its premise the cyber distribution of information as *source* of dramatic conflict. So, too, did the mega hit British import *The Curious Incident of the Dog in the Nighttime* (2012) and The Public's presentation of the National Theatre's *Privacy* (2016), that deliberately invaded the audience's sense of social media privacy. The response to *Julius Caesar* held the mirror to nature in ways not intended in the Shakespearian text or even in the concept of The Public Theater. The production deliberately reflected a contemporary leader and his lofty and sometimes dictatorial inclinations. But this, actually, is a fairly standard tactic in the presentation of the play, going back to its first showing in 1600. Inadvertently, and perhaps more powerfully, the Eustis *Caesar* mirrored and instigated a contemporary need to connect, to be outraged, and to share that outrage online with a global community. Eustis approached that conclusion when he noted, "I think the core function of the show had nothing to do with the demonstrations or anything else. I think the core function of the show was cathartic." But actually, the demonstrations provided that. If drama requires conflict and obstacles, the social media response to *Caesar* allowed for a complex and powerfully appropriate response to the production that mirrored the conflict in Shakespeare's text, creating multiple levels of performance, indeed a meta-performance. That response, then, was the immediate and lasting power of the production.

---

[25] https://www.youtube.com/watch?v=1eZQr72JJto.

INTERLUDE

Kenny Leon and Beowulf Boritt

FIGURE 3.3 (a) *Kenny Leon. Courtesy Walter McBride.*
(b) *Beowulf Boritt. Courtesy Michael Loccisano.*

Kenny Leon directed the 2019 Park production of *Much Ado About Nothing*. He placed his play in a suburban Atlanta neighborhood, and Beowulf Boritt's set design featured an enormous brick mansion set amid a bucolic orchard. Emblazoned on the side of the house was a campaign poster: "Stacy Abrams 2020." The play was noteworthy in that its cast was made up entirely of Black actors, a first at the Delacorte. It starred Danielle Brooks and was filmed for PBS's *Great Performances* series. In 2022, Leon and Boritt reflected on the process of bringing the play to the stage. The following is a shortened version of a longer discussion.

Leon: I don't want to do Shakespeare for rich folks with fur coats on. So, I set out to do what Shakespeare wanted. I want the everyday person to understand what I'm trying to say. I want to have real laughter, belly laughter. Nothing about this is phony. …

Boritt: Kenny and I had our first meeting, we were on the phone, and we were chatting about the show. And he said "I want it to be set in the Atlanta suburbs." He gave me a few things that were specific. And I immediately loved that because it was going to be, I think we said it, like eighteen months ahead of where we were in time. But it was essentially a modern-day production.

And that's really my favorite way to do Shakespeare ... Kenny said, "you know, at the beginning of the play they're coming back from the war."

So, I said, "oh, do you mean they're coming back from Iraq or Afghanistan or something?" And Kenny said, "no, they're coming back from the war that's happening in America right now." And I stopped for a second and I was like, shit, Black Lives Matter was in the news, but this was before George Floyd, we'd been watching Black people being killed in this country for longer than I'm alive, for the history of the country.

As a middle-class white boy, I would not have described that as a war. I would have described it as civil rights violations and killing, but not war. And that—when Kenny said that to me, it reset my head for the production, and I was like, well, of course it's a war. ...

At some point Kenny was clear that they're not carrying weapons, they don't have guns. It's not that kind of war. And we worked through a bunch of different options and what those signs might be. You know, at the time I think we stayed away from saying Black Lives Matter. We didn't actually have that logo out there. And I think in a weird way that was, it was maybe too controversial to put on the stage in 2018, 2019.

Leon: I'm interested in how the play speaks to the people in the seat today.

So, when I'm given an assignment like *Much Ado*, first thing I ask as a director is, OK, where does it take place? What's the city? I remember, there was a city that has the same exact name like fifteen minutes from my house. I live here in Atlanta, Georgia. So, it was like fifteen minutes from my house, it was the exact town that Shakespeare talked about in Italy.

I know it's in the future. I know it's in America. ... It's a play about upper-class people. Wow. Atlanta has the highest upper-class Black community in this country. ...

So, you just start slowly making choices. And then, given what's happening in our country now, there was a lot of racial strife. And I was like, well, one misconception that the white community has about Blacks is that we don't love our country. ... They hated when Kaepernick got on his knees and knelt. ... I said, OK, let me try to paint that picture. "So, Beowulf, I think that there needs to be an American flag in the backyard of this house."

We know it's in Atlanta, Georgia now. We know its in a city that's in a state that's turning blue, so it's kind of purplish now.

We've got a community of Black folks; we've got an American flag. We also know this is a comedy. So, we've got to always walk that line of comedy. We can't make it a drama. We've got a flag there. I said when you see Black folks sitting in the back of the yard, they're dancing, they're laughing, and they've got an American flag. That says "I love my country."

So, no matter what you bring to the theater, you come away saying, hey, those Black folks, they love their country. They're not that different than we are. We love our country. ...

Landis: This was, I think, the first play at the Delacorte that had an all-Black cast. That must have been one of the very first decisions. Because a lot of these design choices come out of that conversation about race in America. Is that right?

Leon: I didn't take the job with the idea that it's going to be a Black company. I was just given *Much Ado*. [I asked] "what do you see?" And I love Oskar because he's like, "no, you're the artist. What do you see?"

Like I said, it came to me in a natural way. Where does the play happen? ... Oh. Most of those people are Black. I remember one time during the process, Oskar said, "well, do we want to have a multiracial cast? Or do you think it's all Black?" ...

I thought that diversifying around the edge with one or two white folks ... it would dilute what we were trying to say. Because then you would have to put the—maybe the kind of silly police group of guys. They would have to be white. So, some are saying, oh, he's trying to make the white guys be the butt of the joke. No. ...

I said, "Oskar, no, I think it's all Black." And he supported me with that. ...

That doesn't mean that we don't have a beautiful white community, too. But Atlanta is economically controlled by whites, politically controlled by Blacks. So, when you talk about the community of it, and the city of it, the heart of it, that's pretty much Black.

Landis: That's really interesting. I mean it gets to Atlanta-ness being sort of the germinal phrase of this play in a certain way. And so much develops out of that.

Leon: And if you want to go deeper than that, me and Beowulf started talking, it was like, well, when we sit in the audience, how will the audience know that we're in the future? How will they know, because I don't want to change Shakespeare's words? And at that time my friend Stacy Abrams, had been in the governor's race and that was over. And I was like, you know what? I know Stacy Abrams. I don't think she would mind us putting a political sign, "Stacy Abrams."

Boritt: Also, in retrospect, a year later I called Kenny and I said, "how did you fucking see the future as clearly as you did?" Because a year after we did this production, the entire country is in massive civil rights marches. And six months after that, the Democrats are in control of Congress because of Stacy Abrams. Even though she didn't run in 2020, she was probably the most potent politician of that year. And it just like—it just got done.

So, I said to a bunch of college students or a bunch of high school students in Atlanta—we were doing a Zoom, and I said, "if Kenny Leon tells you something about the future, listen to him."

Leon: When she came to see the production—that was really special, that she came to New York and saw the production and spent time with the cast afterwards.

Landis: Well, I have to ask. What was her response to that design choice?

Leon: She loved it. Because I asked her about it first, and then she came to see it. She was honored by it. What people don't know is that she studied a lot of theater in school. She was really pleased at the production. She was pleased at what it said.

Landis: Beowulf, could you jump off some of the things that Kenny was saying, especially, you know, around Atlanta-ness, and Stacy Abrams?

Boritt: Well, what I think it did for us is—we were very specific and that in turn made the show universal. We were very specific about the choices. I think we probably could have set it a lot of places and been as specific. But Atlanta was Kenny's world, and so that's what we were doing with it.

But that specificity I think landed the reality of it in a way, because it started to answer every choice. Like in the script they talked about Beatrice walking in the orchard at one point. And so, I put some orchard trees over there and made them peach trees, of course, because it was Atlanta. It started to answer those kinds of questions for us in a really, just a sort of easy way almost.

As Kenny is saying, once you start going down that path, that choice starts answering a lot of questions and making the world cohere and feel real. And you don't have to do Shakespeare realistically. ... For *Much Ado* it works really well. In part because it's one of the few Shakespeare plays that basically all takes place in one location.

It's at Leonato's house, maybe Dogberry is somewhere else. But there's no reason Dogberry can't be at Leonato's house.

The only location in the script that ever gave us trouble was after Hero is dead, there's one brief scene where they go to her grave, or what they think is her grave. And it's a really important scene. And I kept saying, I think if I have them walk out with a Styrofoam gravestone and plunk it down in the middle of the stage, it's going to look ridiculous.

And we came up with this idea: instead, there's going be like a little memorial they set up in the backyard with a picture of her and some flowers. And we'll play the scene there. And the audience obviously knows she's not really dead. It's all about Claudio repenting for what he'd done. But another thing that I just loved about this production is that I've never seen anyone make sense of the character of Hero the way Kenny did.

I think as written, she has about six lines in the whole play. She's important but she doesn't have anything to say. And Kenny put her in every scene she could possibly be in. We had a great actress playing the role. So, she was very present. And she seemed as important a character as Claudio or Beatrice and Benedick. And I've never seen that happen in *Much Ado* …

Another thing Kenny said when we first talked is he said "they're coming through the war at the beginning, they're going from the war at the end. But this isn't a play about war. It's a play about living and loving. And laughing" …

And they finally all come together. And then when that police siren started blaring at the end, and you watch them all say, "oh shit, we're married, we're happy, but we've got to go back and fight the fight again," it gave the play a gravity that I've never seen *Much Ado* have before. …

It gave the story life and death stakes, and it ran them in parallel with the life and death stakes going on in the country at the moment. And I think that's why there was the reaction to the production that there was—and why it was so powerful. It's certainly why it was so powerful for me.

Leon: I think that one of the things that we do well together, we make choices, and we follow those choices, as director and designer. So, for instance, the biggest choice I made was to cast Danielle Brooks as Beatrice, a plus-size chocolate woman, you know, dark skin, beautiful. Right away it questions what we call beautiful. What's beautiful? You know, and all these years and you hardly can remember ever seeing a Beatrice that wasn't thin and white.

So, it was like, OK, why can't she be chocolate and beautiful? And she was. Then you cast Hero now, as the typically thin one now, now that dynamic is off. So subtextually you're watching that whole relationship. ... Just by making that choice that way, it affected almost everything else in the play. And all we have to do is just be true to the choices that we made.

Landis: Beowulf, I want to go back a little bit to the specific set. I saw a hyperrealism. I know the story about the ducks who came on the stage and laid eggs during the process because they believed it was real. You had nature happening right in front of you.

Boritt: The raccoons tried to eat the peaches on the peach trees that were made of Styrofoam. But we found peaches shredded on the ground because the raccoons were pissed off that they weren't real food.

Landis: Could you talk a little bit about how you made that real life suburb of Atlanta come alive? What were some of the revelations you had during the process of creation of that set?

Boritt: You're accepting the trees are part of the image, that part of the world is these real trees in the park. ... We brought fake grass and fake trees onto the set, but it sort of blurs the lines between the stage and what's behind it. And I don't know that I would have realized to even do that my first time out, but I talked to John Lee Beatty—he's a great set designer, he's worked in the Park a lot—and when I knew I had the job, I called him and I said, "John Lee, you've worked there a lot, do you have any pointers for me?"

One thing he said was, "you know, you can use greenery as masking. You can use greenery to sort of fill out your set." And I think I might have been scared to put fake trees against the real trees. But in fact, it works really well.

The other thing that was really important, was that the house felt absolutely real and absolutely solid, and it felt like it had been there for a long time ... at one point I had done a version and Kenny said, "Leonato's house has to feel really grand. It's got to feel like, you know, thirty people showed up at the house for the weekend and it wasn't a problem. There's enough room for all of them." ...

We dressed out the whole interior of the house. Every one of those rooms had furniture in it and pictures. Most of the audience couldn't see much of it, but when the door opened you've got to see something inside there that looks like real life. And my favorite piece of set dressing ever is, once we had the whole set built, we had enough money left over that I got to go buy a Shepard Fairey print of Obama, a Hope portrait.

And so, we bought a real authentic Obama Hope picture and we put it over the mantelpiece.

Landis: This is an unfair question. I'm jumping off of something both of you said. You said, Beowulf, that Kenny is seeing the future. This play happened a year before the death of George Floyd and a lot of the racial reckoning happening within our industry and America. Is it a fair question to ask, or may I ask—How would the play be different now? What are some of the choices that were made then that suddenly are different by the happenings of the last couple of years?

Leon: Go ahead.

Boritt: Go ahead, Kenny.

Leon: Like for me, I'm treating it like a new play. So, you know, I have to take a lot into what's happening with Covid ... simple things ... why can't people do something together like get vaccinated ... our hate, our separateness from each other. All those things will find a way.

And I think I have to honor Brianna Taylor. ... It probably would have been a production about the sacrifice of Brianna Taylor, what that meant ... the parallels of her life and Hero's life, of Beatrice's life. But it's all, you know, going with the truth of what's happening today and how this play speaks to it.

Boritt: This is just a detail thing, but I would say we made the conscious choice not to say Black Lives Matter in any of our writing on the set. And we were kind of skirting that line. And when we did *Merry Wives* last summer, we had a Black Lives Matter mural planted right on the wall there. And we got the rights to use one of the real murals that was painted in Harlem, and we recreated it on the set. ...

I would have been afraid to say that in 2019, for fear of being controversial. And it's a phrase I would be afraid *not* to say now. Because why should it be controversial? The fact that the right wing turned ... what should just be a statement of fact into a controversial statement is crazy. ...

Leon: Well, for me—and we're different this way—like I probably would still not use Black Lives Matter because it has been, you know, politicized in such a way so you have an opinion based on whatever you think about that. ...

I sort of look at what would be the same. And what would be the same is an American flag waving in Central Park and a cast of Black folks saying, "we love our country, why you all keep doing this to us?" And so those things will still be the same and it would end the same way too. ... We start, we came from war, but then life happens. And then we still have to go back to war.

We still have to fight our battles in life. And in between we can have families, we can love on each other, we can keep talking to each other, we can try to keep getting rid of racial disharmony.

Lafayette

4

Four Twenty-Five

FIGURE 4.1 *Lobby of the Anspacher Theater overlooking Colonnade Row. Courtesy Kevin Landis.*

Disembarking at Astor Place from the southbound 6 train on the east side of Manhattan, one takes the stairs up directly into the middle of the bustling East Village. The square is anything but square—in a city laid out in a grid, Astor Place is one area in which that grid scrunches into a confluence of roads; a distorted "H," really. East 8th Street, Cooper Square, Lafayette Street, and Astor Place converge in a haphazard mess, with the flow of traffic speeding uptown. The area has changed enormously in the past decade, and as you emerge from the subway, you are greeted first by a massive Starbucks, then the undulating glass façade of the Astor Place Tower directly in front. The building sits at the south end of the "square" and to its left and just behind it is the Cooper Union, the famed brownstone structure in which, in 1860, Abraham Lincoln gave a now-legendary speech resisting the spread of slavery. Several months later he would win the presidency, catapulted there in part due to his remarks at Cooper Union.

On the west side of the tower is another structure of the same era, a looming façade based on Staatsbibliothek in Munich. It's a grand, three-story building with imposing columns and arches, topped with wedding-cake adornments. It looks entirely appropriate for what was its first tenant, the Astor Library. Now, as the banners out front proclaim, it's more famously known as the home of The Public Theater.

There is history everywhere as you exit the subway, though you might not immediately sense it today. The glass towers, the chic gyms selling wheat grass juice at the door, and the countless coffee shops and food trucks cover over a history of social unrest, political protest, and even violent insurrection. Astor Place was the location of one of the deadliest riots in American history. On May 10, 1849, supporters of the British theater actor William Macready came to blows with followers of the American actor Edwin Forrest. In the streets of New York, the dueling theater patrons fought out who was the greatest actor in the world, and by the end of the melee at least twenty-two people lay dead or dying and over a hundred were injured.

The Astor Place Riots and the history of the neighborhood as a location for political tumult makes it, in an unusual way, the perfect location for America's most famous theater. While the history of 425 Lafayette Street is covered in the grit of that history, the grand entrance to The Public Theater is now an architectural paean to New York-ness, a little Grand Central Station that veritably buzzes with the business of theatergoing. On a busy evening in February, it's easy to be awestruck by the lobby and the phantasmagoric panoply of options. Grand white archways on either side of the room lead to staircases and to the theaters. To the right, bright red lettering proclaims the LuEsther Theater and The Newman. To the left, Joe's Pub, the Anspacher Theater, and the Martinson. In front of you, behind the barista serving wine, cookies, and coffee, is the box office, and the smaller Shiva Theater behind that. Overhead flies Ben Rubin's Shakespeare Machine, an octopus-looking LED-lit chandelier that illuminates phrases from the Bard. On either corner of the lobby, two screens, like the ticker boards at Grand Central, guide audiences to their desired venues. Hovering above the lobby is a mezzanine, where people mingle, sip drinks, and discuss what they have seen or are on their way to see, all the while peering down on the traffic below. Now, after the full overhaul of the lobby, there is a sumptuous restaurant, The Library, that sits just off of the mezzanine. It is not at all uncommon to expect that you might run into the actress you just saw on stage having a drink with castmates around the bar in The Library late in the evening.

It's clear that Giorgio Cavaglieri, the famed architect who Joe Papp tapped to design his lobby and theater spaces, and the Ennead Architect group who oversaw its renovation in 2013 were focused on creating a space that straddled old and new, with multiple nods to the history of the building situated in a decidedly contemporary milieu.[1] Classical columns are juxtaposed with red tinted glass overhangs, while the bold theater signage bellows out the various spaces' existence and demands, like the streets in Astor Place, an almost haphazard traffic pattern. Chelsea Clinton, a frequent patron, comments: "I love the kind of chaos in the lobby when you're trying to figure out where you're going. Are you going left or right or up two flights of stairs or three flights of stairs? But you always know that wherever you're going to wind up is exactly where you are meant to be."

Building The Public

The history of the library in Astor Place is gloriously and richly "New York," and once known, it is difficult *not* to read its history into everything that happens there. While it was based on the Bavarian State Library (begun in 1831), the largest library of its kind in Germany, the Astor Place Library defies any easy architectural categorization. Articles and historical documents variously refer to it as Victorian, Byzantine, Early Renaissance, Northern Italian Renaissance, Rundbogenstil, or a combination of them all. The latter, which features prominent rounded arches, was typical for Germany at the time, en vogue elsewhere in the nineteenth century, and gives The Public its definitive façade.

In his *An Historical Sketch of the Old Astor Library Building 1895, 1980, 2002*, Dan Dalrymple tracked the history of The Public back to well before "architecture" even occupied the location of The Public Theater.[2] In an elegant foreshadowing of the mission of The Public, the land upon

---

[1] Ennead is also the design architect for the revamp of the Delacorte Theater.
[2] A technician at The Public Theater, Dalrymple created a passion project history of the building that is now enjoyed by his colleagues, but was never published. I am indebted to him for his exhaustive research, and lean heavily on what he has chronicled in his study. Not only has he drafted schematics of the building at various points in its history, but also included numerous

which it stands was first granted to the slaves of the West India Company in 1640. By 1804, it was purchased by John Jacob Astor and subsequently leased to create the Vauxhall Gardens, a verdant pleasure park based on its London namesake. Dalrymple notes that with its first public manifestation being a location of musical performance, The Public can thus claim deep-seeded roots as a location of entertainment and cultural creation. Vauxhall lasted about twenty years, at which point Lafayette Street proper was built. The west side of the avenue was subdivided to make Colonnade Row, an architecturally distinct series of grand row houses. The Greek Revival mansions were lined with columns, and of the nine, four exist to this day. They stand directly across Lafayette Street from The Public Theater and provide a dramatic vision as one exits the theater.

Continuing its deep history as a location of entertainment, what remained of Vauxhall, which was almost precisely on the spot of the present-day Public, was leased to the great circus impresario P. T. Barnum. Eventually, however, the area was urbanized and, according to the will of Astor, $400,000 was allocated for a library to be built on the site. The project was overseen by the Harvard librarian Joseph Cogswell, who would be the original curator of the holdings. Over the years, three architects—Alexander Saelzer, Griffith Thomas, and Thomas Stent—designed and built the sections of the structure that now stands on the spot. After the final building was erected, for good measure, a false fourth floor was added, replete with decorative urns, and the entrance was moved to the central building. Though it all holds together, it is no wonder that succinctly stating its architectural style is perilous, which is exactly why, when one exits the subway at Astor Place, eyes are drawn to the grand and unusual building a little way down Lafayette.

It is well to imagine the Astor Library as you stand at the entry of The Public Theater, a place now known for its dedication to diversity, free Shakespeare, and universal access. While that was the mission of Cogswell's library, when it opened it was not a circulating library, and due to hit and miss electricity, it closed when it became too dark to read. Access, in other words, was not its greatest asset. But the place was grand: a marble staircase, wainscotting in pink and black marble, frescoes, and busts of Homer, Plato, Brutus, Seneca, Cicero, Pompey, Euripides, and so many others. In an area that attracted other libraries and booksellers, the Astor Library was the jewel.

In 1895, as the Astor Library outgrew its space and plans were being hatched for the future of public libraries in New York, the Astor, with its 260,000 volumes, closed its doors to the public. By 1897, the trustees partnered with their counterparts at the Tilden Library and the Lenox Library and formed what would become the New York Public Library.

---

articles and resources that allow a better understanding of its development. Where possible, I will directly site those resources, but here acknowledge Dalrymple's deep influence, passion, and expertise.

While it operated temporarily out of the building on Lafayette, it relocated to its permanent and current home on 5th Avenue and 42nd Street in 1911. The building at 425 Lafayette Street would stand vacant for eight years.

The second tenant looms just as powerfully to this day in the moral and cultural makeup of The Public. In 1920, the building was purchased by the Hebrew Immigrant Aid Society (HIAS) and was subsequently opened as a space to shelter new Jewish immigrants to the United States and aid in their immigration processing. To accommodate the influx of immigrants and the new necessities asked of 425, the grandeur of the library was lessened; the central staircase was taken out, and spaces were turned over to create offices, a dining hall, and a synagogue. For forty-four years, 425 Lafayette was a safe house of sorts, registering over 250,000 immigrants through the height of the Second World War and the regime of Adolf Hitler. However, after the war, the need for the large building decreased for HIAS, and by 1964, the organization moved uptown, and the Astor Library was again vacant.

The vacancy of 425 came at a particularly challenging and yet somehow fortuitous moment for New York architecture. In 1963, the original Pennsylvania Station, a Beaux-Arts style building occupying two blocks between 31st and 33rd Streets, was razed to make way for the construction of Madison Square Garden. The destruction of the landmark train depot did not go unnoticed or critiqued. The elimination of what Michael Kimmelman of the *New York Times* recalled as the "Parthenon on steroids" caused uproar in New York City, not just from insider architectural critics, but also citizens.[3] Was a forward-looking New York City of the 1960s eliminating its noble past for a brave new future of contemporary blandness? So great was the dissatisfaction with the 1960s New York wrecking ball that Mayor Robert Wagner created the New York Landmarks Preservation Commission in 1965. And, to add to its illustrious history as the genesis of the New York Public Library and the location for the sheltering of Jewish immigrants, 425 Lafayette was among the first group of buildings saved by what is now the largest municipal preservation commission in the United States.

But in 1965, it was far from certain that 425 would be long for the world. In fact, when HIAS sold the building to a developer, its razing was all but assured. Enter Joe Papp. To assure its historical status, the building needed an interested owner, and as Kenneth Turan describes, Papp and his associate, Bernard Gersten, arrived just in time. The two theater makers, already famed for their New York Shakespeare Festival, toured the building and found it to be a shell of its glory days; skylights boarded up, dust and debris, and overseen by a single caretaker, Arthur Abraham, who had stayed on from the HIAS years. Papp described what he found:

---

[3] Michael Kimmelman, "When the Old Penn Station Was Demolished, New York Lost Its Faith," *New York Times*, April 24, 2019.

The entire building was littered with old pictures and file cards, thousands of them, lists of people who had applied to come over, all kinds of things lying around abandoned for forty years. With all the damp and disarray and leaking ceilings, it was very, very sad. It looked like there had been a pogrom in the place.[4]

But the old structure—sitting as it was on the site of a former slave sanctuary, a location of an English-styled pleasure garden where P. T. Barnum produced spectacles, the site of the first major library in New York, and the landing place of European Jews—seemed just right for what Papp wanted for the permanent home of the Festival. With an interested champion and the newly created Landmark Preservation Commission, 425 was close to being spared. Helped by a donation from Florence Sutro Anspacher, Papp secured $250,000 toward the $575,000 asking price. With partial funding, Papp also lobbied the newly created Preservation Commission to allow renovation, and it was granted on the grounds that, while he could renovate the interior, the façade had to remain as it was. Papp was to invest $1.8 million into renovations, with subsidies from the City of New York. For the first time, tickets would have to be put on sale to help pay the loans.[5]

Papp selected the renovation architect Giorgio Cavaglieri to transform the inside of the old library into two 300-seat theaters—what are now the Newman and the Anspacher. Ming Cho Lee, the renowned set designer, helped with the theater layouts, and the initially identified spaces were added to in subsequent years. In the north building, the 200-seat Martinson Theater was created, the new LuEsther Hall occupied a large room in the south building, and a small rehearsal space called "The Other Stage," now the Shiva, replaced the former synagogue. To top off the extraordinary transformation of HIAS and the success of the new historic building renovation plan, the kickoff of the New York Shakespeare Festival's residence in the East Village was a musical about hippies from the East Village protesting the Vietnam War, expressing love, equality, and freedom. In 1967, *Hair* was an exclamation point on the transformation of 425 Lafayette and a statement that the Joseph Papp Public Theater intended to be a New York institution.

And just as it had been in the Delacorte, Papp quickly realized how close his relationship would be with the city. By 1970, it became clear that The Public could not pay its debts on the building and a lien was placed on the theater. In April, the City of New York agreed to cover the $2.6 million that Papp needed to pay off the purchase of the building and its renovation. The Public secured a fifty-year lease from the City at a cost of $1 per year

---

[4]Joseph Papp quoted in Turan, *Free for All*, p. 175.
[5]Richard F. Shepard, "Shakespeare Festival to Acquire Old Astor Library for a Theater," *New York Times*, January 6, 1966.

(the length of the lease was later increased). The "full circle" nature of the evolution of the Astor Place building was complete. The Public Theater would forever be owned by the people of New York.

Getting in the Door

FIGURE 4.2 *Lafayette façade. Courtesy Kevin Landis.*

When the lobby and the façade of The Public was renovated in 2013 by Ennead Architects, great effort was made to create a gathering space, a hub of activity before and after a performance. The $40 million renovation included a glass canopy built over the vaulted front doors, rebuilt outdoor steps that invite lounging on warm days, and an entire front restoration that was to be spectacularly lit, making the building a glowing center of Astor Place life. During the design process, the architects referred to the expanded stoop and the theater's "seventh stage," calling attention to the theatrical performance of the New York populace gathering in front of the building. To accommodate that "stage," the sidewalk had to be expanded and the street narrowed. The effort was to give New Yorkers a place to congregate, to feel the ownership that came with their buy-in as residents. As Oskar Eustis noted of the newly added mezzanine: "Looking down on people milling about is 'part of the social act of going to the theater.'"⁶ A social act or, really, a performance of the everyday. Like the gurgling frogs in the Central Park pond, the raccoons at the Delacorte, and the police helicopters, folding "city-ness" into the fabric of the theatrical infrastructure has been a consciously intended goal of the organization. The groaning 6 line subway at Lafayette actually rattles the theater walls, making it easy to be taken out of a dramatic moment knowing that not too many feet below the seats are other New Yorkers, sitting on the train heading south and out to Brooklyn.

While the performance of permeability at the building is consciously orchestrated, as in the Park, the reality of who is sitting in the seats at the Anspacher or Shiva Theaters attests to the continuing challenge in American theater. By the time of the 2013 renovation, Astor Place and the East Village was a gentrified neighborhood and the patrons lingering in the lobby were not at all an accurate cross section of New York. Unlike at the Park, the seats at the theaters at 425 Lafayette come at a price, and the glowing façade, the glass canopy, and the high-end restaurant all come at a social price as well. Who is this for, one might fairly ask?

"Getting in the door" means something more than the literal interpretation and the fact that the building is technically open to all. For a company that is often seen as a national theater, getting in the door means "access" not only for audiences, but for artists as well. While the theater at Central Park is largely the province of William Shakespeare, the promise of Lafayette is that it is the laboratory of new American work. Who are the new American playwrights whose stories need to be told and how are they offered a platform? That is the central question, and infrastructure has its affect and influence on the answer. There is a dedicated effort at The Public and at other theaters around the country to challenge the reality that their buildings can be seen as arts cathedrals for the wealthy, and that their structure, replete with high-end restaurants, can actually be a hindrance to a mission of inclusivity.

If The Public is a consistent feeder to Broadway, and if its stars are given their star power through the spotlight of an Astor Place show, it is no wonder many want to know how to get through that door. And of course, to the frustration of many, there is no real answer, though we can look at historical examples and plans for the future. The taste of Oskar Eustis—and Wolfe, Akalaitis, and Papp before him—is easily the most determinative factor. If Eustis loves the work, it will likely be produced. But to get something in front of the artistic director is obviously a challenge, especially as the Theater has grown and its offerings expanded. There are several artists whose work goes right to the top—people who have a long history with the company or a close relationship with Eustis. Artists like Suzan-Lori Parks, Tony Kushner, and Richard Nelson are often asked by The Public to create

---

⁶Quoted in Robin Pogrebin, "Come for the Drinks, Stay for the Drama, at The Public," *New York Times*, September 21, 2012.

or direct plays, knowing that their position in American theater broadly makes their work an easy producing bet. Similarly, the Theater has, over the years, developed relationships with designers and directors who they return to time and again—people like Ming Cho Lee, Jennifer Tipton, Clint Ramos, Alex Timbers, Jo Bonney, and many others.

Likewise, there are "go-to" actors who continuously work with the theater and are invited back over and over again. Jay O. Sanders, Liev Schreiber, Maryann Plunkett, Nikki James, and others are commonly seen on The Public stage and, like in rep companies of old, become audience favorites. Casting directors Jordan Thaler and Heidi Griffiths have been at The Public since 1988 and 1995, respectively, and note that every show has a different trajectory from a casting standpoint. Some productions arrive at The Public already cast from another theater company, or carry a star whose presence is essential to producing the work. The 2018 production of Jane Anderson's *Mother of the Maid* was clearly a vehicle for Glenn Close. Similarly, a play like *Hamlet* will not be produced unless the lead actor has already been decided, as in Kline's version in 1986 or Oscar Isaac's 2017 rendition directed by the New York wunderkind Sam Gold. (The latter became a mini controversy for The Public as it was originally slated to premiere at Brooklyn's Theater for a New Audience, but due to differences between Gold and Artistic Director Jeffrey Horowitz, the director pulled the show and took it to Lafayette. The rift between the two theater companies was splashed all over the press.)

A show's arrival with a famous director and lead makes for a different process than a play that starts small, as an idea within the walls of The Public or from a plucky writer who winds her way through workshops and dramaturgical sessions. Griffiths and Thaler describe the process of casting each new work as uniquely complicated and evolutionary—some casting choices have to be rethought and people let go. Newly created Public Theater musicals like *February House* (2012), *Soft Power* (2019), or *The Visitor* (2021) can be especially difficult because the number of interested parties in the casting process grows, inclusive of other coproducing theater companies. Thaler remarks: "When you get into a room with a musical, you have a director, a composer, potentially a lyricist, a choreographer, all of their associates and assistants, depending on how much voice they're allowed or brought to the table. So, you have a gigantic room of people, and you are looking to try to find consensus." Still, at the end of the process for most shows not already managed by a commercial producer, the final casting approval lies with Oskar Eustis. He is particularly hands-on in the audition process, and often joins the casting directors in callbacks, mostly guiding without being prescriptive.

With casting directors who have been in their positions for thirty years reporting to an artistic director who has the final say, with agents pushing certain actors, and with favorite authors, directors, and musicians slotted into the season, producing is a messy endeavor, and not always as egalitarian as some might like. Nor, of course, is the capitalist system under which the American experiment operates. But with a name like The Public, how can an institution stay on message by appropriately diversifying and expanding its artistic offerings? The short answer is that it is a constant struggle.

What is often lost in conversations about the structure of The Public Theater is that it isn't egalitarian and never was, and the movement in the recent past to decenter leadership sometimes underestimates the necessity of structure, especially within the history of the company. The effort at The Public, though, has been to identify places where positive growth can occur in the midst of capitalist mayhem, where a focus on leadership can and should be about "accountability" rather than "power." As Saheem Ali, the new associate artistic director, notes, "It doesn't matter that we are, in some ways, progressive in our current moment … there are blind spots that The Public has just because of the huge machinery of the institution and the huge volume of work … it's like the subway in New York. When do you repair it when you are constantly moving?" Those blind spots are evidenced in the reality that when the machinery is constantly moving, leadership tends to go with what works, and to go with the people that they know best. Ali and Shanta Thake, in addition to their artistic skill, were brought into senior leadership to help expand access and act as conduits between Eustis and his growing staff; to be sure that all voices were heard, so that decision-making would not seem remote from the needs and interest of a talented artistic staff.[7]

Getting the balance right and hearing from a multiplicity of voices is essential since The Public Theater's producing choices dramatically affect the tastes and trends of the American theater. The stories heard on the stages of the hallowed grounds of 425 Lafayette are often of the greatest playwrights in contemporary American history. There is a chicken and egg question embedded in that formulation, however. Does The Public Theater attract that talent, or does it provide a platform for potential to be achieved? As with Papp's Shakespeare Festival, the answer for the contemporary Public is: a bit of both.

The artists described in the following pages demonstrate both sides of this equation. Some—like Tony Kushner, Jeanine Tesori, David Henry Hwang, and Suzan-Lori Parks—have had an established connection to The Public over decades. They are among the best known of The Public Theater playwrights, people whose careers, while varied and connected to many other companies, have a strong tie to 425. Their trajectories at The Public are told here in short form, but it is noteworthy for the fact that they all are tied together. All four are friends and collaborators with Oskar Eustis and, in fact, with his predecessors as well. While these first stories demonstrate the interconnectedness of some of the American theater's most well-known

---

[7] In 2021, Shanta Thake left The Public to become the chief artistic officer at Lincoln Center.

playwrights, the second part of this chapter looks at ways that the Eustis Public has made efforts to be a location of dramaturgical development, his expertise and passion. How might the theater continue to expand access to artists and diversify by creating avenues of new work creation that assures greatness into the future?

Home Base for Legends

Oskar Eustis and Tony Kushner have developed their friendship into a professional relationship that makes them one of the most important duos in American theater. No story of Eustis's contemporary Public is complete—or really can even begin—without some focus on that now famous friendship.

The relationship is over forty years old, and *A Bright Room Called Day* figures as a linchpin work of art that connects Eustis, Kushner, Joe Papp, George C. Wolfe, director Michael Greif, and so many other pillars of The Public. The play, a takeoff of Bertolt Brecht's *The Private Life of the Master Race*, parallels Reagan's America of the 1980s and the Republican Party to the rise of the Nazis. It premiered in 1987 under the direction of Eustis at the Eureka Theater in San Francisco. And, in the interconnecting worlds of theater in the late 1980s and early 1990s, it was also the play that connected Kushner to The Public. Kushner remembers:

> From the time I first arrived in New York in 1974, The Public always seemed to be the most important theater in the United States—the place that was doing consistently the most daring and interesting work, the most heterodox aesthetics, a theater that routinely explored areas of artistic production that are of great importance to me, art that is on some level politically engaged, art that is interested in antecedent form, Shakespeare, the permission to be both a validly public, political theater but also a theater that can investigate the canon and classic dramatic texts and productions, and a theater that's always had a lively connection to the avant-garde.

Kushner came to New York City as a student at Columbia University and remembers that Joe Papp was producing the same people who were central to his education and understanding of the theater: from Lee Breuer and JoAnne Akalaitis and their company, Mabou Mines, to the avant-garde artists Stuart Sherman and Richard Foreman, and the Ontological-Hysteric Theater. Foreman's 1977 production of the Brecht and Kurt Weill musical play *The Threepenny Opera* was formative to Kushner: "I remember every second of that production. I think I saw it eight or nine times. He was an artist I adored and was in awe of. Having him do Brecht fused a link that was enormously important and enormously generative for me in many ways."

The other plays that Kushner points to are *Hair* and *A Chorus Line*, the biggest successes in The Public's history. "I was a gay kid from Louisiana. My father came up to visit me. I hadn't really come out at all, but I made him come with me to see *A Chorus Line*. ... I wanted him to see it because of Paul's monologue about his father discovering that his son is gay. I think he got the point!" In identifying those major hits alongside an obscure production of Brecht by one of the brilliant and yet mystifying avant-garde theater directors in history, Kushner ratifies the deep legacy and influence of the "cutting edge" side by side with the Broadway megashows. In story after story, and interview after interview, many of the famous creators in the history of The Public have talked about how important the unusual, the avant-garde, and the transgressive have been in their upbringing and love of The Public Theater.

As an artist, Kushner's entry to The Public coincided with that of the director Michael Greif. After a surprise visit to see Greif's work at the Naked Angels Theater, Papp, who was ill at the time, invited the director to The Public to be a "resident director," to helm up to three plays in 1990–1 season with $1 million as a budget. It was an extraordinary act of trust, and Greif chose Sophie Treadwell's classic *Machinal*, Constance Congdon's *Casanova*, and Tony Kushner's *A Bright Room Called Day*. Kushner and Greif were elated, remarkably elevated to produce at one of the most respected theaters in the country and, seemingly, given carte blanche. It was the beginning of a long partnership between Greif and the Public. He has been one of the most prolific directors in the company's history and has worked for each of the four artistic directors. Papp was a real fan of Kushner's work when Greif came on board and Kushner looks back on those times fondly: "I couldn't believe I was going to have a play at The Public Theater. I couldn't believe I was sitting and talking to Joe Papp."

At around the same time that *Bright Room* was gearing up at The Public, *Angels in America*, commissioned by Eustis and Tony Taccone, had just finished performances in San Francisco and Los Angeles. Papp had read the script and invited Kushner to his office to discuss the possibility of switching shows. Kushner recalled that Papp didn't express any doubts about the quality and validity of *Bright Room*, but that he was taken by *Angels in America* in a stronger way:

> "This is a very, very, very good play," said Papp. "This play is really quite remarkable. This play is really going to be a very important play, and I would like very much to do this play."

Of course, Papp was right about *Angels*, but it was commissioned by Eustis at Eureka, and it would premiere there. And so, *A Bright Room Called Day* was Kushner's first production at The Public Theater. It would be followed during the Wolfe years by *A Dybbuk, or Between Two Worlds* (1997), an adaptation of Shloyme Ansky 1941 play, and *Caroline, or Change*, a musical collaboration with Jeanine Tesori. *Caroline* premiered under the direction of

Wolfe in 2003 at the Newman Theater at The Public before transferring to Broadway, where it was nominated for six Tony Awards. During the Eustis years, Kushner continued his collaboration with Tesori and Wolfe with the epic Meryl Streep-led production of *Mother Courage and Her Children* (2006), *An Intelligent Homosexual's Guide to Capitalism and Socialism with a Key to the Scriptures* (2011), and a remounting and re-visioning of *Bright Room* in 2019 with Eustis as the director.

* * *

Kushner's tie to Jeanine Tesori was integral to her early involvement at the Public Theater, and now her presence and influence at 425 is deeply felt. Several years ago, I was asked by the staff if I would be willing to moderate a conversation with important company artists during the annual staff appreciation. Honored by the request, I went about helping curate a conversation with Jay O. Sanders, Jo Lampert, who was playing Joan of Arc in David Byrne's *St. Joan*, and the costume and set designer Clint Ramos. As we were walking across the crowded lobby on the way to the Newman Stage, I saw Tesori walk in, heading upstairs to a meeting or rehearsal. With her recent Tony for the music of *Fun Home*, Tesori was a star, a luminary in the New York theater world (though she resists the praise). I didn't know her well, but greeted her and somewhat offhandedly asked if she would join us, knowing full well that she couldn't. Beat. "Yeah, why not?"

That is the way in the lobby of The Public, where brushes with some of the most influential theater makers in America are not unusual. And Tesori's response, I have found, is not unusual either: "Sure, let's talk theater." And when she talks, Tesori, like so many others at the theater, demonstrates both an awe for The Public and a deep warmth and gratitude for the fact that it has become a home. Of her first meeting with George C. Wolfe, she recalls:

> I remember the first time going there and it was like Anne Hathaway in *Devil Wears Prada* where there are racks going and costumes. Everybody seemed so important. They had important things to do, in quotations. And I met with George and the next thing I knew we were going down there all the time. And the thing that I loved about going down there was every nook and cranny was filled with people doing something ... someone tap dancing to a metronome in one corner and then there was a tech going on in another corner. There were deliveries, and in another place, there were fittings. Outside someone was painting. There was a band rehearsing in the Pub. It was just a crazy hive. ... There was no difference between the people on the streets of New York and the people who were working at The Public.

Her history, like many at The Public, started back in the Papp years, when going to The Public and seeing plays there was something every New York theater lover just did. As her career developed, she made the acquaintance of Tony Kushner, the director Joe Mantello, Craig Lucas, and others. Kushner had heard some of her compositions from the musical *Violet*, which premiered at Playwrights Horizons in 1997. Intrigued by her work, he sent her the libretto to a new play, *Caroline, or Change*, hoping that she might be interested in working on the score. "I didn't quite see my place or any composer's place in *Caroline* because it seemed so complete, and it had no repetition in it. It seemed less like a libretto than a play." They each started working on other things, but eventually Kushner came back to her and encouraged her to have another look. They agreed to develop it further, this time with the backing of Wolfe and a workshop at The Public Theater.

While Tesori was undoubtedly a musical theater success before she came to The Public Theater, she found her place at Lafayette with *Caroline*:

> When at a time when I had no money and George found $30,000 for me ... *Caroline* would never have been written because I didn't have any money. And we had a kid and I had said to George, "I can't take the time to write a piece like this." He said, "Oh, I'll find you the money. I'll find you the money," and he found it, and $30,000 for me was the difference between writing something and not writing something. I think great artistic directors like that find artists and what they need. If they need an office or if they need money or if they need an idea or if they just need a place where they can come, and that to me was what The Public has always been good at.

It didn't start that way. Tesori was intimidated by Wolfe, especially because he and Kushner had created such a strong bond due to *Angels*. In the early days of their collaboration, she found it difficult to even get into the inner sanctum of the upstairs offices at Lafayette. At one point she remembers just giving up and saying, "I'm Tony Kushner's assistant." Eventually she confronted them: "How are we going to do this because I can't compete with the history that you have?"

Tesori was brought into The Public fold by Kushner and Wolfe but quickly became friends with Eustis, who was head of Trinity Rep in Providence. He invited her to Brown University to speak to one of his classes and present a small sample from *Caroline*. During her time there—in fact, in the guest room of his house—she wrote part of the second act of the show. Tesori says of Eustis, "He has a gravitational pull." Their friendship blossomed at Trinity and when he became the head of The Public she continued there with the Brecht/Streep/Klein/Kushner/Wolfe/Eustis megalith, *Mother Courage* (2006). That was followed by the full development of *Fun Home* from The Public Lab in 2012, to the Newman Theater in 2013, and then its Broadway debut at Circle in the Square in 2015. *Fun Home* won five Tony Awards, including Best Musical and Best

Score for Tesori. In October 2019, Tesori joined with David Henry Hwang for the musical *Soft Power*, a coproduction with the Center Theater Group in Los Angeles.

And the connections continue. Tesori's *Soft Power* collaborator David Henry Hwang has had a relationship with The Public perhaps longer than any other playwright, and notes that the theater was part of his consciousness since he was a child growing up in California. It was the mystical company that did renowned plays and musicals that young playwrights of the 1970s followed closely; he knew that he wanted to be there, or at least just see the place. And so, in 1979, during spring break of his senior year of college, he flew out to New York on a red eye, got a ride into the city and, at five in the morning, saw the legendary theater for the first time. Remarkably, Hwang booked his first show at The Public in 1980, almost exactly a year after his predawn wander around the East Village. In the spring of 1979, he wrote a play called *FOB* ("fresh off the boat"), which was performed in his dorm in March, just before his visit to New York. After his dorm production, he sent it to the O'Neill Theater and it was accepted for a summer production, directed by Robert Allan Ackerman, a friend and collaborator with Joe Papp. It was a confluence of extraordinary young talent and remarkable luck.

Further adding to the serendipity of the moment, at the same time that *FOB* was performing at the O'Neill, Papp had a challenge on his hands. His new production, Len Jenkins's *New Jerusalem*, featured a Caucasian actor cast in an Asian role, prompting protests—what Hwang recalls may have been the first "yellowface" protests in New York theater history. Papp, given his mission to create theater that looked like New York, realized his glaring blind spot and invited the protesters into his office to discuss their grievances and find solutions. In response, he decided to hire one of them, David Oyama, with the brief to find more plays for Asian actors. Over the course of a year, he solicited plays and auditioned actors from the Asian community with other producers from The Public. *FOB*, after its successful run at the O'Neill, rose to the top.[8] Says Hwang, "So, all these things coincided, and I feel like I was really the beneficiary of affirmative action, because that's what affirmative action does. It identifies a social need and then creates a program to try to address that. I was the guy who got to walk through the door."

Hearing of *FOB* from Ackerman and Oyama, Papp asked Hwang to come to New York and do a reading of the play, not long after Hwang's twenty-first birthday. After the reading, Papp took him into his office and gave him notes, most of which Hwang didn't actually agree with. But, eager to make an impression with the legendary producer, he said he'd go back to San Francisco and rework the script and send him another draft. "[I] waited

---

[8]David Oyama, "Asian-Americans Take Center Stage at The Public," *New York Times*, April 27, 1980.

three or four weeks. I sent him back the exact same script, and then about 10 days later the phone rings, and it's Joe Papp. He said, 'okay, the script's great; now we're going to do it.'" And that is how David Henry Hwang got in the door.

FOB was paired in the spring of 1980 with Wakako Yamauchi's *The Music Lessons*, and they marked the first time Asian American plays had been performed at The Public. Papp later told Hwang that he would produce anything he wrote. He was good to his word. In 1981, The Public produced Hwang's *The Dance and the Railroad* and *Family Devotions*. In 1983, *Sound and Beauty* was performed in the LuEsther at The Public. David Henry Hwang was a staple of the repertoire at The Public Theater when his star really rose with his Broadway hit *M. Butterfly* (1988), his adaptation of the Puccini opera about the ill-fated relationship between a Peking opera star and a French diplomat. George C. Wolfe subsequently produced *Golden Child* in 1996, a play that explored the effect of Westernization on a Chinese family after the patriarch converts to Christianity. Hwang's themes of Chinese identity, cultural heritage, and immigration run through much of his work at The Public.

Hwang met Oskar Eustis when he was hired by Jon Jory at the Actors Theater of Louisville to direct Hwang's one-act *Bondage* (1992), with a companion piece called *Devotees in the Garden of Love* by a young playwright named Suzan-Lori Parks. Eustis was still at the Mark Taper Forum under Gordon Davidson, but at Louisville he and Hwang struck up a lasting dramaturgical relationship: "I came out of that experience feeling like, 'oh; well, Oskar, for me, is the best dramaturg in America. He's the person who I want to read all my work.' There are a lot of people who feel this now, whether or not he ever produces it." Eustis continued the relationship with Hwang when he became the artistic director of Trinity Rep in Providence, and invited him to do an adaptation of Henrik Ibsen's *Peer Gynt*. In addition, Hwang developed a playwright/dramaturg relationship with Eustis and sent him scripts over the years—not for production, per se, but for suggestions and thoughts about development. That sort of trust takes time, of course, and Hwang now consults with Eustis on most everything he writes, in addition to Leigh Silverman, who has directed many of his plays.

In 2019, Hwang was commissioned by Michael Ritchie at Center Theater Group to write a play for the Mark Taper Forum's fiftieth anniversary season. Hwang had an idea for a play that turns into a musical that reverses the exoticized paradigm of *The King and I*; in this case, a Chinese businessman comes to America and meets Hillary Clinton, with ridiculous references to American culture and customs, including a dance with a giant box of McDonalds French fries. Hwang wanted to work with Jeanine Tesori and The Public agreed to take on the commissioning expense of adding her to the project. It grew from there, and was presented with a 23-piece orchestra at the Ahmanson Theater in Los Angeles and then premiered in New York on the Newman Stage at The Public. *Soft Power* joined a 2007 production of *Yellowface* as the two Hwang productions produced under Eustis at The Public Theater.

As is so often the case at The Public, each story and play seems inextricably linked to another playwright, another tale, another tie in the story of contemporary American theater. That young playwright that paired with David Henry Hwang at the Actors Theater of Louisville has become perhaps the most important writerly voice at The Public in Oskar Eustis's tenure.

Suzan-Lori Parks and Oskar Eustis have been friends for a long time. Like Hwang, she moved to New York City shortly after college and recalls standing in line at the Delacorte and wandering by the East Village headquarters: "I would save all my hard-earned money from doing temp word processing and self-produce my plays; and only walk by The Public Theater and look into the lobby; and ooh—every once in a while, I'd save up money and go see something in The Public Theater. You knew when you walked in the lobby that you were in the presence of the greats; the great writers, the great actors, the great directors, the great designers."

In 1992, George C. Wolfe told Parks he wanted to produce one of her plays. She had won an Obie Award in 1990 for *Imperceptible Mutabilities in the Third Kingdom* and Wolfe, soon after he became head of The Public, added her *The America Play* (1994) to the season. The two collaborated again on *Venus* (1996), *In the Blood* (1999), *Topdog/Underdog* (2001), for which she won the Pulitzer Prize, and *Fucking A* (2003).

Parks says that Wolfe and Eustis are similar in many ways, especially as they approached supporting her career. She says that as directors they both have a deep understanding of the way she writes and the ideas that she wants to express, not just from their sterling intellects, but "through the guts and the heart," and thus can communicate that to actors. Both Wolfe and then Eustis knew that Parks would be a critical part of the story of The Public Theater's history. Wolfe, who promised to produce her plays at the Pubic *before* he was even appointed artistic director had, according to Parks, "a long game plan that involved me." When Eustis took over the job, he continued that game plan. "He asked me one night, when we were watching the end of *365 Days/365 Plays*. 'Would you like to come home?' I said, 'what does that mean.' He said, 'would you like to become …'—I don't think he had the title at that moment. He had a long plan that involved me."

What Eustis had in mind for the playwright was a position that was embedded in the theater and allowed an artist to work without pressure. As artistic director, what he hoped to offer was two things—a stable job and support:

I've discovered that writers really like being offered jobs. The master writer chair here is so important to me because the whole point was that it was a job which had no obligation other than for her to write. Even though the job is for her to write plays, and The Public Theater is paying her salary and her pension and medical benefits, we don't own a jot of the plays. We didn't even have options on the plays. That was terribly important to me, because I wanted to really replicate what I think is the best of academic culture.

The master writer chair was created with *no* expectation that Parks must complete and produce plays on any set timeline, and the academic reference is notable and reveals Eustis's ties to the academy from his youth. Eustis uses the university model as something to strive for, where resident academics own their work and are given space to think and develop. He says, "The understanding is that the social role of the university is to provide a place for philosophers to work. That's what the theater should be. It's providing a place for writers and artists to work."

Parks describes her role as master writer chair simply and clearly: "I write the best plays I can. I try to involve as many people as possible in the building in the creation and development and workshopping and production of those plays." While that is the core, she does other things at The Public as well. She began a weekly event in the lobby mezzanine of 425 called Watch Me Work. The premise is so simple that its almost laughable when described. Parks sits at a desk behind a cordon and writes for about twenty minutes: quite literally, a playwright on display, cordoned off, head down, working on a script. But lest it feel only like an avant-garde performance, members of the public show up and work on their own scripts, and don't simply watch Parks (though how could you not?). After the work is completed, Parks answers questions and offers advice. And that's basically it.

Parks describes the offer of Watch Me Work as something similar to Free Shakespeare in the Park—it's free and it's about the attendees as much as it's about the performance. Watch Me Work is, in a way, an amazing piece of meta-theater, where *working* is the performance, both the work of Parks and the student attendees. What is created is an almost sacred space; the use of 425 Lafayette both as a classroom and a production. It is a show, and one cannot help smiling at the structure of the event—the cordon, the clacking of Parks's typewriter, the comings and goings in the lobby, and the kitchen timer she sets at the beginning for twenty minutes. It is performance art, really, or a "meditation on the artistic process" as The Public's website proudly proclaims. It has become an important part of her role as master writer chair and relates to the process of dramaturgy that Eustis subscribes to. Dramaturgy is more than research on a singular production. Rather, it is a longitudinal commitment to the development of theater in a society, an acceptance that a theater company owes something deeply to its constituents. Parks sees it as her obligation: "I thought that, as a master writer chair, I could offer that to people, people who perhaps can't afford to enroll in a formal writing program but who still long to have feedback and advice, if you will, from a person who has been writing for a long time and has had some success in the field ... I was just looking for a way to be available to people in the local community and also the worldwide community, since livestreaming was a basic component of it pretty much from the beginning. It's called Watch Me Work, but the 'me' in the title is 'you.'"

Parks keeps to the philosophy that the performance-like meditation is about the participants, not her. If they ask her about a play she has written, she turns it around and asks them about their writing. As a yoga practitioner, she believes that Watch Me Work is a communication of energy—*Shaktipat*, the transmission of energy from the spiritual guide to the pupil. In that way, she doesn't see it as teaching: "I don't know if 'educational' is a good word. It doesn't feel that way. I don't feel like I'm educating. I feel like I'm *light housing*. I'm going to make up a word right now. I feel like I'm being present for people. I'm providing an example." In that way, what is notable about Suzan-Lori Parks at The Public Theater is that she has managed to fully commit herself to the hard work of playwrighting—she continues to be one of the most respected playwrights in the world—while taking on a play development methodology that complements that of Oskar Eustis.[9]

Finding Future Voices

The integration of Parks as playwright, master writer chair, and educator of new talent makes her a fulcrum of the basic structure of the Eustis Public: that is, a company dedicated to established great artists and an incubator for the new. The Public would like to believe that a young, talented playwright from an underserved part of the country can find her way to having her play produced at the theater, and years ago began developing tributaries of new work development. To that end, the company has tried to expand its outreach by developing programs that attract new talent around the country. Eustis had been concerned that perhaps that hadn't always been intuitive in the past, and his goal has been to ease the process by creating new paths: "We said, 'All right, we are not getting all of the work by artists of color that we wish we were. What's the issue?' Education, economics, access." In 2008, the Emerging Writers Group was formed on

---

[9]Suzan-Lori Parks's *365 Days/365 Plays* used The Public Theater as its New York hub in 2006, in the first full year of Eustis's time at the theater. The production was coproduced at theaters across the country. She also wrote *The Book of Grace* (2010), *Father Comes Home from the Wars (Parts 1, 2, 3)* (2014), and *White Noise* (2019).

the principle that The Public Theater would be a place that nurtures the next voices of American theater, with an attempt to decentralize standard ways of getting attention—agents, degrees, connections, and the like. The program consists of two-year fellowships for new writers, overseen by the New Works Development Department with a goal of diversifying that pipeline of new work in American theater. Knowing that graduates of MFA programs are automatically going to have their work seen by the big theaters, Eustis wanted a program that upended that paradigm. He says, "You can't be in the Emerging Writer's Group if you already have an agent. Why? Because if you have an agent, you know how to get to us. You can't be in the Emerging Writer's Group if you've already had a New York production. Why? If you've had a New York production, we know about you. You have access to us." With the new program, everything revolved around opening up access.

Jack Moore, who codirected the program for several years with Jessie Cameron Alick, further described the goals: solicit plays from writers who don't have graduate degrees but who show enormous promise; bring them to New York City for two years for crash courses on development, the business of theater, and the process of getting an agent; and, importantly, grant them full access to The Public, its staff, and shows. "And that cohort becomes its own little mini community," Moore says. Sometime during those two years, each playwright stages a full-length show; not on a main stage, but *seen* by the heads of the theater. The program counts many successful alumnae, including Dominique Morisseau (*Detroit'67*, 2012), Branden Jacobs-Jenkins (*Neighbors*, 2010), and Mona Mansour (*Vagrant Trilogy*, 2022).[10] About five hundred applications come in every two years for admission to the Emerging Writer Group.

Another tributary in the watershed of new work is the popular Under the Radar Festival, a January celebration of innovative work from around the country and world, focusing on new approaches to performance making and, often, marginalized voices. Under the Radar is devoted to what was once (and often still) called "devised theater" that celebrates contemporary performance that is often not based on a traditional script or dramatic format—"experimental," "avant-garde," and any other word of that ilk that has a general understanding but stands alone, means little. Under the Radar brings in productions that are ready for presentation, but sometimes also acts as a development entity, nurturing new artists and their vision. The festival has become an institution unto itself and is an eagerly anticipated event every year.

Under the Radar was founded by Mark Russell, an avant-garde theater professional who cut his teeth on the European auteurs Jerzy Grotowski,

---

[10]*Detroit '67* received a full production at Classic Theater of Harlem and The Public under the direction of Kwame Kwei-Armah, *Neighbors* had a full production at The Public and *Vagrant Trilogy*, in rehearsals when theaters shut down, premiered in April 2022.

Tadeusz Kantor, Peter Brook, and Antonin Artaud. He wanted to create a theater that mattered to his aesthetic, something that could continue the avant-garde tradition of shock and transgression, to upend expectations. In 2005, while working at the theater at St. Ann's Warehouse, Russell produced a conference of new work that Eustis attended just before he took the job at The Public. Taken by the experience, he invited Russell to continue the idea at The Public in an effort to get back to some of the experimental roots of the company and to provide a platform for devised new work. JoAnne Akalaitis, after all, was the founder of Mabou Mines, one of the most famous avant-garde theater companies in the United States, and The Public has produced the work of the experimental provocateur Richard Foreman many times over. Russell's codirector, Meiyin Wang, described art that would be "form-forward," meaning that the *way* that the performances were developed, and their unexpected structures, would identify an Under the Radar piece. A contemporary performance group from Chile could be in a festival with the drag performer Martha Graham Cracker, and it would be thematically acceptable. That's because, rather than theme, Russell and Wang preferred a governing *question*: "Why do theater, now?"

So, by using buildings and open spaces all over The Public Theater, at New York University, and around the city, Under the Radar presents unusual new work that ranges from concerts at Joe's Pub, to audio tours in museums, to performances from prominent experimental groups paying with new forms and technologies. The output is delightfully eclectic. The musician Reggie Watts created *Audio Abramović* in which he composed and performed an original song created for each singular audience member as they sat across from him. It was a riff on Marina Abramović's famous and satirized piece, *The Artist Is Present*, which featured the artist sitting face-to-face for hours on end with museum goers. Stan's Cafe, a British company, presented *The Commentators*, a work that featured artists acting as soccer announcers, commenting in real time on the comings and goings in the lobby of The Public Theater, and then livestreaming the event on the web. Elevator Repair Service, the group that went on to create new plays at The Public and other experimental houses, presented their much-lauded *Gatz*, a full reading (and acting) of *The Great Gatsby*, word for word, on stage in the inaugural year of Under the Radar.

The festival sources art from all over the world and has deepened and expanded the ways that it fosters the growth of that work. By creating the Devised Theater Working Group, for example, several selected groups are able to meet together and discuss new ideas and proposals as they create "works in progress" for Under the Radar. Russell says, "Theater is a really great way to get those disadvantaged or not-included voices to the forefront. Often, I feel that this work that goes around playwriting is another way of getting at that. ... I want things that open up and use that idea of 'coming together in the theater' in a radical way." That process includes working groups, in-house workshops, and university residencies in advance of a festival showing.[11]

Andrew Kircher, who was the director of devised theater, speaks of the essential importance of creating new work outside of usual means. While Under the Radar does not shy away from playscripts and traditional drama, there is too often a presupposition that theater must have certain designations, set structures, and methodologies. The Public, he says, turns that on its head and proposes that through programs like Under the Radar and the Devised Theater Working Group, its spaces can be used in myriad ways to harness artistic potential: "The idea is that we all benefit when we stop trying to define the boundaries of theater. The question isn't 'is something (for example, a show at Joe's Pub or Under the Radar) theater?' Rather, the question should be: 'What happens, what becomes possible when we call this performance "theater?" What magic happens when we leverage this great organization, all the staff ingenuity, everything, to realize a work with the scale and ambition that only theater affords?'"

Whatever it's called, the word "workshop" is important, and Eustis's Public has created a veritable buffet of development options. The Public Studio (or Public Lab) is a process of dramaturgy and audience-invited workshopping that allows a testing ground for artists. Generally reserved for early career playwrights but also there to assist seasoned authors, Public Studio was a remount of Public Lab, and supported Suzan-Lori Parks's *Father Comes Home from the Wars*, Michael Friedman and Alex Timbers's *Bloody Bloody Andrew Jackson*, and Jeanine Tesori and Lisa Kron's *Fun Home*. Studio, in recent years, has seen the development of *Wild Goose Dreams* (2018) by Hansol Jung and *Ain't No Mo'* (2019) by Jordan E. Cooper, which was slated to transfer to Broadway in 2022.[12]

Development Case Study: *Cullud Wattah*

The process by which a full play comes to the stage is different for every project, but one case study is illustrative. In the fall of 2021, *Cullud Wattah*, after a circuitous routing, made it to opening night in the Newman Stage,

---

[11]The companies 600 Highwaymen and Manual Cinema, for example, workshopped their new Under the Radar performances of *The Fever* and *Frankenstein* at universities including my own, the University of Colorado.

[12]Lest one spend time trying to distinguish between Public Lab and Public Studio, don't. Lab essentially grew into Studio and while there are slight differences (Lab had rehearsals between performance weeks while Studio frontloads rehearsals and dramaturgy, and then does six performances in a row), no one at the organization seems to be able to succinctly identify why they are separate programs.

just after New York theaters reopened after the pandemic. The play, by Erika Dickerson-Despenza, is a syncretic work about three generations of Black women living in Flint, Michigan. It focuses on the polluted water crisis that has gripped Flint for years, and a family's connection to the corrupt politics and civic choices wrapped up in that environmental disaster. Using poetry, African spirituals, and a set packed with hundreds of bottles of dirty Flint water representing the days that the family had endured the poisoning of their city, the play is a devastating tragedy of one family's experience in a corrupt capitalist system, a system that promotes what Dickerson-Despenza calls "environmental anti-Black racism." Actors clad in white ethereal vestments begin the play singing the spiritual "Wade in the Water," but here it's "Lead in the Wattah," a remake by Avery R. Young. The narrative is at once poetry and prose—human blending with the divine—as spiritual musical interludes intermingle with the quotidian. Dickerson-Despenza says that she draws from the Afro-Surrealist manifesto by D. Scot Miller that posits that all art created from the lived experience of "other" is always surrealist. Miller's contention that "Afro-Surreal presupposes that beyond this visible world, there is an invisible world striving to manifest," is thus evidenced in Dickerson-Despenza mixing of styles.[13] Moving from theory to practice, *Cullud Wattah*'s visioning of an inner-city water crisis takes on an outsized theatricality, an unusual elevation of surreality. Water is elevated to symbol. Dickerson-Despenza says:

> Water, which is a life-giving force, is a life-sustaining force ... it's that important, because our relationship with it historically has been so tumultuous. I think about those who jumped over on the way to what we would know as chattel slavery, who liberated themselves through that. ... I also think about baptisms, and I think about how integral water is to agriculture. ... I think about what it meant for Dorothy Dandridge and others in swimming pools that had poison put in because they didn't want Black people in the pool. ... I say all of this to say chiefly, writing about water is my way in, in talking about environmental racism.

Cullud Wattah at The Public was met with praise, and Dickerson-Despenza won the Susan Smith Blackburn Prize for women playwrights in 2021.

Though Dickerson-Despenza had been a playwright in residence at The Public, *Cullud Wattah* got "into the building" through its eventual director, Candis C. Jones, who had met the playwright at the Lark, another New York-based experimental development laboratory. The Lark focused on centering marginalized voices and became a mainstay of BIPOC (Black, Indigenous,

---

[13] D. Scot Miller, "Afrosurreal Manifesto: Black Is the New Black—a 21st Century Manifesto," http://dscotmiller.blogspot.com/2009/05/afrosurreal.html.

and People of Color) and LGBTQ+ literary circles.[14] Jack Moore, whose job is to scout new writing talent, was always interested in Jones's directorial work. In an early meeting, he posed his "dream scenario" question: "If you had a mainstage slot, what plays would you pitch? Who is exciting to you right now?" She sent him a few plays to read. He recalls that he wasn't able to finish *Cullud Wattah* before he texted Jones, "Who *is* this person?" Then he wrote to Jeanie O'Hare, the head of New Work at the time, and said, "I haven't felt this way about an artist since I met Jordan Cooper for the first time." O'Hare was similarly smitten, fighting back tears due to the power by which the play expressed women— Black women—in the context of such an unusual existential crisis. As Jones later recalled, the poetry of the play uses the Flint crisis to position water as a powerful symbol of Black oppression, but Dickerson-Despenza's writerly approach made that poetry and symbolism accessible. Jones says, "What stood out to me was that she was writing something that felt political in nature but wasn't screaming. Like it didn't feel like she was holding a flag. It felt like she was talking about something that was important, that we all needed to pay attention to."

With so many of The Public Theater's New Work staff on board, *Cullud Wattah* was added to a group of plays that was sent to Eustis as possibilities for the 2019 Public Studio season. It was quickly approved, and the studio process began. The Shiva Theater was given over for workshops that were open to the public, a designer was brought on board, and the play was performed over several nights as a "beefed up" staged reading after a short rehearsal period. The Studio rehearsals coincided with the season planning process for 2019–20 and, with *Cullud Wattah* powerfully fresh in the minds of the artistic team, they took a risk and went ahead and added it to the full season the next year—green-lit before it was performed in Studio. It was put in a season that began with a revival of *for colored girls who have considered suicide/when the rainbow is enuf* by Ntozake Shange, Dickerson-Despenza's hero.[15]

Cullud Wattah was postponed due to Covid just as rehearsals were starting in the spring of 2020, but after a sixteen-month hiatus, it returned as one of the first shows presented in the fall of 2021. It was epic in every way; a two-and-a-half-hour play/song/meditation that recalled the choreo-poem style of Shange but with the distinct new young voice of Dickerson-Despenza. Designed by Adam Rigg, a scaffold of a house devoid of walls showed the interconnectedness of the family and, indeed, all of the marginalized communities devastated by the political choices of their municipality. The hundreds of bottles of dirty water, which were present in the Studio version,

---

[14] The Lark closed in the fall of 2021 due to financial reasons related to the pandemic. Editors, "The Lark Is Grounded: New-Play Incubator to Fold after 27 Years," *American Theater Magazine*, October 5, 2021.

[15] The revival of *for colored girls,* directed and choreographed by Camille A. Brown, transferred to Broadway in 2022 and garnered seven Tony nominations.

were now everywhere—on strings, in cabinets, lined up in rows, columns—overpowering in their ubiquity, almost an infestation. They served, just as did the play, as a morbid reminder of the power of the unheralded commodity that we take for granted. Jones, Dickerson-Despenza, and The Public set up avenues of donations in the playbill and elsewhere to contribute to people of Flint. Due to the unavoidable world circumstances, this offer was far from what Dickerson-Despenza wanted when the project was conceived in 2019. Ever the teacher and community organizer, her plan had been to workshop *Cullud Wattah* in the Midwest, in conjunction with local churches, and to tour historically Black colleges and universities, thus truly bringing the work to people most deeply affected by the crisis.

With its process of development, its elevation of new voices of color, and its commitment to social issues illuminated in policies of systemic inequity, *Cullud Wattah* seemed like exactly the sort of project that the Theater has always been committed to. Jacob Padrón, the artistic director of Long Wharf Theater Company and former staff member at The Public, said of the play, "It felt like it was a play that was activating a conversation that we are still having right now." This was the work that spoke to the mission—of a company that could change the way Americans thought about their country and their role in it, especially around the intersection of marginalized communities and politics. And, to Padrón's point, it met the moment, and "activated" a conversation that was already in the national consciousness. In that way, it was reminiscent of what *Hair* did for the anti-war movement, what Larry Kramer's *Normal Heart* did for HIV/AIDS, and *Hamilton* did for conversations on fluid casting and a reimagining of history.

Building Dramaturgy

Cullud Wattah is but one example of the dramaturgical trajectory at The Public. What it and other examples highlight is a complex and varied process of creation. If *process*, then, is synonymous with *dramaturgy*, it is appropriate to say that the stories related in this chapter—stories of famous American playwrights, of the Under the Radar, of Emerging Writers, of the Devised Theater Working Group, of the steps in bringing *Cullud Wattah* to the stage—are all examples of dramaturgy. The building at 425 Lafayette, then, is a location of dramaturgy, as much as it is a precinct of entertainment. Oversimplified, perhaps? An avoidance of a true definition of a word? Not really. The Public Theater attempts to be a location of dramaturgy, however nebulous that term may be, and Eustis clearly wants his legacy to reflect his dogged desire to open pathways and support artists.

As a purely academic term, "dramaturgy" essentially references the study of plays and their structure, inclusive of directing choices and textual research. Gotthold Ephraim Lessing wrote *Hamburg Dramaturgy* in 1767, in which he compiled a series of essays about the structure and function of the Hamburg National Theater, from acting practice to the role of a theater in a society. If one looks at Oskar Eustis as America's foremost dramaturg of the late twentieth and early twenty-first centuries, it is certainly in the role of advocate for the power of drama. In 2018, in a lecture for TED Talks, Eustis made his claim for theater as the cornerstone of democracy: "Theater matters because democracy matters. Theater is the essential art form of democracy, and we know this because they were born in the same city. ... I'm asking you to switch your mind and imagine what it feels like to the other person talking. I'm asking you to exercise empathy. And the idea that truth comes from the collision of different ideas and the emotional muscle of empathy are the necessary tools for democratic citizenship."[16] This form of oratorical dramaturgy is not uncommon for the leaders of American theatrical institutions, though there are few who do it as publicly and intentionally as Eustis. It bears resemblance to the writings of Lessing, with the flourishes and dedication to the lofty goals of the dramatic art. But giving speeches or publishing articles on the power of art is only part of the story of the dramaturgical process.

What constitutes dramaturgy in the Eustis model is far removed from what many regional theaters and universities have in mind when they hire a dramaturg for a production. Generally, the job is a series of often thankless research projects, delving into the meaning of words, unpacking a historical outline of the time period of the play, and perhaps the organization of a packet of materials for the actors and designers. For Eustis, it's different, and he identifies a description in an article in the *New Yorker* by Rebecca Mead as the most flattering and accurate definition of what he tries to do as a dramaturg. Mead sat in on a dramaturgy session of a new musical and later wrote: "Eustis had described their musical to them in a more ambitious form than actually existed—telling them not what he had seen but what he had seen in what he had seen."[17] In other words, at least in Eustis's reading of Mead's definition, he is in the room to help the writers imagine what the show *could* be, and then support and inspire the artists to achieve it. He elaborated in an interview with me, "The thing that I should stress within that is that it only works if you're seeing the artist's vision of the show. The danger of it is if you supplant your own vision. And if you supplant your own vision, you're not helping artists realize their work anymore; you should go work in Hollywood as a script doctor. So, you have to be enough attuned with the artist so that you're actually responding to the impulses that they have, and then you have to figure out what does it mean practically to help them achieve that?" Lisa Kron, who worked with Eustis

---

[16]https://www.ted.com/talks/oskar_eustis_why_theater_is_essential_to_democracy?language=en.
[17]Rebecca Mead, "Stage Left: Oskar Eustis, The Public Theater's Latest Radical," *The New Yorker*, March 15, 2010.

most famously on *Fun Home*, reinforced that idea of a dramaturgy that is attuned to the entire artist and the expression they wish to convey: "I think that a good dramaturg looks at the whole system and says, you know, this arm is numb. Where in the spine is the problem that's keeping the blood from flowing there? Where's the structural problem? The best dramaturgical experiences I've had have been about that."

Eustis says that in the role of artistic director, his ability to be the dramaturg he wishes to be is more achievable because he has the power to offer workshops, retreats, talking sessions, or even facilitate meals and conversations. He recollected one dramaturgical strategy, employed with his friend Tony Kushner. Deep into the writing process for *Homebody/Kabul*, Eustis realized that he had a big idea that was quite different from what Kushner was envisioning. So, he got in his car and drove up to Kushner's house in upstate New York, stopping on the way to buy some groceries. He arrived, told Kushner the idea he had, and then went into the kitchen and prepared a chicken casserole. "And by the time I came out, he had restructured the outline. And for me that act of saying the idea and then going away and making him dinner that felt like dramaturgy to me. I mean, here's the little thing I have to offer, now I'm going to feed you while you do the work."

Eustis says that the dramaturg is the person in the room who knows more about the play than anyone with the exception of the author, and who has to care about the script more than anyone in the room other than the author, but who cannot own any of it. *Angels in America* is definitively Tony Kushner's epic play and yet it would have been impossible to create without the guidance of Eustis. Yet the dramaturg must take a back seat, settle perhaps with a mention in the acknowledgments. It's a difficult negotiation with an artist, Eustis acknowledges: "Janet Malcolm wrote a book called *Psychoanalysis: The Impossible Profession*, and she called it the impossible profession because of exactly this dilemma. A psychoanalyst has to be totally open to their client; has to receive on multiple, three dimensional, conscious and unconscious ways, what they're getting from their client, and then has to not own it themselves. They have to be in a relationship that is deep and not mutual. That's really tricky. It's really hard to do, but it's also necessary."

Listening to Eustis, I had a sense of déjà vu from my conversations with so many of the playwrights he has worked with. The Eustis world of dramaturgy asks for a listening ear, an empathetic and intellectual person who can focus the artist on the story that they want to tell, not a story that the dramaturg thinks will be "successful" or find a strong revenue stream, or have the possibility of a Broadway transfer. This dramaturgy is about the playwright's "song" and facilitating the other elements of the process to serve that mission, that need, that voice. David Henry Hwang concurs: "I feel like there's a strange kind of therapy analogy, because if you're the therapist, and I'm the patient, you're trying to understand what it is and the person I want to be, and then you're going to try to help guide me to achieve that. That's how I experience dramaturgy with Oskar."

* * *

The Public Theater, the building itself, is that place of guidance, in its purest form. Joe Papp wanted a theater that supported American Shakespeare and intertwined the words of the Bard with mid-century America aesthetics and cultural mores. The founding of 425 Lafayette, in the former home of the New York Public Library, utterly altered the mission of the theater. Free Shakespeare in the Park would continue but the permanent home and the new name, The Public, would mean that the company would have to shift to a place of development, a place of dramaturgy. This is where Eustis has had his greatest impact on the Theater. Because of his lifelong commitment to play development, he has reinforced that aspect of The Public ethic, perhaps more than anyone else, Papp included. And befitting the previous residents of the building, from the library to HIAS, the place has become an intellectual sanctuary, where artists work in collaboration, develop their own skills, and—hopefully—edify and support a broader democratic community.

5
Coming Home

FIGURE 5.1 *Waiting in the Newman wings. Courtesy Kevin Landis.*

When you stand in the wings of the Newman Stage at The Public Theater, its notoriety as a legendary location of American theater history can feel powerful. But you'd have to know something about it because the theater itself isn't all that impressive. Though it's the largest theater at The Public, it's a pretty standard performance space, a bank of parallel rows of seats with a very gradual rise. It's a reasonably deep proscenium stage, brick walls, and an utterly unusual foyer at the entrance, where you have to climb one of two short flights of stairs—like fire escapes, really—to get in the main doors. To the side of the stage is the building's loading dock, a scene shop, and a fairly substantial props shop. It's probably right to just note at this point: The Newman isn't really a pretty theater. Rather plain, actually. Utilitarian.

But if you have the good fortune to have the opportunity to stand on that stage or in the wings, and look out into that space, even its blandness and smallness is strangely impressive. The feeling is similar to the standard effect people get when they see the Mona Lisa: "Amazing, and it's so small!" As you stand there and you hear the audience buzzing, it's easy to wax poetic about the little theater that could. And if you took a theater history class in college, you might even call up thoughts of the director Peter Brook's famous words: "I can take any empty space and call it a bare stage. A man walks across this empty space whilst someone else is watching him, and this is all we need for an act of theater to be engaged."[1] It is the simplicity of Brook's framing that makes those words so indelible; the idea that theater is basic, a communion between a viewer and one being viewed, the exchange of an idea in a generative act of community.

My first time standing in those wings was for precisely those reasons. I was asked to lead a conversation between audience and actors after a show, a simple talkback—the most basic communion of audience and performer.

"Sure," I said. "I'll swing by the theater after the show."

I stood there, waiting for the actors to join me, looked at stage crew set up the chairs that we would use in our talk, and was surprised to feel goosebumps; to register that growing anticipation and excitement that so many schoolchildren know from their very first play. "I'm a theater professor," I reminded myself. "This is my profession, it's what I do. Why am I so moved?"

I found the magic of the connection that Brook describes in the basic and simple thrill of knowing that the audience members, who were sitting mere steps from me, did not yet know I was there. Illusion intersecting with the promise of communion. Of the participants that evening, I was the least

---

[1] Peter Brook, *The Empty Space* (New York: Touchstone Press, 1968), p. 9.

important; simply the person who would help move the conversation along. But even in that role, there was magic in my personal anticipation.

More than that, much more, the empty space, as it always does, calls to nostalgia, that *thing* that theater and theater spaces do better than any other artistic precinct. The power is in the ephemerality of the form, the knowledge that everything within the walls will only last in memory layers within the individual imagination. With the side lights blazing in my eyes, I could almost see, like a ghostly palimpsest, the original actors of *A Chorus Line* on a fall evening in 1975. In my imagination, they were there, on the opposite side of the stage, gold suits and top hats in hand, adrenaline filled as they prepped for their spectacular final number: "One singular sensation, every little step she takes ... One thrilling combination..."[2]

Another layer of memory, perhaps, for spectators that evening: a wooden scaffold set, the brick wall of the theater showing through, and the creaking parquet floor. The first chords of *Hamilton* start up, "ba-badada-da da," as Leslie Odom Jr. steps forward into the spotlight and sings about an orphan, "dropped in the middle of a forgotten spot in the Caribbean by providence, impoverished, in squalor..."[3]

The smaller, less famous shows come back just as powerfully, as you stand in the wings. Tarell Alvin McCraney's *Head of Passes*, starring the incomparable Phylicia Rashad, is a memory that lasts, if for nothing else than the privilege of remembering watching the entire stage rock and groan, as the set broke apart and sank into a massive onstage pool of water, the matriarch sitting regally as the world fell apart. There, in my memory, is Daniel Radcliffe among a pile of Amazon boxes in James Graham and Josie Rourke's *Privacy*, while information from the phones of the actual audience members is projected on giant onstage screens. Or, in another memory, there Rachel Weisz stands, stoic, in a revival of David Hare's *Plenty*.

Up two flights of stairs and into the back door of the Anspacher Theater, one is met with another avalanche of remembrances of experiences they perhaps never even had. That's the other power of the place; it connects you to memories you actually didn't experience, creating what the philosopher Roland Barthes calls "counter memories"—plays you maybe saw, perhaps heard about or read about in a book.[4] My favorite time in the Anspacher is in the evening on a night with no performance at all. I crack open the door into a dimly lit cavern, the original Public Theater stage. Like every space in the building, it is strange. A three-quarter audience configuration, steep risers, banks of red velour seats. The ceiling seems impossibly high—this must be a waste of real estate—while masses of now dark lighting units are

---

[2]Marvin Hamlish and Edward Kleban, *A Chorus Line*, 1975.
[3]Lin-Manuel Miranda, *Hamilton*, 2015 (as with subsequent *Hamilton* quotes).
[4]Roland Barthes, *Camera Lucida* (New York: Hill and Wang, 1981), p. 91.

clamped onto a complex metal grid. Up in the rafters, somewhere, is a stage manager's booth—is it a booth? A nest?

A singular ghost light in the center of the stage casts a glow on the quiet, abandoned set. The pillars that seem to be everywhere in The Public break up the space; they have to be incorporated into any set design, since they hold up the building. From the distance, in this dark winter evening, some psychedelic music starts up, wafts through the empty space: "When the moon is in the Seventh House, / And Jupiter aligns with Mars."[5] And there we are, 1967. Joe Papp's Public Theater has just opened, and the streets of the East Village are part of the internal architecture of the old HIAS sanctuary. The war-protesting hippies gather around a fire and sing, make love, and, famously now, take off their clothes and burn their draft cards. You can close your eyes and still hear *Hair*. Let the sunshine in.

Like the Newman below, this strange space is a memory box of American theater. Martin Sheen in *Hamlet* (1967), Ntozake Shange's *for colored girls who have considered suicide/when the rainbow is enuf* (1976), Kevin Kline in his second *Hamlet* (1990), Suzan-Lori Parks's *Topdog/Underdog* (2001), Heidi Rodewald and Stew's *Passing Strange* (2007), McCraney's *The Brother/Sister Plays* (2009), and James Ijames's Pulitzer Prize winner, *Fat Ham* (2022).

And just one story above that is the less well-known LuEsther Hall, named for the donor who saved the organization in its early days. A narrow room with the ever-present pillars that one accesses by a nondescript stairwell, like a walkup apartment. There is an elevator, too, that, like the whole building, rumbles and creaks and is often undergoing repairs. When the door opens, you are in a space that saw Larry Kramer's epic *The Normal Heart* (1985), Kushner's original *A Bright Room Called Day* (1990), David Byrne's *Here Lies Love* (2014), Danai Gurira's *Eclipsed* (2015), and Richard Nelson's *The Gabriels* (2016).

And on the other side of the building, a couple floors above Joe's Pub, the Martinson Theater still echoes the music from Elizabeth Swados's *Runaways* (1978) and the dramatic poetry of David Henry Hwang's debut production of *FOB* (1980), Sam Shepard's *True West* (1980), José Rivera's *Marisol* (1993), Suzan-Lori Parks's *Father Comes Home from the Wars* (2014), and Lynn Nottage's Pulitzer-winning *Sweat* (2016). Even in the tiny Shiva Theater, tucked in the back of the lobby, the former home of the HIAS cafeteria, history reverberates: George C. Wolfe's *The Colored Museum* (1986), Diana Son's *Stop Kiss* (1998), Jeanine Tesori and Lisa Kron's original Lab production of *Fun Home* (2012), and Nia Vardalos's adaptation of *Tiny Beautiful Things* (2016).

It is a small fraction of the plays and performances that have performed in the now hallowed halls of The Public Theater's East Village home. And

---

[5]Galt MacDermot, Gerome Rangi, and James Rado, *Hair*, 1967.

while the larger ones that have gone on to Broadway receive so much of the attention, it is the intimacy of the space and, thus, of the plays themselves that define The Public Theater. "Large" doesn't quite fit as a descriptor of The Public, and even those epics aren't known for their spectacle and grandeur. *A Chorus Line*: a lineup of dancers on a bare stage. *Hamilton*: a wood scaffolding. *Fun Home*: a family's living room. The plays here are intimate and always close to the audience.

This, of course, is a luxury for Oskar Eustis and The Public. "The largest theater I have down here is 300 seats, which means the delta between a successful show and an unsuccessful show is pretty small. It's kind of a rounding error for our annual budget … so I never have to be afraid financially." This means that the theater relies on contributed income and the spaces can be mostly used for what Eustis and staff want to present, not what must make money. The intimacy of the theaters of the old Victorian/Byzantine building is reinforced by Eustis and his marketing team's instance that The Public is driven by its not-for-profit, do-good, social justice artistic platform. Indeed, Eustis and The Public team do create work with the understanding of the power of their spaces, knowing that the most affecting art can often be small in scale. For many, this is how it should be, and so the tensions about what it means to be a small, plucky theater company in the midst of the allure of Broadway's lights is continuously debated among staff and artists.

Selling The Public

As noted, Joe Papp's Public never ran on surpluses and, in fact, it is generally understood that it was only the success of *A Chorus Line* and the funding of LuEsther Mertz that allowed for much of the experimentation of the 1980s. As one member of the current financial team put it, The Public back then was "a fatted veal of an organization," and so Papp basically disbanded the development department—a reflection of the disgust he felt for the whole capitalist enterprise. That may be too easy a historical revision, but it is at least true that fundraising was not his passion—in addition to *A Chorus Line,* he had the good fortune to have had lots of city support and the backing of major donors. Financial realities, though, would soon catch up with the company. A few things happened to significantly crimp the organization's moneymaking abilities that eventually had to be addressed: *A Chorus Line* closed on Broadway in 1990 and Mertz and Papp both died in 1991. A significant organizational retraction met Akalaitis and Wolfe during their years and, indeed, the impact of 9/11 nearly folded the company altogether. It wasn't really until after the arrival of Mara Manus and, later, Patrick Willingham, who both brought in a level of business acumen, that The Public started running with some rainy-day coffers. While much of that would be erased with the closures of the theaters due to Covid, the company ran fairly robustly for many years.

In addition to stronger financial oversights and a more considered fundraising infrastructure, the arrival of Eustis and his insistent reframing of the organization around the original Pappian goals contributed to the larger-than-life image of the company, and its artistic director. The growth over the Eustis era has been enormous and is very much due to his drive that the many theaters should be chock full of new work and collaborations with other theaters across the country and world. In fiscal year 2010 and 2011, The Public was about a $10–12-million organization. By 2020 (pre-Covid) it had grown to about $57–60 million. Not a fatted veal, but a company running at breakneck pace.

One should not mistake that this sort of assiduous marketing of "Publicness" began with Willingham and Eustis. In a move that would redefine the post-Papp Public, George C. Wolfe hired Paula Scher in 1994 to create the new look for Theater's marketing. The changes that were implemented were dramatic, the results in stark contrast with equally iconic design that had come before. During Papp's tenure, the artwork of Paul Davis—elaborate paintings of actors in full costume—was the recognizable aesthetic of Public Theater outreach, and had been since his hire in 1975. Davis's work was as beautiful as the productions themselves: a painting of Meryl Streep as Alice in Elizabeth Swados's 1981 *Alice in Concert*, or a stoic Kevin Kline posed next to a glowing globe/skull for his 1990 portrayal of Hamlet. The walls of the theater are still covered with the Davis portraits, a permanent installation that includes the striking image of Papp in a suit and natty black coat smoking a cigar that graces the entrance of the Newman Theater.

While Davis was interested in the likeness of Papp, Streep, Kline, and others in glorious, rich colors, Scher's early work, a style that continues to this day, focused on words and lines of text, printed boldly. One has to stop and read to fully understand; something that is often antithetical to many marketing trends. Wolfe had wanted to get away from a sense of a company based on one man (Papp) and a look that focused on individuals and, rather, turn attention to content of the plays, the themes of the season, and the intellectualism of the offer. In Scher's recent book, Ellen Lupton described Scher's change as nothing short of converting "the Papp" into "The Public."[6] Indeed, Scher recalled a visit to the theater in the mid-1990s and the challenges that she would have to address: "They didn't even have a flag up. Nobody knew what the building was. The press called it either the New York Shakespeare Festival, or the Papp." Finally, she says of the branding, "it's about the place," but it took over ten years of image redefinition to get there.

---

[6] Quoted Steven Heller in Paula Scher, *25 Years at The Public, A Love Story* (New York: Princeton Architectural Press, 2020), p. 15.

Wolfe ushered in, and now Eustis oversees, a graphic identity that is bold and distinctly urban; a moniker that quite literally looks like an exclamation point, with "Public" written vertically, and "Theater" at the bottom like the point in the exclamatory punctuation. Scher recalled Wolfe saying, "I want the work to feel POPULIST, but in a smart way ... the design should include people without dumbing itself down."[7] Again, the description is beautifully telling in its need to create an intellectual populism, something that was at once for all the people of New York, but which also had an erudite caché. What has developed over the years, influenced by old time Victorian wood type, was something of a playbill of old—a broadside, packed with information. The evolution of the style at The Public played up certain words, so that Free Shakespeare in the Park would become "FREE WILL" in block lettering, or *Bring in 'da Noise, Bring in 'da Funk* would be marketed as—again, boldly—"NOISE FUNK."

A detour into marketing is relevant to the framing of the contemporary Public more broadly since "The Public" as a place and idea in contemporary American theatrical life is due to Scher, Wolfe, and Eustis's vision of brand identity. Like all good marketing, it is indelible, and much of that comes from the essentialization of the message. While the broadside style of selling the work is artfully wordy, the "pop out" of certain words and messages has made clear—quite literally, in bold—what the company believes in, what it promises, and what it *is*. For example, while the Broadway version of the *Hamilton* poster is that now iconic star with the titular character atop, the original Public version was an old bust of the founding father with highlighted text taking up more space than the title of the musical. One poster proclaims: "Revolutionary. Bastard. Founding Father. War Hero. Scholar. Immigrant. Mastermind. New Yorker." Another simply reads: "WHO LIVES WHO DIES WHO TELLS YOUR STORY." There is no punctuation. In a way, it's the brief version of the theme of the show—a Cliff's Notes, really. For Eustis's controversial *Julius Caesar* in 2017, a poster featuring a bust of Caesar was adorned with the text "Danger knows full well that Caesar is more dangerous than he." The title of the play, in small lettering, is dwarfed by the word "Danger."

When Scher was asked to fully incorporate the graphic look into the 2013 building renovation, it became a permanent part of the entire organization—PUBLIC, written in its now definitive font, is emblazoned across the glass awning and engraved in locations around the lobby. The glorious banners that are now so iconic at 425 quite clearly sell an ethic more than a play. Though colors and style are swapped out year to year, the three banners out front read "Joe's Pub," "The Public," and "Free Shakespeare in the Park." On each banner, another proclamation: "Artist Centered." "Radically Inclusive." "Free for All."

---

[7]Scher, *25 Years at The Public, A Love Story*, p. 33.

What Oskar Eustis and the contemporary Public Theater have done so well in the past two decades, with massive help from Scher and the initial idea and push from George C. Wolfe, is to turn the entire company into an ethic—to separate it from the singular man who founded it, Joseph Papp, even as he is continuously revered. No more is it the Joseph Papp Public Theater; rather, it is "Radically Inclusive," or "Free for All," or simply "Public." The Public has become a business of culture-making and with its enormous success, Eustis himself became the face of that success. It helps that he is vastly charismatic, but by the time the theaters closed due to Covid, he was aware that the image of "Oskar Eustis as General" was the prevailing view, and not what he thought was healthy for the theater. In 2021, I asked Eustis if that placement of the singular artistic leader as a central voice of the organization was a problem. "Yes," he said. "And I think it's really important to change that. And yes, that definitely means rejecting a legacy that runs from Joe through George to me." Even in that formulation, as Eustis and others recognize, it is an embarrassing admission—the image of The Public is often wrapped up in the tenures of three men, with the sole female artistic director driven out by the board in less than two years.

* * *

The stature, image, and brand of The Public has grown over the last two decades for all sorts of reasons: because of the notoriety of *Hamilton* and *Fun Home* and other Broadway transfers, for bold takes on Shakespeare in Central Park, for a continued focus on radical inclusivity and new work creation, for the enormous output at 425, *and* because of the positioning of Oskar Eustis (even if inadvertent) and the theater he leads as being guardians of and champions for social justice. In 2016, I asked Eustis about the myriad events and artistic endeavors that were coming out of 425. Was it too much, I wondered? No, he insisted. "Elevator Repair Service is happier when their work is being seen next door to Shakespeare and next door to new plays. Shakespeare feels more robust when it's being performed in the same building as musicals and in the same building with Joe's Pub. It actually is good for the artists, and hence good for the art form. ... What we also know is that art doesn't like being put into categories." While that sort of output eventually could not last, diversity of programming is reflective of his thinking about what the building should be, and one of his most important contributions to the company.

It is well, then, to look at some of the work that has happened inside 425 Lafayette, to see how priorities are made, and productions created. While ties to commercial success will be explored in coming chapters, here we consider a few plays by some of America's most prominent playwrights that lived and breathed and thrived in the intimacy of the LuEsther, the Anspacher, and the Martinson. Standing in the wings of those famous stages, the magic is real—any contradictions fall away. It's The Public Theater, it's legendary, it's inclusive, it's radical. Often, more simply, it's just great theater. Richard Nelson's *The Gabriels,* Suzan-Lori Parks's *White Noise,* and Lynn Nottage's *Sweat*, though perhaps not the most widely known works of the Eustis years, well illuminate the way plays can develop, thrive, stumble, and, eventually, find their voice.

The Gabriels

FIGURE 5.2 *The Gabriel family,* 2016. *Courtesy Joan Marcus.*

The need of Eustis and The Public to be seen as champions of the common person in a world of outsized capitalist greed is curiously wrapped up in the themes and ideals espoused in the plays of Richard Nelson. In the midst of his epic series of works, set in his hometown of Rhinebeck, New York, we learn a bit about the little community in which this American version of Chekov takes place. It is a location, befitting the theme, of working-class humans interspersed with opulence and wealth. John Jacob Astor IV, we are told—and it is true—is the town's most famous resident. While not lingered upon, the relevance is delicious—a wealthy business magnate who was born on a family estate in Rhinebeck and died in the north Atlantic aboard the *Titanic*; a man whose grandfather, John Jacob Astor, was the wealthiest man in the United States, the namesake of Astor Place, and the financier for the building that would become The Public Theater. The referencing to the Gilded Age is never lost on Eustis and he sees Nelson's work, writ large, as a response to or at least in dialogue with the fact that we live in the new Gilded Age, where the unmoneyed feel powerless, where the community feels like hamsters in a wheel, while a billionaire becomes president of the United States. The Gabriels and the Apples, fictional families that represent all of these complexities, graced the stages of The Public for much of Eustis's tenure.

"The Gabriels," in particular, fills a niche that perfectly incorporates the Eustis/Nelson aesthetic, the dialectic of wealth and working class at the intersection of contemporary politics. In his introduction to the published version of "The Gabriels," Eustis writes, "Nelson's characters, like Chekhov's, are undeniably appealing people, but lack the power, the agency, to become heroes."[8] When Eustis and The Public commissioned the trilogy, Nelson was given three opening dates that coincided with the 2016 presidential election: the Friday after Super Tuesday, the middle of September on the eve of debate season, and election night, Tuesday, November 8. Nelson reflected, "This is an incredible challenge and an incredible opportunity because it allows me to feel some kind of participation in my country. I'm relating to it. The plays are not finished until three o'clock on the opening night, meaning during previews I'm rewriting it. I rewrite on opening day. The actors know they're going to get a few new lines. The reason why it's three o'clock is that's determined by the press department. [They] need the script. ... That's the three o'clock deadline."

Eustis and Nelson had known each other for years before Nelson was produced at The Public under his leadership. He had presented *Il Campiello, a Venetian Comedy* (1981) with Joe Papp, and in 2005 George C. Wolfe produced *The Controversy of Valladolid*. In 2007, Nelson had been working on a new play, *Conversations in Tusculum*. A historical piece set in the time of Julius Caesar and featuring Brutus, Cassius, and Cicero, the work was actually a reflection of America post-Iraq War. He asked Eustis to read the script. Eustis liked it, produced it, and began what would be a decade-long partnership largely revolving around stories from Rhinebeck.

But the path was unexpected. After *Tusculum,* Eustis went to Nelson and asked him if he could do something else focused on the Iraq War. Nelson recalls:

> I said, "That's really interesting. I'm really flattered. Let me think about it." I called him up the next day and said, "Well, here's what I would like to do. I would like to do a play with six people in Rhinebeck sitting around a dinner table, just talking about the next election coming up, and open it on election day—just human beings talking in conversation, somewhat related to *Conversations in Tusculum,* but this is just people

---

[8]Oskar Eustis in Nelson, Richard, *The Gabriels: Election Year in the Life of One Family* (New York: TCG, 2018), p. IX.

from Rhinebeck, my town." I said it would have to open on election night, because that's when it would be set. It's set on that night, before the polls. He laughed and said, "Okay, I get it. I get it completely. That really would be thrilling."

Indeed, for the next series of plays, "The Apples" (2010–13), Eustis did something fairly unusual for American theater—he gave the author carte blanche; he could do whatever he wanted. It would be granted again with "The Gabriels." Eustis said:

> I basically said, "Richard, I believe that if I give you the opening nights you will create work that will deserve those opening nights." He says that he had never experienced anything like that in his career ... and that he's never heard of anyone getting that in their career. And what that vote of confidence did was make him a better writer. I totally believe that.
>
> One of the ways that I think you can feel that is the style of the plays, the very form of them, are totally distinctive because they're not trying to sell you anything. The plays are just letting you watch life.
>
> Suddenly, when I think about this I say, "oh my God, there's a connection because these plays never had to sell themselves because they were sold before they were written. They were committed to before they were written, so at no point in the act of writing the play did Richard even have to think about, 'How do I impress somebody?' and it allowed a different kind of art to happen, and I think in many ways, manifestly, a better kind of art."

The resulting work is pure Public Theater and, true to form, Eustis frames them through the lens of capitalism. *There is nothing being sold.* But, of course, there is always something being sold if you unravel the layers of the market. While Nelson wasn't selling Eustis a script, he was indeed selling a concept, which Eustis immediately saw as potentially electrifying. It's not capitalist in the sense of ticket sales and revenues, or the selling of a very specific political viewpoint; rather, it is the selling of the ethic of the theater and the proposition that human communion is *enough*, just watching life unfold. Added to that, the form of the plays and the choices around producing them felt exciting and new. This, in fact, is a beautiful bit of selling. One enters the LuEsther Theater and immediately thinks, "ah, this could only happen here."[9]

So, what is happening in "The Gabriels"? It's hard to describe and, at the same time, extremely easy. A family gathers in a kitchen and cooks dinner.

---

[9] "The Apples" cycle is *That Hopey Changey Thing, Sweet and Sad, Sorry,* and *Regular Singing.* "The Gabriels" trilogy consists of *Hungry, What Did You Expect?,* and *Women of a Certain Age.*

They talk. When the food is ready, they go to an offstage dining room and eat. Lights go down. End of show. The audience leaves. Nelson says, "Human beings are the only animals who cook. No other animal cooks. It is one of the things that makes us human. If you are trying to celebrate the complexity of the human being, here's an opportunity to show in the context of one of the definitions of what makes us human."

Typical of "The Gabriels" and of Richard Nelson is that format. The plays revolve around a Rhinebeck family on a very specific evening and a very specific set of circumstances. The plot is perhaps less important than the style. The basics are the following: A family is grieving the death of Thomas. The story centers around his widow, Mary (Maryann Plunkett), Thomas's brother, George (Jay O. Sanders), his wife, Hannah (Lynn Hawley), Thomas's sister, Joyce (Amy Warren), his first wife, Karis (Meg Gibson), and Thomas's mother, Patricia (Roberta Maxwell).

Each of the plays begins the same way: The audience enters the LuEsther Theater to a bare stage, the Peter Brook empty space. Actually, it is not empty per se, but rather "un-lived"—no signs of life. There is a refrigerator, a table, a sink, a cupboard, and other things that make it look like a kitchen in an abandoned home. Then "Wilderwoman," from the band Lucius (or another Lucius song, depending on the play), wafts through the theater. Actors enter carrying trays of kitchen things and, as Nelson writes in the script, "create the life of the kitchen." The work is not so much about decoration as creating a sense of use, of warmth, of—forgive me—intellectual populism: iPod docks, dirty towels, food, bowls, books, coffee, and oven mitts. Mary begins to knead dough as the play begins. But, of course, the evocative dumb show at the start *is* the beginning of the play and, in fact, carries so much of the information that we are to receive. These are the people we will meet: a doctor, a teacher, a cabinet maker, a piano teacher, an assistant costume designer, and a caterer. None is John Jacob Astor IV. They enter and we watch for ninety minutes as they create life through the necessities of life, cooking, and then, we presume, eating. While they reminisce about Thomas and his life, Mary and others busy themselves with cooking. Typical stage directions include "Mary takes out a frying pan; she will go and get oil from the pantry cupboard." Or "timer goes off." Or "Mary will taste the vegetables, add salt and pepper." Or "a short time later. As Hannah prepares her salad dressing; the middle of conversation."[10]

Reading this on the page, one is forgiven for an eye roll of incredulity at the precision with which Nelson prescribes the actions of the stage. *Add salt and pepper?* It is as if the entire play is a recipe. But of course, it is. Nelson writes the story, refines the words, selects the Brooklyn-based hipster music, and directs the plays. He generally works with the same actors over and over again (especially Sanders and Plunkett), and acts as the grand auteur.

---

[10]Nelson, *The Gabriels*, pp. 48–9, 57, 74.

And it works, for many who witness it. The feeling of authenticity, as if you are an unseen voyeur in the Gabriels' house, is created through elaborately considered dramaturgical choices and effects. Pendant mics hang around the stage so that none of the actors needs to speak above what would be normal in a small kitchen. The choice gives the designers the power to adjust the levels, making it possible for the audience to hear but often having to lean forward to make sure they are getting it all. Plunkett recalls in the discussions with the director, "Do you project? No, don't project. He says, 'If people are eavesdropping on you, they don't necessarily hear everything you say.'" In that lies a certain kind of theatricality.

Nelson speaks with humility about his directing ability:

> I learned that when I write my plays, I do not see them and do not hear them. Instead, I feel them. The plays are written out of a kind of dynamic, which means I walk into a rehearsal room, and my first job is to convince the actors—because they see me wearing two hats, the director and the playwright—and convince them that I don't know how to do it. I tell them I really do not know how to do this play. However, because I have within me a dynamic, a feeling of the play, I know when it's wrong.

In this way, trust in a team is important to the process and why he continuously uses the same actors and designers. He asserts that he has been lucky to find people who are able to work in this way. Jennifer Tipton, the prolific American lighting designer, has a long history with Nelson and designed all of his Rhinebeck plays at The Public. Of the technical aspects of the work she notes:

> It's just a very human experience. The light is simply the light. It's not trying to be realistic in any way. In a sense, it's less challenging for me as a lighting designer but as a theater person, it's so exciting ... rather than being hyper real lighting, it's just lighting that totally surrounds the actors and the room somehow.
>
> What happens in lighting is tricky because you want the actor to be able to use his or her face in a way that communicates. You don't want the light to make the expression. ... In Richard's way, you want to eliminate that possibility, and just reveal totally.

Tipton gets to the core of The Public's experiment with the Rhinebeck plays—the idea of a total reveal of the human condition. There were no lighting cues within the scenes, itself a bold choice when working with one of the most famous lighting designers in the history of American theater. Tipton and Nelson himself demonstrate a style of minimalism by patiently allowing moments and images to reveal themselves. So, too, what Eustis has done—offering Nelson free rein over the writing, directing, and process is also an exercise in staying out of the way.

The Rhinebeck plays somehow create—even when witnessed in the very present tense structure of opening on the actual day they are representing—a sense of nostalgia, a wistfulness of familial connection, of the pleasures of creation, through smells of food, the whispers of families and friends, and the carefully curated soundtrack. Each play is tightly structured, and just as they begin in the same way, they all end on a similar note. From *Women of a Certain Age,* the final installment of the election year trilogy:

> Mary continues to collect cookies and listen to the short piano piece. … Music: Lucius's "Until We Get There" plays from the theater speakers. She looks over the table and the room, puts on oven mitts, picks up the shepherd's pie; after one more look across the kitchen table, she goes to join the others in the dining room.[11]

Amid the hyperreal atmosphere, the plays have a certain surreal nature—an over reality—that is at once soothing and bizarre. Mary is the only one who hears the piano and, as Eustis notes, it acts as a palimpsest or a reminder of the past.[12]

Since the subtitle of the series is *Election Year in the Life of One Family*, it does indeed feel disingenuous to claim that the plays are not political. And yet, the works are noteworthy in that they do very clearly avoid politics. This may be another way that the Rhinebeck plays are so elegantly reflective of the institution that housed them, at once clearly liberal but also attempting to avoid embedding partisan politics within the greater role of a theater; that is, to promote equality and access to art. To define the Gabriels as Democrats (they likely are) would stand in the way of the communion, quite literally here of breaking bread. Hillary Clinton and Donald Trump are cursory figures, deeply of the consciousness of the audience and yet quite obviously less of a concern to the family Gabriel. Nelson says, "I don't see myself as a writer with a political agenda at all. I see myself as doing one thing, and one thing only. It's really quite simple, and it's really very hard: to celebrate the complexity of people, of the human being."

But that structure is not to be ignored. *Women of a Certain Age* opened on election night and took place on election night. The Gabriels casually discussed voting and getting to the polls. Thus, *when* one saw the play defined how they experienced the play. I witnessed it on one of the few preview evenings, the weekend before the election—one of the several evenings that Nelson was given to make final adjustments and see how it all worked. On election night 2016, The Public Theater hosted watching parties, with televisions set up around the theater, and Joe's Pub staged an evening of election themed

---

[11] Nelson, *The Gabriels*, p. 282.
[12] Ibid., p. X.

entertainment. As Eustis recalled, those seeing "The Gabriels" entered the theater confident of a Clinton win. When they left, he noted, "We could feel it instantly in the uncomfortable atmosphere of the lobby and Library, and the numbers on television bore out that unease."[13] In the heart of Democratic America, a play captured a moment that was, presumably, for most of the theatergoers devastating. Due to the style in which it was written, that created a one-two punch. The blending of worlds of reality and fiction that is the forte of Richard Nelson was piled onto by an election result that was met with disbelief and incredulity, the stuff of fiction.

"The Gabriels" needn't exist as a curious footnote to a specific election. As this is written, other elections have come and gone, some with even more remarkable and fantastical outcomes. Jay O. Sanders frames it well: "What you really get is Chekov. You get people in a society talking about the world. Some are very lucid when they're young, but often it's the older characters seeing things from a perspective of history. I have a line in *Hungry* which I say, 'It's all just politics. What about history? Now it's just politics. Whatever happened to history?' And I think that sense is that we are our own history and that we have to learn from it, and politics grows out of it."

Eustis is so drawn to Nelson as a second "house playwright" (Parks is the official one) because he does what Eustis preaches about the theater. In Nelson's words, "Everybody is in the same room at the same time—the very essence of theater and its value and moral obligation. I've said this many times to students and friends: It is the only artistic form that uses the entire live human being as its expression. That's what theater is." Now, the critique of the Nelson plays, especially within the organization, is that they are far from representative of the population that the theater purports to represent as a *theater for all*. While the characters are financially insecure, working within unfair structures, they are all white intellectuals. This is both absolutely correct and a flawed critique—missing, perhaps, what these plays are trying to be and do. The challenge is that the plays, in their presentation of American middle-class struggle, inadvertently construct a monolithic version of that reality. Like a Norman Rockwell painting, Americana is undeniable here, and yet it is clearly only one version. But is the offer uniquely American or even broadly American? Is that the point? It's hard to fully say, though Nelson, Plunkett, and Sanders point to the world tour that the trilogy took as evidence that the work translates—in fact in multiple languages. It seems, rather, the immediacy of the style and the connection between audience and actor in real time and space is both the stylistic point and source of the beauty of the work. Sanders states of the Rhinebeck plays: "It's not uniquely American at all, but it is *exotically* American. ... This is so Chekhovian in its understanding of people. You want the sense of something that is so specific, that it's absolutely universal."

---

[13]Ibid., p. VIII.

Father Comes Home from the Wars and *White Noise*

FIGURE 5.3 *Daveed Diggs in* White Noise, *2019. Courtesy Joan Marcus.*

Suzan-Lori Parks is an American theater icon and her affiliation with The Public Theater is perhaps one of the most glorious feathers in the company's hat. Consider her output. Of the years that The Public has been her artistic home, it is the place where most of her plays received their off-Broadway premieres: *The America Play, Venus, In the Blood, The Book of Grace, Father Comes Home from the Wars 1, 2, 3,* and *White Noise*. Her canon is a list of required American theater reading; like August Wilson, a meticulous and phantasmagoric tracing, compilation, and deep dive into the American experience told through its intersection with race. Still middle aged with years of work ahead of her, that Parks is a staple of The Public, both on the stages and on the staff, is a source of great pride for the company. As beacons in the American theater, The Public and Suzan-Lori Parks stand side by side. Of The Public, Parks says, "They get what I'm doing. So why go—it's like, why go anywhere else? It's like being married."

To fully describe the work of Suzan-Lori Parks is a fool's errand since whole books are dedicated to understanding the scope of her contribution to world drama. I will not do that here, and in fact, to pretend to do so, within the context of a broader study of The Public, would be grossly reductive. Her style is mercurial and unfathomable, surreal and epic. Rather, looking at the development of two plays at the Theater gives insight into one avenue of creative process at Lafayette, and how the position of writer in residence, or master writer chair, speaks to her essential and unique place at the Theater.[14] Beyond the sheer talent of Parks, the way the chair-ship was conceived (for her) and has flourished speaks to the commitment that the organization has made to the creation of new work. She works, she teaches, and lives as a creative force, an artistic guru, and a celebrity, in the best of ways, among the staff. In the time that she has been writer in residence, she has developed the epic masterpiece trilogy *Father Comes Home from the Wars* and the prescient and fully of-the-moment *White Noise*, which premiered in March 2019 with Oskar Eustis as the director.

White Noise, though perhaps not yet a classic or a financially successful Parks piece, is compelling as a subject of artistic development, because it is actually far less obscure than some of her more dreamlike, anti-structural work. It marks a break of sorts in her style and, as with any brilliant creator, drives one to ask, "What will come next?" She told me once, "I could not tell you what any of my plays—what the meaning is, but I can tell you the story." In the juxtaposition of "story" and "meaning," Parks's statement is reminiscent of a Susan Sontag reflection about the Swedish film and theater director Ingmar Bergman's masterpiece *Persona* (and really many of his films): "Instead of having a full-blown 'story' on his hands, he has something that is in one sense cruder, and in another more abstract: a body of material, a subject."[15] The filmmaker had, Sontag notes, a subject of "opacity" and "multiplicity" and, indeed, the same could be written of Parks's plays. Even as her work fluctuates, evolves, and grows more narratively clear, she demonstrates a long-term commitment to challenging organizational structure and literary form.

While vastly different, *Father Comes Home from the Wars* and *White Noise* are interconnected works of art. *Father*, a play that blended story and music (Parks is a musician, as well), began in workshop in the Shiva Theater where she actually performed one of the roles, as a musician. True to the Lab format, Parks recalls that on the stool next to her—upstage, so it couldn't be seen—was a little notebook to which she would turn to jot notes and questions that she had as the play unfolded around her—thoughts for its development, and ways that she could edit and evolve.

The epic play, based on the *Odyssey*, traces the story of a slave named Hero, who joins his master to fight for the Confederacy in return for his freedom. Hero has a talking dog named Odd-See, who often acts as a Greek

---

[14]Parks now prefers the title "Writer in Residence" and is shifting to that verbiage from "Master Writer Chair." She says that writer in residence better captures what she does, and that's probably correct. But the change coincides with a general push in the United States to move away from the use of "master" where possible, as it can be seen as too tied to racial and gender-fraught historical implications. I use them interchangeably since the original title is still widely used.
[15]Susan Sontag, "*Persona*—Review," *Sight and Sound Magazine*, Autumn 1967.

chorus member, an interlocutor or conscience, connecting the audience to other happenings and scenes. The sprawling play is genre-bending, and true to Parks's style blends naturalistic impulses with fantasy and ethereal magic. The dog talks, after all. But at the end, it is a play that contemplates the "after" of freedom and emancipation, the unknowing future for Black people in a world that has suddenly changed. Parks said: "It was going to be a long, many part thing; long, long, long play." It was truly epic in scope.

To create something that big required the ability to work in the way the chair-ship allowed—with staff support but, more importantly, with time for personal reflection and no requirement of deadlines. The labor of a writer is solitary, as the cliché goes, even if one is working at a company that has invested so much in resources to the development of that work.

> I have to go in between the rock and the hard place, to go in there, like *White Noise*. I have to go places that—most people can't go ... which is why my plays, I think, look like they do, because I'm sort of a deep undersea water diver who goes places very difficult. You can't breathe. It's very pressurized. It's scary. You feel like you're going to die or something. That's where the story is for me. It's been that way over and over and over, so I'm not depending on a kindly, brilliant dramaturg person to help me figure out the story. ... There's nobody who can help me. People can cheer me on. It's very helpful to know that. Once I've retrieved this thing, fleshed it out, added some—now it's a fire we can all gather around.[16]

The privacy and lack of *need* of a "kindly, brilliant dramaturg person" is a telling comment related to a play in which the director is the most famous dramaturg in America and the sitting artistic director of one of the most well-known theaters in America, and the author is one of the most famous playwrights in America. But the ability to support is, as described before, a chief role of the Eustis model of dramaturgy. He says that working with her on a "brilliant" play like *White Noise* is the height of what that floating definition of dramaturgy can be:

> She does not use a dramaturg in a conventual sense of sending a draft, getting notes etc. What we do is we talk about the plays a lot. For *White Noise* we talked for a year and a half. And the conversation didn't change when we were in rehearsal. We kept talking about it. She was at every moment of rehearsal. The division of labor was really clear which is that I led the room, but Suzan-Lori could say anything that she wanted ... she mostly talked to me. It was completely congenial.

---

[16] Parks is famous for her use of syntax and Gertrude Stein-like challenging of grammatical rules. It is a style that is expressionistic, surreal, aural, and yet fully "Suzan-Lori Parks." As with her writing, she sometimes speaks in that layered and evocative way and, as such, any transcribed interview does not fully capture the tenor and feel of the poetry.

For me, that conversation is the best kind of dramaturgy there is because you are not actually telling somebody how to write the play, you are hopefully helping them to deepen their understanding of what they have written. See it, reflect it back at them in the way you talk about it, and that allows them to change it more easily than if it was all just in their head. All of the great long-term relationships—with Suzan-Lori, with David Hwang, with Tony Kushner—involve less and less paper and more and more just talking. That is the sign of the successful depths of the relationship.

White Noise evolved for Suzan-Lori Parks out of the work that she did on *Father Comes Home from the Wars*, watching it unfold in 2014 in the Anspacher Theater under the direction of Jo Bonney.[17] One moment in particular kept catching her eye—and ear. Hero, the lead character, a slave, asks Smith, the Union soldier, what he thinks life will be like in the future when he is free. He wonders aloud that if, in that idealized future, he is walking home from work and a law enforcement individual stops him and asks who he belongs to, that he will be able to say, "I belong to myself." That line was the seed of *White Noise* and Parks realized in that moment, "Oh, shit, I've got to write that play."

What Parks created was a story about two friends. Leo is, in Parks's description, "a brother of African descent who doesn't feel protected, is roughed up by the cops and thinks the best way to deal with it is to have his friend [Ralph] buy him." The premise and structure are shocking on the page, and watching Ralph slowly be convinced that this performative ownership will be the best way for him to help his friend grapple with the deep-seeded identity damage of racism and ownership is, unquestionably, chilling. For $89,000, part of Ralph's inheritance, Leo can pay his credit card debts and college loans and be in servitude to his best friend. The experiment would last forty days, heightened in the theater by the projections that tracked where the characters were on their journey. In this calculation, Leo figures he might come to a better understanding of his ancestral horror and the societal rot that allowed him to be roughed up by the police and seen, continually, as "other." In addition, the society around them would see how America has not lived up to the promise of equality and demonstrate just how far we have *not* evolved.

Over the course of the writing process, Parks introduced the characters of Misha and Dawn, the partners of the two men, who had story arcs that both related to and mirrored the complex and anxiety-inducing relationship of Leo and Ralph. Each character is fundamentally flawed and blinded by their self-righteously liberal identities; their belief that they are the "good guys." For example, Misha, we are troubled to discover, glibly playacts racial identity in a cringy podcast called "Ask a Black" that reveals an on-air personality that bears no resemblance to the other Misha that we observe

---

[17] The production subsequently played at the Royal Court in London, ART, and Center Theater Group.

with her friends. Dawn, too, is a lawyer whose moral rectitude is exposed to be something of a fraud.

The production received positive reviews that encouraged the sort of moral questioning that Parks wanted. London's *Guardian* noted that the play incited one to ask, "What is so wrong with the audience that no one intervenes? What is still so wrong with America?"[18] Two years after the production, Eustis reflected on its continued power and, contrary to the London review, ability to viscerally provoke the audience to act, or at least react: "It's a play that really dangerously played with internalized oppression . . . The way that it wanted to explore how the Black characters had internalized slavery . . . The legacy of slavery and what they needed to do to try to understand and overcome it was very upsetting to a lot of people. That's what art is supposed to do, I think. We had walkouts almost every night."

White Noise contained a sort of literalism that reversed other Suzan-Lori Parks conventions that were seemingly more experimental, spiritual, and even avant-garde. Famous for upending punctuation and syntax in plays like *Venus* and *The America Play*, in *White Noise*, there is something more, for lack of a better descriptor, realistic. Eustis agreed, and noted that an evolution for playwrights in a similar vein is not unusual: "I think of Brecht. I think of Caryl Churchill. I think of O'Neill; writers whose fierce experimental profile of their early years continues to mature until it develops into something that Georg Lukács called great realism."[19] Brecht's *Mother Courage* and *Galileo*, he notes, show an author's evolution away from "estranged epics" such as *A Man Is Man* to a more realist and, well, Brechtian approach. Eustis continues that Parks's "mastery of form has led her to be able to be more and more supple about her formal innovations. So while *White Noise* is more realistic than anything she has written on the surface, it still encompasses some wildly improbable events. Its formal concerns and focus is still there, but it's merged. The formal innovations aren't on the surface calling attention to themselves." To connect back to Lukács, an audience can watch and identify with *individual* characters, while a style of heightened realism allows for a clear articulation of the broader social problems and contemporary realities.

The telltale blending of literal and symbolic shines through in the play, showing an artist who, while finding a new epic form, is still true to the playful nature of abstraction; what a *New York Times* critic referred to accurately as "marginally heightened reality."[20] Leo is an insomniac, allowing for the title of the play—a white noise machine, that thing that drowns out reality

---

[18] Alexis Soloski, "*White Noise* Review: Suzan-Lori Parks Provokes and Disturbs," *Guardian*, March 20, 2019.
[19] In Lukács's *Realism in the Balance*, great or "true" realism is a response to modernist and individualistic literary movements that lack collective and revolutionary power. See David Krasner, ed., *Theater in Theory 1900–2000* (Malden, MA: Blackwell, 2008), p. 116.
[20] Ben Brantley, "Review: Hearing the Roar of Racism in 'White Noise,'" *New York Times*, March 20, 2019.

and allows us to be calm and sedate, not by eliminating the bad, but by painting over it. And then there is the fact that Suzan-Lori Parks is extremely funny, irreverent, and tongue-in-cheek in even her most distressing works. In her deep-sea dive into the human psyche, she allows herself to have fun and to explore the areas of irony and just plain silliness. In a discussion about the writing process of *White Noise* she tossed out, as an aside, "I didn't know what their names were, but very quickly when I started writing it, I thought—their names are Leo, Ralph, Misha, and Dawn. The Ninja Turtles: Leonardo, Raphael, Michelangelo, and Donatello. So, their names come from the Ninja Turtles."

"What?!" I said.

"Yes," apparently her child was playing with Teenage Mutant Ninja Turtle figurines at the time of the writing.

> Right when I started laughing, I thought oh shit, it's going to be a deep dive. I'm going to have to go to a deep place to write this one because—while I write in many different styles, I have to suit, like Hamlet said, the action to the word—I have to suit the style of the play to the content. ...
>
> When I heard that, many years ago hanging out in the East Village at St. Mark's Church Poetry Project, I was like oh, yes, that makes sense to me. Form is not some arbitrary thing or some cookie cutter thing. Form is an expression of what it is that I'm writing about, the story, if you will. So, while I write in all these different kinds of forms, there is a constant in that: one, they're always expressing the content. And two, most of them start with a dumb joke.
>
> So, *Topdog/Underdog*: two brothers, Lincoln and Booth—ba dump bump.
>
> *Fucking A*: I'm going to write a play about fucking. Isn't that funny?
>
> Same thing with *White Noise:* I named the characters after the Ninja Turtles.

The shock of the play, and the reason for the walkouts, was due to the extraordinary intersections of content, style, and form, and the emotional effect that it had. Dawn is a lawyer, Ralph an English professor, and Misha a vlogger. Parks created the most hipster of duos—two sets of middle-class friends (mixed race couples), tight since college, bowling friends, former rock band members, living in New York City in 2019. And so, the play evolves and decorum devolves, and by the time Daveed Diggs's Leo has a slave collar affixed around his neck to affirm his slave status to his best friend, the audience almost invariably gasps. The evening I saw the play, as Eustis noted, a visibly upset woman on the other side of the audience stood up and headed for the exits. It had the look *not* of someone offended by the conventions that Parks was using, but of someone who needed to get out quick, perhaps to get air, to throw up, to escape.

The play is one of her most complexly challenging. In fact she says it was the hardest play she has ever written. In the frame of the play, she attempted to encapsulate four points of views on race in America and noted that there was a huge amount of anger in the work, and a lot of despair. "It's not just a play about, the Black guy's right; or the white guy's right. ... We're following four characters at the same time." She notes that whoever is speaking makes good sense, and she feels forced to like and agree with them. And yet, there is so much contradiction in their viewpoints. "So, it's like my brain, my mind, myself, was being pulled in four different directions. I was being quartered, drawn and quartered. It was that kind of horrible feeling. At any moment I was just going to rip into four pieces. It was really hard to write because I loved them all."

As hard as it was to write, the prevailing sense is that it was not as complicated for Eustis to direct. Indeed, what was staged was simple and befitting the style of the play. Realistic, unobtrusive direction that allowed the gut punch of a play to resonate so powerfully with so many in the audience. "When you do a world premiere of a new play, the director has an extra obligation to try to make sure that you not only try to do the best production possible, but that you do a production that is in some fundamental accord with what the playwright thinks they wrote, because that first production will determine, in a lot of ways, that play's future," Eustis said. Its presentation at The Public received a glowing review from the *Times*. And yet, aside from a couple of other productions, *White Noise* has not taken off. True, the pandemic came on only a year later, and in 2021 there was a prominent London production for which Parks reworked the script. But Eustis believes that it did not receive the attention it deserved because it truly upset people; it affected people deeply while other plays on internalized racism only lightly provoked or titillated. This, he thought, cut to the core.

Only two years after *White Noise* premiered at The Public, I asked Eustis how it has held up. Without hesitation he reaffirmed his belief in the genius and "miracle" of Suzan-Lori Parks. But, he added, his work on the show could not be possible anymore. It would be far too transgressive. "There is no way that Suzan-Lori could choose a white director at this moment. Certainly not for that play. That's not because there is a law against it, it's not because she's being bullied into it. It because what feels clear about this cultural moment is that there is a cry for agency and authenticity of viewpoint that is irresistible in the culture. And I don't think that's a bad thing. I think it could become a bad thing. I think it could lead to bad consequence. But I don't think it's a bad thing."

"How could it become a bad thing?" I asked.

"The bad consequences would be an essentialist, identitarian culture taking root. Sadly, this has always been the strategy of oppression. It's the strategy that invented racism ... we'll be arguing for equity, empathy and equality while articulating a world view that embodies the opposite." Two years on, the reality that the artistic director of the company and perhaps even Jo Bonney, Parks's longtime directing collaborator, might not be appropriate people to direct these plays is at once a fascinating comment on the rapidity with which conversations around identity and representation have evolved in American theater, and a realization that the industry is in a moment of great questioning, with still variously defined goals. *White Noise*, in fact, captured some of that questioning.

Class and *Sweat*

White Noise and *Father Comes Home from the Wars* are, unquestionably, plays that primarily confront race and the legacy of slavery, as is the case with all of the works that Suzan-Lori Parks has added to the American canon. Coupled with that, and in fact essential to her work and the work of so many other playwrights presented at 425 Lafayette, is a deep evaluation of the placement of class in the American cultural fabric. This, too, is almost baked into the ethos of the theater—a company founded by a socialist and currently run by someone for whom Marxist ideals run deep. It is critical to *White Noise* that the four central characters live a decidedly middle-class life, making their confrontation with institutionalized racism focused through the lens of privilege. "The Gabriels," too, is deeply class-based, even if the working-class heroes of Richard Nelson's plays are firmly positioned within the milieu of white intelligentsia.

Increasingly, over Eustis's tenure, the output of work at 425 Lafayette has framed class and the American inability to appropriately address wealth disparities as a central focus of many of the plays of their season. In 2016, I asked Eustis where he felt The Public had come up short, where he wanted to focus attention going forward.

> I feel like as a field we're short on writing about the working classes of this country. The theater tends to be an activity of the intelligentsia. It is hard to really break through to different classes. I think the work we've done with Stephen Adly Guirgis I feel very proud of in that way. ... Lynn Nottage has just written a gorgeous play about Reading, Pennsylvania and the destruction of the steel mills there and what that's done to the classes. And even though Lynn herself is not working class, she has immersed herself so thoroughly in that community and with those people that she has born back an authentic voice that I feel great about. But those are exceptions. In general, I haven't done a good job of articulating those concerns.

In the intervening years, Eustis has worked on that articulation, and the Nottage play that he mentioned in 2016, in fact, turned into something of an exemplar of class-conscious theater making. *Sweat*, which won the Pulitzer Prize in drama the following year, shows one of the many ways that stories come to the stage at 425 Lafayette.

Lynn Nottage is the only woman to have won the Pulitzer for drama twice, for *Ruined* and *Sweat*. For her, the research on *Sweat* started five years before, when she was brought on by the Oregon Shakespeare Festival (OSF) as part of the American Revolution History Cycle. Nottage decided that the revolution she wanted to address was the Industrial Revolution, and further wanted her work to have a life in New York after Oregon. She recalls, "My dream was always for it to be at The Public Theater, because I think that Oskar's social justice mission is very much aligned with my own social justice mission and the way in which I want to use theater as a tool for healing and also a tool for change." Eustis came on board early, before the production was staged at OSF, reading drafts, attending rehearsals, and giving notes. From the beginning, *Sweat* was to be a partnership with OSF, The Public, and Arena Stage in Washington, DC.

It is a story about a group of steelworkers who have worked in a factory in Reading for twenty-five years and realize they will have to make concessions to continue in their jobs. The drama takes place in a bar in 2000 and 2008 (the latter being a prologue and a flash-forward that features a racially tense parole hearing that frames up the happenings eight years before). The story is told through conversations over drinks, all related to their work and financial insecurities. One friend is promoted while others find their wages cut and job security under siege. Her promotion, one speculates, may have been related to her race. Others lament that jobs are being outsourced to Mexican immigrants. The busboy, Oscar, takes a job at the factory even as others are protesting the company.

The tribulations of the nine characters across a decade represent and reflect the destruction of the promise of the Industrial Revolution in middle America. Nottage wrote of this descent into tragedy after spending over two years interviewing residents of Reading with her director and longtime collaborator Kate Whoriskey. *Sweat*, prescient as it was, showed deep working-class resentment for the loss of the American promise, and forecast the rise of anti-immigrant sentiment. The play was striking in that it outlined a tragedy in ways that were deeply tied to the social and political zeitgeist without seeming to be polemic about contemporary politics.

I asked Nottage how conscious she was about speaking to a conservative element in American culture—speaking to the "red":

> So, I think, more so than speaking to red, we wanted to speak to purple. People who were undecided, who were feeling a certain level of disaffection. First in the form of voting for Obama, and second, the disaffection took the form of voting for Trump. But what they were looking for in both instances was some form of radical change. It was important, I felt in particular, because a play like *Sweat* ... is politically neutral and just telling a story. [It] has empathy for all of the characters.

A person who has very strong conservative, red allegiances can come to that play and be moved, and vice versa.

She resisted, though, my framing of the work as political since *Sweat* was meant to speak across spectrums. To reduce it to politics, to Trump voters versus Obama or Clinton voters, would seem crass, an anathema to the real goals of the work: "I believe that my work is socially engaged and that I always want to be in conversation with what's happening in the moment." Even as politicians and their decisions feature prominently on the television screen at the bar and in the denigration of the lives of the characters, the play is about the people of Reading and the fact that they are, according to Nottage, a microcosm of the state of America; their anxiety, their dreams deferred, or even crushed. Rather than a direct commentary on American politics, *Sweat*'s articulations about race and class tension in 2000 and 2008 actually predicted the political instability that would flip the Rust Belt and lead to the election of Donald Trump in 2016.

This is exactly the sort of work that Eustis wanted The Public Theater to do more of and where he felt that he had fallen short. For Eustis and Nottage, the creation of *Sweat*, the successful Broadway run, and the Pulitzer were not, in fact, the end goal. The Oregon Shakespeare Festival, Arena Stage, The Public Theater, Studio 54 on Broadway: These are elitist institutions, as psychologically far away from Reading as possible. While 425 Lafayette nurtures and houses artists and their work, *Sweat* actually demonstrated a different way of working. It was born in deep relationship between Nottage and a hardscrabble Pennsylvania town and nurtured through multiple performances across the country. The Public Theater was but one stop on that journey, one that eventually culminated in a tour back to Reading. That journey, both literal and symbolic, was, according to Kate Whoriskey, essential to Nottage's form: "We're wanting the theater to be an alive, dynamic conversation that has civic questions that we can all answer together or examine together. ... I think both Lynn and I were really interested in how we get more people, more diversity in the theater, or how do we get the stories out to them?"

Getting stories out to the people, geographically, while embedded in the interview-style dramaturgical creation of *Sweat*, became obvious to Eustis after watching a now-famous interaction at the Richard Rogers Theater on Broadway. One evening in 2016, after the election of Trump, the Broadway cast of *Hamilton* created a stir when cast member Brandon Victor Dixon gave a post-curtain speech to the Vice President-elect, Mike Pence, who had been in the audience. The audience, upon hearing Pence's name, started to jeer. "There is nothing to boo," Dixon said. "We are sharing a story of love ... we hope that you will hear us out."

Pence had left the auditorium when the speech began, but could hear it in the lobby. He stopped and listened to the remarks.

Vice-President Elect Pence ... we sir, are the diverse Americans who are alarmed and anxious that your new administration will not protect us, our planet, our children, our parents, or defend us and uphold our inalienable rights. We truly hope that this show has inspired you to uphold our American values and to work on behalf of all of us. ... This wonderful American show, told by a diverse group of men and women of different colors, creeds and orientations.[21]

While Lynn Nottage had always hoped that her play would serve communities beyond Broadway houses ("embedded in the mission is that we wanted the play to reach beyond the proscenium," she said), for Eustis, the Pence-directed speech at *Hamilton* crystallized something strong and problematic about the elite "cathedrals" of entertainment. The headquarters at Lafayette, the home at Central Park, did not speak to the country in any way that could rightly allow The Public to deserve the recognition as a de facto national theater. The *Hamilton* speech eloquently and briefly addressed diversity and anxiety, inalienable rights, rights of people of all colors, creeds, and orientations. But was there anything that reflected the anxiety that got Mr. Pence elected in the first place? Eustis recalls the day after the speech feeling very happy, especially when Trump called for an apology from the producers. He started altering his view, however, as *Hamilton*-backlash ensued, and it became clear that an American story actually was being ignored:

> As a result of Trump doing that, there was an online move to boycott *Hamilton* ... and I thought to myself, "that's insane." None of those people are going to see *Hamilton*. They can't afford a ticket. It wasn't going to come to a city near them. And even if they could afford a ticket and it did come to a city near them, they don't have the "ins" to get on the list.
>
> And I realized, *we've* actually been boycotting those people for a long time, they are not boycotting us, they are returning a boycott. We have taken half the country and turned our backs on them and said, "you don't want us, we don't have anything for you. You can't support us; we are going where we want."

As if on cue, the *New York Times* posted a map of American counties, with each county colored in red and blue based on party preference in the recent election. Eustis realized that if the blue was identified as the location for nonprofit theaters and the red as where they weren't, it would probably still be an accurate map. "We had done the same thing that the economy did, that education did, that the culture as a whole did. Abandoned."

---

[21] https://www.npr.org/2016/11/19/502687591/hamilton-to-pence-we-are-the-diverse-america-who-are-alarmed.

For him, at that moment, the idea of getting *Sweat* out of New York City revealed itself as the essential thing to do. At the time, it was in production at the Martinson Theater at The Public (it opened the weekend before the election) and was slated for a Broadway run beginning in March 2017.

The morning after *Sweat* closed at The Public, the cast, crew, and producers left 425 Lafayette and got on a bus to Pennsylvania. Reading, they decided, needed to see the work *before* it went to Broadway. At the same time, the company was percolating on the idea of expanding further, into a national tour. The initial idea was that a new model of leaning into the red, or the purple, would allow for plays like *Sweat*, about class and race, to go out to the country—to red counties, to swing states, to the Rust Belt—to reach people that the elite coastal theater houses miss. Eustis noted that the idea behind it is something he believes in fully, and that it is his hope that, post-pandemic, theater emerges strong enough to examine that sort of work again: "We in the non-profit theater movement have a responsibility that extends beyond our own demographics." Nottage reflected that sentiment almost precisely: "I think that too often we're preaching to the converted. ... As a result we're not really shifting the dial."

But for that reading in Reading, The Public Theater attempted to try out the viability and power of getting out of town. It's the same sort of ethic that gave rise to the revamped Mobile Unit and Public Works, which will be explored in detail in Chapter 9. Nottage recalls the power of the mini tour of *Sweat*:

> We performed it in the evening, and we were kind of shocked by the response. It was almost like going to church. People saw the play as a reflection of who they were, and then at the very end, they got up, and they testified. People shared their own stories, and it was incredibly moving, not just for me but for the actors involved and, in particular I think, Oskar. I think that he was overwhelmed by the experience, bringing theater to audiences that are not used to entering into the space.
>
> When I was interviewing people in Reading, talking about being a theater artist, they said they don't often feel invited into certain art spaces. They don't know how to dress. They don't know whether the stories will be interesting to them. So, we did a lot of work when we went to Reading to make sure that people felt very invited within the space. We had a diverse audience. It was diverse racially but also economically.

An economic diversity in the audience was what Nottage had been searching for since she began the project. Like the other plays considered in this chapter, positioning class within the context of American theater culture-building is a longstanding goal. The repositioning of the work outside of the building at 425 Lafayette began to affirm that goal and pointed toward future development—ways of making The Public Theater, if not *the* national theater, at least a company that could facilitate national and even international conversations.

* * *

While history does echo through the halls of The Public Theater, through the posters, the old rickety auditoriums, and the calls to the past and promise of the future, it is evident that the headquarters of The Public, the building itself, functions as a laboratory of sorts. These are not fancy theaters; none of them has even a fraction of the audience capacity of the Delacorte. Four Twenty-Five is The Public at its best—a place where artists work, where they develop and toy with their creations, with the support of dramaturgs, designers, and producers. Most productions perform there for a limited run and then, perhaps, have a few engagements in smaller theaters around the country. While The Public is famous for those Broadway hits, a transfer to the Great White Way, as will be considered in the next chapter, is never the goal. This is the workplace of Suzan-Lori Parks, Richard Nelson, Tony Kushner, Tarell Alvin McCraney, Jeanine Tesori, and hundreds of others. The Public Theater is the place that so many artists and producers, most not widely known beyond a small circle, proudly call their artistic home.

But the great realization of the past several years, perhaps illuminated best by *Sweat*, is that *that* is not enough. Just as the Delacorte in Central Park has become financially and socially elitist, so too has 425. No longer can it just say that it is an Eden of artist support; The Public has to transform again and see itself as a conduit between those artists and the communities that they reflect. Broadway transfers demonstrate exactly the challenge that faces The Public Theater. What happens when socially important shows become inaccessible to the people who need to see them and for whom they were written? What do *Sweat, Hamilton,* and *for colored girls …* mean when taken to Broadway? Through all, the question is, "What does by, for, and about the people actually mean?"

INTERLUDE

Justin Vivian Bond and Bridget Everett

FIGURE 5.4 (a) *Justin Vivian Bond. Courtesy Burak Cingi.* (b) *Bridget Everett. Courtesy Kevin Yatarola.*

One of the great venues at The Public, and in New York City broadly, is Joe's Pub. Started by George C. Wolfe in 1998, the unusual experiment of creating a nightclub off the lobby of The Public quickly proved a success. Guided by Serge Becker, Bill Bragin, Shanta Thake, and now Alex Knowlton, the stature of the Pub is large and attracts artists from Taylor Mac to Adele.

Justin Vivian Bond and Bridget Everett are among the most produced performers at Joe's. In addition to being a musician, Bond is an actor, a visual artist, and a trans rights icon. They are also one half of the comedy act Kiki and Herb. Everett is a singer, monologist, and television actor, recently starring in the HBO series *Somebody Somewhere*.

I spoke with Bond in their dressing room above the Pub in 2017 and with Everett in the Library Restaurant at The Public. The following are selections from those interviews.

Justin Vivian Bond

Landis: *The New Yorker* calls you the best cabaret artist of their generation. What is cabaret to you and is that the right term to describe what you do? And, if not, is there another way you could describe it?

Bond: Well, I think what I do is cabaret. I call myself a trans genre artist. I write. I am a visual artist. I'm a singer. I'm an actor. And cabaret is really a genre where I can incorporate all my practices, all rolled into one ... basically what I think what I do at Joe's Pub is a site-specific performance. ...

Landis: What are some of the defining factors of cabaret, or your specific cabaret, if you categorize it in that way?

Bond: I'm perfectly, delightfully comfortable being known as a cabaret artist because I feel like, not to toot my own horn too much, but I think, on a certain level, Kenny [Mellman] and I, as Kiki and Herb ... we really redefined what cabaret was for a new generation. And many of the artists that are successful today were artists that were influenced by us. Bridget Everett, Taylor Mac, acts in the UK that are really successful, Bourgeois and Maurice, Jonny Woo, all these people. That's their livelihood, that's what they do and the way that they present their work and the anarchy in it was inspired by us.

It was about harnessing an energy within the zeitgeist and exhibiting it to the audience through a lens that let them feel like they weren't crazy, basically. Because you know, when we are being told this story that is so counter intuitive and not healthy, malfeasance on the part of the government or the culture ... we can go in there and sort of like let the air out of that tire that's carrying this horrible load of bullshit. When we started Kiki and Herb, it was AIDS, you know. It was the time when so many people were dying, and the government was seemingly doing nothing about it. And people were out on the streets—activists—and we were the entertainment for the troops.

Landis: I like what you said about letting the air out of the tire. Is there almost a sense that coming to a show like yours is a catharsis and a release?

Bond: I think it was, especially in time of anxiety, when the people in the room ... can go, "oh, there are other people here that agree with me, there are other people that are feeling this too," which is the wonderful thing about cabaret. And even when we took Kiki and Herb to Carnegie Hall, my parents—I mean there's twenty-eight hundred people there—my parents and their friends came and I was making these cracks about Ronny and Nancy Reagan, you know, critical comments. And 2,720 people were cheering like mad and my parents and their group of friends were like "oh my god, what the hell?" They had no idea people thought that or would ever agree with that. That's not their world, their worldview. So, it gives people a chance. I like it when people say they bring dates to my shows as a litmus test. (*laughs*)

Landis: Why do you like that?

Bond: Because it means they're looking for somebody who sees the world in the way that they do, and they figure like I'm the

	person that will help them find that out. I'm like a shortcut. ...
Landis:	Do you think when you're creating a show, do you think toward your audience of liberal blue state sort of people who think like you, or not? Is there an effort to reach into other communities beyond that base?
Bond:	Well, you know, the thing is I'm from "other communities beyond that base," so I have a way of doing things or saying things that can be really the antithesis of what that world and what that base is. But because I can talk to them, I don't talk down to anybody. I assert my superiority, but I don't talk down to people if I can help it. I don't do it intentionally, anyway. So, I feel like a lot of times when I'm in those places, they are not threatened by me. ...

I can see those people and I know, if it's like Republican people, whether they're rednecks or whether they're bourgeoisie. I mean I know them. I know how to talk to them. I know how to infiltrate and survive when I'm surrounded by them. And they're not my allies by any means, but I know how to, in general, engage with them in a way that I don't feel like I'm in danger. And I don't always alienate them or make them angry. Although I want to, sometimes, and then I do it. |
Landis:	So, you're just trying to entertain you're not trying to necessarily to change certain political views.
Bond:	Oh, I want them to see things differently than they thought of before, but I don't accuse them of being horrible. I just show them different ways of looking at things than they might have ever thought of before. ...
Landis:	Obviously, gender and sexuality is a huge part of the history of cabaret. Can you say a little more from that perspective about what is it about the genre that lends itself to it? And what is an audience seeking perhaps through that?
Bond:	Well, I think that's a broad question, first of all ... I'll just pick a little something. To speak to in that very broad question. ... The thing about cabaret is that artists such as myself get to speak with our own voice and say what we have to say without any committee, without any approval and either sink or swim. Somebody who's writing a script for theatrical presentation, you have all your producers, you have all these things that they have to go through ... what's the next step, what's the next stage, what's the next step to get it to where people are going to invest their money? blah, blah, blah. My work is contingent on two things, me showing up and having something to say and people showing up and paying their money to hear it. That's all.

That has been my MO for my entire career. I do not do subsidized work. I do not do work that I get paid for whether people show up or not. That's the thing about Joe's Pub, I get a percentage of the door. If people show up, then I make money. If people don't show up, then I don't make money. So, it's incumbent upon me to be interesting, to have something fresh to say, and to entertain them. And that is what I love about it. I mean, that's just a very nuts and bolts thing. The people that come to hear me perform want to hear what I have to say and I, as a cabaret performer, am free to say whatever I want. And that plays to the strength. When I started out, there weren't places where people like me got to say things that much. So now people can. But that's what cabaret is about, I think. That's why it's threatening. That's why it's dangerous. That's why they had those cabaret laws here in New York for all those years because people want to be able to control what other people say.

Landis: The fact they're showing up is an experience of empowerment. Is it not? You said it's your living room. ...

Bond: The people that are there looking around seeing there are other people there that want to hear the person. ... So, it is to a certain extent preaching to the choir, but the choir doesn't know that they are necessarily members of the same choir until they show up.

* * *

Bridget Everett

Landis: Why does the Pub, a small venue, why does it loom so large for artists? What is it about it that people are drawn to?

Everett: Well, I really think it's largely due to what Shanta has created, which has been fostered by Oskar. They are risk takers. First of all, it's a beautiful room. It feels intimate wherever you sit. And I've performed all over the country and world, and there's no place like it. It just has such a warm, radiant feel. But within the beautiful room you can sort of do whatever you want. So, it's cool to get to be a little bit dirty on such a beautiful stage. And I've done some really dirty shit. ...

You can be a misfit and an outlier. You can sing in your diapers, which I've done many times at Joe's Pub. Or you can be Adele, and you want to be in the room because you want to be part of the fabric of Joe's Pub.

Landis: Could you say a little bit about how your career has noticeably changed in your eyes because of your affiliation with The Public Theater and with Joe's Pub?

Everett: Well, it's changed enormously. I'm in two movies that are coming out next month. And those are people that saw me singing in Joe's Pub that wrote parts for me because they saw me here in Joe's Pub. There are people ... specifically, all the people that have come to see me based on my performances here, based on the opportunities I've been given by Joe's. But also, the opportunity to come and do your show once a month, with regularity and develop a core audience of people that push you to do more and try to go further. And knowing that you're at Joe's Pub, so you can't slack off. Whenever I do a show at Joe's I want to try something new. I give it 150 percent because I know that the place I'm in is an institution. I don't want to let it down because it's never let me down. Does that sound corny?

Landis: No, it's true, exactly. And to that point, performing in front of a Joe's Pub crowd must be unique. Is there a way you can describe the type of people who show up downstairs versus other venues that you work?

Everett: Yeah, I mean you get art freaks and geeks and people that are Pulitzer Prize winners and major actors and writers—also just DJs. And the cross culture that you get there—trans, queer, gay, straight, rich, poor—

Landis: What is the producorial process in your relationship with the Pub? Do they just say, "Here's your time. Have a good show?"

Everett: Typically, it's like, "Here's your time. Have a good show." At one point I used to get on top of the piano all the time. They were like, "Could you please not stand on it. We've got a brand-new piano." "Are you saying I'm going to break the piano? I know I'm a big girl, but I'm not going to break the fucking piano," "But out of respect." *(laughs)*

Landis: Could you talk a little bit about how you perhaps view your work as political, if you even think about it in those terms?

Everett: I mean I think it's political in the way that a six-foot-tall blond woman who's not ashamed of her body and there's partial nudity, and it's very sexualized. And I talk about abortion and shit like that. But to me, I'm not trying to be political. I'm just trying to be myself. And it's not to say that there aren't plenty of things that are political here, and that people that see my show might not think that it's political. I'm not trying to normalize anything or be a champion for anyone. I'm just trying to do something that would make me laugh and that would make me feel powerful if I were an audience member.

Landis: And if I could go a little further on that, if someone said, "What is your type of performance?" someone who's never seen your work, other than describing some of the things you do, is there a way that you would describe what sort of an artist you are?

Everett: I'd say something like, "It's rock n' roll cabaret with great tits and a heart of gold," or something like that. I can never really describe it. Some people are like, I'm not really a standup comic. There's a whole world of new cabaret which is thriving and thriving at Joe's Pub, people like Taylor Mac and Meow Meow and Cole Escola, Justin Vivian Bond. The list goes on of people, trans, queer, straight, gay, but risk-takers, and Joe's Pub has them all.

Landis: You use the word "cabaret" which is often the way I describe what goes on in Joe's Pub, and yet it's limited. Could you describe the way you look at cabaret and how it's changed and how you fit into this new cabaret that you described?

Everett: Yeah, for me cabaret lies somewhere between storytelling and just singing songs. I mean there's the old guard, which would perform at the Carlyle and sing beautiful songs like Sondheim and whatever else ... but now there's this new world of cabaret. If I could go see a show five nights a week it would be all those people that I mentioned. ... All these people that are weird, subversive, and so fucking funny but also with so much heart. And it's not just like standing around singing songs that are beautiful. I mean they have great voices and stuff, but I think it's a cool world to be a part of.

Landis: What do you think? Do you see an integration between the two aspects of this institution, the Pub and The Public Theater?

Everett: I do. I see that there's the same heart that beats behind all of it. It's like risk-taking and care for the artist. You feel really well cared for. You feel like you can do anything. I've seen plays here. I've seen musicals here. I've seen things at Joe's Pub, but you always feel like there's an integrity and risk involved. And that's just so cool. I can't think of any other building, theater in this city, let alone the world, that does that, that has Shakespeare and then club acts and cabaret and musicals and plays. And they have incredible taste. Oskar and Shanta have incredible taste. They somehow know.

When I started here, I was pretty raw, even though I'd done the stuff at Ars Nova. I was still figuring it out. But they have a great way of knowing who to get behind and who to stick with for the long haul. And I think that's what makes this place special. And they get actors that did their first play here that go off and do movies and *Star Wars* and whatever and come back—Meryl Streep, Shakespeare in the Park. And for me, I will always come back to Joe's Pub, and it'll be my home because you just get treated so well here—from the sound guy to the guys that bring you the French fries, to Oskar Eustis … he's had a really full, wonderful, dynamic, crazy life with some real heartache. And he still manages to give everybody a lift when they see him. I feel so legit because Oskar used to give me the seal of approval.

Landis: This is another impossibly broad question, but I'm going to throw it out anyway. Are there a couple that you could relate, of extraordinary, in the moment experiences that you'll never forget?

Everett: Oskar was there one time, and he was sitting in a booth all by himself, and the show was sold out. And I was like, "That motherfucker's sitting at a table all by himself with a martini. Let's make this a memory." So, I got up at the end, and I got up on top of his booth and table, and I had my leg up there. And he was drinking his martini, and I was just like … And I don't even think about it at the time. But walking away from him I'm like, "Oh my God, I just spilled half of Oskar Eustis's martini and shoved my pussy in his face."

Landis: And I'm sure the audience loved it.

Everett: And the audience fucking loved it. … One night I'm going around the room. I'm singing the song "Titties" that I do, which you'll see. And somebody walks in late, and I hate when people walk in late. I want them to see the whole thing. Otherwise, it doesn't feel like … It's like missing the first act of the play, or whatever. And I turn around, and I'm like, "You're late."

And I'm like, oh shit. It's Gloria Steinem, and I'm singing the song "Titties," which I thought, for some reason, she wouldn't like. And I felt at that point I'm a disgrace to feminists. But she's seen me before, and she loved it. It just was like you don't know who's going to walk in the door. And you start mouthing off to everybody. But slow down every once in a while, Bridget, because it's Gloria Steinem that's going to be sitting there sometimes.

Broadway "Bound"

6

Building the Disco

FIGURE 6.1 *Set rendering for* Here Lies Love. *Courtesy David Korins, Javier Ameijeiras, and Alex Kuhn.*

> *The Public has never made a top priority of transferring any show [to Broadway] ... you have to remember that I'm a Marxist, which means that I believe that everything is in contradiction. That's dialectics, that's how history moves forward. So, the fact that there is a contradiction doesn't bother me. It's a question of how you manage that contradiction, to be as progressive as possible.*
> —OSKAR EUSTIS

Climbing up four flights to the LuEsther Theater at The Public is a bright white stairwell. There is an elevator, but it's small and there is often a line to get on. Making the journey up by foot seemed right when heading to the David Byrne and Fatboy Slim musical *Here Lies Love*, as it prolonged the mystery. It was hard to know what to expect from a play advertised as a story about the deposed dictators of the Philippines, Ferdinand and Imelda Marcos. The posters were psychedelic, multicolored drug trips, visioning a disco diva, elegantly dressed, mic in the air, surrounded by bright lights and adoring throngs. Even the text—HERE LIES LOVE, in all caps, each letter a different color—at once screamed at the viewer and seductively enticed them in.

Making the way up those steps, the distant thumpa-thumpa coming from the "attic" of The Public grew louder, until that final turn; a blast of neon and a wave of music leading to the open door of a swanky club. The theater space was no more, replaced with a disco floor, surrounded by modular platforms, disco balls, rotating lights, screens, and a bellowing DJ on a platform overseeing the mayhem: "Americans are wearin' those sexy jeans. Americans are usin' technology. Americans are surfin' that Internet. Americans are listenin' to 50 Cent."[1]

Wait a minute, *50 Cent? Internet?* Weren't the Marcoses in power in the 1970s? It didn't matter. The room was shaking. As the first song of the discotheque died down, the stages rotated, audience/dancers adjusted, a projection on a back wall flickered on—"Tacloban, Philippines, 1946"—and the sound of rainfall filled the now-still room. A young woman emerged in a plain white dress, sat and sang, reminiscing about her youth, "I'd see the people smile, when I would sing for them. How happy they all seemed—when I would dance." As the tune progressed, the humble girl emerged as Imelda Marcos, in full color, with backup dancers carrying white umbrellas, and a band, sound popping again as she sang of the hopes for the inscription on her tombstone, "Just say: here lies love ... here lies love ... here lies love." In four minutes, the complete trajectory of a life of a megastar.

---

[1] David Byrne, *Here Lies Love*, as with all other *HLL* quotes in this chapter.

And *Here Lies Love* itself represents a fascinating study of the trajectory of a musical. Too often, the judge of musical success is the transferability to Broadway (spoiler alert: *Here Lies Love* never made it uptown). It's a facile barometer for a nonprofit theater, as Eustis pointed out. Yet, The Public Theater would not have survived had it not been for *A Chorus Line*, and its early success was defined by *Hair*. Joseph Papp will always be associated with those shows and the other Broadway transfers, like *The Pirates of Penzance* and *The Mystery of Edwin Drood*. George C. Wolfe, despite his major success in the Park, the establishment of Joe's Pub, and his nurturing of artists like Suzan-Lori Parks, will also be defined at The Public as the producer of Jeanine Tesori and Tony Kushner's musical *Caroline, or Change* and the director of the 1996 Reg E. Gaines *Bring in 'da Noise, Bring in 'da Funk*, both Broadway critical hits. Similarly, no matter how much is written about *Caesar*, the challenges of dealing with Covid, and the growth of programs like Public Works and the Mobile Unit, Eustis's professional profile will always highlight *Hamilton* and *Fun Home*. "Broadway 'Bound'" realistically reflects a reality at The Public Theater: Despite its mantra of inclusivity and accessibility, its financial model and image has, since its inception, been tied to commercial success. As anyone who has seen a show on Broadway or caught a touring production, "Broadway" is not defined by *accessibility*. That fact was spotlighted in garish lights when *Hamilton*—a show about immigrants and people of color, created by an artist from the Bronx, with lines that glorified "scrappy," "hungry" people getting their shot—was such a hit that tickets were being sold for $800 or more on Broadway. That doesn't seem "public."

Transferring to Broadway has, by some necessity, grown during the Eustis years, and in fact a new division called Public Theater Productions was established to help shepherd those plays and musicals. Again, a Broadway production of a Public Theater-created show does not guarantee significant revenue for The Public; shows are often not viable financially. For example, during George C. Wolfe's tenure, The Public sunk almost $5 million into its revival of *On the Town* in 1998, and was the primary funder. It was a labor of love for Wolfe but went on to middling reviews and limited success. Producing on Broadway had become too risky. Now that commercial producers are involved in almost all shows that have even the potential of transfer, The Public never controls the same share of the revenue that it did with *A Chorus Line*. The Public remains a general partner, acting as a coproducer; thus you see Eustis onstage at the Tony's when accepting awards for those hits.

Early in the Eustis years, four shows in quick succession went to Broadway: *Passing Strange, Hair, The Merchant of Venice,* and *Bloody Bloody Andrew Jackson*. With those massive lifts as examples, and with early missteps, it became clear that a nonprofit theater should not bear the burden of fundraising for those transfers. As will be discussed in a later section on financial realities at The Public, *Bloody Bloody* actually lost the company a significant amount of money—almost a million dollars—and resulted in deep animosity and mistrust between the board and the finance team, feelings that had been building since Wolfe's financial flops *The Wild Party* and *On the Town*. Due to success and failure, authors, agents, and the board began desiring for commercial producers to sign on before a show received a strong review in the *Times* or success at Lafayette, indeed even as it was in development. This new necessity, born out of financial constraints, increased the need for a codified relationship between commercial producers and the originating organization. Thus, Public Theater Productions was mandated by the board to help assure financial stability in Broadway transferring. Associate artistic director Mandy Hackett was tapped to lead up the division.

It is clear to see how tensions can rise in the milieu of commercial arrangements, especially in an idealistic young staff devoted to a nonprofit model that celebrates the "necessary" work that they signed on to do. Ergo, the contradiction. If *Hamilton* makes millions of dollars for The Public by selling out to wealthy tourists at the Richard Rogers, that *feels* wrong. But if the income saves the company in an unexpected pandemic, delays furloughs, and allows for experimental new work at 425, that *feels* okay. A complex dialectic—Marx and Hegel, I suppose?

So, does that put The Public, and other companies like it, in bed with commercial producers? Yes, of course. But as Eustis says, the contradiction is consciously managed. The Public negotiates enhancement deals with commercial producers, assuring it some funding for development and the possibility of a percentage of the financial windfall, should there be any, after it transfers. The Public producers, Hackett and Eustis mostly, insist that they never want to get in a position where they are saddled by transfer burdens, and that organizing and codifying the relationship between The Public and commercial producers helps the company actually *not* be "bound" to the Great White Way. Hackett remarks: "We felt, as the leadership, that at that point in The Public's life, it was not worth hoping for that greater profit share, because the burden of the obligation of raising that money just felt off message, off mission for us." The Public will get involved in the commercial relationship if the show is something that leadership believes in as a viable and appropriate transfer, and if they are fully on board with the artistry.

Since those early transfers, The Public and Public Theater Productions have been in relationships with commercial producers consistently, even if the show doesn't end up making the move uptown. *St. Joan*, the follow-up to *Here Lies Love*, had a commercial producer from the outset, as did Michael Friedman's *Fortress of Solitude*. Neither transferred. Other shows have—from Stew's *Passing Strange*, to Danai Gurira's *Eclipsed*, to Nottage's *Sweat*, to the post-pandemic opening of the Bob Dylan musical *Girl from the North Country*. Of course, the two most famous transfers, *Fun Home* and *Hamilton*, would be major successes and win back-to-back Tony Awards for best musical for The Public and its producers. Hackett notes that even if a show has a commercial producer and doesn't end up transferring, it's a win–win: "The basic rule of thumb is, you're a guest in our home when the show is here and then we get to come be a guest in your home when the show transfers." In that way, there is automatically another voice in the room, offering assessment and feedback. Making sure the right commercial partner is on board is thus critical. They have to offer gut feedback but also understand or at least appreciate the ways that plays develop at The Public. Hackett does not believe that this arrangement negatively influences the creation process; rather, it only adds a certain amount of "sting" if it doesn't transfer. The addition of a commercial producer, in a sense, announces that the show will be great. Coming up short, then, will necessarily upset the expectation.

This chapter and the next look at three musicals and the process of their creation, both at The Public and in relationship to their potential of transferability. *Here Lies Love*, a show that didn't make a full transfer, is considered in detail, from concept to production. *Fun Home* and *Hamilton* are addressed mostly through the process of writing, development, and technical design; an exploration of how the mark of The Public Theater as "laboratory" is indelible, even as productions change locations, accommodate different theaters, and transfer to film.

Here Lies Love

"It's not about the shoes!" David Byrne kept telling the cast of *Here Lies Love*. An important reminder for a group of young New York actors whose only memory of Imelda Marcos, the corrupt former first lady of the Philippines, might have been the story of her three thousand pairs of shoes that she spirited out of Malacañang Palace in Manila on the evening of her exile to Hawaii in February 1986. It was a juicy international story at the time; the glamorous once and future politician, a disco maven who danced with presidents and movie stars, whose personal fortune ran into the billions of dollars, was ousted by a people's revolution. And she insisted on bringing her shoes. It all had the feel of Marie Antoinette. That it was her husband, Ferdinand Marcos, who was *actually* the politician—the president of the Philippines—eventually was lost on a press eager for the gossipy story. He faded quickly and died in Hawaii. Imelda returned and was eventually elected to parliament. Imelda and Ferdinand Marcos were incomprehensibly corrupt, brutal, and unapologetic. It wasn't about the shoes, to be sure.

David Byrne, the rock star and former front man for the band Talking Heads, was always fascinated by the Marcos story, especially Imelda. "What really kicked me off was when I read that she loved going to disco. She loved going to Studio 54 and other clubs like that. She had a disco installed on the roof of the palace in Manoa. She had a mirror ball installed in her New York townhouse. I thought, this is real commitment." At the beginning, he wasn't sure if there was enough of a story there or, rather, just an infamous individual for whom enough had already been said. Then someone sent him a video of Marcos dancing under the disco ball in her apartment with someone who appeared to him to be an arms dealer. It was so odd, amazing really. "I'm not hearing it, but the music is obviously ever-present," he recalled about the video. There was a sense in that reel that the uplifting disco music was the soundtrack to the life of the narcissistic and autocratic leader.

"There *is* a story there," he thought.

Byrne started comprehensive research on the life of Imelda Marcos, from her youth in Tacloban to her exile in the 1980s, compiling reams of research that would eventually be poured into the creation of something. Though he didn't know what it could become, there was enough at least for Byrne to start composing songs from the various episodes of her life, with a particular emphasis on her relationship with her childhood maid and friend, Estrella. He saw in Imelda Marcos's life story a challenge to write from a place of empathy about a person who was universally loathed, someone of whom most adults of a certain age had preconceived notions, and whose actions, along with those of her husband, were nothing short of criminal and dictatorial. What would happen if a story was created, centered on a disco, with dancing and uplifting music, but with a catch—it's about a late-twentieth-century criminal with a penchant for shoes?

That *Here Lies Love* eventually found itself to the stage, to The Public, to a commercial production, and an eventual transfer to London's National Theatre was not that much of a departure for one of the most famous rock stars in the world. While he had never written a musical before, Bryne had always had an affinity for theater and the theatrical, as was evidenced in the Talking Heads aesthetic. He was friends with the cellist Arthur Russell, who, in the 1970s, invited him to see an interpretation of Samuel Beckett's radio play *Cascando* at Mabou Mines, the experimental theater company around the corner from The Public in the East Village (directed, incidentally, by JoAnne Akalaitis). Byrne was taken by Mabou Mines and started following other experimental theater-based companies including the Wooster Group, the theater artist/musician/auteur Robert Wilson, and The Public. The work of those legendary 1979-era avant-gardists planted a seed in his head, he recalled. It made him wonder what ways he could "open up" his own work, perhaps make it even more theatrical.

As the story that would become *Here Lies Love* began to percolate, Byrne had the initial thought to set it *not* in a theater like The Public or Mabou Mines, but in a place more apt to the story: a megadisco. Thinking of the warehouse-sized clubs that were ubiquitous in New York City, he imagined filling one of them with little stages that could platform the vignettes of Marcos's life: "So people could be dancing while getting a story and characters at the same time, rather than it just being the arc of the DJ getting everybody excited, then calming them down, then getting them excited again. I thought it might add an emotional and 'story' level to that world."

The warehouse-disco-blended concert never happened, since *Here Lies Love* had a long gestation period. Years passed between the idea for the performance and its opening at The Public Theater. In that time, Byrne feverishly researched, went to the Philippines to play music to see if he was getting the story right, and visited the Marcos mausoleum and Imelda's birthplace. As Byrne recalled, by the time they had something to show, most of those megaclubs that he dreamed of presenting in had gone away, evaporated in the quickly changing New York City:

> If I'd known that, I might not have started, but that's how things go. You do something. You try it one way and it doesn't work, but by then you've got something written. You've got the momentum going, and in some ways it's harder to let go than it is to push on into the unknown.
>
> ...
>
> I'd fallen into this middle ground of being a popular performer who's doing something that more fits the model of those theater groups. People thought, well, what is this, then? Is this pop music? The music was very much pop music. Is this pop music, or is this a concert? Is this art-theater ... ? Well, it's both.

Byrne began to think that his collection of songs about Imelda Marcos wouldn't come to the theatrical stage. And so, he shifted direction and decided he would make an album, using a collection of well-known singers. Alongside the album, he published a booklet that told the history of Marcos, complete with images from his copious research. The concept album was released in April 2010, in collaboration with Fatboy Slim and lead vocals by Cyndi Lauper, Florence Welch, Martha Wainwright, St. Vincent, and Tori Amos, among many others. It was performed live at the Adelaide Festival of the Arts and at Carnegie Hall. It was a modest success, not a great seller, but something about which he was proud.

While there is never one way a musical makes it to The Public stage, the contracting and producing of *Here Lies Love* may have been the strangest. Around the time the album was released, someone came up to Byrne, an avid cyclist, and said, "You know, Oskar Eustis rides a bicycle. Maybe you should talk to him."

That's it.

Someone made the connection that they both loved cycling, which gave the rock star the idea to take a meeting with the artistic director to see if opening a show based on a concept album with contemporary pop stars might make sense. With the recording mostly done, he could just hand the album over and describe his vision for the staging. The meeting worked—Eustis was enthusiastic and encouraged workshops for the show. Finding the right director would be critical and Byrne himself did not want to do it.

Byrne, who had lived with *Here Lies Love* for years by that point, already had ideas. Both he and Eustis came up with names of directors, and on the shortlist for both was a young artist named Alex Timbers. While Timbers's biggest works were still in development, his reputation had already begun to be established as an immersive and innovative theater director. His *Peter and the Starcatcher* premiered at La Jolla Playhouse in early 2009, and he was, that fall, workshopping a Public Theater musical with his friend Michael Friedman about the seventh president of the United States: a rock ballad opera called *Bloody Bloody Andrew Jackson* (which would transfer to Broadway the following year). Immersive theater, already a limited and facile description for what Timbers does, would continue to be his aesthetic. He went on to direct *Beetlejuice* (2019), Byrne's *American Utopia* (2020), and *Moulin Rouge*, for which he won the Tony Award for direction in 2021.

In the fall of 2009, Byrne was familiar with Timbers, having seen his *A Very Merry Unauthorized Children's Scientology Pageant* (2003) and *Hell House* (2006), and Eustis was deep in development with the director on *Bloody Bloody*. Timbers quickly became the obvious choice to work on *Here Lies Love*, a musical that would need the guiding hand of someone who understood the theater/disco immersion that Byrne envisioned for the piece. The seed of the album, its reason for being, was the image of a twentieth-century dictator's wife recreating disco culture in her mansions around the world. That "feel" had to be paramount.

Both Byrne and Timbers agreed to a structure that could recreate that sense of a megadisco on a smaller Public Theater stage, but also knew that the play had to be taken apart, dissected, and mined for the core of the story. In other words, the idea was there but it needed heavy dramaturgy. It couldn't be a bunch of vignettes glorifying a dictator; a through line had to develop. To that end, Timbers decided to work on the album in thirds, as he had with *Peter and the Starcatcher*, finding a different venue to workshop each part. The first third would use the Black Box Theater at New York University (NYU) as its development sandbox, the second at Massachusetts Museum of Contemporary Art (Mass MoCA), outside Williamstown, Massachusetts, and the third at The Public. Through that triad of development, Timbers recalled a breakthrough of sorts, when he realized that the artistic team would have to look at comparable musicals, stories that similarly put an audience in the position of having to grapple with complicated and mostly negative views about the dangerously glorified central character. Timbers recalled, "I think the issue with Imelda is that she did terrible things and so in the end, if your goal is just to make Imelda sympathetic, I think you're doing something politically irresponsible."

The "comps" that they selected were *Evita, Sweeney Todd,* and *Gypsy*. Friedman and Timbers's *Bloody Bloody Andrew Jackson* similarly centralized a deeply problematic historical figure as the "hero" of a musical, treading the line between provocatively illuminating and in poor taste, depending on its execution and reception. With the three comps in mind, Byrne went to work studying the similarities. *Evita* was almost too spot on. The Andrew Lloyd Webber musical about the former first lady of Argentina had many striking similarities to *Here Lies Love*. Eventually both Timbers and Byrne decided that the closest one, the musical that they would particularly focus on, would be *Gypsy*.

With *Gypsy*, the Sondheim musical about a domineering stage mother, Timbers recalls that he and Byrne saw a character in Mama Rose, who "comes to the precipice of self-knowledge," almost like a Greek hero, and then backs away. That felt like a comparison with the journey of Imelda Marcos, or at least a soupçon of a theme that could help flesh out the depths of the Marcos story. That moment in *Here Lies Love* is the song "Why Don't You Love Me?" in which the "hero," on the brink of expulsion, laments: "I gave you my life, I gave you my time. What more could I do? I'm broken inside ... Why don't you love me? Do I mean so little to you?"

Here is the baleful wail of an almost deposed dictator, the vulnerable core of the character at her moment of deposition, seeing, finally, that her people have turned against her. This is that important "precipice of self-knowledge" that they identified in other musicals, and in Byrne's original album, "Why Don't You Love Me?" is the final song of the Marcos story. Timbers remembers that, in the conversations and comparison with *Gypsy*, the "ah ha" moment came with the simple realization that the show is called *Gypsy*. It's not *Mama Rose;* it's called *Gypsy*, the put-upon daughter of the domineering lead character. What is that comparable in *Here Lies Love*?

Well, there wasn't one.

For the story to be fleshed out, to have the structure that it needed as a complex and multifaceted musical, it needed, in a way, a different heart. That character was staring them in the face. Ninoy Aquino, the leader of the Philippine opposition movement, was a constant presence in the life of Imelda Marcos up until, and including, his assassination at Manila International Airport after returning from the United States after a self-imposed exile. Here was, in dramatic terms, the ultimate foil; the opposition leader, a person, it's speculated, who had a serious relationship with Imelda for years, and was gunned down by the Marcos regime, precipitating their exile and the elevation of his wife as the new president of the Philippines. The mirroring of the Marcoses and Aquinos which is evident in the historical record, was the stuff of extraordinary musical exposition and dramatic arc. And yet only half of one song in the original album was sung by Ninoy Aquino. Timbers recalls: "Aquino is actually the heart of the piece ... David ended up building that out, to being a really important character that intertwines with the life of the Marcoses. And I think he's the real heartbreaker of the piece. I think any musical that doesn't have a big emotional center is going to be unsuccessful, and I think that that was one of the many key things to *Here Lies Love* succeeding and connecting with the audiences in a big way."

The workshopping model made for a detailed exploration of dramaturgy, one that lasted years. They were sometimes small explorations, "proof-of-concept" work that allowed the team to jump to the next level, allowed Byrne to rewrite, for Eustis to visit the various workshops and suggest cuts and additions, and for direction and choreography teams to elaborate. By the time the play arrived at The Public, no longer did it end with Imelda's lament; rather, Timbers and Byrne had discovered through the identification of the "heart of the piece" a new ending, a way to tie up the show with a view of the ramifications of the regime. Ruthie Ann Miles, the originator of the role of Imelda, described the ending: "What I love about the arc that Alex took the audience on is that after you have these heart thumping songs and the audience is dancing, they are swept away by the Marcoses ... and then he turns on all the ugly lights, we call them. Like at 4 a.m., you know, at the bar. It's last call and the ugly lights come on. ... 'Wow, did that just happen?'"

A ukulele player stepped into the center of the brightly lit "last call" theater space and the feeling was exactly as Miles described. Though it was in the relatively small LuEsther Theater, the unmistakable feel was of the megadisco that Byrne originally envisioned: sweaty exhausted patrons caught in "ugly light," smiles on their faces melting away into realization. The musician strums and the final song isn't a dictatorial lament, but a transcription of a description of a freedom fighter on the day of the expulsion of the Marcoses—"God Draws Straight": "I saw nuns on their knees. Some who were weeping. Saw a middle-aged man. And a government clerk ... I didn't feel fear or terror. It felt like a movie. Like the end of an era."

Ruthie Ann Miles remembers: "God draws straight, but with crooked lines. And that's one person's takeaway. God is in control, even if I don't understand the path. So, these are all people's words, and not David's ... his genius was putting it all together."

The critical success of *Here Lies Love* came in no small part due to the seamlessness of music, direction, and choreography. Timbers and Byrne seemed to speak the same artistic language and knew that a musical set in a disco needed a copacetic movement aesthetic, a choreographer who understood the work of David Byrne. It turns out that Byrne already had someone in mind, a person who had been studying his style and the style of the Talking Heads since she was in college. By the time *Here Lies Love* was in workshops, Annie-B Parson had established herself as one of the finest choreographers in the Unites States, having worked with David Bowie, Martha Graham Dance, and St. Vincent. Byrne, too, was a big fan of Parson's company, Big Dance Theater. He came to many of their performances, and they began to know each other socially through their mutual friend, Jonathan Demme. When Byrne went on tour with Brian Eno in 2008, he asked her to choreograph several songs. Parson recalls being duly intimidated. "As a young artist, I was inspired by the Talking Heads aesthetic ... obsessed aesthetically with them. When I was hearing the Talking Heads for the first time, I was young and really had no aesthetic ... their work appealed to me primarily because it was dry rather than wet, it was cool rather than warm, it was detached rather than connected, it was wide shot rather than a close up. I was so involved with what David was doing that it was not a leap for me to work on his work. It was like I had been practicing since I was twenty years old how to choreograph his work."

The Byrne/Eno tour prompted a strong working relationship and when Byrne went to Timbers with the suggestion that she be the choreographer, it was agreed she'd guide the disco. It *was*, in fact, a bit of a leap. While Parson was a noted choreographer with a decidedly Byrnian sensibility, she had never directed a musical, and, in fact, had no desire to. "I'm not from the American musical theater family tree," she remarked:

I didn't train in musical theater and don't have much knowledge of it, and I often don't respond artistically to a typical musical—my body doesn't move naturally to that kind of material, but instead I see all the trope-y movement material that is associated with the derivative work that came from that tree. Other people can explore and animate it better! But anything that's experimental, experimenting with the musical form, which David was very much doing, I'm interested in.

Byrne, Timbers, and Parson worked closely together, copiously pouring over the massive amounts of research that Byrne had collected—boxes full, with videos of the Marcoses at clubs and discos and at parties with world leaders. Parson was interested in Filipino folk music, which was incorporated into one of the pieces that made it into the final work, but much of the movement language came from watching videos and from Parson's yearslong connection to Byrne's musical style. "I am interested in the way people move," recalls Parson, and one gesture in particular caught her eye. It became the most odd, stylized movement in the show. "Imelda had this action that she would do with her butterfly sleeves, where she would flip them. Jose [Llana, who played Ferdinand Marcos] told me that his mom used to do it, too. It was a way to get the sleeve to stand up in the right way and it became a central gesture in the dance for 'Please Don't.' That's verbatim material, flicking her dress. ... A vanity, a peacock gesture. A gesture of self-grooming."

From the very literal proofing of a dress, Parson gave Ruthie Ann Miles a germinal phrase: a flick of the wrist slightly above her head. There is no reason that the audience would understand it to have originated from that necessity of couture, but it had an undefinable weirdness, something so "spot-on-Imelda Marcos" that it didn't really matter what it actually meant. Miles noted her own interpretation of how the gesture could have been read and how it fed her character choices: "Like inviting money in and chasing evil spirits out. And it's just—it's like nothing ... just flicking her fingers." The "sleeve poof dance" in fact adorns the poster, the psychedelic image of Miles with one hand grasping the mic and the other derisively flicking away.

Jose Llana talks of Parson's movements as creating an overriding energy in addition to a choreography. For those who do not know her unique physical vocabulary, there is something almost akin to miming. Llana described the choreographer and her assistants breaking down the movement into easily digestible phrases: "machine gun," "whack a mole," "strawberry picker," "kitty kitty." "But when you see everyone doing it in

FIGURE 6.2 *Ruthie Ann Miles and cast in* Here Lies Love. *Courtesy Joan Marcus.*

unison and then you see it in the context of the show, it's fascinating. If I try to explain it the way that I understand it, it's not going to be same that someone else might see it."

How much did Parson think about the audience in the creation of her work? It was a full disco, after all, with the audience dancing in and among the actors the whole time. None at all, she said. Her job was to come up with over twenty dances and Timbers would integrate the audience. She did suggest the incorporation of a camera with live feed so that Llana's Ferdinand Marcos could venture into the crowd and be followed by television cameras that would broadcast his image on screens around the theater.

The other major contributor to the show was its dramaturg, Oskar Eustis. There were many meetings with Timbers, Parson, and Eustis and some of the feedback gave rise to song rewrites and the creation of entirely new numbers. So, while Eustis is not a trained dancer and didn't directly give Parson notes, his choices and suggestions for new directions certainly influenced her work. But he offered more than that. Oskar Eustis is a mover. If there is music in a room, especially rock music, he cannot help but move. Parson remarks:

> If you are a dance person, you read bodies, and particularly in a show like that where the audience is standing, so they can dance whenever they want. So, I would observe when and how the audience would dance. I saw when they were dancing, I saw when they were not dancing and wished they would dance—and when Oskar was in the house, would

observe Oskar, who loves to dance! He was a great litmus for how things were working. And then I would take these observations to make the stage choreography more kinetic.

With an artistic team that worked together about as smoothly as possible, with a concept for a disco musical, and with a producer willing to assist in its development, the next step was gathering a cast. Jordan Thaler and Heidi Griffiths had a challenge, as they do in any development workshop. One, it was necessary that most of the actors be Filipino and specific to the world that Byrne, Timbers, and Parson were creating. They all needed to be dancers, rock stars really, who exuded charisma. Workshops are also challenging because, by their very nature, things change; scenes and songs are written out, characters expand or are eliminated altogether. Most actors going into a workshop know those risks, but the slow development of new work can be a stressor on their career. Do you stick with the tortoise speed of a new musical with world famous musicians, or jump ship when a surer and more lucrative gig comes along? Many in the cast, including Ruthie Ann Miles and Jose Llana, stayed with the show throughout its development. Others, like Conrad Ricamora, came in later when it became clear that a newly developed Ninoy Aquino would be necessary.

***

Ruthie Ann Miles was terrified when she showed up to her audition. She struggles terribly with stage fright and notes that many of her earlier big works allowed her to hide. When she was in a national tour of *Annie,* she wore a wig and disappeared into the ensemble. In John Doyle's revival of *Sweeney Todd,* she played the accordion and flute and was happy to hide behind her instrument. In her breakout role in *Avenue Q* in 2011, the hit off-Broadway musical by Robert Lopez and Jeff Marx, she got to hide behind a puppet, performing as the character Christmas Eve. So, when her agents sent her to an audition for a strange workshop production associated with David Byrne, she was perfectly happy to see that it was for a part in the ensemble. The actors had no idea what they were getting into. In those early auditions/workshops they were rolling around TV carts, being told to pretend they were projections and speakers, while Alex Timbers and Chris Giarmo (Parson's associate) helped along with instruction and training. Miles remembers turning to Llana and asking, "What is this? What exactly are ... what is this?"

Miles is not a trained dancer—her upbringing is as a musician—so when they took her aside and told her they were going to give her something else to work on, she was certain she was done. In fact, they asked if she would sing some songs for the character of Imelda. David Byrne and Alex Timbers were pushing the shy performer into the center of the spotlight. She grew up in Hawaii and so knew something of the Marcoses, but like so many people, it was a recollection of lots of money and shoes. The audition workshop went well and, even though she didn't quite know what she was getting into, she was cast as the lead in David Byrne and Fatboy Slim's buzzy new musical.

Jose Llana, who played Ferdinand Marcos, has had a long relationship with The Public Theater. He had his first Broadway gig when he was nineteen years old in a production of *King and I* (1996). One year later, his agent sent him to an audition for the George C. Wolfe-directed production of Leonard Bernstein's *On the Town* at the Delacorte Theater in Central Park. He scored the part of Gabey and within one year had a Broadway credit and feature at the Delacorte under his belt. In addition to other productions, Griffith and Thaler went to him for many readings and workshops. He performed again in Central Park in The Public Works production of *Twelfth Night* (2016).

In 2011, upon the premature closing of a Broadway show, *Wonderland*, Llana was told of a mysterious show about Imelda Marcos that was supposed to be auditioning at The Public. He had his agent send him to read for Aquino. Filipino-American, Llana's parents were fiercely anti-Marcos activists and so when he was asked to read the role of Ferdinand he thought, "ok *great*." Paralleling Miles's memory, Llana noted that the rehearsal/audition at NYU was just bizarre. Llana was put onstage with a camcorder and asked to sing into the camera, while people danced around him. But from the mayhem of those early rehearsals came a couple of showings for an audience of about thirty people. They moved it to PS-122 for another set of showings and then, by the summer of 2012, a fuller production at Mass MoCA. The editing, adding, and trimming kept coming. Llana recalls:

> I remember the day it happened where Alex comes to say you know, "so Oskar was here yesterday. He has really great points, really great things to say. We're going to cut these songs." And the first time you hear that, you're like "ugh, whose song is getting cut?" You know? And then we're going to add a song for Aquino. He needs a bigger—he needs a bigger entrance song.
> ...
> But it was one of those things where we were all really tired and we're like, "oh no, is the show in real trouble. Is this bad? Is this a bad thing?"
> ...
> And I tell you, two days later when those two songs were cut and then Conrad came in with the new song, it was so—we're like "oh, we're getting to the point. We're getting to what we need—what the audience wants to hear right now."

By the time *Here Lies Love* arrived at The Public, it had gone through exhaustive research, years of revising, and a decade of work from David Byrne. Eustis says that it was one of his favorite works of his tenure at The Public: "We all worked really beautifully together. I thought the development process on that was, as far as I was concerned, just about ideal." It was extremely popular, received wide critical acclaim, and was extended several times. Critics took note of the contradictions, the incongruity of what was happening in the telling of the story. Ben Brantley in the *New York Times* pointed to the "insidiously infectious" songs that feel like the "aural equivalent of amyl nitrate."[2] When the ugly lights came up, audiences left the theater with vastly different takes. Llana recalled, "There were people who came up to Ruthie and me in the lobby of The Public Theater and said, 'thank you. You presented Marcos and Imelda with such sexiness and showed the world just how amazing they were.' I'm like 'did you see the same show that we just did?' People see what they want to see." Miles, too, recounted that the Marcoses' grandchildren came to the show, gaze affixed on her the entire time: "They wanted to know what was being said about their grandmother. And afterwards they said to me when they introduced themselves, 'thank you for telling the truth. Thank you for telling the story of our family.' You see what you want to see because this show does not demonize her, but it certainly doesn't romanticize her."

The production was created in the midst of the Obama years. Following four years of a celebrity/talk show president in the United States, the regime of Rodrigo Duterte in the Philippines, the 2022 election of Marcos's son as president, and the ever-present and nefarious elevation of social media driven culture furthering political apathy, *Here Lies Love* and Byrne's interest in the politics of celebrity power feels awfully prescient. Jesse Green wrote in *Vulture*, "The horrible truth beneath the coyness and danceable beat of *Here Lies Love* isn't so much about the Marcoses as about our vague and distant response to them."[3]

The show did exactly what Byrne set out to do, and that is why it may be one of the strongest illustrations of the development of a concept musical in the contemporary history of The Public, even in American theater history broadly. He created a contradiction, which is his wont. It came from an obsession of a rock star known for musical passion and frenetic oddity. It was augmented by movement that was stilted, stylized, and also deeply authentic, by a famous choreographer with a long professional relationship with the musician. It was helmed by the director of the moment, who happened to specialize in immersive storytelling. It was produced by a company that was in no hurry to get it to the stage, but rather wanted to create a generative process of editing and developing. And yet, of the three musicals considered in these chapters, it is, without a doubt, the least well known.

Here Lies Love may have been a transformative musical, but it was drowned out, pushed beyond the spotlight in the Eustis years for several reasons. Certainly, one was the fact that *Fun Home* and *Hamilton* were

---

[2]Ben Brantley, "A Rise to Power, Disco Round Included," *New York Times*, April 23, 2013.
[3]Jesse Green, "Theater Review: Imelda Is More Than a Woman in 'Here Lies Love,'" *Vulture*, May 1, 2014.

quick on its heels, and while they weren't as theatrically inventive as *Here Lies Love*, they were brilliantly conceived and destined to take the focus of American musical theater for several years. Most importantly, though, *Here Lies Love* never made financial sense. Eustis recalls:

> We had this beautiful hit show and people tried like crazy to figure out some way to make money out of it and they just couldn't because it was designed unbelievably labor intensively. It was never going to pay for itself. But we could do that because we were non-profit. And of course, I don't care. I think David and Alex ended up quite frustrated that it couldn't transfer, but for me it's like, we did a great show, we did what we were supposed to do. And I loved the show.

Byrne and Timbers were eager to see the production transfer to Broadway, especially since its popularity seemed enormous. Movie stars and celebrities—Tyra Banks, Patti LuPone, Kevin Kline—flocked to the LuEsther, there to dance, sing, and sweat with the former first couple of the Philippines. The problem was the same as it had been all along. Broadway is not made to be a disco; tourist audiences cannot flock to a show in which they have to stand, move, and dance for ninety minutes. And, most critically, try as they might, the producers at The Public couldn't find a venue in Manhattan that could do it. Circle in the Square was considered, and plans drawn up, but scrapped when they realized they would have to cut through the grid. And so, it was decided that a commercial producer, Joey Parnes, would pick it up and continue the search for a venue. Mandy Hackett recalls that they faced the exact same problems that Byrne had discovered years before: "I always believe if this were ten years ago we would have found—there was just so many more interesting spaces in New York. ... This city is really changing, and all those cool, old clubs and nightclubs and spaces that you could have put a show like *Here Lies Love* into [were gone]. ... We wanted to maintain the whole design and structure of the show. We looked for months." In an unusual decision, rather than transfer to Broadway, *Here Lies Love* transferred back to The Public. Parnes produced the show one year later at 425 Lafayette.[4]

In retrospect, it was a bad idea. On the one hand, thousands more people would get to see the show, but on the other, having a commercial producer operating a show within the walls of The Public Theater felt wrong. It placed the nonprofit Public in the position of landlord to the commercial producer, and the time between the original show and the "transfer" was a year, causing the show to lose some momentum. Even with Eustis's Marxist embrace of contradiction, this arrangement didn't work. Tension abounded between the staff and the producers, and actors resented the unhappy comparison between the family nature of the first year and the corporate nature of the

---

[4]Parnes had a close relationship with the Public, serving as an executive producer at the company in the 1990s and as an interim executive director in 2011.

second. In addition, it was an expensive show, with a large cast, technical complexities, video projection, and a standing audience. It would require a lot of marketing energy since the subject seemed odd and distant, perhaps, to the average theater attendee. Mostly, though, they could not really figure out how to increase capacity, which made it a tough Broadway sell. It did have professional productions in Seattle and at the National in London. David Korins, the set designer for the original production, figured out a way to significantly increase the seating capacity for the production at Seattle Rep by essentially "decking up" the stage and jutting it onto the main stage apron, thereby making the horseshoe of the mezzanine front row seats to the club. It showed that it could be done, making it still a Broadway option. Indeed, there is consistent chatter that it could, one day, come back. Annie-B Parson said that that dream of a remount, however unrealistic, would be ideal: "David ... wrote music that told the story that was necessary to tell, music that was great. ... I can hear the tropes of musical theater, the melody lines, the stuff that you'd expect ... he didn't do that, and it was groundbreaking. The reason I want it to come back is so that people get inspired to write differently. I think it was a hugely important piece theatrically and musically."

* * *

Is there a contradiction in a Public-created musical operating in 425 Lafayette under a commercial producer? The answer, as with all things at The Public, is complicated. The lines consistently get blurred. In fact, the "conflict" between downtown success and Broadway lights is as old as The Public Theater's existence. Joe Papp was clearly drawn to the lights of Broadway, even as he tooled around New York taking Shakespeare to the people. The mission was always clear with him. At the end of his life, his great pride was that he expanded opportunity to Black, Asian, and Hispanic populations. But, of course, Broadway and commercial success isn't the antithesis of progressive and inclusive theater. In fact, it can be a helpful tool in spreading the mission of "one public." Reflecting on his immediate predecessor, George C. Wolfe, a man who has been nominated for sixteen Tony Awards (inclusive of producing)—from *Jellies Last Jam* to *The Iceman Cometh* to *Gary: A Sequel to Titus Andronicus*—Eustis comments:

> I think George understood correctly that there's a cultural impact to shows being on Broadway that can't be matched by being on any other stage, because it's just so visible and just so prominent. It's a huge megaphone for the work. So, it *does* mean something to get a show to Broadway.
>
> The only correction I'll make is I'm trying very hard not to push shows to Broadway. I'm trying very hard to let Broadway take the shows that want to be there. Because it isn't our mission to produce on Broadway. It's our mission to produce shows that have a wide enough appeal that

some of them will be manifested by being on Broadway. It means we have to get our hands dirty with the commercial system.

This means partnering with people who profit off of the theater in an entirely different way—the Marxist contradiction that he alluded to—and buying into a capitalist system, driven by profit. He insists that The Public must have distance from it but, "if we're going to actually impact that culture, we cannot completely turn ... and segregate ourselves from it."

And so, it is well to look at what productions actually *did* go on to commercial transfer in the years of the Eustis artistic directorship (as of 2022). They are generally plays that live up to the mission—plays that aren't "pushed" there, but make good sense to the goals of the company: *Well* (2006), a play by Lisa Kron about mothers and daughters and family health histories; *Passing Strange* (2008), Stew and Heidi Rodewald's concert exploration of Black identity; *Hair* (2009), the revival of the original rock musical that made The Public famous; *The Merchant of Venice* (2010), the Al Pacino-driven transfer of the Park show; *Bloody Bloody Andrew Jackson* (2010), the controversial rock concert telling of the story of the American president; *Fun Home* (2015); *Hamilton* (2015); *Eclipsed* (2016), a devastating production about sexual violence during the Liberian civil war; *Sweat* (2017); *Latin History for Morons* (2017), John Leguizamo's solo show about, well, Latin history; *Sea Wall/A Life* (2019), a monologue play featuring Jake Gyllenhaal and Tom Sturridge; *Girl from the North Country* (2020 and 2022), a Bob Dylan jukebox musical about Depression-era Michigan; the revival of *for colored girls ...* (2022); and Jordan E. Cooper's *Ain't No Mo'* (2022), a play that explores what would happen if Black Americans chose to move to Africa. All are examples of plays that in some way buy in to a pattern of workshops, tryouts, and multiple stops in the development process.

Some at the company actively worry about losing their soul to Broadway and its celebrity culture. It took Lupita Nyong'o winning an Oscar before *Eclipsed* was produced, and then transferred. *Sea Wall/A Life* happened mainly because Gyllenhaal was involved. Glenn Close's *Mother of the Maid* wasn't groundbreaking, but it starred Glenn Close. Leguizamo had been doing *Latin History* for decades and its director, Tony Taccone, had been friends with Eustis for many years. It was a good play, but people came to see Leguizamo. It is easy to lose sight of a basic question: Is popularity and celebrity buy-in a problem? Of course not. Being on-mission really refers to the ongoing need to find balance between revenue, quality, and social good. That is the balance that Eustis, Hackett, and the rest continuously evaluate.

* * *

Oskar Eustis smartly surrounds himself with the best artists in the business and consciously uses all advantages he may have as the head of the most prominent theater in America. His success is not luck. He is sharp and shrewd. But when there is a confluence of good happenstance as well—when a show meets a moment and is thus seen by a far greater number of people—important things can happen. Ambassador Samantha Power, ever eloquent about the theater, vividly remembers seeing *Eclipsed* at The Public. She recalls that of the one hundred and ninety-three countries in the UN, only thirty-seven were represented by women when she was the American UN ambassador. She brought them to see the show.

> The Liberian ambassador to the UN was one of the attendees that night, along with these other women ambassadors. ... She grew up in Liberia and had heard accounts of sexual violence, but again, by the time you're hearing the accounts ... it's the verdict. It's the results. You've escaped or your relative has died or you've been raped multiple times, and you were telling it in whatever way you have learned to tell your story.
>
> But what theater does is, it brings you in at the beginning, and you are living it with these women ... and you watch them learning to regularize this kind of ritual, of rape, of sexual slavery.
>
> And after the play, she said, "You know, I lived it, I knew it, I've talked to people. Until I saw this play, I think I never really understood what sexual violence meant to the people it's being perpetrated against."
>
> And how could she? How could any of us, when unless you're living it forward, there is something inevitably stilted, however authentic. I mean, everything she heard or I might have heard would have been accurate, but by not being in real time, it lacks some of that ability to bring you in and really—not experience, mercifully—but feel as though you are internalizing some version of what they're actually experiencing.

How do you tell a story that is essential, that forces a broader group of people to lean in and listen and hear and feel? More could feel the power of *Eclipsed* on Broadway at the 800-seat Golden Theatre. But moving a show is not always the right path, even though Eustis may well be known for the hits that land uptown. While it is no coincidence that some of those shows represented the best of The Public, his resistance to the assumption that transfers are necessary comes from a real place of frustration about the lack of nuance in the expectation. So much of what he and his coproducers see as the essential in art is represented in the great successes that somehow don't *need* to make a transfer; plays that perhaps may have a greater life at 425 and in regional theaters around the country. *Here Lies Love* didn't go to the next New York step, a step that is unfortunately seen as the pinnacle of American theater. But the story of its creation mirrors others that did. And *that* is the point. The Public Theater is the American theater laboratory that every so often captures the attention of a great many people.

Waiting in the wings was a little girl named Alison who, with her ring of keys, was ready to change the world.

7

Listen to Me

FIGURE 7.1 *Beth Malone, Sydney Lucas, and Emily Skeggs. The three Alisons in Fun Home. Courtesy Joan Marcus.*

The Radio Studio Music Hall stage for the Tony Awards in 2015 was about as psychologically far from Alison Bechdel's Vermont artist studio as one could get. From the peace of her now iconic drawing desk in the countryside to the 6,000-seat home of the Rockettes and an international television audience of millions, *Fun Home* had become an unexpected theater hit. Bechdel sat in the audience that evening and watched the story of her youth, a tale about her and her father confronting their sexual orientation in 1980s Pennsylvania, win out over *An American in Paris*, and take home the biggest prize in American theater: Best Musical. Her friends and collaborators, Jeanine Tesori and Lisa Kron, won in the category of Original Score, Sam Gold for Direction, and Michael Cerveris for Lead Actor (incidentally, Ruthie Ann Miles won that year for Featured Actress in *The King and I*).

"I did not know what I was in for. I didn't really grasp what Broadway meant," Bechdel says. "I remember one day coming out of the theater, I was actually literally mobbed by schoolgirls. This whole bunch of kids in plaid jumpers who had just seen the show and they all wanted my autograph. That sort of thing never happened to me before."

In so many ways, it was a breathtaking moment. *Hamilton* would win the Tony Award the next year and its success would crowd out the conversation for years to come, and likely cement it as the most important show of its era. *Fun Home*, though, should be seen as transformative in many of the same ways, and is demonstrative of a major leap for American theater. While Lin-Manuel Miranda was able to tell the story of the founding of America through the eyes and bodies of people of color and immigrants, powerfully demonstrating to its viewers and listeners that history and legacy belong to everyone, regardless of race and class, Bechdel, Kron, and Tesori did the same thing for an ordinary young woman named Alison, and for women all over the country and world. In that way, *Fun Home* dared to say that the story of a young lesbian learning who she is and how she fits into society was worthy of deep consideration. They trained the theatrical spotlight on women in a way that had not yet been done on the biggest stages in America. That *that* only happened in 2015 should make *Fun Home* a social and cultural touchstone akin to *Hamilton*. By 2021, Bechdel noted that she was still, seven years later, trying to assimilate the whole experience of watching her life story play out for legions of Broadway spectators: "It felt unreal. It felt surreal. It still does. I'm always trying to figure out what was this moment in the culture that enabled that to happen."

The stories of *Fun Home* and *Hamilton* share more than simply their transfers from The Public to Broadway and their subsequent wins at the Tony Awards. Part of their success was due to some sort of cultural moment that allowed them to flourish and become a focus of American theater for a brief moment in time or, in the case of *Hamilton*, for years. Perhaps America in 2015 had arrived at a point in time in which a story about a young lesbian coming out and discovering her unique, autonomous self was somehow ready for a national spotlight. In 2016, at the tail end of the presidency of

Barack Obama, maybe the country and the world were particularly focused on telling stories of diversity and turning their attention to new readings of history. And yet, both shows arrived at a time of great turmoil and fractious debate and anger related to social justice and progressive politics. Both plays were running on Broadway when Donald Trump ran for the presidency, propelling a new politics of fakery, division, and hate-fueled outrage. The story is not as simple as we might like to believe and likely needs even more time to be fully folded into the broader history of American theater.

And so, focusing too much attention on an ethereal zeitgeist as a reason for the recognition and success of *Fun Home* and *Hamilton* misses a perhaps simpler point; both productions took extraordinary work and years of pushing by some of the strongest voices in American theater to get to that stage at Radio City Music Hall. It is the contention here, too, that those productions were able to find their legs and their wings due to a mode of development at The Public Theater that had become, by 2015, a fairly well-oiled process of artist support. Add to that, the graphic novel of *Fun Home* was and is a cult classic, beautifully drawn, and evocatively captured, and *Hamilton* was penned and conceived in the mind of a wunderkind of American musical theater. How could they miss? In fact, they could have "missed" disastrously; there was no assurance that *Fun Home* and *Hamilton* would lead to Broadway success. Looked at from a different angle: A musical about a young queer woman in Pennsylvania and a hip-hop concert about the original secretary of the treasury—how could they not flop? It is here, then, that we need to take Eustis at his word: "The Public has never made a top priority of transferring any show." In both of these cases, the Theater and its artistic director saw something unique and thus invested time to see what might work, with no assurances. The following pages uncover just a bit of that process: from the writing and laboratory versions of *Fun Home* to the discussions at The Public about how the design of Lin-Manuel Miranda's musical creation could be realized at the Newman Theater and then on to other locations around the world.

The *Fun Home* Laboratory

In a 1985 comic strip called *Dykes to Watch Out For*, Alison Bechdel identified a problem in American filmmaking: women on screen are massively outnumbered by men, they rarely talk to each other, and, when they do, they generally talk about men. From that original strip, the "Bechdel Test" has grown to be a well-known judge of gender progress in American filmmaking. Essentially, "passing" the test means that a film (or play, in this case) features the stories of women and their lives, not only in relation to men.

While Bechdel and many others had been calling attention to the problem for a long time, even by the time that *Fun Home* premiered, the situation was just as acute. Indeed, by 2019, a USC Annenberg study of 1,200 popular movies showed that most films still did not come close to passing the Bechdel Test. Women accounted for about 30 percent of the speaking roles, 11 percent were women of color and 11 percent were over the age of forty-five.[1] While shocking when starkly laid out, any astute consumer of film knows this to be true and a blight on American entertainment.

Theater has not fared much better. Any number of studies confirm this, and have for quite some time. The glaring disparities, in fact, accounted for some of the early conversations between Lisa Kron and Oskar Eustis. Playwrights Julia Jordan and Marsha Norman famously published "The Count" in 2015, which showed gender inequality across American theater to be dismal.[2] In 2018, the League of Professional Theater Women published a report that focused particularly on Off-Broadway institutions, showing that female playwright representation accounted for 29–37 percent of plays over a three-year period with similar inequity in most design positions (stage management and costume design positions, as reflected in other studies, remained disproportionately held by people identifying as female).[3] This would not have been a surprise to Kron, who had been encouraging Eustis for years to increase representation at The Public. A year after her 2010 production of *In the Wake,* she took a meeting with Eustis to discuss her version of a count, and he agreed about the problem. But the proof of the commitment had to be in the producing. The years 2011–12, remarkably, featured no female playwrights. The 2012–13 season presented works by Lisa Kron, Jeanine Tesori, Sybille Pearson, Vanessa Redgrave, and Dominique Morisseau. It was a step.

Gail Papp, too, has noted the broad challenge that The Public has had over the years in producing female playwrights and employing women directors. In the early days of The New York Shakespeare Festival, there was one notable exception to a lineup of male directors. Gladys Vaughan directed *Richard II* in 1961 and codirected *King Lear* and *Merchant of Venice* with Joe Papp in 1962, the premiere year of the Delacorte. While she became a staple of early Public Theater directing, only a small handful of other women have ever directed at the Delacorte; among them, Jane Howell, JoAnne Akalaitis, Phyllida Lloyd, Lear deBessonet, and Laurie Woolery. At 425, the numbers have been better but still reflect a major problem in New York and country-wide. Gail Papp recalls, "I chafed on that a hell of a lot, it's one of the reasons I divided part of my energy into finding directors as well as playwrights. Hopefully I thought maybe playwrights would bring along the directors, and they sometimes did."

---

[1] Dr. Stacy Smith, Marc Choueiti, Dr. Katherine Pieper, Kevin Yao, Ariana Case, and Angel Choi, *Inequality in 1,200 Popular Films: Examining Portrayals of Gender, Race/Ethnicity, LGBTQ and Disability from 2007 to 2018*, Annenberg Foundation, September 2019.
[2] "The Count" 2.0 came out after the 2017 season demonstrated some improvement, but marginally. https://www.dramatistsguild.com/advocacy/the-count.
[3] *American Theater* editors, "Study Shows Women Still Under-Employed Off-Broadway," *American Theater Magazine,* May 2018.

Eustis has made great strides to right this inequity. Public Theater seasons of late have featured the work of directors like Marissa Wolf, Jo Bonney, Carrie Cracknell, deBessonet, Woolery, Leigh Silverman, and Candis C. Jones, among others. But, to have to name a handful of exceptions truly highlights a problem that "The Count" continually reminds us of.

Similarly with playwrights, the Theater has had to make strides in the past twenty years to accomplish what should have been obvious for a company with a mission like The Public. The female playwrights who have attained a national presence from work that they have done at The Public are, as with directing, few and far between, though that has changed quite a bit in the Eustis years. Some of America's most accomplished authors have seen their work at The Public, including Suzan-Lori Parks, Lynn Nottage, Julia Cho, Shaina Taub, Sarah Burgess, Danai Gurira, Rinne Groff, Kron, and Tesori. It is also without question that the Theater and the industry in America have broadly recognized the problem, even if they have been very slow to evolve. When The Public returned to production in the 2021–2 season, two productions, *Cullud Wattah* (by Erika Dickerson-Despenza, directed by Candis Jones) and *Suffs* (by Shaina Taub, directed by Leigh Silverman), a new musical about American suffragists, were focused on female stories with female artistic leads. Both were received as highlights of the season and widely critically acclaimed. However, more plays in the season were directed by men.[4]

The problem with counts and charts is that, as demonstrative as they can be about inequalities, they rarely get at the difficult challenge of illuminating the weight of a problem, especially in the reception and perception of the challenge; that is, optics. This assessment of gender parity in directing and playwrighting does not even begin to address the transgender community and its representation, or lack thereof. This was precisely at issue with a 2016 production of *Southern Comfort* that will be considered in Chapter 8.

While one could look at the history of The Public and identify many extraordinary women associated with the company, including Gail Papp herself, that misses a critical and ineffable issue that is far bigger than The Public Theater: What are the plays and musicals that continue to grab the attention of audiences, critics, and awards? Even as The Public had, by 2015, showed a stronger commitment to female playwrights and directors, when Jeanine Tesori and Lisa Kron accepted their award that year at the Tonys for best score, they were lauded as the *first* female team to achieve the honor. In other words, a "first" in a seventy-year-old award ceremony was celebrated as progress for an industry whose audiences are about 70 percent female.[5] In 2017, when Nottage's *Sweat* and Paula

---

[4]*The Vagrant Trilogy* by Emerging Writer's Group alumna Mona Monsour also was staged in that season.
[5]Broadway League publishes a report yearly: https://www.broadwayleague.com/research/research-reports/.

Vogel's *Indecent* were nominated for Best Play at the Tonys, it was J. T. Rogers's *Oslo* that went home with the top prize. The vagaries of taste aside, it was well noted that the shut-out of two of the finest female playwrights in America was odd, especially when *Sweat* went on to win the Pulitzer.[6]

Perhaps this is a labored way (albeit necessary) to underline a critical point: *Fun Home* was an important musical—for The Public, for Broadway, for women, and for the LGBTQ+ community. In Bechdel, Kron, and Tesori, *Fun Home* had a writing team that represented not only three of the most important artists in America, but three people who have been integral in conversations about gender equality for years. When Kron was commissioned to write a musical based on Alison Bechdel's graphic novel, she knew immediately that she wanted to bring in Jeanine Tesori. Bechdel, who had no experience with theater, was able to let go of her work and trust Kron and Tesori to transform it for the stage. "I knew that Lisa would get this story right. She wasn't going to make it all glossy or flossy or stupid. And she didn't."

The real Alison Bechdel stayed away from the process even as she occasionally had some check-ins with Tesori and Kron. She remembers in late 2010 being sent a CD with rough versions of a first draft of the score and script. The script was complicated and hard to follow, but as soon as she listened to the songs, she *got* it, and understood the direction in which they were going. She recalls that it was magical, and she immediately sent a dozen red roses each to Tesori and Kron. "I'd never done anything that ... demonstrative before in my life. But it felt like the only real gesture that I could give back to them. I felt just so—so seen—and validated."

Sam Gold, who in 2012 was already a well-known director of Annie Baker's *Circle Mirror Transformation* (2009) and Dan LeFranc's *The Big Meal* (2012), was slated to direct *Fun Home*. He found out about the work when he, Tesori, and Kron attended the Ojai Playwrights Conference in California. He remembers asking them: "You're taking a memoir written in the style of a graphic novel and adapting it as a musical theater piece? *How?*" He had no sense that there was any place for him in the process; he was mostly interested in it as a fan of Tesori, Kron, and Bechdel. Months later, they called him up and asked if he'd be interested in working on it. He jumped at the chance.

Like *Here Lies Love*, *Fun Home* demonstrated the power and possibility of The Public workshopping process and in-the-moment development. Kron had received a Mellon Grant to begin work on the play at Arena Stage in Washington, DC. When that production fell through, she was able to

---

[6]Three women have won the Tony for Best Play: Francis Goodrich, Yasmina Reza (twice), and Wendy Wasserstein. Joining Kron and Tesori for wins in musical theatre writing and score are Betty Comden, Lynn Ahrens, Lisa Lambert, Cyndi Lauper, and Anaïs Mitchell.

transfer to the Lab and help pay for its original workshop staging. This was critical since the writing and dramaturgy of *Fun Home* was so complex. The play exists in the mind of its central character, a middle-aged cartoonist named Alison Bechdel. As Alison sits at her table, drawing her cartoon, the existence and presence of a "Small Alison," a "Medium Alison," and her family are theatrically brought to life. While it eventually worked on stage, the presence of three versions of the central protagonist, most existing in memory, created a muddy script. Kron has said as much, noting that the character was overwritten from the beginning, and it wasn't until David Zinn's set concept was developed that the character was fully unlocked. The set consisted of a writing table placed at the side of what would become something of a "memory room." Adult Alison was able to walk around the set with a pad and record her past life in drawing, while projections and furniture were added to flesh out the memory. In that way, time and place could be received as fluid. And yet, in the beginning, many of the people helping develop the workshop of *Fun Home* thought that Adult Alison, the cartoonist, should be taken out. "It's a coming out story," several suggested. "Why are we focused on the adult version? She's not interesting."

Eustis attended many of the rehearsals once it got to The Public Lab and helped them chip away at the play. Like others, he was unsure of the Adult Alison character, but Kron and Tesori insisted on that narrative through-line, and they got their way. Kron was adamant: "I know she's not interesting yet. I don't know if we can make her interesting, but I dare you to show me what the story is without her. It doesn't exist. There is no *Fun Home* without her." Bechdel, too, says that *that* is the essence of her story. "The book is about becoming an artist. It's about what it's like to be engaged in the creative process. I knew that Lisa had, herself, been grappling with the problem in her own way and then came up with this new parallel version of everything. And it just felt—I don't know, sort of wondrous."

The early workshops revolved around this problem. Three Alisons had to live in the world and equal weight had to be given to each. But there couldn't be too much exposition. It had to be able to become a play not just about coming out, but about a middle-aged woman dealing with the struggle of writing *that* story. What we see, then, is meta-theatrical in an extraordinary way. Can a musical really be about the author writing the story of the musical? Conceptually, it's a very odd place to start—a nostalgia piece, structured from a cartoon with no scenes. Kron recalls an early meeting with Tesori: "She said 'I cannot picture how this,' and she was holding the book, 'how this can become a musical.' And my heart just sank. And she said, 'and *that's* why I'm interested in it.'"

As with the Studio process described previously for *Cullud Wattah*, Public Lab was set up in a way that allowed for great latitude for change and adaptation. Over three weeks, the *Fun Home* team rehearsed on Tuesday, Wednesday, and Thursday and then performed for an audience on Thursday, Friday, and Saturday. They were creating new work, rehearsing it and showing it to an audience, adjusting and then representing it in the tiniest theater at The Public on an incredibly busy schedule. Gold recalls: "We were giving actors sheet music and they were hiding it in the props and trying to sing songs they'd learned that day, in front of an audience." Public Lab allowed for shows to be made in tandem with an audience, akin to the process of *Here Lies Love*, however under one roof and on a much tighter schedule. Gold recalled that it was not dissimilar to the way that he had worked before at the famed avant-garde company The Wooster Group, where he had been an assistant director. There, they made all of the performances in open rehearsals and did not mind—in fact relished—that they were making their unfinished work available for public viewing and critique. One week, Tesori came in with new songs for Beth Malone (Adult Alison) to learn at one o'clock in the afternoon for a workshop audience that night. While taxing for the performer, to be sure, that spontaneity can also be electric. Gold notes, "Don't be precious, show it to an audience. See how it's going. Cut it, change it, throw it out. Make it different the next day." That was the modus operandi of Public Lab.

If some were concerned with the fact that Adult Alison was uninteresting, it was in part because she was, perhaps, given too much weight in the early workshops. In the Lab production, they recreated Bechdel's writing studio on that tiny black box stage. The artists visited the studio, took pictures, and even copied the same green paint that she used on her floor. The Lab rehearsals showed that Adult Alison was important, but also that the three Alisons had to have equal importance and that the play would have to move through time, backwards and forwards, simultaneously. For those who have read the book and then seen the musical, that was a fairly major leap of understanding that finally made it clear how to create the multiple memory piece. What the Shiva audience did was show that merely by watching Adult Alison watch the unfolding of her life on stage, the audience would get the various levels of memory building and pained nostalgia. That was the thing that couldn't be understood in a script, but that came to life in the cartoon and, eventually, on the stage.

The two writers wrote seven or eight opening numbers in an attempt to set up the complicated framework for the musical. Nothing worked. Kron wrote and Tesori advised her on what could be a lyric and what could not. Kron recalled, "I'd write, write, write. She'd say, 'there's something here, there's something here.' We'd talk, talk. This back and forth would go on for weeks and little by little we'd home in on something." Tesori remembers that the opening number, "It All Comes Back," was impossibly complex because it felt like so much had to be conveyed so quickly. Frustratingly, what that created was a beginning that seemed too expository:

> I really, really thought that we needed to know more about the protagonist. I thought that we needed to place her in space and time, to understand why she was doing something in that typical opening, and it

turned out we didn't need it at all. And it took so many openings to find out that all she needed to do was come on stage, grab a ring of keys, sit down and start drawing, and then you hear a motif, and we were off. That was it.

The simple motif, followed by the ring of a bell. Adult Alison stands at her desk, Little Alison enters and sings to her father: "Daddy! Hey, Daddy, come here, okay? I need you. What are you doing? I said come here. You need to do what I tell you to do. Listen to me. Daddy!"[7] The meta-theatrical complexity melted away, as did any need to explain to the audience what was happening. It was clear. A woman watching her younger self identify her need to be seen, to be heard. She held a ring of keys, a symbolic element that foreshadowed the scene of her younger self singing "Ring of Keys," the coming-out anthem of the show, perhaps of the decade. These symbolic elements were further identified on Broadway, when Zinn's set became more fully realized by actually *paring down* the scenic elements. Furniture could rotate around on wheels, or raise and lower from trap doors in the stage, and the entire world could exist in the swirling mind of Adult Alison.

The discoveries of those interlocking worlds made the end of the show click. By the time that the audience had wound its way through the three stories of the "three" protagonists, the penultimate songs, "Telephone Wire" and "Edges of the World," packed a power that could only be appreciated once it was on its feet. Adult Alison, after watching and interjecting here and there into the story of her younger self, *becomes* her younger self, gets in a car (stylized, non-realistic), and joins her father Bruce (Michael Cerveris) for a drive in the countryside. They both sing past each other about their experiences, as they pass through a Pennsylvania landscape of youth and nostalgia. The two characters recognize, on different terms, that they are gay: "Telephone wire. Long black line. Telephone wire. Finely threaded sky. There's the pond where I went wading. … Say something! Talk to him! Say something! Anything!"

Even though it was a song that was written early in the process, it perfectly captured the moment of overlapping realities only after the intricacies of the dramaturgy were sorted out in Lab: father and daughter, center stage, singing a song both about nostalgia and being caught speechless in the present moment. Beth Malone now performing the role of Medium Alison; the father, now gone by suicide, played by the same character of memory. The worlds collide and it all makes sense. The audience invariably weeps.

Sam Gold established the casual nature of the Lab each night. He'd wear a silly hat, drink a beer, and tell the audience: "You're going to leave

---

[7] Lisa Kron and Jeanine Tesori, *Fun Home*, 2013, as with all other quotes from the play.

here and say God, that needs work, and you're going to be completely right." As Tesori recalled, it "de-snarked" the audience, and gave license for failure. Bechdel herself attended a couple of the Lab workshops in the Shiva. Both Kron and Tesori remember it going very badly at first, and Tesori says that she was mortified when Bechdel came to them and said, "What happened to the play?" Tesori: "I had to sit down because I had this feeling in my stomach that my pancreas had switched places with my liver, and I said to Lisa, 'I don't know what's happening,' and she said, 'You're having a panic attack.' And it was the worst feeling artistically—not in terms of true disasters, but it was an artistic disaster for me because I couldn't find my way out." Kron took it in stride, knowing that it was the first Lab production of the play, that it was textually a bit incoherent, and had a long way to go. But that sort of feedback was essential and every bit of nuance that they could wring out of the author was helpful. They emailed back and forth with Bechdel, to be sure they were getting details just right. Bechdel's family came to Lab workshops, too, and watching them watch the show was helpful to Kron and Tesori. While they knew that all of the dialogue was made up and that the story diverged from the full accuracy of their lives, their response was that the musical felt true to their experience. All of the creators affirmed that Public Lab allowed work to percolate, gave space for ideas to flop, and for others to take flight.

Bechdel was invited back to the Shiva late in the workshop process. By that time, the play had come together: "And that, too, was incredibly moving. I'm not a terribly overtly emotional person. But I did cry seeing that first version of the show. But Oskar put me to shame. I was sitting to the left of my partner, Holly. And Oskar was sitting next to Holly. And he apparently had been sobbing on her shoulder for the whole show."

After its successful development at the Lab, *Fun Home* returned to The Public Theater main stage season the following year. It moved to the Newman Stage, the same illustrious space that housed *A Chorus Line* so many years before, and played from September 2013 to January 2014. The following year, on March 27, 2015, it began previews at Circle in the Square Theater on Broadway. It ran until September 2016. It had to change dramatically to fit the much larger stages at the Newman and Circle, but the basic idea remained the same. Gold actually believed that the theater in the round at Circle was ideal for many of the discoveries that were made at the Lab, noting that the round staging, with rotating furniture, allowed the audience more access to multiple perspectives. In that sense, the literal stage nodded to the meta-theatricality of the script and the music, and put the audience in the mind of Adult Alison, in a swirl of memory.

Why did *Fun Home* work? Almost everyone I have talked to about the production has said something about its ability to meet a moment. Like *Here Lies Love*, it was also about compiling a team of creators that clicked in a way that no producer could ever predict. Mandy Hackett says, "I've never seen an artistic team pull together and do such good work in previews; and on *Fun Home* they had such a good relationship, they knew exactly what to do." The core of that was Tesori and Kron. They describe that they were able to push each other, to debate, to allow each other to be freer, to dare, and to take risks. Tesori has said that Kron taught her how to work with the moment in front of her and to respond to the ways things developed in the rehearsal room. "I eventually called it 'painting on the actors.' I would paint on them all the vocal work that we would do and (ask them to) come over to the piano, 'I want you to sing this,' in response to what they were doing on their feet." Painting on the actors, actually, is the best way to identify the process of *Fun Home* and the importance of a Public Lab, as it centers the artists and the immediate needs of the show before all else.

The Lab also gave Tesori time to convince Kron to push, to understand their fears and take risks. Kron was nervous about hitting a "lavender ceiling," not knowing what people would do when faced with a lesbian coming-out story on a national stage. She didn't want the work ridiculed. Tesori said: "Let's do it because the moment calls for it, and that I think is how change happens … the behavior happens and then the times catch up to it or the times allow the behavior to happen. It is a chicken and egg situation, but someone has to put it on stage, and it turns out that we were the ones to do it."

The time was right. On June 26, 2015, the Supreme Court upheld marriage equality for same-sex couples.

Historians like to look at trends and analyze "moments in time" and the "how" and "why" an event or movement comes to pass. *Fun Home* and *Hamilton* were an incredible one-two punch for The Public Theater. They won Tony Awards in consecutive years but also elevated social, gender, and racial issues in American theater as well as, if not better than, any other musical pairing in the American theater canon. Utterly different, they actually are of a piece. Mandy Hackett, looking back on the two, says: "They're really different, but at the same time there are such strong similarities in terms of the impulse to do all these things. And I'm saying, the impulse to connect people to a larger moment in our time."

Many of the plays of The Public that find success on Broadway meet that moment. A lesbian coming-out play set to music in a time that coincides with increased openness to equity for LGBTQ+ rights. A story of people of color and immigrants retelling the tale of the beginning of American democracy, just as the country basks in the glow of its first Black president and renewed conversations about race and the American stage. Every so often, though, lightning strikes, and those plays do much more than reflect the time; they meet the time, and become the guide in the deepening of the conversation. *Hamilton* did just that.

Constructing *Hamilton*

FIGURE 7.2 Hamilton *set rendering. Courtesy David Korins.*

The story of *Hamilton* has been told over and over again, and with each retelling there is more nuance and investigation into the reasons and pathways for its enormous success. By now, every theater lover can envision the famous image of Lin-Manuel Miranda, laying in a hammock by the ocean, enjoying Ron Chernow's *Alexander Hamilton*. Or we can hear Miranda at the Obama White House in 2009 singing what would be the opening song of the new musical he was composing. Though every high-profile artist who ever touched *Hamilton* can now use it as a theater calling card, the designers who brought the world to life are often less known to the public. If *Hamilton* altered the trajectory of musical theater and our views on casting and inclusivity, it is well to regard an oft-ignored part of the influence of that story and the cultural game changer. While Miranda's music is extraordinary, the dancing electric, and Chernow's story riveting, the elegance of the design of the show and its transferability propelled its success as well. Moving to Broadway was on the cards before *Hamilton* even reached opening night at The Public.[8]

---

[8] The definitive story of the making of *Hamilton* is Jeremy McCarter and Lin-Manuel Miranda's *Hamilton: The Revolution* (New York: Grand Central Publishing, 2016). My effort here is in no way to recreate the history of that show, though some of the stories told to me in the archive are also embedded in that comprehensive work. Rather, I here offer some insight related to its part of the broader story of technical theater dramaturgy and development at The Public Theater.

No one knows the complications and challenges of building for Broadway better than David Korins, who has had one of the most sterling design careers of any working New York designer. Korins designed *Passing Strange, Chinglish, Dear Evan Hansen, Here Lies Love, Beetlejuice,* and *Hamilton,* among many others. And, as addressed in Chapter 6, an acclaimed show with extraordinary and unique design doesn't always make it beyond The Public. In fact, overly unique design can actually inhibit a transfer.

Hamilton, though, was not nearly as complicated as *Here Lies Love* since Korins came to the project distinctly understanding the need for it to be representational, and to resist the urge to render the spaces realistically. He lobbied hard to get the *Hamilton* design job. He wanted it badly, and even though he was a design star before he was hired, he left nothing to chance. He had heard about the project years before he was brought in, first from its eventual director, Tommy Kail, who mentioned it to him back when it was simply known as *The Hamilton Mixtape.* Kail, Korins, Andy Blankenbuehler (choreography), Alex Lacamoire (composer), Paul Tazewell (costumes), and Lin-Manuel Miranda were all at the height of their artistic productivity when *Hamilton* was a glimmer in Miranda's eye. All of them, except Korins, were in the midst of another Broadway success story, *In the Heights,* at the same time that Korins was designing *Passing Strange* at Berkeley Rep, The Public, and then on Broadway. In 2008, *Heights* won the Best Musical Tony Award over *Passing Strange,* though the latter won for Best Book of a Musical.

Korins saw his group of contemporaries, all award season regulars, as his friends, and he wanted to work with them at The Public. He was clear about his interest and when the time came for The Public to put together its team, Ruth Sternberg called up Korins to interview with his friend, Kail. "And I remember saying to him in the meeting, some version of 'I'm not going to throw away my shot,' quoting the show. 'You've got to hire me for this, man.' And I felt young, scrappy and hungry, and I was like, 'we are like the founding fathers!' " By that time, he knew the music well, having listened to it over and over again, and he felt clear then that the show was going to be important in the annals of American theater history. He also knew that the commercial producer Jeffrey Seller was on board, as he had been with *In the Heights,* and so a Broadway production was likely. But first, the producing team wanted the play to find its legs at what Seller considered the "quintessential New York downtown theater laboratory."[9]

Knowing of a potential transfer would deeply influence Korins's design of *Hamilton,* and so questions revolved around creating a world that could move to other theaters. With that in the back of his mind, Korins had to also consider that he was to design a setting for a musical that was retelling of thirty years of American history with fifty-one songs in a cadence, intensity,

---

[9]Seller quoted in McCarter and Miranda, *Hamilton,* p. 103.

and speed that would be highly unusual for a typical musical theater audience member. How, then, does one even start with a design?

Obviously, the great gift that Miranda created was that it actually was reasonably easy to follow textually, and it was eventually helped, according to Korins, by Howell Blinkley's lighting that effortlessly carved up the space such that a single set could stand in for so many locations. Whereas *Here Lies Love* was highly focused on the disco aesthetic that was embedded in the music and David Byrne's conception of the ideas, *Hamilton* needed a set that was a backdrop, that allowed for the story to be told in front. It couldn't be simple, to be sure, but didn't necessitate something overly articulated either. Early in the process, Korins and his associate Rod Lemmon continuously sold Kail on the idea of a double turntable, which would become the main scenic gesture of the play. Not only would a turntable inside a turntable allow for furniture to smoothly move around the stage, Kail also saw it as symbolically relevant to the story that Miranda and Kail were telling: "My impulse for it was the fact that Hamilton and Burr kind of have this cyclical relationship. Hamilton was swept off the island by a hurricane. There was something poetic and cinematic. We would go in and out of time. It was a story about growth and the travel of the country." The director was not fully convinced and so asked Korins and Lemmon to come up with at least ten different moments in the show in which the double turntable would be effective. They did, and eventually everyone consolidated around the idea.

Kail and Blankenbuehler rehearsed around the "double donut" idea, and were surgical in their approach to the choreography. But for a show in which dance, rhythm, and movement are absolutely essential to the aesthetic, it was impossible to know how it was all going to come together until they actually had the double turntable to work with. The Public Theater producers, knowing this, allowed the company to come to the Newman Theater before technical rehearsals began so that they could give the stage a try. It did not go smoothly. Exactly how much the actual set could be used for choreography was not understood until they were on the stage and dealing with the hazards of multiple moving floors. The original choreography did not account for that, and the dancing and blocking was clumsy. Simply, the timing was off in the double donut. But after the trial run on the stage, Kail and Blankenbuehler could go back to the rehearsal room and reinvent the movement and staging of the show so that it could seamlessly work with the set design. Korins states: "I would say, out of all of the things that we are all most proud of about that show is the exemplary collaboration on that show, in which you don't know where the scenery ends and the directing and the choreography begins ... you don't know what is lighting ... what's Paul Tazewell's, what's mine. You just don't know."

The turntable influenced so much about what the show was and could be, and it developed into its permanent form that has been recreated all over the world. It isn't, though, a wildly scenic element. That's only to suggest that one doesn't look at the turntable; it literally propels the production in ways that are visual but is itself invisible. That could also be said for much of the design of the play since many of the other visual elements are remarkable for their role as "supporting character." There is no barricade à la *Le Misérables,* a landing helicopter à la *Miss Saigon,* or a wall of technology à la *The Curious Incident of the Dog in the Nighttime.* Most audiences do not leave *Hamilton* remarking on the complexity of the set, but rather the complexity of the show itself that is made possible by the integrated sets and costumes and lights. Korins: "Tommy said to me in one of our design meetings, this is not really a show about America's Founding Fathers. This is a show about the people who created the framework from which the country was built. And if you think about the set design for *Hamilton,* it is an aspirational kind of half-built space." Jumping off from that offer from the director, the set team created a tapestry of early American architecture; a structure that is not completed, merely a scaffold.

Oskar Eustis, too, offered thoughts on the set and his own dramaturgical nudges to the creators. When he saw what Kail and Korins were constructing, he mused that it was interesting that so many of the early carpenters that were flooding into New York at the time of the play were skilled ship builders. He suggested to Korins that that might be something they might like to lean on since what they had already brainstormed looked like a bow of a ship. It was a mini revelation. In addition to the bow of a ship, the designer was playing with ideas of rope and hemp and "kinetic and dynamic" movement: "The very first thing that one of the performers does when they come into the town square is pull up these big ropes and fly them up into the rafters. That's all Oskar. Oskar said to think about nautical influence."

The scaffolded nautical set created places for actors to play, to live, to dance, to sing. But it existed, like the musical itself, as a symbol: a metaphorical space that spoke to the *process* of building, of upward momentum and of aspirational thinking. A nautical setting of rope and wood and turntables that tells a story of an immigrant who washes into town, the victim of poverty, of a hurricane, and wanting to make a new start. In that light, the simple scaffold, like the turntable, contains worlds of imaginative impulse and perfectly blends deeply complex design thinking with a stage aesthetic that could ideally platform the intricate music and cadence that so worried Korins when he made his pitch.

That the original production didn't have a lot of money did not ultimately matter in the creation of the play. In fact, the design, like the titular character, had to be scrappy. The back wall of the original production was the back wall of the Newman Theater. The two turntables were borrowed from Hudson Scenic, with on-the-spot revisions and additions—"Frankensteined" together, says Korins. His daughters came to tech rehearsals, and they carved their initials on one of the beams at center stage. When the show moved to the Richard Rogers Theater on Broadway, that beam was taken uptown, too.

Since the stage at the Newman has a similar footprint to the playing space at the Rogers, the transfer wasn't all that hard. It had to get taller, slightly rescaled, a proscenium added, and a few other flourishes were embedded. Korins: "I always felt that performing that show at the Newman was like being in a roadside chapel and moving to the Richard Rodgers was like moving into a cathedral ... the message can be the same, it's just the physical structure and how it's supported." The original set from The Public Theater, a set that grew out of metaphor and symbol, is basically the same on Broadway and around the world. In fact, the initials of Korins's daughters are carved into the center beam of all of the versions of *Hamilton*.

Hamilton has the advantage of being able to be assessed through several iterations, including a "transfer" to film at the height of the Covid pandemic. Do those changes in location and modality affect the story that is being told, or does that same "roadside chapel" performance still shine through? Kail recalls being asked multiple times when the Disney+ version of *Hamilton* was released in the summer of 2020 how he was able to rescale the show to fit the film format. The short answer was that he didn't. In fact, the camera was able to build back the closeness and the proximity of the original production, and nothing really needed to be altered. "I never spoke to a single actor about that. That's how they were performing the show. They were performing the show in a way that would work in a 130-seat theater, or on the road in a 2,000-seat theater. And it also worked for camera, because they were interested in being honest in their storytelling and trusting the material. I mean, if you have good material, you're not going to have to put a lot of spin on the ball."

"Simplicity" is the opposite of "complexity" linguistically, but not scenically. That the *Hamilton* set was so seemingly simple and unobtrusive belies the detail, research, and time that went into its creation. While Korins and his team had a series of seminal fragments—base scenic ideas that they wished to play through—they were rigorous in getting the fine points precise. The musical features myriad locations that had to be distinguished clearly, and so extensive research of the lavish setting possibilities was crystallized down to a perfect fabric or an ideal piece of furniture. Korins: "There's a bench that is the entire location [so] that bench is gilded with a very specific turned leg."

Jay Duckworth, who created the props for The Public Theater version of *Hamilton*, recalls the determination to get specific elements as perfect as possible. This, he says, is often more important for the actor, who relies on small details to fill out their performance, than it is for an audience member who may never see the period-appropriate cursive on a small piece of parchment at the back of the stage. He recalls one moment in which Eliza Hamilton (Phillipa Soo) burns letters from her husband as she sings "Burn." A simple moment, perhaps. Except not. Rather than burn multiple letters and risk waste and danger, they designed a receptacle that had a separate compartment so that the actress only had to light one letter, and then place the others behind the partition. Even the one letter that burned had to be a carefully researched type of paper so that when it finished burning (for exactly two minutes and nine seconds, he remembers) the remnants and ash wouldn't fly up and float away causing a fire hazard. Duckworth: "So you have to cut down pieces of paper and check different weights. It's things like that that you have to think about. And then the candle that she walks off with—that's a hanging candle, so you have to do an extra ring on it, covered in leather, so that the heat of the candle doesn't burn her when she's picking the stuff up and taking it out." Nothing is simple.

Much of the color palate for *Hamilton* at The Public and at the Richard Rogers came from Paul Tazewell's bright costumes that purposefully bounced off the parchment color of Korins's set. Much like his design compatriots, Tazewell had had enough experiences at The Public to know that the process could be organic and develop in whatever way was needed. He designed costumes for Suzan-Lori Parks's *Venus* (1996), the Delacorte production of *Henry V* (1996), Kushner and Tesori's *Caroline, or Change* (2003), and Eustis's *Julius Caesar* (2017). When *Hamilton* started as a staged reading at The Public, Kail and Tazewell decided to use the costume stock at the Theater and fully clad the cast so that they could get a sense of what the production could eventually be. While not the full lab that *Fun Home* had been, every "version" of *Hamilton* influenced the final product. Tazewell: "At that point I wasn't sure if it was going to be jeans and T-shirts and sneakers or if it was going to be boots and breaches and corsets." It was trial and error. He originally focused on a neutral look, concentrating mostly on silhouette, saving color only to distinguish between the Americans and British—a practical storytelling choice.

As *Hamilton* moved from staged reading to full production on the Newman, Tazewell's costume design mirrored some of the representational choices of Korins's set. Rather than elaborate eighteenth-century flourishes, he designed a stripped-down version that wasn't overly fussy, so that one might subconsciously note a row of buttons without focusing on it. "It spoke to the fact that it's an American story, as opposed to, say, a French story. And I think that it also allowed for it to stay modern, so that modern audiences can engage with it and not get bogged down in the fact that it's a costume musical drama."

Like everything else, costumes were additive. Tazewell created a base level of neutrality for all of the actors that mirrored the parchment color of the world that had been established. As characters came forward and developed, he added color, from the green jacket that Hamilton wears when he becomes a politician to the ice blue dress worn by Eliza, a look that Tazewell believed conveyed a sober and sympathetic character. But it was not only the characters that the designers responded to, but also the actors who were bringing the characters to life for the first time. For a production as iconic as *Hamilton* now is, it is hard to separate what we know to be true about the show from the reality that these designers were coming to the script with utterly fresh eyes. American history itself was the greatest inspiration and, in a way, hindrance, since designers and performance had to forcefully break out of the historical frame. Daveed Diggs's Thomas Jefferson was one such breakthrough. At the staged reading and in early conceptions of the character, Tazewell notes that he was influenced by the *idea* of "Jefferson," collected from his research and the Romanticist paintings of George Trumbull. It didn't really work because Trumbull is decidedly not Diggs, and so Kail, Miranda, and Tazewell collectively decided to not be beholden by assumptions, and rather embrace what was in front of them. By celebrating Diggs's big persona, Jefferson became a contemporary celebrity, clothed in purple, triumphantly returning to America from his post in France. No wig was necessary. "What'd I miss?" asked Diggs's rock star Jefferson. "I've been in Paris meeting lots of different ladies. I guess I basically missed the late eighties."

Contrast that look with King George III. Simply from the standpoint of silhouette, the role had to be stodgy, impish, and immobile. While Tazewell eventually steered away from old portraiture when it came to the upstart rock star founding fathers, he consciously embraced that aesthetic for the British King. Here, then, Brian d'Arcy James's monarch came out laden in costume and accoutrement, the exact opposite of the production's image. Fully weighed down by his office, he can barely move; the crown bobbles on his head. Of course, the character is played by a white actor, in eighteenth-century wig rather than his own hair, underlining the racial contrast that the production utilizes in telling a new history. This was a critical fact, and Tazewell and his cohorts wanted to be sure that the design represented the uniqueness of each actor portraying the role. While there are some prescriptive elements, the design still allows for actors to wear their hair as they might every day.

Costuming, too, didn't alter that much when it transferred. Tazewell notes that the only thing that really affected the look was that he was given bigger budgets to assure that his costumes could be crafted to his exact specifications. "I had my dream shops that I wanted to build the costumes in because I knew that they could make them the ultimate version of what the design is. Because the production was so very popular, I was able to realize that. I went to the best theatrical tailor in town to build all of my principal men. ... I went to the best dressmaker for the type of dresses that I wanted for my principal ladies. That shop is able to build those costumes impeccably, and they still do."

In previews for *Hamilton* at The Public Theater, in the final moments, when Alexander and Eliza are on stage and the audience hears the indelible line, "who lives, who dies, who tells your story," Eliza walked across a bridge toward the turntable. There, where stagehands had pulled up sections of the deck, was a magically revealed eight-foot diameter pool of ink-black water, beautifully lit, with glimmers and glisters of light reflecting on the bodies of the two lead actors. It was a stunning moment of design—an exclamation point to a show that they knew, at that time, would be transformative. It was an ode, in a way, to the reflecting pools at monuments to founding fathers all over Washington, DC—another grand symbol of time, of remembrance, of the challenges of national storytelling. Korins was in the audience watching those three preview performances. Finally, Kail turned to him:

"We are cutting the pool."

Korins agreed. The reflecting pool, no matter how gorgeous, was overwrought—that wasn't the show. Audiences were left, at the end, not asking the central question of the play—"Who tells your story?"—but rather wondering, "Is the water real, was it there the whole time, how heavy is it?" They drained the pool.

Hamilton was conceived and written long before it was green lit for workshops and production at The Public Theater. As with *Fun Home*, the show landed at The Public because the artists who created them wanted it there. Kail noted that he could trust that The Public would never try to remake their show, but rather try to help them find the best version of it. "Oskar is not prescriptive. He doesn't say take this and put it in the second act. He forces you through his insight and his questions and his conversation . . . The understanding of process was in place from the very beginning and Oskar ... understands the practical challenges of that within a rehearsal period, within the tweaking period."

As shown in all of the case studies in this history of The Public, "The Tweaking Period" is just another name for "longitudinal dramaturgy." Artists and producers know that it is critical, even if they are eager to take the next leap. Despite gossip columns to the contrary, Kail confirms that Jeffrey Seller was fully on board with the continued working and reworking of the play at The Public Theater, even though they had the opportunity to bolt for Broadway earlier than expected. It wasn't an easy choice. On the one hand, wages on Broadway would be far better than at The Public and the national attention would be greater. But on the other, Eustis, Seller, and the artists knew that there were many things that they wanted to improve, and the only way to do that was continuing at The Public through the winter and the spring, into May. Kail told Seller that there was so much more that could be discovered off-Broadway and that they would create a better, more lasting show. He agreed, and *Hamilton* stayed. The tweaking period would go on. *Hamilton* opened on Broadway in August, thus kicking off a new uptown season and all but assuring the back-to-back Tony wins for The Public and their commercial producers.

* * *

With the 2020 Disney+ version, *Hamilton* became a rare show that was able to reinvent itself yet again. Perhaps more accurately, *Hamilton* has been available for years of re-analysis in a country that has changed and evolved politically and socially in a relatively short time span. The film adaptation of the show was edited between 2015 (when it was filmed) and

2018. Kail took 2019 off and then relooked at it in 2020, just before the pandemic hit. He reflected on that hiatus and the subsequent evolution of the musical: "This is a piece of theater that is fiction, fashioned from fact ... now being looked at and talked through a lens five years later. We hadn't changed a word and yet the world had completely changed it. I think what art in its highest form can do, it stays the same and we change, and so our conversation around it changes." And so, when *Hamilton* was released that summer, debate revolved around things that weren't deeply part of the conversation when it was workshopped at The Public years before. Phrases landed differently. Moments resonated in new ways or seemed somehow off-key. The fact that *Hamilton*, a play about the founding fathers featuring people of color, mostly avoided the topic of slavery became a Twitter talking point in the summer of 2020. Lin-Manuel Miranda tweeted a response: "All the criticisms are valid. The sheer tonnage of complexities & failings of these people I couldn't get. Or wrestled with but cut. I took 6 years and fit as much as I could in a 2.5-hour musical. Did my best. It's all fair game."[10] In 2021, Kail concluded: "For a Broadway musical to be part of a cultural conversation is a rare thing. To have it happen a few times with the same show is—it's almost impossible to imagine, and yet that's what happened to the show."

Times certainly had evolved, but also Disney+ changed who got to experience *Hamilton*. Within two days, more people had seen *Hamilton* on film than had ever seen it on Broadway. Kail and Miranda say that their job is to present work with an understanding that it is a reflection, a time capsule even, of 2015. Re-viewings of it in 2020 and beyond necessarily presented a different reality, through the eyes of millions more people, thus allowing for a stronger democratization of the conversation that *Hamilton* began.

The passage of time, too, put into context some of the design decisions. Looking back at the last-minute cut of the reflecting pool now seems prescient. At a time when memorials to racist leaders are being torn down all over the United States, the idea of another version of *Hamilton* that featured a reflecting pool is imbued with all sorts of new meanings. Kail: "We didn't build our film as a monument; we built our film as a way to have conversations and take humans down from pedestals and put them right in front of us. And I feel like that's relevant in a new way, as is the conversation about black and brown bodies, using a black and brown art form to tell a story about white men."

* * *

This section began with a rejoinder from Oskar Eustis when I asked him if Broadway was antithetical to the mission of The Public—a contradiction. "Yes," he said, and he was fine with that. He is also fine with the fact that

---

[10] From @Lin_Manuel, July 6, 2020.

he has been in charge of a theater that has allowed space to develop a show about a gay kid from Pennsylvania and a story of the founding of America told by people of color. The money and the fame that comes from these outsized successes may not feel right in a conversation about socialism, but how one manages that contradiction is essential to Eustis and his ideology. He notes, "You make it clear that that's not what The Public's setting out to do ... if it's going to make money, go ahead, move it uptown to make money ... as long as we keep that clear, I don't think that's a contradiction."

Broadway casts a grand light, and often that light is important, if not crucial, to the expansion of the ideals of The Public. Eustis says, "I look at *Fun Home* which takes place in a small town in Pennsylvania ... We're a big urban area with a centuries-old tradition of gay liberation where it is possible, and has been possible for generations, for gay people to be out. That allows us to create a show about being gay that would be very hard to create in a lot of other places in the country ... I came here from rural Minnesota, and it's not like I've forgotten that." Similarly, with *Hamilton* performed all over the world and existing now on film, engagement in the conversations about the representation of traditionally marginalized people expands by the millions. That, then, is radically inclusive.

INTERLUDE

Lin-Manuel Miranda

FIGURE 7.3 *Lin-Manuel Miranda. Courtesy Theo Wargo.*

Lin-Manuel Miranda wrote and starred in *Hamilton* at The Public Theater. The production went on to Broadway and won eleven Tony Awards. I spoke with Miranda in March 2022.

Landis: What's your first knowledge or experience of The Public Theater either as a professional or just as a young person going to see something?

Miranda: The Public looms large in my family's history. The day my parents got married they went to see *Runaways* on Broadway.

They wanted to see a Broadway show and that's what they wanted to see. You know, they were both so tired that I think they each saw an act, and then slept through the rest of it. But they love musical theater and that was one of the things that they had in common when they met. And as far as my memories go, I think my first Public experience was probably the somewhat, I think, notorious at the time imported *Midsummer Night's Dream* at the Delacorte with the naked roller-skating fairies. You have to check what year that was.

(This is a reference to the 1991 Cacá Rosset adapted production, performed with his Brazilian company, Teatro do Ornitorrinco, in Portuguese. It was an exuberant production with belly dancers, jugglers, and fire-eaters.)

Miranda: Definitely the first naked women who was not related to me I'd ever seen in person!
... But that made an impression. And then, as I became more obsessed with musical theater, really beginning by doing the musical in high school, I became more aware of how many shows came out of The Public.

When I was a junior in high school, my girlfriend, who was a senior, directed *A Chorus Line*. And so, I was her assistant director, and it was a student-run theater at my high school. We learned the history of the show and the interviews with the dancers and how they workshopped that show into being. We felt very proud at the time that we, basically, got the uncensored show. Now as a dad, I look back and think about our parents watching us kids singing "Tits and Ass." (*Laughs*)

You know, in a padded bra ... how weird that must have been. But we were very proud. We had a really amazing theater advisor named Gina Dooley who let us do the show.

Landis: I was going to say, that's ambitious for high school.

Miranda: It's very ambitious for high school! And so, yeah, I think that was my first interaction with a show from The Public—mounting that in high school.

Landis: So fast forwarding to the early days of *Hamilton*, could you talk a little bit about why it was important—if it was important—why you decided you wanted to work it at The Public Theater?

Miranda: Well, it's interesting. It really is all Jeremy McCarter's fault. Jeremy and I are the rare duo where one of us is a critic and one of us was a playwright and we became friends anyway.

I think Sondheim and Frank Rich is the other example. I don't think that friendship really blossomed until after Frank Rich wasn't in the gig anymore. But Jeremy really wrote what I felt was the first review of *In the Heights* that truly understood what we were trying to do. It wasn't a unanimous rave, but it really got what we were going for.

And so, I reached out to him once the show was up and running and we struck up a friendship. And, you know, you can't take him to Centrale because the other theater artists are there and they're like, "Oh God, there's a critic here." He was the critic for *New York* magazine at the time. And he left that gig to write for *Newsweek* for a while. And then he left *Newsweek* to work at The Public. And he knew I was working on this *Hamilton* project. And he said, "You really should meet Oskar Eustis, you really should bring it to him."

At this point I was still thinking of it as an album. But when he said that, what I got excited for was not the show of the *Hamilton Mix Tape,* which is what I was calling it at the time, I thought, "Oh, maybe we can do—like if I finish this song cycle, we can do a concert at the Delacorte."

That was my initial pick—can I get the Delacorte for two nights and put on this concert of songs I'm working on? I had like two or three demos at the time. And Jeremy basically took them to Oskar, and we had a meeting about that. And he just responded to the material. We didn't end up talking about like "Yes, you can have the Delacorte." He said, "What you're doing is so exciting. Please keep writing." And we stayed in touch from that initial meeting that Jeremy facilitated.

And then I learned very quickly, I don't work well without deadlines because I was averaging about a song a year. So, Tommy Kail saw me perform the second song I had written for it, "My Shot," at an Ars Nova benefit and he said, "You should be going faster than a song a year and let's pick a deadline and you'll write a bunch of songs for that deadline."

I had been offered a slot in the American Songbook Series for "Jazz at Lincoln Center" and, auspiciously, the slot they offered me was January 11—Alexander Hamilton's birthday. So, it was a sign. This is a sign! And Tommy and I worked toward that. I wrote eleven songs for a concert. And that concert was the first sign of proto-*Hamilton.* We basically said, "What are the songs that *if* there were a musical of *Hamilton,* there would be songs in these spots?"

The bill was not the *Hamilton Mix Tape.* The bill was an evening with me. I had my friends perform a bunch of rap songs—I really liked to show the internal workings of my brain—and then we kind of launched into the *Hamilton* tunes. And Oskar was there and flipped out. Everyone kind of flipped out.

Landis: How do you mean? What do you mean flipped out? What was the response?

Miranda: I mean just like—it was just like "When do you want to do it? When can we have the show?"

Landis: They were ready to produce.

Miranda: Yeah. It was the thing that Jonathan Larson dreams about in our movie of *Superbia.* Like that was the experience of everyone seeing those eleven songs. It was like "When are you going to be done?" And that was really exciting.

Landis: I want to frame up what you're already talking about: how The Public Theater acts as a midwife for American theater, or an incubator for dramaturgy. Could you say a bit about why working at The Public is helpful and specific reasons or examples of how it's helpful in developing work that you're pretty sure is going to go on to Broadway?

Miranda: Well by the way, we never talked about Broadway, honestly. We did one more workshop up at Vassar at the Powerhouse Stage and Film and after that we were like, "We feel ready. We don't want to wait three more years." Then coming out of that we kind of went to Oskar and were like, "How soon can you give us a slot? We want to go. Lin's pregnant with this thing." (*Laughs*)

All along they gave us a home base. I remember a really seminal workshop which was the first time I reached the end of the story. I really wrote this thing chronologically, which never happens.

In one reading—at Vassar—we only did Act One. And then the next reading, I got all the way through "It's Quiet Uptown." And then I was like, "Oh, that's a rough place to end a show." But it's what I had. It's how far I got. And we just kind of kept going—and The Public would facilitate that. … They had secured us a rehearsal space across the street, on the fourth floor, and when I walked in, I remembered, "Oh shit, I used to do an after-school theater program here."

Landis: Oh wow.

Miranda: It was a free theater program called Creative Arts Team, and they would give you tokens so that you could get home. That was the only thing. And it just felt, again like January 11, it felt like it was a great sign that this was the space they got for us.

I think Suzan-Lori Parks was—she was in residence, but she was kind of on sabbatical. So, they let me just like hang in her writing nook. And I remember writing "It's Quiet Uptown" in a day at The Public. And I kind of felt like the ghost of The Public. I was like padding around in slippers and pajamas talking to myself like Hamilton in the song: "if you see him in the street walking by himself, talking to himself, have pity." Like I was that guy walking through the lobby in my pajamas trying to find the words for this devastatingly sad song. And then when I had enough, I would cross the street where the actors were rehearsing everything else I'd written. That was a really vivid, wonderful memory.

Landis: I know that you ended up having to decide about staying at The Public for a little while or going straight to Broadway. And you spent another couple of months at The Public. Can you talk a bit about what doing the show at The Public helped you learn and change before you made the transition to Broadway?

Miranda: Oh, 100 percent. You know it was interesting, what happened with *Hamilton* was the thing that you fantasize about, but you cannot pay for, and you cannot buy: which is everyone who left that show told everyone they knew about the show. And again, that was not from some crazy advertising budget. ... It was just the word of mouth on the show. It was really crazy. And so, everyone kind of assumed we were going to just sort of leapfrog to the next thing. But that was never our plan. Our plan was do this run—I think it was through April or May, learn what we learned so that we have a really good checklist of things if we're lucky enough to move. And the people should demand that we move. (*Laughs*)

Because again, you can also just say I had a great run at The Public and that could be that. That also would have been a wonderful life. I think we could have made our way to a cast recording if that were as far as it went. But because of the word of mouth, there was a lot of speculation and Jeffrey Seller, our producer, was like, "It's my job as a producer to present the case for that." And here is how we could do it. He presented it to Tommy, and Tommy really weighed the pros and cons. Like really sat with both the options. The thing that was always the dealbreaker for me was that we basically honor our commitment—and I think it was to run through April or something—and then we'd have to put it up. Like basically it would allow no time for changes. It would basically be like the show that everyone loved Off-Broadway is moving to Broadway.

And I always thought I'd have another crack at everything if we were lucky enough to move. I cannot tell you enough how the experience of being a playwright in the thing helped me. Because it's not like I'm sitting in the audience trying to read tea leaves. I'm on stage experiencing the audience's reaction in the Newman every night.

And so, by the time we did our run, I had so much information. I was like "this is a 100 percent laugh every night. This is a laugh when hip hop heads are there. This is a laugh when the history nerds are there. This is where I fucking lose them because they don't know where we are in the song."

The list that we were compiling was just so laser-oriented. ... I am going to cut this LL Cool J reference. I have to clarify "One Last Ride" into "One Last Time" because it's just about too many things right now. I can feel on a chemical level that I'm losing the audience because they're like "western Pennsylvania? Where the fuck are we?"

And so, that was the most incredibly useful information—experiencing the show every night with a different audience. And again, this is pre-cast album, too. So, no one knew the words. It was just happening to them. And so, I really got a sense of when they were with us and when they weren't like in my bones. So, we had a lot of intel. ...

Oskar was in a tricky position ... they were transferring *Fun Home* that season. And if we had been in the same season as *Fun Home*, like two Public darlings would be sort of in a kind of competition. You're never asking to be in competition, but we'd be in the same season. And you know, I love *Fun Home*. I think it's one of the great musicals of this millennium. I had no interest in being in that narrative of *Hamilton* versus *Fun Home*. That was just not interesting to me. I could see that brewing in other people's conversations, and I felt I would rather take the time to make the changes I know I want to make.

Landis: I wanted to ask as a follow up on Oskar, I love what you talked about as a writer developing your work there. How involved was he and his team in that process? Did you go to them for dramaturgy questions? Or how hands-on or hands-off were they?

Miranda: Yeah. So, here's Oskar's big secret. I'm sure someone else has said this to you in different words or maybe in the exact same words. Oskar, when he talks about your work as a writer, he envisions an infinitely better show than you could possibly write. (*Laughs*) By which I mean he emails with the tenor of like "Lin, if you accomplish this, you will have brilliantly reclaimed our history ... and taken these men off of pedestals and using it in today's language and, basically, you're our Shakespeare."

Landis: But no pressure.

Miranda: Well Jesus Christ! But he really—he builds you up in a big way. So that's one part of it, that's just great. And I think every writer has felt the Oskar effusiveness which is when you're alone for long periods of time which is what being a writer is, it's oxygen. It's just pure oxygen being pulled into the casino.

But on a more micro level, he has really strong opinions on stuff. And I respected those opinions. ... I'll tell you one really good one which was I had a lyric in a song called "Take a Break" where Hamilton is quoting Shakespeare. I mean catnip to Oskar Eustis for fucking sure. But the quote I used was [*sings*] "my dearest Angelica, they have tied me to a stake I cannot fly. They're like I must fight the course. I trust you'll understand the reference to another Scottish tragedy without my having to cite the source."

And that is a reference to Act Five, Scene One. It is the most sordid scene in *Macbeth*. It's a scene where young Seward, poor motherfucker, comes up and goes, "I'm gonna kill you." And Macbeth is like, "No, you're not." Macbeth kills him and goes, "No one of woman born can kill me" and proceeds. And Oskar said to me, "Lin, that is such an obscure reference. I run the Shakespeare Festival and I didn't catch the reference. So, if you want to fix the reference you might want to think a little more quotable." So, I swapped that out for "tomorrow and tomorrow and tomorrow."

Landis: That's great.

Miranda: But our biggest difference of opinion—and I've talked about this in other places—but I think it's where our debate led to the most interesting stuff was, he really believed Burr was a scoundrel and was trying to push the case for Burr being a scoundrel. And I think I viewed Burr more sympathetically than Oskar did and the debate in that, particularly as it pertained to the final monologue. Because there's a case to be made—and Oskar had a valid case—that Hamilton putting his gun up in the air is his last revenge on Burr, like "I'm going to die but you're going to be a villain for eternity." And there's a case to be made that that could be a motivating factor. But I don't think it's the only motivating factor.

And I also wasn't interested in answering why. People have been speculating for centuries why that motherfucker didn't aim at Burr or maybe did or didn't. There's conflicting accounts. And what was more interesting to me was sort of a CAT scan of Hamilton's final moments in thinking about this, and thinking about this, and thinking about this, and his hand goes up. And it could be any and all of those things that make his hands go up. And after those debates, I clarified that that's what I wanted to do.

And then the last piece Oskar added because again, he was getting nowhere with me using the monologue as a Burr revenge piece, he said, "Well the other thing I'll say is that right now when the monologue starts, he's already made the decision. Is there a way in which you don't make the decision until the last possible second?"

And that was so valuable because I want a Shakespeare gasp. You know, we go into *Romeo and Juliet* knowing how the story ends, but she wakes back up and gives that gasp, but you're drawn in anyway. And so, by changing the language to make it a continuing question until the last second, we got those gasps. And Oskar really pushing and pushing on the monologue is what got us there.

Landis: That's fantastic. Obviously, Oskar is not retired yet, and he probably will be there for a few more years. But looking at him as someone you know fairly well, can you say what you think may be his stamp on the American theater? That's probably impossibly broad, but some of the reasons for his importance and The Public's importance in contemporary theater.

Miranda: I just think he loves writers. Do you know what I mean? That's been my experience and the experience of other writers who worked there is again, it's such uncertain, lonely work. And to have an Oskar Eustis sweep into your life and go, "You may change American theater if you finish writing this" or "What you're doing has this immense power." It's everything you could want. And then backing that up with institutional support. I mean God, my season, where the late, brilliant Michael Friedman is there with the members of *The Fortress of Solitude*. Cush Jumbo is doing a show in Joe's Pub across the hall, and just to be in and among that laboratory, to even be able to tell you, "I was in Suzan-Lori Park's writing spot when she wasn't using it!" What an incredible feeling that is and what an incredible privilege that is.

That was the joy for me was to have this place that has been an incubator for so many great works of theater. And then be able to call that a home base. Because Oskar really welcomed you and goes like "What do you need? Do you need a cot? Do you need a cot put up in your office? Get a cot." It's quite a thing.

Landis: Well I suppose he's right. You and *Hamilton* did change American theater. So, he put the pressure on, and I guess you all met it.

Miranda: You know, he stands on that bar and he says, "Dear comrades" and lifts you up in this sense of community. And community is really why we all do this. It's the collaboration and the sense of community that is the biggest takeaway.
Landis: Lin, thank you so very much.
Miranda: Absolutely.

To the People

To the People

8
Courting Controversy

FIGURE 8.1 *Cast of* Bloody Bloody Andrew Jackson. *Courtesy Joan Marcus.*

An exchange on Facebook in the fall of 2021 reflected a confused culture of skepticism and anger that permeated the American theater in the wake of a tumultuous two years. The exchange was about a controversy related to an actor who left the cast of a Public play. On the surface, and what was reported, the conflict revolved around the use of an accent and representations of race. The actual intricacies of the incident, which are always more complicated, are not the focus here. Rather, it is the response. Someone wrote to The Public, "It's about time you be even a LITTLE transparent with your audiences about what is happening?" Another rejoined, "What, exactly is happening?" Another speculated on motives, and true to contemporary form, commentary was breathless and uninformed. The Public had to just weather bad press, unfocused anger, specious accusations, and demands for transparency. The seeds of this particular brand of internet-based speculating and gossipmongering were planted long ago, and have permeated American culture.

In the theater, suspicion and distrust of "organization" and "corporation" is acute, and in the past year, I have heard multiple forms of the sentiment: "The American theater is eating itself alive." The comment comes from people of all ethnicities and gender identities; a sinking feeling that not all is right in the theater business. It is something deeper than a pandemic closing the doors, though that certainly focused the attention. That gut feeling that is shared by so many reflects the state of affairs for the art form as it grows out of the pandemic and the racial reckonings in the aftermath of George Floyd's murder. On the one side, people argued that The Public, and organizations like it, *should* eat themselves alive, course correct through massive reorientation and righting of past wrongs. On the other, as we will see, there has been a perception that a leftist organization with a mission fully devoted to inclusivity is not exactly a fair place to focus a purge for mistakes and missteps. As I have watched the conflicts and challenges of the past few years from afar, I am reminded of a conversation I had with Lynn Nottage in 2019, reflecting on the state of the world and what she was thinking about in her writing: "I can tell you what I'm interested in now is the moral corruption of our culture, which I think goes beyond the political. I think it's spiritual. ... I think, we culturally—and I say we, and I think it's global, not just the country—need some form of healing." Any sentient being knows that the state of contemporary discourse is at a nadir and that healing is necessary and maddeningly far off.

And yet.

Controversy has been in the blood at The Public from the very beginning. I would argue that it's the foundation upon which the organization is constantly reified and rebuilt. And so, the story of the present need for healing must go back further and look at how the organization evolved and grew during Eustis's tenure, financially, morally, and tactically. What does it cost to be The Public? With idealistic goals of radical inclusivity, culture for everyone, and a phalanx of programs that espouse values of social justice, cost here is literal and figurative. Precisely because the country is caught in a vortex of structural distrust, The Public's size and influence will, for some, make it suspect. It is necessary to first offer that it is of course impossible to know what lies on the horizon, but, as this is written, enough can be said about The Public's economics of the past and forecast for the future. For a company with Marxist underpinnings there should be no surprise that morals, economics, and their contractions are fully entangled.

If we understand Pappian and Eustisian senses of Marxist ideology, we know that the value of a human being at The Public must be separated from their value as a laborer. Yet the argument on the other side points out that the reality of the American capitalist system always reinforces hegemony, and elevating human value when beholden to economics and labor becomes improbable. P. Carl, who studied theater companies for years at *HowlRound*, succinctly identified the problem in the industry: "As subscribers began to wane and as the idea of any kind of civic life was ever more eroded by late-stage capitalism, nonprofit theaters went into survival mode where money became the bottom line and Broadway deals and rich board members the path." What are the economic realities of The Public Theater that have to be balanced by its commitment to inclusivity and the value of human ethics? The following is a sketch.

Paying to Be Public

As indicated in earlier chapters, after the deaths of LuEsther Mertz and Joe Papp and the closing of *A Chorus Line*, The Public went through a decade of fairly lean times. When Eustis arrived, the yearly budget was about $12–15 million, but by fiscal year 2019–20 that rose to close to $60 million. By contrast, the National Theatre in London had a 2020 fiscal year budget of approximately £110 million (about $150 million). By any standard, the twenty-year growth at The Public is enormous and much of it is due to the rapid increase of programs, more mainstage productions, and enhanced contributed revenue. The growth necessarily strained staff. By "programs" one means the additional output of the theater beyond the plays of the season, though those plays increased in number as scope at the same time. The addition of Public Lab, the Mobile Unit, Public Works, Public Forum, Under the Radar, the various development projects, and other offerings made the theater a content machine, daily churning out new programs and additions to the schedule. In-season added programming (ISAP) was commonplace and could add millions to the budget. Many of those programs and additions do not actually create any great revenue for the company. Since the organization cannot add much in earned revenue from ticket sales (the theatres are small and are not going to get bigger), the company is dependent, especially with added programs, on increasing contributed revenue. Mobile and Works, which are considered in the next chapter, exist on a promise of social good and access; ticket sales are contradictory to the entire model and reasoning of those programs. While not able to earn ticket revenue, those programs, like Shakespeare in the Park, are excellent and principal sources of foundation giving. The Mobile Unit was supported from the outset by Stavros Niarchos Foundation and Bloomberg. Public Works was set up with funding from NYC Theater Subdistrict Council and the Tow Foundation, with other foundations coming on board after the proof of concept. The Mellon Foundation gave $2.7 million for the inception of Public Lab and $1.9 million for Works and Mobile. The Ford Foundation similarly gave generously for the support of Works and Mobile, to the tune of about $1.3 million.

In addition to underwriting the 1970s productions of *Two Gentlemen of Verona* and *A Chorus Line*, LuEsther Mertz left a legacy of about $100 million to the New York Shakespeare Festival upon her death in 1991. The Mertz family was the owner of Publishers Clearing House and the revenue associated with that brand helped support three New York cultural institutions: the Joyce Theater, the New York Botanical Gardens, and The Public. By 2021, as that revenue source was winding down, Larry Condon, the remaining Mertz trustee, established The Mertz Legacy Trust, with revenue going to those three institutions. The anticipation is that the interest from the Legacy Trust will be divided at The Public between the annual budget and the endowment. That endowment, as of 2021, sits at about $30 million (from an original corpus of around $20 million), a majority of which is Mertz money. Eight million dollars of money from the trust went to building the "business side" of the organization, as championed by Patrick Willingham. This influx, even more than *Hamilton* revenue, helped increase marketing and development, and thus the recent growth of the company. Clearly, the late LuEsther Mertz is a pillar of The Public's past and current financial viability.

The Public also significantly increased individual donor support in the last two decades, and a large amount of energy now goes into those efforts. Individual programs often have the support of corporations, such as Delta Air Lines and Bank of America. When Delta pulled its funding after the controversy surrounding *Julius Caesar*, it was press-worthy but actually only represented a small drop in the bucket of The Public's annual contributed revenue. The Public rallied social media resources and more than accounted for the losses from the withdrawal of corporate sponsors.

But what about Broadway? That is always the question.

It is not fair to imply that The Public Theater, the not-for-profit paragon of social justice, is beholden to Broadway, as the title of the previous part may suggest, and as some people like to believe. As noted, "Broadway 'Bound'" simply acknowledges the financial allure that Broadway gives and the need now to manage Broadway transfers as an integral part of the operation of the organization. *A Chorus Line* and *Hamilton* are outliers in an industry that never sees receipts anywhere close to those behemoth shows. The rise of commercial producers also means that companies that nurture and help create Broadway hits (and flops) don't receive all that much revenue. The days of The Public earning *A Chorus Line* money (as the primary producing entity) are long gone.

Yet, there is money to be had on Broadway if one is lucky. Or smart. Hackett and Eustis, in building Public Theater Productions and creating commercial partnerships, have learned to navigate this liminal production space (not quite commercial, not quite nonprofit, dabbling with low risk). During Eustis's tenure, *Hair* and *Merchant of Venice* brought a decent return to The Public. But they, too, are outliers. One was led by massive Hollywood celebrities (Pacino and Rabe) and the other had the benefit and cachet of ubernostalgia. *Bloody Bloody Andrew Jackson*, though critically lauded, did not succeed on Broadway, and in fact The Public was left on the hook for several hundred thousand dollars of unredeemed revenue promises to early investors. It was a devastating blow to the organization and strained trust with the board. Smaller productions, like *Fun Home*, *Eclipsed*, *Sweat*, and the in-house commercially produced "season two" of *Here Lies Love*, brought in some revenue but ultimately did not have a huge financial impact on the company.

And then there is *Hamilton*. It is an unquestionable success and by the time the pandemic hit, it was performing on Broadway, on the West End, in four tours, and in a new production in Australia. In total, The Public's share had risen to almost $25 million annually. Eustis, Willingham, and the board were clear that the mistakes of the past would not repeat, and that *Hamilton* money would be mainly placed in reserves. The money would go into three places: a financial safety net, the annual budget, and to improvements on the physical plant.

When Covid-19 closed theaters, The Public was in far better shape than others, with a reasonably significant safety net and, surprisingly, a fairly substantial outpouring of support from its donors. In addition, government Paycheck Protection Program funds and the Shuttered Venues Grants were enough for The Public to sustain its full staff into June 2020, before furloughs became necessary. The programming during the pandemic—mainly digital—did not require much of a financial footprint. As the theater opened back up in the fall of 2021, the reserve funds were still available, but there was an expectation that building *out* of the pandemic might necessitate drawing on those monies. In addition, ticket sales were expected to remain low in hyper-Covid-conscious New York, denting earned revenue.[1]

Is The Public Theater awash in cash? Absolutely not. Is their programming and content output replicable for most other theaters? No chance. Through smart financial stewardship, The Public has weathered several financial

---

[1] Though things will invariably change before this is in print, on the day that I wrote this, The Public Theater announced that, due to the Omicron variant of Covid, the annual Under the Radar Festival for 2022 would be cancelled. This is a clear example of the challenges of "building out" of the pandemic, and Oskar Eustis admitted that he was very nervous about the future. Spring and summer productions went on as planned.

crises, but some ask, has it grown too big? Is a company that has a division dedicated to for-profit Broadway transfers really true to the founding principles? I'd venture here my authorial opinion. The Public *has* grown, and the skeptical questioning of revenue models and Broadway hits is appropriate and fine. In fact, the Public was producing a huge amount of content in 2019 and likely straining its staff. However, the dedication and devotion to the founding principles is clearly genuine from the executive staff to the interns. In 2021, in the midst of huge pushback against the corporate culture of American theater, Oskar Eustis's salary—at least $850,000—was "leaked" on Twitter. That's a generous description of a contemporary scandal. An intrepid tweeter "discovered" publicly available information and posted it to social media, inciting performative outrage—proof that the business was corrupt. Might it be a bit high when placed next to the mission and espoused philosophies? Yes. In purely financial terms, is it in line with Eustis's worth to the board and the company? Without question. But does it, then, undercut the mission of the company? Not in any appreciable form other than the symbolic. But when ethical promises are espoused, when brand is dependent on unimpeachable moral credentials and socialist ideals, everything is liable to be called into question, and cannot be dismissed. That is where The Public Theater and American theater writ large found themselves by the winter of 2021.

While finances and the perception of bloated funding creates buzz of controversy for those dissecting what it means to be a non-profit theatre, outrage relating to programming and artistic choices, too, is not new at The Public. From the takeover of Lincoln Center to the outpouring of anger that propelled Papp to program more plays from Asian American communities, to the hiring and firing of JoAnne Akalaitis, to the Broadway misses in the 1990s, and the *Caesar* outrage, The Public has grown and evolved (and even thrived) on the pain—sometimes very deep pain—of controversies related to inclusion, mission, and growth. In Eustis's tenure, the productions of *Bloody Bloody Andrew Jackson* and *Southern Comfort*, perhaps more than any others, encapsulated the conflict between marketed vision, reality, and unrealistic expectations. They also represented moments of communication failure, where the company missed perceptions and reactions to their work and yet, as before, attempted to have those low points become platforms for social growth within the company and in American theater. Those conflicts of praxis and optics, exemplified by *Bloody Bloody* and *Southern Comfort*, seem to have hit their apex in the confluence of crises that met the beginning of the third decade of the twenty-first century. The Public would be held to account even if—especially if—the idea of accountability for the theater company, its conscientious and justice-oriented critics, *and* its internet-rage-driven detractors was unfocused, ill-defined and, at its worst, vituperative. That is not to imply that The Public and other institutions did not need to be held to account. The intersection of Covid and the racial reckonings of 2020–2 created a complex emotional environment in which everyone at the

Theater—and in American theater in general—was caught up and seemingly unprepared.

Bloody Bloody Andrew Jackson

In April 2009, a sexy, disaffected rocker, with heavy eye shadow and leather pants, sauntered onto the Newman Stage at The Public. In front of a set adorned with nineteenth-century chandeliers, red velour curtains, oil paintings, and a grotesque amount of taxidermy, he grabbed a microphone as his backup band screeched out the opening number of *Bloody Bloody Andrew Jackson*: "But it's the early nineteenth century / And we're gonna take this country back, / From people like us who don't just think about things ... Populism, Yea Yea." The Newman had the feel of a western style saloon, where drunk patrons might belt out an off-key song. Set designer Donyale Werle's saloon was populated by young hipsters, dewy and plucky, idealistic and narcissistic; self-righteously convinced that *this* was *their* time, a time to take their land, to express their rights of manifest destiny, to explore the frontier, and eliminate opposition. Populism indeed.

Bloody Bloody Andrew Jackson was a pean to American political and social brutality and a reflection on the original age of American populist anger and nationalist identity. Its tagline "History just got all sexypants," while cringeworthy to some, expressed the happenings on stage. It was presented through a historical lens, albeit distorted and reflected through early twenty-first century ways of thinking. And it was certainly sexy. The tight-pants-wearing rocker with emo makeup was the titular president, played by the impossibly handsome, wavy-haired Benjamin Walker. The play was created by two prodigies of American theater, the composer Michael Friedman and writer and director Alex Timbers.

It is important here to note, since he is not featured extensively in other places in this study, the importance of Michael Friedman at The Public. He was the resident composer for years, the creator of *Fortress of Solitude* (2012–14) and a musical version of *Love's Labour's Lost* (2013) in Central Park. He led up the popular Public Forum talk series and was integral in the operation and the spirit of The Public. Friedman died in 2017 from complications from HIV/AIDS at age forty-one and his loss is painful for everyone at The Public. Photographs of him hang behind Eustis's favorite booth in The Library at The Public. His career was already a shining light even as he was just reaching his most productive years.

* * *

Freidman and Timbers's *Bloody Bloody Andrew Jackson* ran successfully at The Public and, with underwriting from the company, moved to Broadway's Bernard Jacobs Theater. It won the Drama League Award for best musical and, when it transferred, garnered Tony buzz and critical acclaim. Peter Travers in *Rolling Stone* described it as the best show of the downtown season: "Jackson's scandalous history as a frontier kid, brutal soldier, husband to a woman who was still married and racist Indian fighter are all grist for this wild, surreal ride of a show."[2] The *New York Times* was equally impressed, noting, "*Bloody Bloody* takes precision aim at its central target: an impatient electorate ruled by a hunger for instant gratification."[3] It was nominated for two Tonys but went home with no wins. It closed on Broadway after 120 performances. It rarely receives any revivals.

Bloody Bloody Andrew Jackson was satirical and revelatory to some, and utterly unconscionable to others. In fact, it may have been the most controversial production in Oskar Eustis's tenure as head of The Public Theater. For every review that commented on its youthful energy and humor, there were others that noted that it was sarcastic, disaffected, and unsophisticated. Why does history have to be sexypants? Why are we laughing at crass humor? Is it really *that* funny? Is Andrew Jackson an appropriate character to be placed at the center of a musical comedy? As one critic queried: "Am I too old for this shit?"[4] And for some, the hardest question of all: "Isn't this sort of racist?"

The Chicago critic Chris Jones writes of *Bloody Bloody* as a compelling predecessor to *Hamilton*—a play with similar traits that didn't quite find its voice. He rightly addressed a difference between the two since, on the surface, they seem to be of a thematic piece: "Whereas Jackson felt like a cautionary tale of celebrity excesses and populist megalomania, Hamilton reminded us of ourselves."[5] That, Jones concluded, was the main reason one was a success and the other had a short life on Broadway. While that may be true, the reasons for their divergent paths are far more complex than that. I first heard about *Hamilton* from Eustis when I was in New York seeing *Bloody Bloody*. I was bemused when he told me of it, wondering why The Public would present two rock musicals in quick succession about American politicians. The fact is the two musicals share almost nothing in common structurally and thematically. One is sarcastic and critical; one is hopeful and uplifting. Where they converge is in the fact that each incited conversations about racial representation on the American stage. *Hamilton* was celebrated for its unique approach to race and American history while *Bloody Bloody* was sharply critiqued.

---

[2] Peter Travers, "'Bloody Bloody Andrew Jackson': The Best Original Musical of the Theater Season," *Rolling Stone*, June 24, 2012.
[3] Ben Brantley, "Ideal President: A Rock Star Just Like Me," *New York Times*, October 13, 2010.
[4] Jason Clark, "Am I Too Old for This Shit?: *Bloody Bloody Andrew Jackson* at The Public Theater," *Slant Magazine*, April 6, 2010.
[5] Chris Jones, *Rise Up: Broadway and American Society from Angels in America to Hamilton* (London: Methuen Drama, 2018), p. 159.

Ten years on from *Bloody Bloody*, the fact that a play like this cannot and perhaps should not be restaged actually defines the state of American theater in the latter part of Oskar Eustis's tenure as head of The Public. The problem with the play—one that wasn't recognized by The Public Theater, by Broadway producers and others—was that the subject and content undercut and demeaned Native Americans. This was by no means the intent, but certainly the result and likely an even more compelling reason for its failure.[6] Andrew Jackson was a brutal president, and in his tenure oversaw the forcible removal and slaughter of Native Americans. The play does not shy away from that reality and, in fact, lambastes Jackson, not just as a populist hero but also an American Hitler. Friedman and Timbers tried to create a show that satirically eviscerated Jackson, planting purposeful stereotypes of Native Americans to demonstrate the racist tendencies of America broadly and of Andrew Jackson specifically. "Ten Little Indians," a song that comes midway through the musical, uses the racist nursery rhyme as a base, and reframes the lyrics to describe the various way Americans slaughtered Native people. From syphilis to shooting and hanging to religious persecution, the song painfully chronicles the killing of a race of people at the hands of those manifest destiny-obsessed youths. True to the form of the show, the way that the horrors were retold was sarcastic, satirical, comedic, and even juvenile. That was, to be clear, the point.

In production, white actors adorned themselves in stereotypical Native American clothing, with beads and feathers in their hair. The satire was fairly clear, both to those who loved and hated the show; the production posited that American politics is a tenure of ineptitude, of adolescent rage, impulsive decision-making, and hero worshipping. At the end of the play we see those adolescents, having played "dress up," looking back and admiring their accomplishments. It is then that the effect of their incompetence settles in. Similar to the end of *Here Lies Love* and the rise of the "ugly lights," audiences saw the destruction of Native Americans in the face of political and social brutality. As Jackson speaks in the final moments, the audience sees the consequence: the Trail of Tears is enacted in the background.

When *Bloody Bloody Andrew Jackson* premiered at The Public, it had been workshopped in several locations. In 2006, Timbers was working at Les Frères Corbusier, an experimental theater company that he co-founded in New York. It was and is a company committed to historical theater, though its mission reveals a twist: "aggressively visceral theater, combining historical revisionism, multimedia excess, found texts, sophomoric humor, and rigorous academic research."[7] The cockiness of the mission is evident and, in a decade worth of twenty–twenty hindsight, one can perhaps see the ire the Ivy League

---

[6] For full disclosure, I directed an academic production of *BBAJ*, and similarly missed the problems with the show and didn't appropriately address its racially insensitive content. I can attest to and speculate on some of the reasons for those blind spots.
[7] https://alex-timbers.squarespace.com/about-1.

graduates might incite from "sophomoric" retelling of racially fraught history. Timbers and his team were in the midst of creating a piece about New York Parks Commissioner Robert Moses and turned to Michael Friedman to compose a couple of songs. Friedman was part of The Civilians at the time, a company that produced new plays through a process of residency work, intense research, and in situ community interviews. Friedman couldn't commit to the Moses project but the two struck up a conversation and friendship, and continued to talk about their shared interests.

Timbers recalls that he was going through a phase of interest in emo music and Friedman, after taking a class on Andrew Jackson at Harvard, was interested in the history-altering tenure of the seventh president. Timbers remembers Friedman asking, "Isn't Andrew Jackson kind of the ultimate emo president?" And I was like, "That's a show!"

Friedman and Timbers developed much of the play through a fellowship at Williamstown Theater Festival in 2006. From there, they sent a demo CD to Michael Ritchie at Center Theater Group in Los Angeles and to Eustis. Ritchie brought it in to his season and Eustis consulted from afar. The production in Los Angeles, according to Timbers, was overblown and perhaps not true to the spirit of the concert version that was started at Williamstown. He had Broadway designers and he wanted to use all of the bells and whistles that he could, to create a slick and gorgeous historical narrative. Eustis was not impressed with the product. He encouraged them to rework, especially the final third of the show, and to consider designing it with a "do it yourself-ness" with downtown designers to recenter the growing nation that the play was attempting to put under the microscope. The Public brought it on as part of its Public Lab—perhaps a perceived demotion from the heights of the illustrious version in Los Angeles, but purposeful so that the artists could feel like they were getting back to the show's roots. They called it *Bloody Bloody Andrew Jackson: The Concert Version*. It was utterly pared down, and it worked. The focus was on the roughness, the grit, and the music. The show clicked into focus at the Shiva Theater and eventually became a full production at the Newman. That "internal transfer," according to Friedman and Timbers, happened in part due to Ben Brantley's glowing review of the laboratory version. The show had no enhancement, meaning no commercial producers were brought on board early, but the positive *New York Times* review gave it a shot in the arm, and it was quickly added to the 2010 season.[8]

When the production premiered on the Newman Stage, there were protests from the Native community, rejecting not only the portrayal of Jackson as a badass hero but also of the visioning of Native Americans stereotypically, furthering a damaging and inaccurate trope. The political

---

[8]The producer, Jeffrey Richards, came on board after it was fully developed and a critical success at The Public.

journal *Politico* even got in on the coverage, and interviewed furious Native audience members who felt blindsided by the production. Steve Elm, the artistic director of Amerinda, a Native American arts organization in New York, stated: "The audience was 99 percent European, and they were all laughing uproariously at jokes about Indians .... And that was very, very uncomfortable for me and made me feel very ashamed that I was sitting in there."[9] At the time, The Public Theater had been engaged in a multiyear effort to prioritize Native American voices through its Native Theater Initiative, supported in part by the Ford Foundation. Reflecting past efforts to engage with Latin American and Asian American artists, the initiative was something that Eustis saw as important to his furthering of the inclusive goals of The Public. With the context of that initiative as part of The Public's portfolio, recognizing that *Bloody Bloody* might be offensive to the Native community should have been clear. But beyond The Public-specific oversights, the content of the show resonated beyond New York; the musical performed regionally to much the same critique. A 2014 production at the Minneapolis Musical Theater incited protest from the local New Native Theater and an open letter from its director, Rhiana Yazzi, who wrote that the play "reinforces stereotypes and leaves me assaulted."[10] One year later, an essay in *HowlRound* by Suzan Shown Harjo reflected on the saga of *Bloody Bloody*, observing, "The dehumanizing, objectifying portrayal of Native People in *Bloody Bloody*, as well as in other contemporary performances of red face, perpetuate the nineteenth century American story that Native People are less than human."[11]

The preparation for and execution of *Bloody Bloody* missed the mark. It is not my intent here to challenge the quality of the musical. More central here is to understand why the show stumbled and how The Public dealt with that controversy. Ten years after the production, Oskar Eustis reflected on what he saw as two "terrible" mistakes. One was political and one was procedural. "I simply didn't recognize what a hot button topic Andrew Jackson was going to be in the Native community. ... I just underestimated and was flatly insensitive to the idea that this was going to provoke some very strong reactions," he said. "It's not as if they [protests] damaged our box office. It's not as if they killed its chances. What's much worse is that we reaggravated a wound that we had created 400 years ago."

---

[9]Quoted in D. M. Levine, "Native Americans Protest 'Bloody Bloody Andrew Jackson,'" *Politico*, June 24, 2010. Accessed January 11, 2022.
[10]Rhiana Yazzie, quoted in "New Native Theater Protests 'Bloody Bloody Andrew Jackson,'" *Minneapolis Star Tribune*, June 4, 2014.
[11]Suzan Shown Harjo, "Andrew Jackson Is Not as Bad as You Think—He's Far, Far Bloodier," *HowlRound*, February 26, 2015.

The other mistake was in relation to the Native Theater Initiative and his commitment to Native representation. With the Initiative, with Ford Foundation support, and with an in-house representative on the program, *the* major mistake was not bringing them in to the conversation on the show earlier. Betsy Richards, the Ford Foundation-appointed in-house lead on the Initiative, was not part of early discussions about the project and felt blindsided when she saw a preview performance. Eustis says, "It was a terrible thing for me to do in my own institution because it meant that we were divided in a way that was inappropriate, and it was really stupid of me to be working so hard on Native American issues and not realize that *Bloody Bloody* needed to be folded in as part of that conversation." Friedman recalls that he and the artistic team made changes to the script to more fully "fictionalize" some of the Native characters, in hopes to highlight the satire and distance the dark humor from real historical figures. He acknowledged, though, that many of the changes didn't really move the dial. Despite the conflict at The Public, *Bloody Bloody Andrew Jackson* was critically popular and moved to Broadway.

The mistakes and insensitivities in the creation of art are constant in any institution, and The Public often attempts to weather these challenges by hanging a lantern on the problem, thus allowing the industry to grow through the process. In the case of *Bloody Bloody*, Eustis invited in members of the Native community, in some cases flying people to New York to see the show. Criticism, he says, "is not something to be solved, it is something to be embraced and if we do it right at all it should make us a better theater and expand our relationship with the community." In his estimation, by bringing members of the Native community to the production, he was actually helping organize protest against his own theater. This, in and of itself, is fairly controversial because it posits a challenging dialectic: the support of a community over the support of vulnerable artists. "Boos" were hollered from the audience, small skirmishes happened in the lobby. This, he believed, was an appropriate thing for him to facilitate in the wake of his late realization that the play was seen as toxic to many in the Native American community, a community that did not have a voice in the process. He said, "We're not supposed to batten our hatches against criticism and exclude people who feel powerless. We should invite them in."

In 2016, I asked Michael Friedman to reflect on the process and the controversy around his Tony-nominated show. He was clearly hurt, not only by the reaction by some in the general public but also by the response of The Public Theater. In his mind, the show was about the impossibility of governing this nation, a country that is full of "nutballs." He said of the themes of the play, "I think it's the conflict between populism, direct democracy directly applied, as it were, between true populism and actual government ... [where] land has been stolen and in which people have been taken from their land to also work that land. So, in a land of slavery and genocide, in effect, in a land built on slavery and genocide, populism becomes insane, and that he [Andrew Jackson] is the first 'id' expression of that." The play for him was deeply political and his thought process around presidential power and populism was researched and nuanced. The character was an amalgam of Reagan and Bush populism, with a dash of the executive power of Lincoln and Roosevelt.

In his reflection of the show, he said that he did feel proud of the work and the message it conveyed about American populism, but said that a play about Native people being created and conceived by white men furthered a long historical problem:

> To me, the protests against our show ... where they've succeeded, "hooray." And at the same time, I stand by my show. I know those are two ideas that are hard to hold in your head at the same time. ... I think all questions have representation, where sometimes the point of representation is to say it doesn't matter if your show is good, bad or indifferent, your show is part of a structure that is oppressive. And I think in the end, the American theater—when it comes to that community, unquestionably—has been part of a system that is oppressive.

In 2021, Eustis, too, saw that despite its flaws and insensitivities, *Bloody Bloody Andrew Jackson* proved prescient in a current era of dangerous and out-of-control populism. Friedman and Timbers envisioned an Andrew Jackson in an era that had produced George W. Bush and the Iraq War. In a country that now has Donald Trump and his ideologies embedded firmly in the national psyche, the play is suddenly much darker, and the disaffected apathy all the more frightening. While Eustis acknowledges that *Bloody Bloody* cannot be done again, it provided rich insight into the Trump phenomenon and an understanding of the historical roots of a country that could allow populist fervor to unleash destruction and megalomania. The idea that *Bloody Bloody* and *Here Lies Love* occurred years before the game show host president came to power is, in fact, a remarkable statement on the artistic prescience of the pieces, if one takes away the racial politics of *Bloody Bloody*. Which, of course, one cannot and should not do. Eustis was able to take direct aim at Trump several years later with his *Julius Caesar*. When *Hamilton* became the quintessential example of a revisionist historical musical, *Bloody Bloody* was largely forgotten. That is unfortunate, since it gave rise to important questions. It was a painful expression of American existential crisis; from the maniacal power brokers in Washington to the slaughter of its own citizens, *Bloody Bloody* showed a more dangerous and corrupt version of America than did *Hamilton*. But it also demonstrated the limits to which sarcasm could work on the stage, and the responsibility a theater company would have to take for the hurt that, even if inadvertent, illuminated the need for the company to grow with the times.

Southern Comfort

In the late winter of 2016, another controversy was brewing around a new production in the Anspacher Theater called *Southern Comfort*. The story, in fact, was not new at all. The musical started its life as a documentary film, produced by Sundance and directed by Kate Davis, that traced the final years in the life of a transgender man dying of ovarian cancer. The film won the Grand Jury Prize at Sundance and was critically lauded. Three young artists—Tom Caruso, Dan Collins, and Julianne Wick Davis—took an interest in the film and began to develop it into a musical.

At first glance, it was an unusual choice. As Caruso noted, the group took on the project long before trans rights were even a whisper in a broad American theater conversation. In that, there was something risky in figuring out how to produce a musical comedy that was also about a decidedly tragic topic. On its face, *Southern Comfort* is a deeply traumatic story about transgender identity being challenged by a biologically gendered disease. It chronicles both the physical and emotional tumult and terror of Robert Eads, the patriarch of a trans community in Georgia. And yet, the production focused on family, community, and the idea that one can choose who those people and communities will be; the tragedy was consistently underscored with a theme of trans belonging and familial love. The show struggled to find producers and over the course of ten years had workshops in small theaters, fifth-floor walk-ups, and the like. Finally, after a production at Barrington Stage in Massachusetts, Eustis was made aware of the script, read it, and asked for a reading. He was moved by it and committed to doing it in the 2016 season.

Southern Comfort feels like exactly the sort of play that The Public should be doing; one focused on traditionally marginalized communities with dedicated time and resources for development. The problem with *Southern Comfort*, and in line with many of the controversies that befall institutions like The Public, is that it somehow did not meet a moment, even as the *New York Times* and other critics were generally positive in their reviews. Perhaps it is more accurate to say that the moment that it was meeting was in the rearview mirror, and life and circumstances had made the play feel somewhat academic and heavy on the sentimentality. By 2016, it was much easier for a theatergoer to look at the play and *not* say, "What a leap forward" but rather "Why are there so few trans actors onstage?"

That does not mean that *Southern Comfort* wasn't groundbreaking. The Public committed to casting trans actors and brought in dramaturg and scholar P. Carl, then at Arts Emerson, to help ground the piece and incorporate his expertise and scholarship about trans communities and trans art. He notes that in 2016 it was remarkable to see and work on a project about a trans man. "It was the closest I had ever come to anything that was even remotely something I could connect to, of seeing myself.

And so, the idea of a trans show and The Public trying to take that on felt really important." And yet, *Southern Comfort*, in its failures, ran into what actually became a generative conversation. Why, indeed, was a cis woman playing the trans patriarch? Why was the musical created and led by a cis creative team at a company with cisgender management? These questions and more were asked in an open letter by Taylor Edelhart just before the opening of the show. The letter was seconded by over three hundred trans and cis artists in New York City. The author pointedly asked questions for the theater to address and culminated with, "If you're going to produce a story at the expense of the community whose history it's meant to focus on, why produce it at all?"

The fact is that the company was not trying to produce something at the expense of the community it aimed to serve and when the project was approved, Eustis insisted that trans actors be cast. The casting team faced a fairly substantial challenge, though, in that some of the cisgender actors in the production had been with it for a long time and the creative team had a loyalty to them. Once it was clear that those actors were coming with the production, they knew that it was likely going to cause a stir in the trans community. Eustis acknowledged, "By the time we started performing it, the fact that anybody *wasn't* transgender and playing a transgender person had become a big [deal]." No longer was the casting of two trans actors enough; it wasn't complete and actually seemed like a glaring nod to the lack of representation.

Eustis thought the debate good and noted that that letter and the support that it got from the trans community actually showed something that was exciting to him as a leader of a cultural organization. "It means that history is moving. Politics is moving. What's progressive yesterday is not progressive today."

Eustis called Edelhart, engaged with them, and then asked Michael Friedman, the head of Public Forum at the time, to organize a town hall to discuss the controversy that was building. Friedman had the idea to conduct it in the style of a Quaker meeting. That meant that there would be no crosstalk; people could speak and others had to listen. Nobody's truth would be eliminated or challenged, no one had to be defensive. Stephanie Ybarra, the head of Special Artistic Programs, moderated the talk and it featured Michael Silverman, the executive director of Transgender Legal Defense and Education Fund; Cecilia Gentily, a trans program coordinator at a local community health center; Kate Bornstein, the famed theater artist and activist; and the dramaturg, P. Carl. Each panelist spoke and then the audience was asked to share stories and reflections.

By most accounts, the evening went well, and Eustis later noted that he was proud of the way The Public handled the outcry—they highlighted exactly what the Theater is there for, to lead the conversation about its own biases so as to make positive change. It was not just soft critique and convivial agreement. In the course of the evening, the organization was asked to confront its own nearsightedness and the casting of *Southern Comfort* was called out as the gender version of blackface. Edelhart ended with, "Mr. Eustis, you have to put trans artists first."

After the talk, Eustis was approached by someone wishing to convey their empathy about their perception that Eustis was too boldly persecuted. He was taken aback: "I'm artistic director of The Public Theater with an extraordinary amount of cultural power in the city of New York. They are not persecuting me; they're criticizing me. I have the power. I need to be criticized ... you are not getting the way power works, and it's actually a beautiful thing when people who don't have power come together and try to speak truth to power."[12]

As with so many of the controversies at The Public, blowback for choices generally revolves around missteps related to access of expression and full representation. With *Bloody Bloody*, the largest complaint was that members of the Native community weren't brought into the development process inside The Public. With *Southern Comfort*, similarly, the number of trans people in the room where it was created was not high enough. One can debate percentages, numbers, and the correct evaluation of representation in certain scenarios, but for Eustis and The Public, having the conversation about *Southern Comfort* seemed right, a starting point for growth. P. Carl recalled years later: "I remember thinking [about] the rage that we have at each other, those of us trying to do something that makes some dent in the conversation. And even if you fuck it up, fine, fuck it up and have the conversation, which is what was happening."

A historical diversion is perhaps apt here. When it comes to casting and representation on the stage, this is not a new conversation, and in fact the center of the debate that has swirled around The Public and its controversies since its inception, when Joseph Papp insisted on what was then considered "race blind casting." Of course, the discussion has shifted and evolved with the times and has expanded to "race-conscious" casting so as not to imply that race is something that we are "blind" to. Many of the early actors of the Theater reflect back on how extraordinary it was that Papp founded a company that was dedicated to its core to boroughs that were ignored, especially neighborhoods that had higher percentages of Black or Hispanic residents. A James Earl Jones or Raúl Julia tour of the city with American Shakespeare boldly made claim that the theater of New York was expanding its reach. But the American theatrical contradiction was staring the New York Shakespeare Festival in its face, even then: a proposition of radical inclusivity certainly should reach beyond the cast. The *vast* majority of the Shakespeare in the Park productions were led by white directors (in fact, all of them in the first fifteen years). Long ago oversights, perhaps? Not so. The disparity continued through Wolfe's tenure and into Eustis's time. Only recently, with that lack of equity becoming clearer and more

---

[12] The entire town hall can be accessed at: https://www.youtube.com/watch?v=N1aZmzWcMDg&t=2510s.

glaring, has that begun to shift. The majority of the directors in the Park since 2018 have been people of color.

Reaching, then, and sometimes falling short, is part of The Public's existence. Those sorts of nuances were less prevalent in conversations about trans casting in 2016, only a few short years ago, and the *Southern Comfort* town hall helped foreground the dilemma. Should all trans parts be played by trans performers in the same way that race must adhere to appropriate standards of casting? What about a gender expansive actor whose identity exists between traditional structured gender "norms"? Even in 2022, the dialogue is fraught, exciting, and ongoing. That is generally where The Public thrives: in the middle of important social conversations where it risks exposing its own shortcomings.

Caruso acknowledged that *Southern Comfort* was developed and presented at a time of rapid change and visibility for trans theater. "I think some of the things we did now might seem a little quaint or a little soft. And I think if we were to go back into *Southern Comfort*, I would probably work even harder with the team to make it even more—the intricacies of their characters to make them more character-driven ... it would behoove someone to have an entire trans cast." Casting director Jordan Thaler reflected that the show altered a conversation, pushing forward new practices and allowing theater to grow: "It started with *Miss Saigon*, it has rolled out now, and other communities have now said 'we're not going to be represented by actors who are not from our community anymore. You can't tell our stories with people who don't know us.' It's really exciting, and that's going to change how casting works. And other casting directors will benefit from having that pressure put on the people who program and produce theater."

The town hall, in the midst of previews, was not a moment to rework the play. It was essentially set and ready for its run. *Southern Comfort* went on and received a warm to mixed reception from many critics, owing to its spirit and content on the one hand and overly earnest sentimentality on the other. Like *Bloody Bloody*, though, there was very little mention in the press of the controversy that was actually more socially compelling than the play itself. In the American "newspaper of record," gender casting choices were a source of happy astonishment and theatrical awe. Charles Isherwood, who was anxious to see the accomplished actress Annette O'Toole in the lead role, wrote: "Only halfway through the first act, as I was wondering when she was going to show up, did I realize that Ms. O'Toole had been there all along, playing Robert himself, the reed-thin fellow in the black cowboy hat. ... It's not a matter of mere cosmetics. ... More important, Ms. O'Toole has disappeared inside her character, drawing a moving, indelible portrait of a man who retains an unflappable spirit even as death draws near."[13] Though clearly a rave about the performance, rather than a conversation

---

[13] Charles Isherwood, "In 'Southern Comfort' a Family Not Bound by Blood," *New York Times*, March 13, 2016.

about ethics of representation, the marvel here was that the actress *passed* as a man. In these terms, the *act* of acting gender can so clearly be read as an affront to the trans acting community. The Public engaged in those conversations, even if the popular theater press did not.

*   *   *

The consistent question that Eustis and The Public must face, as the face of American theater, is how to *lead* the conversation while also espousing the genuine need to *listen* to the conversation. This gets to the central aspect of "story" and "controversy" in this moment of American theater, and begs for the invocation of the most famous and overused quote in the contemporary Public Theater canon: "Who lives, who dies, who tells your story?" P. Carl notes, "I think that now the theaters in this kind of scary place of imagination, all the things that make theater great, there are now rules about. And I'm not trying to sound like a cis white guy who feels oppressed by that. I mean, it's just a weird way to think about art." In a world of rapidly changing rules, the skill and speed with which a theater company pivots, reassesses, and makes changes is an important marker of its genuine commitment to progressive ideals.

Carl said of The Public and of Eustis, "There were a lot of theaters that were in some ways prepared for what was coming in terms of the reckoning, and I think some of the leaders that have been most condemned in this period of time were people who were actually trying to do the right things in acknowledging the white supremacy of the theater." And yet, he notes, the structures of American theater and the "white frameworks" set in place have ended up biting them in ways that they hadn't expected. The Public Theater places itself at the center of cultural conversations, right in the midst of debates on representation and inclusion, and literally asks for critique, saying that that is how it grows and reflects its society. It is obvious then that it, as an institution, and Oskar Eustis, as its leader, will receive much of the focus of the increasing digitally based ire and rage in the American theater conversation. For some, that *is* growth. A person who feels ignored can go to social media and be heard and can find a community of empathetic allies. The problem, of course, is the rise of invective that has accompanied platforms that ostensibly allow for voices to be heard.

As established, The Public Theater has had extraordinary control of its image, and "selling" The Public is finely tuned. For an art of imagination and dreaming, this is not a critique, and indeed, storytelling is as much about the plays as it is about the organization. "One public." "Culture belongs to everyone." "Radically inclusive." These are mantras, at once deeply held beliefs that form the foundation of the organization, as well as considered image-makers. But in 2020, when a pandemic struck and when an innocent Black man was suffocated in the streets of Minneapolis, the theater world shifted its outlook on what it means to *be* inclusive rather than *selling* inclusive. Fair or not, The Public Theater was ground zero for that debate and that cultural shift.

Twenty–Twenty

The year with a name that is synonymous with "hindsight" was a year that American theater was forced to look in the mirror and ask, "What have we been doing?" Oskar Eustis acknowledges an obvious fact for him, and indeed for many in the American theater: It was the hardest year of his professional life, by far. In early March, Eustis went to the hospital with respiratory problems. He was there for several days. When he returned to health, his theater was closed. Patrick Willingham and the executive staff made the early decision to close up shop in response to the pandemic that was starting to circle the globe. In fact, Eustis himself was in the hospital battling Covid.

In the weeks that followed, The Public began to shift its programming to digital platforms. Richard Nelson was tapped to write a new "Zoom play" and Jessica Blank and Erik Jensen wrote another, *The Line*, about medical workers on the front line of the crisis. Like all theaters in the country, The Public scrambled to find relevance and to reassert its necessity in a plagued world. The pandemic fundamentally challenged the ideas that Eustis always espoused about the theater: It is necessary and essential for the functioning of democracy. What happens when it's absolutely not possible? While the world is still groping for an answer, we have seen enough in 2021 and 2022 to know that theater is surviving—struggling, but moving. It is reevaluating how it can and should be relevant and how the financial models of old have to be revamped to accommodate market realities.

It wasn't only Covid that was occupying the lives and psyches of the staff at The Public.

On June 8, 2020, a group of BIPOC staff members—collectively, the BIPOC Affinity Group—distributed a detailed letter to the staff of The Public Theater. "A Letter from the Margin" was a call to action, a summary of not only two months of frustration, but of years of feeling invisible, sidelined in favor of white-centric programming and staffing. While they had been meeting for three years, the time felt right to make some of their findings and feelings public. The letter began: "In the midst of a global pandemic that disproportionately kills marginalized communities, a popular uprising over the state-sanctioned murders of Black people, and a sociocultural reckoning with regard to systemic violence, we—the Black, Indigenous & People of Color (BIPOC) Affinity Group at The Public—cannot make sense of the ways in which The Public has structured its priorities and operations within the aforementioned contexts that, for our communities, amount to life and death."

The letter, the circumstances that led to it, and the response to it (which is ongoing) is not only an extraordinarily painful chapter in the history of The Public—for those who felt the marginalization and those who were blind to it—but also a moment of recognition and movement that perfectly encapsulates what The Public has always stood for. As Stephanie Ybarra observed from Baltimore, "The minute you say 'free for all' and when your name is The Public, you immediately open yourself up to all of the folks being like 'but that's not what you said over here. I can point to this, this, this, this. And this doesn't line up with what you just said.'" This is exactly what the letter did by outlining the happenings of the spring of 2020 as illustrative of a broader sense of inequity that needed to be addressed. The group asserted that executive leadership was prioritizing whiteness in its programming choices and said that during the first months of the pandemic it was clear who was moving toward the middle of the organization as essential workers versus those who remained at the margins. The announcement of a white-focused season of plays was a flashpoint that led to the first draft of the letter.

Then, on May 25, George Floyd was murdered in Minneapolis. At the time, The Public was in production of a digital fundraiser called *We are One Public*, to be hosted by Jesse Tyler Ferguson, directed by Kenny Leon, and featuring the stage stars Anne Hathaway, Antonio Banderas, Glenn Close, and others. The BIPOC Affinity Group asserted that the leadership of The Public failed to recognize the murders of Black people and were behind in responding to the national and international trauma that was unfolding. Instead, according to the letter, they focused on the star-studded fundraiser. When the Theater released a statement about Floyd, there was little input from Black staff members. "It is unconscionable that The Public should fail to affirm that Black Lives Matter, fail to acknowledge the tragedies of stolen Black lives, and fail to care for its Black employees, artists, and audiences. It is both abhorrent and telling behavior that The Public continued to promote the Gala instead." The letter asked that The Public acknowledge that, in its current moment, the Theater upheld white supremacy, and also to adhere to a list of demands. Some of those demands included: programming 75 percent of the season with work that centers BIPOC, gender non-conforming, and/or disabled artists; require anti-racist training; shift from top-down decision-making; include salary transparency; and honor the legacy of George C. Wolfe.

The letter was seen as a shot across the bows and was met with surprise. How could an organization so focused on equity, diversity, and inclusion be subject to critique that it wasn't appropriately anti-racist or that it was, actually, prioritizing whiteness? Jesse Cameron Alick, who was one of the affinity group leaders, noted, "No one in the theater world, none of the leaders in the theater world were actually ready to have this conversation." A full staff meeting was held, and tensions ran high. Through the late spring and into the summer, Eustis and the executive leadership faced withering criticism about how the Theater was run and their failure to appropriately address inequity. In those first months after the conversations began, the anger directed at Eustis was pointed and personal. Some openly wondered if he would survive as artistic director. He recalled, "There was a great desire for blood. There was a great desire for punishment that underlay a lot of the first few months of dialogue about this. There were people who were absolutely clear, and that would even say that what they wanted is for me and people in my position to suffer and to be forced to give up power. And part of that is legitimate, and part of that I don't feel was doing anybody any good."

Alick noted that The Public Theater, in fact, was doing the best job among the large off-Broadway New York theaters in representing, and pointed to the Asian American Performers Action Coalition report of 2019 as demonstrating that The Public did stand above others. It reported that The Public's board was 26.7 percent BIPOC, it employed 60 percent BIPOC actors, and one-third of the season's plays were written by BIPOC authors.[14] On those metrics, The Public was the most diverse major theater in New York, far outpacing other well-known companies. But, as Alick asserted, "The bar is laying on the ground, it's easy to jump over that bar." Indeed, the report showed much starker numbers in New York broadly: 58.6 percent of roles went to white actors, 29 percent to Black, 6 percent to Asian Americans, 4.8 percent to Latinx, and 0 percent to Indigenous actors. What's more, white writers still accounted for 80 percent of the plays being presented. New York City is 42.7 percent white.[15]

The staff demanded that The Public raise the bar.

The Public faced an internal struggle. Was the company really "radically inclusive" and adhering to its claim that "we are one public"? Over the summer months of 2020, executive leadership and staff had many meetings, some overseen by outside professional moderators, to attempt to start rebuilding trust and create more equitable models. What emerged in the conversations was an acknowledgment that, at worst, the mission and focus of America's most diverse and de facto national theater was perhaps lip service, and at best that the mission needed revisioning.

Mission and vision often create tough parameters, especially with a theater like The Public that spent years in massive growth mode with an eminent artistic director and a huge Broadway hit highlighting its public facing image. The well-meaning tendency was to use all of those benefits and national platforms to push hard on mission-centric programming. Alick and others have told me the running joke at The Public pre-pandemic: "I've got an idea! Oh, sounds like an initiative!" Alick continued, "That's the

---

[14]http://www.aapacnyc.org/2018-2019.html. These stats reinforce what was earlier outlined. While The Public has been traditionally conscientious about equity on stage, it is less so when it comes to directors and playwrights.

[15]https://www.census.gov/quickfacts/newyorkcitynewyork.

result of brilliant minds at The Public, it's a result of lots of money at The Public and it's the result of this unending ambition of expansion, expansion."

The playwright Richard Nelson well described the challenge that The Public Theater and American theater faced after the summer of 2020 and into 2021. He said:

> The commercial theater will have no trouble. It'll figure itself out because the commercial theater knows what it's about. It's about making money. The nonprofit theater is a little trickier because the nonprofit theater is based upon various visions. What is the vision and its purpose? And right now, it's questionable what that purpose is.
>
> There is no one that I know who works in the theater who wouldn't love a far greater diverse audience. But diversity, race is only one part of that diversity. It's also age, but also even, maybe most importantly, which relates to both of those, economic diversity.

Indeed, swirling around conversations about race and equity were complaints that The Public was too big and that its staff was overworked and running ragged. Theaters in the country started curbing excessive technical rehearsals and made statements and promises about equitable pay. While the debate that started in 2020 began with the BIPOC Affinity Group's letter, conversation built to a discussion more broadly about commitment to artist compensation and access to theater. Nelson was right. Race representation was central to the challenge facing American theater, perhaps honed and focused by Covid and Black Lives Matter, but it wasn't the entire thing. Just as these conversations were reaching their height, The Public had to start furloughing staff. The necessary move highlighted structure and what it means to be an "essential worker." The timing was horrible.

In 2022, Eustis reflected back on that summer and acknowledged three major flashpoints that ignited a fire. One, of course, was racial inequity and the feeling that The Public was not living up to its promise. The second, in his words, was "that there were too many decisions that were being made by a white person; namely me, and that that was inappropriate for a theater in search of true racial justice." He noted that there was a generalized feeling that decision-making was privatized or perceived as autocratic. The mystery that this book in some ways has tried to unveil—how does an idea come into the Theater and become a show?—is actually just as mysterious to the staff as it is to the general public. Eustis added: "The Public has always been run by an autocrat, or as I've sometimes put it, a charismatic megafauna. So, from Joe to George to me, The Public has always had an outsized artistic director whose personality becomes imbedded with the institution's identity so that it's hard to think of them as separate. I think I've done a lot to reduce that great-man stance that The Public has, but I certainly haven't eliminated it."

The third major problem that he recognized was more amorphous. The dual crisis of George Floyd and Covid led to a set of impulses toward equality that crossed many lines, from race to gender to economics to working conditions.

Eustis spent much of June and July 2020 feeling scared, reactive, and filled with self-doubt. So much of his self-image and identity as a radical, progressive leader, sensitive to racial equality, was being challenged by people he worked very closely with. Broadly, theater leaders were caught off guard by the reckoning, forced quickly to grapple with the realization that their progressive bona fides were perhaps not as deep as they had imagined.

There are many who have asserted to me both on and off the record that Oskar Eustis facing down this sort of fury and pain was a "pile-on" for someone who was, in fact, practicing his progressive ethic like few others in New York theater. In that, The Public and Eustis, to some, were odd places for a theatrical reckoning. Kwame Kwei-Armah, artistic director of the Young Vic and director at The Public, while acknowledging his bias due to their friendship, said:

> I've seen the work that they're doing on all areas of EDI. And I've seen how much Oskar and the staff put in of their spirit, soul and sweat to make The Public get into the most equitable space that it can be. I think most criticism is fair to some degree, it is how it is delivered, and it is whether it is those who are criticizing have the space to give those they are criticizing the benefit of the doubt.

As Alick succinctly asserted, the question wasn't about how The Public is compared to *other* theaters, but rather if it was raising the bar and leading generative change that reflected its mantras.

No doubt, Eustis himself, while weathering the shock and strain of the initial critique, knew that his own ethics demanded that criticism be heard and confronted, and that responsibility for the hurt had to land on him. He was in the position of power, and its use was precisely what the reckoning was about. He couldn't feel sorry for himself—the Marxist dialectic of contradiction, core to his philosophical beliefs, insists that multiple truths had to be correct. "I realized that what my job was, as long as I was running this theater, was to listen really hard to everything that was being said to me. To take it very seriously, to reflect upon it, to decide what I thought was right, and to do it, and to not dwell on how it would be received, because the dwelling on how it would be received was driving me crazy. And that's what I've tried to do ever since."

As summer turned to fall, The Public began to implement changes that could begin to address some of the staff critique and changing nature of theater. The megafauna artistic genius model of a theater did not square with a company with the values of The Public. He has said that going forward, The

Public has to create a mode of leadership where a diversity of voices have input and where power is accountable to those who don't have power. To that end, Eustis has expanded artistic leadership. He elevated Shanta Thake and Saheem Ali to join Mandy Hackett to create an associate artistic director team. He meets weekly with them, managing director Jeremy Adams, and the head of producing, in a sort of senior artistic staff, discussing programming.[16] Eustis made a commitment that all major decisions about the content of the season would be made with those people at the table. Eustis would still be responsible for those decisions and have the final say, as in keeping with his contract with the board, but the move attempts to readjust toward consensus building.[17]

"A Letter from the Margin" encouraged vociferous push back in other organizations and fostered systematic changes. At about the same time that The Public was engaged, "We See You, White American Theater" published its now widely-known manifesto and list of demands, calling for forceful action and accountability in the American theatre more broadly. That some of these conversations were centered at The Public in the years leading up to 2020 is perhaps appropriate. That is supposed to be why the company exists, and that engagement is precisely why it continues.

* * *

Joe Papp founded The Public on a need to get "to the people." It's the sort of ideal that is reminiscent in American politics of populist politicians talking about "real America." On the one hand, it makes sense. On the other it demands a clarification. The rejoinder, of course is, "What is fake America?" That's the problem with slogans and, and as offered in this book, the challenge and controversy of being a theater that is wrapped in slogans. Even if they are all well-meaning, they are perceived differently by each who reads them. Papp wanted to get to underserved neighborhoods and broaden access for the citizens of his city. As The Public has grown, it now serves more than New York. It has expanded to include the millions of people who have seen *Hamilton*, *Fun Home*, *Noise/Funk*, *A Chorus Line*, or *Hair*, attended the hundreds of plays at 425, those who have watched the Tonys, and those who have traveled from around the world to Central Park to queue up for a free ticket to see Meryl Streep play Mother Courage. One Public is *huge*, and for the company to ethically grow with its vastly expanded base, it had to return to its roots, to explore the core beliefs underlying "to the people." The outlet is there. Two relatively new programs, the Mobile Unit and Public Works, would fill that need and, likely, point to the future of American theater.

---

[16]Thake has since left The Public.
[17]Eustis announced a 2022/3 season of plays that focused on stories from artists of color, including new plays from Suzan-Lori Parks, Erika Dickerson-Despenza, and James Ijames. Ijames's *Fat Ham* had just been coproduced in the spring of 2022 by The Public and The National Black Theater. Directed by Associate Artistic Director Saheem Ali, the play won the 2022 Pulitzer Prize for drama.

9

The American Neighborhood

FIGURE 9.1 *The Mobile Unit on tour in Brooklyn. Courtesy Kevin Landis.*

> *For me the mission of the theater is that it creates a space for the humans of this city to gather together and share their humanity through the process of seeing and making theater, telling stories, listening and receiving those stories. There is a fundamental communion about that act. I think democracy and church are similar, in my mind. ... There is a higher ideal that's rooted in the notion that every single person is worthy, and is precious.*
>
> —LEAR DEBESSONET

On a late summer afternoon in 2021, a yellow truck pulled up in front of the old Dime Savings Bank of Brooklyn, just at the bottom of the steps, beneath the columns of the neoclassic facade. Out from the truck poured a group of spry young actors, boxes of props, pop-up tents, bubble machines, an Astroturf floor, a massive sign that read "SHAKE SPEARE," pink folding chairs, prop bookshelf with prop editions of the complete works of William Shakespeare, an impressive array of amps and speakers, lavaliere rock-star mics, and all the trappings of a show.

It was one of those classic New York scenes that afternoon in Albee Square: ninety-five degrees with high humidity, people lounged on curbs, bought cotton candy and Mr. Softee ice cream at the food trucks, and generally waited out the August muck. On this afternoon, at 4:30 p.m., the height of the day's heat, Albee Square played host to the reconceived Mobile Unit. In 2021, it was in fact a third iteration of an idea that dates back to the origins of theater: take it to the people.

The Public Theater's famed beginning as the New York Shakespeare Festival saw tours to parks not far from Albee Square. On the back of Joe Papp's converted sanitation truck, now legendary actors toured the city's boroughs through the late 1950s and up until the creation of the Delacorte in Central Park. This mobility was the founding modus operandi of the Festival, long before "Public" was added to the company's name. To achieve Papp's goal of meeting his fellow city dwellers where they were, in the neighborhoods where they lived and died, movement was key. But with the creation of the amphitheater in the Park and the acquisition of the former Astor Place Library, The Public Theater very quickly became decidedly, oddly, and unapologetically stationary. With the hits, with their takeover of Lincoln Center, with the new tradition of Shakespeare in the Park, with *Hair* and *A Chorus Line*, and all the other legendary plays, the audience would come to The Public, not the other way around.

This reversal of the founding principle is somewhat striking, in fact. In the interview that Joe Papp recorded in 1988, he mused to Steven Cohen on the origins of mobility at The Public Theater:

> It was free Shakespeare, but it needed, first of all, to be good Shakespeare before it could be free. You can't give something poor away. ... I was dedicated to the city of New York and its people and the parks in particular, and the notion that all people can enjoy the works of this great English playwright. As time went by it proved to be true with our mobile unit, which toured this city, the boroughs and the various other parts of the city. We played parks and playgrounds and reached all kinds of people—people with very little academic education. I must make that distinction. You say, "very little education," education is a big word. It encompasses everything people do and live through. We played primarily in Black areas to begin with. We then began to play in Hispanic areas and found the need, in these Hispanic areas, to do plays also in Spanish. We had to do Shakespeare in Spanish. I got Pablo Neruda at the time, who was still alive—the great Chilean poet—to do a translation of *Romeo and Juliet*, which now remains the standard translation of that play. We put on the play with his translation. It was a brilliant translation. We also did *Macbeth* with a Latino audience.

That Papp considered these things as a theater maker in the 1950s showed a fairly forward-thinking producer whose goals tended toward social justice and a keen sense that ownership of the works of William Shakespeare belonged to all people. Sam Waterston said of those early days: "It was a time of a lack of polish, but ... yes, we grew up. We learned how to do Shakespeare that way. We learned it by doing. We learned it in front of audiences. It was rough, but it was ... a great thing, because it's taking theater to the people. ... It's also lefty, wonderfully anti-authoritarian, and populist in the best sense of the term." With mobility came a need for the theater to reflect the communities that it served; sending predominantly white actors to locations supporting audiences of color would not make a lot of sense, and Papp was known for his focus on righting racial wrongs in theater casting. Barry Edelstein, the current head of the Old Globe in San Diego and former head of The Public's Shakespeare Initiative, reflects that:

> We all know that the early years of Joe Papp, he was a pioneer in what has variously called colorblind casting, non-traditional casting ... it's related to that same sense of ownership. What he was saying early on, and what The Public has pioneered and brought to a level of sophistication unlike any other theater in the country, is an idea of who should be on that stage and what they should sound like. ... That's been a monumental contribution to American theater and American Shakespeare in particular.

Does a theater need a $40 million makeover on its lobby that includes a fine-dining restaurant? A glass canopy? Slick polished walls with bright red lettering? A proposed retractable roof over an outdoor stage? The mobile-centric model answers all of these questions with an emphatic *no*. As Steven Cohen said of the early days of the mobile form, "the idea was we were in a schoolyard or whatever small park in that particular neighborhood where the people—the diversity of the people of the community could see the diversity of the people on stage. Was that to encourage them to become actors? No, of course not. It was to say that this was another language, this is theater, this is art, and this is a component that could add to your life. I think it was just a brilliant thing that Joe did."

Getting back to the roots of mobility was important to Oskar Eustis when he took over as the head of The Public Theater, and by the early 2000s, even as The Public had largely abandoned its mobile ambitions, there were models in the United States that reflected those early goals. And lest mobility be fetishized as some sort of unique New York phenomenon, it's important to note that Shakespeare himself performed in various locations, and always with a degree of roughness that we often do not think to associate with the author who so often represents the height of Western literature.

The model of mobility that perhaps ushered in a new era of touring Shakespeare in the United States can fairly be attributed to Michelle Hensley's Minneapolis-based company Ten Thousand Things. The idea was, and continues to be, fairly simple. Started in 1991, the company dedicated itself to creating theater that was bare bones, where the audience could be seen, and the sense of community was paramount. The structure of the theater could be erected and broken down in minutes since it consisted of a square of carpet with audience chairs on all four sides. Famously, Hensley insisted on "all the lights on" (the title of her 2005 book/manual on the style[1]), a mantra that pointed to the fundamental conceit that theater was as much about the communion of people in a shared space as it was about the telling and retelling of famous stories. She says that the core of the Ten Thousand Things way "is respect for [the audience's] intelligence, their imaginations, and their very hard-won life experiences. And those are things that are in very rare supply in most of their lives." The model radically shifted the focus back to the Pappian ideals of humanity and the lives of the audience.

By 2010, Oskar Eustis and The Public Theater had identified a problem, one that is present to this day. Their theater of the people had become elite and out of reach for the audiences that it claimed to champion. While free, Shakespeare in the Park really only served the people who could spare the time to wait all day in long lines to nab prized tickets to see some of the greatest actors in America under the Central Park lights. Eustis says that his initial urge to revive Mobile was to solve the problem of the success of the Delacorte Theater, to reach the audience that Central Park missed. In that way, atmost forty years after the founding of the Delacorte, the new artistic director realized something that is now a bit of a trope in assessing the success and failures of the organization: "Success" has a way of eclipsing the moral fabric on which the mission of the company is written. The mobile

---

[1]Michelle Hensley, *All the Lights On: Reimagining Theater with Ten Thousand Things* (St. Paul: Minnesota Historical Society Press, 2015).

New York Shakespeare Festival turned into Delacorte Free Shakespeare in the Park, turned into the downtown Public Theater, turned into Lincoln Center, turned into the generator of Broadway hits. America's "national" theater was suffering from the same challenges as the country that it represents. From "give me your tired, your poor, your huddled masses, yearning to breathe free," to capitalist market realities that sidelined the people of low socioeconomic class, and, despite The Public's efforts to the contrary, people of color.

In 2010, Eustis hired Michelle Hensley and Barry Edelstein to direct the premiere production of the Mobile Unit's *Measure for Measure*. The initial outing seemed to work, a solid proof of concept. It toured to multiple prisons, homeless shelters, and community centers. In a December 2010 article in the *New York Post*, Hensley identified, "It has a fantastic resonance for people who have been incarcerated or are homeless. It's really a play about how you judge others ... Shakespeare wrote for the groundlings. He expected audiences to shout back at the actors, which is what happens at our performances."[2] In a similar vein, Edelstein commented: "People having the same experience of wonder and joy and being moved and being transported and finding that there are ideas in Shakespeare that are directly relevant to their own experience, but the material circumstances of their lives make it difficult to access. That's what the Mobile Unit does."

Ron C. Jones acted in the 2012 production of The Public's Mobile Unit as the title character in *Richard III*, and described, as so many do, the audiences and how they receive the work.

> [It] is kind of like how the original audiences were in the classic Shakespeare days. They're very vocal and very animated. There's not a lot of theater etiquette that happens. It's something about that—being able to do a play in that environment, where you really get the people involved. It is an experience that you don't feel in the theater because of all the rules and etiquette that go along with it—unwrapping candy, telephones ringing, babies crying, people eating, walking out, going to the bathroom, and coming back, people talking to each other while the play is going on.

The lack of traditional decorum, he noted, had a focusing effect. When an elderly lady yells out, "Hey, can you speak up please?" some of the preciousness of the work is stripped away and the story is more actively engaged. "Oh yeah," you can imagine someone thinking, "she's right, I need to understand this. Speak up!"

As Hensley alluded to, there are true comparisons that can be made between the Mobile audiences and the ones Shakespeare wrote for, a cross section of society that might include nobility *and* the generally poor groundlings who stood in the front. Valuing a multiplicity of voices is the

---

[2] Quoted in Frank Scheck, "Theater in Prison for Good 'Measure,'" *New York Post*, December 9, 2010.

overarching vision of the company, and thus, it should be taken as no surprise that race, class, and accessibility are embedded in almost every conversation about the Mobile Unit.

"What does the Mobile Unit actually do in the 2020s?" is a fundamental question that has to be unpacked with the myriad Ten Thousand Things copycat programs that have popped up around the country over the past decade, from The Old Globe to Cal Shakes to Baltimore Center Stage. Importantly, too, what is it not doing? Is it serving community in the same idealistic ways that Hensley and Edelstein described? In 2016, I had my first opportunity, as a visiting scholar, to go on tour with The Public's Mobile Shakespeare Unit, a production of *Romeo and Juliet* at Rikers Island Prison. The reflections that I wrote down the next morning still resonate for the complex and problematic assumptions that they bring up.[3]

> I can say it was there, at Rikers that I had the most transcendent day of theater since I have been in New York. Maybe ever. I watched 65 inmates and about 20 guards deeply engage with some of the best actors in New York as they performed Shakespeare in a creaky gym deep within the facility. Our advance team of five people showed up at 10:30 am in a Zip car and a white van filled with props, a few benches, some awkward balloon arrangements, a keyboard, and a 20x20 carpet. Thirty minutes of transporting the stuff through the various levels of security, and within another 30 minutes the gym was set up. The actors arrived shortly thereafter, in another white van, and made their way through security. Then the inmates arrived.
>
> I watched the actors spend almost 30 minutes with the Rikers residents and employees before the show began, talking and laughing, answering questions. I watched some of the great theater professionals of New York create shoestring theater, with plastic chairs, a square of carpet, some balloons and quick changes. No backstage. Everyone could watch Capulet change into the Friar. ... But why would they? The communion between audience and performers was happening on that small stage in the middle of the basketball court. Nothing else existed. There were remarkable emotions. When Romeo and Juliet kissed for the first time, the younger detainees hollered and whistled. There were other moments when the noise of the audience escalated—there was general clamor and discussion. Midway through, a group of about 20 inmates from another part of the prison came in and grabbed chairs and set them up next to the established audience. I was entranced by the reactions far more than the performance, terrific as it was. During a particularly raucous moment, I glanced over at the guards to see if they were at all concerned by the "heat" in the room. They weren't, they were engaged too, one

---

[3] Some of these reflections were used in the following article: Kevin Landis and Ciara Murphy, "The Public Theater's Mobile Unit: Lean and Mean Shakespeare," *American Theater*, March 29, 2017.

with her camera out, snapping pictures of the young lovers. It was never worrisome. Just purely electrifying, every element of the experience. In other words, none of the "rules" of theater applied here, and that was entirely ok—great, even.

And then, the moment that gave me goosebumps. A beautifully staged fight scene that, as we all know, ends with Romeo killing Tybalt. The audience erupted in applause, several men stood, rooting passionately for Romeo.

As soon as I had written those thoughts, a creeping anxiety about the wealthy hegemonic nature of Mobile, in a location of great hardship and filled with social stigma, hit me. Within the context of a prison milieu, it is dangerously easy to fetishize the product, to pat oneself on the back for creating an accessible version of William Shakespeare. Those who strongly support its mission are right to point out that the strength of Mobile is that it does not dumb down Shakespeare at all; in fact, it simply places it in communities that have been denied access to the greatest author in the English language. This, it would seem, is a noble effort.

Stephanie Ybarra was the longtime director of the Mobile Unit and says that the focus on William Shakespeare was a struggle for her: "If it were up to me, I would maybe depart completely from what was, and invite my favorite voices from today to write for this context, for this physical structure, for these communities. That is more and more a desire, an interest of mine: to be adding to the canon in a distinctly American way, but in a way that also acknowledges and honors the different cultures that collide in our communities." Therein lies a central challenge at The Public, a company founded on American Shakespeare. The noble effort at bringing the Bard to underserved communities, people with limited financial means, is obviously a consistent through line of The Public Theater's history. However, saying "Shakespeare is for all" still presupposes that the long-dead white poet from Stratford *should* be seen as *the* critical playwright for our time.

In 2021, I revisited the subject with Ybarra, who by then had risen to the top of Baltimore Center Stage, one of America's premier theaters and a company also dedicated to Mobile work. She noted what all agree upon: To meet audiences where they are is fundamentally right and the responsibility of any theater company. Large American regional theaters must release themselves from the static buildings located in city centers and reach into local communities, with new stories that speak to specific needs. How it is accomplished is a challenging negotiation, and one that Eustis and The Public constantly revise. Eustis is unapologetic in his love for Shakespeare and sees that author as central to The Public's artistic mission. He is not alone. Edelstein notes that at the Old Globe, Shakespeare is, clearly, the house playwright. But more and more that idea needs to be negotiated and puzzled through. Ybarra insists that it is right to ask why we make the choices that we do, to uncover the not-so-pretty underbelly of the things that we love. "Because Joe Papp did it" is no longer enough. She says, "In the case of The Public Theater and the Mobile Unit, they need to take a break from Shakespeare. Full stop. That's it. And that's not news. I was saying that when I was there. Because that in and of itself—the fact that he is the only writer is incredibly harmful and problematic."[4]

Breaking bonds with some of the Pappian style is something Eustis knows he needs to do, even as he is completely committed to The Public's and his own devotion to William Shakespeare. But Mobile needn't be solely dedicated to the Bard, just as Hensley's company never was. The thing about Mobile that gets more deeply to Eustis's cares and passions is the ability for it to feel "of the community" and devoted to the principles of accessibility. Eustis: "I think we are seeing a rejection of the idea that what we should be in is the expensive commodity-making business. We are not Faberge eggs; we are not trying to create incredibly refined pieces of couture that can only be bought by the wealthy as a sign of how privileged they are … as a field, we are rejecting it. We are saying, actually, that's not our future."

Not long before Ybarra left The Public, she, along with Chiara Klein, led up a new take on Mobile with the creation of Mobile Unit National that reinforced those egalitarian bona fides. After seeing the power and success of the reading of Lynn Nottage's *Sweat* in Reading, Pennsylvania, and after the backlash to *Hamilton* by the new Trump administration, as discussed in Chapter 5, The Public Theater tried a pilot tour of the Pulitzer Prize-winning play to address the yawning divide between red and blue America in its access to theater. Through sponsorship from the Ford and Mellon Foundations, the play toured throughout the Midwest, the Rust Belt, and essentially pared down the contemporary play from the "largeness" of Broadway to something more akin to the Hensley model. It was presented with all of the lights on, in three-quarter seating and with minimal set pieces—a mirror and a makeshift bar. It would play one night only in each city and be produced in partnership with a local organization that might help tie the company with the community. For example, a presentation in Meadville, Pennsylvania, was performed at the Voodoo Brewery Production Facility and Event Pub, in partnership with the National Manufacturing and Tooling Association. A performance in Rochester, New York, partnered with the Guthrie Theater and the Rochester Diversity Council. The performance in Kenosha took place at the United Auto Workers Local 72 Hall.

The tour ran to about twenty cities and towns in the fall of 2018 and featured post show conversations and the potential of a longer-term relationship with the city. Klein reflected that the promise of Mobile was so vivid with *Sweat* and its national tour: "the uber-thesis of mobile is that plays catalyze conversations," she said. Indeed, in the program notes Eustis wrote, "This isn't a blue play or a red play. This isn't a Republican or a Democrat

---

[4] At the time of this writing, Ybarra was sunsetting Baltimore's mobile unit until she feels that she has a better answer for why it is done and who it is serving.

play. This play does what theater does best: It tells the truth about the lives of people who don't normally get the spotlight, who aren't glamorous or rich, but who are as heroic and deep and complicated as anyone." Bringing plays to the people, they hoped, would expand the conversation beyond New York City and imagine the country in dialogue.

National Mobile began and ended with the mini tour of *Sweat*. The departure of Ybarra and Klein and the onset of the pandemic put a stop to the further expansion of the program. It is within this context and backdrop that the 2021 revisioning of the Mobile Unit, in front of the Dime Savings Bank, was unusual. This was far removed from a gritty *Romeo and Juliet* at Rikers Island, or *Sweat* in Erie, Pennsylvania, with the yellow truck, the props, the expensive amps, and mics. No, this was, in fact, a bit of a Faberge egg, placed incongruously in the heart of Brooklyn. In some ways, the actual "production" and the year on the calendar don't really matter. The palpable sense is that The Public Theater, while striving to live up to its name, often battles with itself. Far from derision, this observation suggests that the struggle is, as noted, what gives The Public its identity.

The production in 2021 was not a Shakespeare play but rather carried the title *Mobile Unit's Summer of Joy!* It was, indeed, joyous, and the bubble machine, bright pink chairs, and the candy store colors of the set created a phantasmagoric visual feast in the corner of Albee Square. Gone was the Ten Thousand Things square of carpet encircled by hodgepodge chairs. While all the lights were still on, so too were the synthesizers and amplifiers. More compelling than that for the famed Shakespeare company was that while Shakespeare was written over the truck, there was no play. Instead, what followed was remarkable and worth retelling insofar as it reflects the struggle that The Public, and perhaps many other theater companies, have in their continuing need to fully engage their communities.

Covid-19 had made a "traditional" version of Mobile impossible. The prisons, community centers, and churches that made up the core sites previously had to be abandoned for outdoor spaces and regulations that prevented audience congregation for more than fifteen minutes. Karen Ann Daniels, the new head of Mobile, and director Patricia McGregor had to reimagine what the division could be in a vastly changed world. *Summer of Joy!* began with Daniels acting as an emcee, welcoming in people from the neighborhood, encouraging people to stop and listen, take a chair, take a seat on the curb, even if for a few minutes. She was followed by an invocation of what was essentially the mantra of the day by the head of the National Black Theater: "You are excellent at living." The hour was punctuated with poetry readings, self-help style speeches, and members of the Fortune Society (an organization supporting formerly incarcerated people) reading from Adrienne Maree Brown's book *Emergent Strategies*. Though everything was moving and expertly produced, one could not help but wonder why "Shakespeare" was emblazoned on the truck that formed the backdrop of this makeshift theater.

The answer came with the second portion of the performance, the McGregor-created "Shakespeare call and response," in which four actors guided the audience of passersby through what can only be described as a Shakespeare lesson. "What is your favorite Shakespeare play?" The audience responded. Shakespeare Mad Libs in which the audience replaced difficult Shakespeare words with easier ones to understand phrases and contexts. "Say what/say word," in which actors had to rephrase their text if someone doesn't understand what they mean. In a section on *Midsummer Night's Dream*, when one actor said "man by man," they were stopped and encouraged to say "person by person." During a lesson on *Winter's Tale*, Paulina, the force of nature nurse in Shakespeare's late drama, was described with a wink and a nod as "Nancy Pelosi meets AOC (Alexandria Ocasio-Cortez)."

It was odd to watch professional actors teach the people of Brooklyn about toxic sexism in a 500-year-old play, that it is inappropriate to use the phrase "man by man," and that Paulina is a cross between two American politicians (of a very certain political persuasion). It spoke to many people, perhaps most, but it seemed off-mission. It underscored elitism in a way that was jarringly evident, if difficult to pinpoint in the moment. Was this "for the people"?

I was reminded of a quote from Oskar Eustis, way back when I first met him in a dramaturgy class: "You may not hold your audience in contempt." The little life lessons on the street at Albee Square inadvertently asserted that the public they were serving *didn't get it* and needed help. As I learned at Rikers, when Mobile is successful it's because the artists know that the audience does get it and, in fact, it will actually read into the play new avenues of understanding. On another level, Albee Square revealed another division that is built into the American theater system. This Mobile attempt demonstrated and doubled down on a huge cultural divide in America that may actually be splitting the country apart. "Culture" is created for people with access, means, *and* specific political beliefs. This is not to imply that a company needs to promote political neutrality, elevate unsavory ideas or political leaders who are antithetical to a progressive mission. However, Mobile, when it stumbles, can be a clear example of hegemonic reincorporation of division. How can a theater assure that efforts at radical inclusivity do not become condescending?

Still, I left Albee Square with a smile on my face and a feeling that I actually did have a lively and engaging afternoon in the Brooklyn heat. I jotted in my notebook, "The Public is trying to be everything to everyone. It's fascinating to watch the struggle." *Summer of Joy!* looked different from Stephanie Ybarra's Mobile, and was, to be sure, a departure from the original goals of reaching deep into underserved communities. But it was a departure bred of necessity, and not a permanent shift. The result was an entertaining Shakespeare lesson, at times joyous, at times trite and didactic, and at all times highly produced. The budget for Mobile in 2021, with all of the regulations, testing, and other protocols, was close to $650,000. That's certainly not the "poor theater" of the early Papp years or the "all the lights on" aesthetic of Michelle Hensley. Similarly, Free Shakespeare in the Park in 2021, a production of *Merry Wives* set in Harlem, saw production costs of about $1.8 million in addition to about $1 million in Covid-related extra expenses. Making Shakespeare accessible and free is very expensive.

In Mobile's successes and failures over the decade, it consistently faces the question: How does an elite, well-funded, predominantly white organization with socialist political underpinnings reach a diverse population? Though I have focused on Mobile's Shakespeare-centrism, a real concern, too, is simply about how a company is *supposed* to serve its community. By putting Shakespeare on a pedestal, does The Public undercut or enhance its mission for social good? Or, like a religious proselytizer, is it only advancing its own dogma rather than the needs of the community? It's a fair question that so many American theaters ask, and it seems that the answer, increasingly, is that the proselytizing of that one man is, indeed, problematic. According to Ybarra, it's actually harmful. However, at The Public, perhaps the more important question of the contemporary era stretches beyond Shakespeare. Is taking work to the people in and of itself at least partly a condescending goal when, in fact, the people themselves are filled with unique skills, needs, wants, and expressions that simply haven't been given the megaphone that The Public Theater can provide? Should the deep pockets be used to fund the work of less financially privileged communities and theaters?

That is the question, then. What is the role and responsibility of a national theater, an organization with outsized influence? *Summer of Joy!* looked at those questions and, with all the unavoidable obstacles in the way, did not elegantly land on an answer. But something noble was being worked through, tinkered with, and unpacked, and it reflected a larger need at The Public. Mobile had a fairly good model that served certain constituents beautifully. It didn't serve *everyone*, but what initiative can? The Public Theater by 2021 already had something else that investigated the mission in a way that Mobile couldn't.

That program just may be the most important development of the Eustis era.[5]

Public Works

Oskar Eustis and his team recognized quickly how traveling Shakespeare can, without care, develop into an enterprise that feels like a colonizer relationship; as he notes, "preaching to people who didn't ask you to preach to them." He recalled that solving that problem and deepening the conversation around partnering and collaboration was important as The

---

[5] About a week before the close of *Summer of Joy!* Karen Ann Daniels was named as the Folger Shakespeare Library's new director of programming and artistic director.

Public grew and evolved. Creating the sort of deep connectivity that he wanted in a metropolis like New York meant going into communities and genuinely asking the people who lived there how the Theater could be of use—asking, in Eustis's words, "What do you want from us? Here's what we do. What's interesting to you?" At the Brownsville Recreation Center in Brooklyn, the answer from the mostly senior clientele was clear: "We want a jazzercise class."

Well, that's a start.

And indeed, jazzercise was a start of a new conversation about engagement. For a year, The Public helped facilitate jazzercise classes for the Brownsville Center's seniors. This, from a renowned theater company, may have seemed incongruous at the time, but the direction would become clear. It was a longitudinal relationship; they could bring the seniors to The Public to see shows, then, out of those connections, perhaps dances that were in those jazzercise classes might show up in a Public-produced play. While they may not be polished actors, they were darn good at jazzercise and that, they concluded, should be celebrated on the stage. Eustis says, if you start with "'We have resources. What do you want?' and the first thing you do is respond to what people want from *you*, that's a way better basis for a relationship than 'Here's what The Public Theater wants you to do.'"

Eustis is the first to admit that this really was not his idea. He is proud that his role has been to surround himself with brilliant minds and facilitate their vision. Enter Lear deBessonet, the mind behind Public Works, a person Eustis refers to as a genius: "My contribution, I think, was to intersect with Lear at a crucial point in her career, take her incredibly seriously, become her dialogue partner about how we could turn these impulses into a program and then throw my institutional support behind turning it into the program it's become."

From Baton Rouge, Louisiana, deBessonet mentions Mardi Gras and the sports and church of her youth as influencing her artistic aesthetic, a style she describes as participatory and intergenerational. Eustis met deBessonet in 2011 when she was creating and directing a whole-of-community rendition of *The Odyssey* at Edelstein's Old Globe in San Diego and saw that it was the beta version of what Public Works would become. In addition, she had spent two years creating a version of *Don Quixote* in Philadelphia with a community performance cast of forty-five people, made in collaboration with a homeless shelter and featuring a live band. A meal was served as part of the show every night—another now common facet of community theater creation.

Even this wasn't a new idea. Peter Schumann's Bread and Puppet Theater in Glover, Vermont, is one of many examples in the United States of theater companies eliding entertainment and eating. Schumann even named his theater in honor of that copacetic relationship. In fact, many of the tactics and tools used in the creation and methodologies of Public Works are ages old, and deBessonet and The Public team combined those impulses at an extremely opportune moment.

When she arrived in New York, deBessonet recalls being "distressed and disappointed by what I saw as professional theater, the way that it was functioning in the culture. And ... looking at the audience ... inside theaters and being like, 'this doesn't look like the city at all.' The separation between what was happening inside the closed space of theater and the city itself just felt so—there was such a shrinkage that felt really depressing to me." When she arrived, there was an ongoing question at The Public that revolved around its commitment to education. In conversations with Shirley Brice Heath, the Stanford anthropologist who Eustis brought in to help dream up community collaboration, the company was looking for new ways to reach New York City. If The Public was about community edification, it was a type of learning mostly for the ticket-buying class, and the learning was a one-way street. In Heath's work and reports on the subject, she outlined a need to focus on multidirectional relationships between community and arts organizations that emphasize bilateral discussions, classes, and performance. DeBessonet went to work identifying key partners within the five boroughs of New York; organizations that wanted to connect with The Public in generative development.

The five original partners included the Fortune Society in Queens, a company that worked with people exiting prison who needed assistance rebuilding their lives, and the aforementioned seniors at the Brownsville Recreation Center in Brooklyn. The Children's Aid Society, an organization supporting disadvantaged youth in Manhattan; DreamYard, a Bronx-based youth arts organization; and Domestic Workers United of Queens, which organizes fair labor standards for caregivers, nannies, and housekeepers, rounded out the originating partners. To that list, only three others have been added over the years, and the original five remain the core.[6]

Within six months of arriving at The Public, deBessonet presented a plan to Eustis that looked remarkably similar to the way Public Works continues to work today. She said:

> We will partner with them, the partnership will be a longitudinal, multiyear commitment. We will devise programming together, in collaboration with each other—these are not arts organizations, they each have a different expertise, so we will work with them to find something that would be exciting for them to do that is in the theater space but that will be open to their ideas of what they want. And the idea was that we would do a class at each of those sites, once a week, or every other week, if that was better for them. And then at the end of that year we would do a production.

The idea for the first production was *The Tempest*, not necessarily because of its authorship but because deBessonet was interested in a 1916

---

[6]The new additions are Casita Maria for Arts and Education (Bronx), Center for Family Life (Brooklyn), and the Military Resilience Foundation.

community-based production of the play called *Caliban by the Yellow Sands* by Percy MacKaye. Devised and directed by the famed playwright, its production at the Lewisohn Stadium at the City College of New York had all the trappings of spectacle that his twenty-first-century successor loved in her Mardi Gras youth. It was massive in scope, a masque commemorating the 300th anniversary of the death of William Shakespeare, with 50 characters and 1,500 performers who took part in elaborate interludes. Like deBessonet one hundred years after him, MacKaye called for full community engagement. A week before the event, the *New York Times* reported, "Specially chosen groups will take part in the interludes. ... The English Folk Dance Society will give the Elizabethan episode, under the supervision of Cecil Sharpe. The Germanic episode will be presented by the German University League of the city. ... Sixty young men, chosen as perfect physical specimens, will take part in the Greek episode ... the Alliance Française, under Lucien Bonheur, will give the French episode."[7] Even at that, the scale was not as enormous as MacKaye had wanted. The original plan was to present the masque in Central Park as part of a huge festival celebrating Shakespeare. Local politics prevented him from using the Park and he had to settle for a five-day run with 20,000 audience members and 1,500 performers.

A century later, deBessonet was positioning The Public to think about another grand festival of New York. Something big. And unlike MacKaye, she worked for an organization that could guarantee her a space in Central Park. With Eustis, she had a fully willing collaborator who was ready to approve the pageant. The historical connections for Eustis were resonant. In 2016 he noted:

> I think that it is not a coincidence that the pageant movement of the early twentieth century really came to fruition in the midst of the Gilded Age and the time when there was the greatest separation of wealth, the greatest concentration of wealth in American history until now. It's happening again and I think you can see those things as linked. As wealth is gathered into fewer and fewer hands, as inequality in the country increases, as the division between rich and the rest of us gets larger and larger you can feel in all fields a kind of manifestation of the desire to have an alternative set of values, the belief that not everything can be bought, you cannot put a price tag on the most important things.

It is an important and relevant observation that reflects the cyclical nature of community-based work and what it means to be *professional* in the creation of art. If wealth inequality is reacted to with a curious need for pageant-like work in which huge amounts of resources are poured into community-based spectacle, a question arises about the necessity, or lack thereof, of professionalism. Again,

---

[7] "Celebrated Actors in Cast for Masque," *New York Times*, May 17, 1916.

these ideas are revolutionary only in the sense that they seem to disappear and reappear throughout history. Even the basic structure of MacKay's pageant and the subsequent pageants at Public Works mirror theater creation as far back as the Middle Ages. It's taught in every theater history course that some of the foundational forms of European theater developed out of the cycle and mystery plays of the fifteenth century, when craft guilds participated in the development of theatrical entertainment by contributing their expertise in areas that helped create the collective, community whole.

With the five partners on board and with *Caliban of the Yellow Sands* as a loose model, deBessonet went to work. The Delacorte was reserved for her for the 2013 Labor Day weekend, and thus she had a concrete date to work toward. While the classes, potlucks, and conversations that are now a staple of Works would never end, at least there was a time-certain moment for a formal presentation. That first year, the ambition was a 200-person musical adaptation of *The Tempest* and, of principal importance, it would be on the crown jewel stage of the foremost Shakespeare institution in New York. Public Works could not function, according to deBessonet and Eustis, if it was seen as a secondary program of the company. Her succinct encapsulation of the relationship was: "Let's extend the treatment that would go to Meryl Streep to the community members, because they are the VIPs of this theater."

The time from deBessonet's hiring to the opening night of *Tempest* was just about a year and a half, underscoring how important this new program was for the company. She had a small budget that allowed her to hire one teaching associate, originally someone who could teach jazzercise to the Brownsville seniors. It grew quickly as the ideas about the ongoing work deepened and became dialectic. The Public was not only looking to teach classes but to also see how the seeds could be planted to allow the organization to *create* in collaboration with their community partner. On the evolution of jazzercise, deBessonet notes:

> That's where we started, which was great. And after they did that first year, after they did *The Tempest*, it was like, "Oh, I love singing and I love acting as well." So the second year became totally different. In that year we [were] devising original work that included dancing and singing and acting. And then over time that class has deepened and deepened. They did their own version of *A Midsummer Night's Dream*, and then they wanted to explore August Wilson, and they did *Jitney*. Then they did Lynn Nottage, *Crumbs from the Table of Joy*.

From jazzercise to Wilson and Nottage was a fairly large leap in just a couple of years. Yet each partner had a different structure and artistic trajectory, and deBessonet committed time at each organization to consider what might work best. In conversations with John Gordon, one of the leaders of Fortune Society, they decided that simple acting classes would be ideal. In his view, Fortune Society clients spent lots of time in group conversation, talking about and assessing the ways that they could reenter society and rebuild their lives. What they wanted, he said, more than group conversation, was a way to access their "new selves," to play out the "personhood that you felt." "Maybe theater could be a chance to act our way into thinking differently,"[8] he offered. In other words, in that first year, Fortune wanted something much more personal, much more individual.

It wasn't easy. DeBessonet sat in on "Alternatives to Incarceration" classes and promoted her acting classes to the participants, generally young adults skeptical of her motivations and, in her retelling, glaring at her as if they wanted her to leave. She says:

> Finally somebody was like, "*Robocop*. I like *Robocop*." And I was like, "*Robocop* is acting. Absolutely. Let's work with that." ... There was a guy in the corner who was like, "I watched *Beauty and the Beast* with my kid." And guys started being like, "oh, yeah, and *The Little Mermaid*," and they started talking about these Disney musicals. Which, for me, was like ... OK. Whoa. I mean, I loved those shows in Louisiana. That was part of my introduction to theater. ... I think that the feeling of trying to drum up interest was really very much part of those early days. We did a lot of improv and physical work, and then they wanted to work on scripts.

Like at Brownsville, acting classes expanded quickly and The Public teachers brought in scripts. Especially popular at Fortune was Stephen Adly Guirgis's *Motherfucker with the Hat*, the 2011 play that starred Chris Rock on Broadway. And as with her ability to secure Central Park for the pageants, deBessonet was able to pull on the gilded strings at The Public to invite Guirgis to attend a performance of his play at Fortune. Similarly, the girls at Children's Aid Society were interested in choir and singing. So, in addition to offering classes, visits from professional artists from Joe's Pub became commonplace.

At Domestic Workers United (DWU), participants were clear that weekly classes were not what they needed, nor could they afford the time to attend. Instead, they wanted a monthly lunch. Perhaps they could all read a classic play in Spanish or English and discuss or read scenes. Since DWU has, according to deBessonet, a strong commitment to equity, they didn't want to assign roles that would unfairly give one person too many lines. Instead, they passed the script and divided it up line by line.

The haphazard way that each of the partner organizations discovered ways of creating and partnering with Public Works actually gets to a basic tenet of what is being attempted. It is, perhaps, a way of thinking that will be increasingly essential as art regroups in the wake of the pandemic. It is a question, Eustis notes, of professionalism and expertise:

> It is genuinely radical and a step further in its radical nature from that of Mobile Shakespeare and the Delacorte, because it actually posits that the

---

[8] As told by Lear deBessonet.

separation between professional and amateur is only a question of scale, it is not a question of a binary opposition. ... And actually, there's a value statement in Public Works that says being an artist is not a binary. It's not you are or aren't an artist—that some people are artists, and some people are content to view art—but that being an artist is inherent in the human condition. ... And some of us get to practice it 10,000 hours or more. Some of us get to spend our lives doing it, so we refine our skills. Some people have genetic gifts of singing or loud voices that make them more successful. But everybody is on that spectrum. It's not a separate class of people. And when you put those people together on stage in The Public Works shows, that's proof of that thesis. It's visceral proof. You watch it, and you go, "Oh my God. I'm loving the whole thing."

Eustis's framing makes sense and identifies as clearly as anything else The Public's commitment to expanding its role as a community connector, an organization that must platform the creativity and potential of underserved communities. The desire to blur the divide between the professional and the amateur illuminates a need to de-center the organization, famous for its professional artists, and instead focus on its ability to facilitate. Some of that facilitation comes in the meetings and gatherings that have absolutely nothing to do with theater. An important part of that are the potlucks, a tradition that deBessonet began in Philadelphia. She says, "I think a lot of artists who do community-based work, the breaking bread together is

FIGURE 9.2 *Opening night of* Twelfth Night. *Courtesy John Lamparski.*

just such a vital opportunity for connection. It's church-like ... without the theology part of it, but it is like a sacred fellowship time."

The pinnacle of Public Works was and remains the presentation of work by community actors on the stage built by Papp, Julia, Streep, and all the rest. For The Public, and for its national and international partners, the Works pageant has to end up on the best and biggest stage available. Now that the classes are codified, taught by teaching professionals and benefiting from years of practice, it is expected that the members of the community who audition for the pageant and are selected are ready for the big stage. The organization thus has to support it and, according to deBessonet, it has to succeed on its own merit.

The pageants of Public Works do, in fact, *work*. If reviews are a guide of success (and, of course, they are not), the years of Works extravaganzas delight the critics. Works has presented productions of *The Tempest* (2013), *Winter's Tale* (2014), *Odyssey* (2015), *Twelfth Night* (2016), *As You Like It* (2017), *Twelfth Night* (2018), and *Hercules* (2019). It returned in 2022 with a revival of *As You Like It*. Befitting her interests and the spectacular magic that Central Park offers, deBessonet created a model that was replicated over and over in which a classic story was set to music, creating something more than a traditional Broadway musical—an amalgam of things, really: part concert, part musical, part variety show, part age-old story, part community party. The Public Works pageant is delightful because it is its own thing. In that way, when a performer is not quite as polished, it does not matter because what one is watching is new; it doesn't subscribe to traditional rules of theater.

For the original *Tempest*, *Winter's Tale*, and *Odyssey*, deBessonet brought in the composer Todd Almond to develop the music and star in a principal role. That model was continued. In late 2015, Shaina Taub, the young rising star in New York composing circles, was hired to write the original score to *Twelfth Night* to be performed the following summer. An actor herself, she would play the part of the narrator/Feste, one of Shakespeare's most popular jesters and clowns. Taub recalled the challenge of the task: create a ninety-minute spectacle out of a three-hour play, make a full score that could be performed by regular people and seasoned actors, be certain that the choices can be justified for a cast of at least 100, and make room for cameos from specialty groups from around the city. What is often created with Works is a folksy mix of R&B and pop, which can give the performances a somewhat docile feel, as if Shakespeare needs to be coy and cute to be fully accessible. So much is lavished on community, good will, and a feeling of connection that occasionally the actual productions dip too far into the saccharine, reducing epic tales into quickie evenings with easy morals. This was most noticeable in 2019, when Works partnered with Disney to revive the largely underwhelming 1997 animated film, *Hercules*, as the summer pageant. While the spectacle was grand and the evening undeniably fun, it was not lost that the annual ode to community partnership and longitudinal relationships with deeply socially worthy organizations was a partnership with a massive international entertainment organization, and music not by the plucky Almond or Taub but by the legendary Alan Menken and David Zippel. It was a bold reach that perhaps underserved the mission.

The massive-scale *Hercules* model aside, some of the success of Works has always been, undoubtedly, due to immense budgets that allow all shows at the Delacorte to have a polish befitting the illustrious stage. The salaries of 200 cast members, including a handful of professional ringers in the lead roles, costumes, mics, lights, composers, and directing teams that are world class is not the sort of theater that any regional company can just do. But The Public can, and has made a commitment to do it. That first year, *The Tempest* ran for only three nights, but the labor and the results seemed to need more—an extended time on that big stage. This, though, is where questions must arise about Public Works and its mission, especially as it grows from its infancy into a staple of The Public season. By placing the pageant in extended runs on the Delacorte with massive production budgets, there can be a feeling of "spectacle" that overshadows the good of the social engagement and accessibility that the program advances.

However, the bigness of the Central Park stage must be part of the equation as it acts as a climax. It is the climax of hours of community connection, a sharing of skills, jazzercise, readings, potlucks, and rehearsals. Shirley Brice Heath recalled a powerful interaction with a participant: "Nobody has ever cared whether I showed up on time or whether I was even there. You never had anybody who cared ... and you come to a place where you are needed, and you are respected. And you are in a play that is about redemption and love." To Heath, this is what live performance at the intersection of community building can do, and the results powerfully display the radical inclusivity and Public-ness that the slogans promise. "It's not poppycock!" Heath exclaimed. This is the essence of theater.

DeBessonet sums up well what Heath was seeing in those first years. Involving an anthropologist in the assessment and creation of new initiatives, they grasped an optimal circumstance for transformation: create a group enterprise with safe boundaries. "That is what the theater is," she says. "And the notion that the recipe of theater is also a fundamental recipe for human transformation, to me, is the reason that it can and must be everywhere."

With the success of this model of socially engaged theater, taking Public Works everywhere became a focus for the Public. Laurie Woolery and Lear deBessonet codified the methodology of Works in an internally published book called *The Public Works Playbook*, and in 2017 the program went national. After years of Works classes and pageants, they had a model that they felt could be replicated in other cities and countries. The founding national partners of the model were Dallas Theater Center, Seattle Repertory Theater, and the National Theatre of London. In addition, in 2019, The Public announced a group of seven "affiliate" theaters—smaller companies that would help integrate theater into communities across the nation. The success of national models and host communities, according to Heath, is very structural and simple. It comes down to access: "One, they've got to know their city and how much their city will take. ... Two, you have to be able to imbue and reflect in your own being that the purpose is deeper than doing good theater, but the purpose is best served when you do good theater. The two are tightly connected. The third is that you've got to understand how people from across class lines can get to the place where you are doing the theater." The final point is actually essential to the success of Public Works. Access to the pageant is of utmost importance as it identifies a central reality in the relationship between the served communities and the organizing theater; if your partners cannot easily get to the venue, the ethics of the relationship are immediately made moot. The New York transit system, one of the most comprehensive in the world, makes the Big Apple an ideal place for the experiment.

For the national version, Dallas Theater Center was a logical place to begin since it had the infrastructure that was needed. In addition, its artistic director, Kevin Moriarty, was a longtime friend and collaborator with Oskar Eustis. He had been brought in as a director of *A Christmas Carol* at Trinity Rep in Providence in the late 1990s and helped Eustis create the MFA graduate consortium between Trinity and Brown University, where he was head of directing. When he arrived at Dallas in 2007, he continued building the relationship with Eustis and The Public, coproducing Tracey Scott Wilson's *The Good Negro*, the musical *Giant*, and Michael Friedman and Itamar Moses's *Fortress of Solitude*.

In 2017, Dallas launched Public Works Dallas with another rendition of *The Tempest*. Moriarty recalled that their first outing mirrored that of The Public. At first it was met by skepticism and misunderstanding from community and staff; then, after it worked, there was a flood of good will and enthusiasm. Transportation was a central consideration and the theater bought subway cards for all of the participants for the first rehearsals. By the time the pageant went up, the mayor of Dallas was onstage with undocumented citizens, all having "conquered Shakespeare," said Moriarty. He went on: "The American theater forever has been saying: 'We care about our communities. We want to engage with the community. We are theater for everyone. We want to connect and open our doors wide.' And yet, actions embedded in the architecture of our institutions often contradict that." Moriarty, like so many of his contemporaries, pointed to something in 2017 that would only be reinforced in 2020 and into 2021 and, likely, for the foreseeable future. According to Moriarty, theater will perish if companies do not deeply connect with the communities that they ostensibly serve; not the donors and the ticket-buying class, but with the people who live in the city, who take the subway, who— back to Papp's formulation—live and die in the neighborhood where they were born. Moriarty: "What's kept theater a living art form is that artists making theater have continued to reflect American society, who are constantly changing the art itself through their experiences."

In relation to the Mobile Unit and Public Works, compelling questions about the nature of performing arts within a community continuously come up: Are the programs serving something fundamentally "New York" or something fundamentally "American?" Or, is this sort of work reaching into something deeply intrinsic to the goals of theater from its inception? Is theater the ultimate democratic art form? Eustis has a clear answer and it is why he believes that Public Works is the most successful innovation of his tenure at The Public. He is often fond of talking about the inextricable link between democracy and theater, of nascent democracy developing on a hillside in Athens in an amphitheater called the Theater of Dionysus. Expressing and deepening democratic values is the entire point of the form.

For proof, he sees the success of Works at the National Theatre in London as evidence of the universality of the experiment. In 2019, Rufus Norris, the artistic director of the National and a friend of Eustis, committed to creating a version of the program in England. In a way entirely different from The Public, Norris believed that his theater had an obligation to the entirety of his country. At the National, a theater actually subsidized in a very real and significant way by the British government, Norris recognized that the values of Works could actually work well in a geographically smaller nation and within an institution *obligated* to serve everyone. He created the Theatre Nation Partnerships that allowed the Theater to directly link to communities that were underserved by art, by going into schools, touring, and creating new theater in partnership with those communities. For example, the National Theatre's megahit *The Curious Incident of the Dog in the Night-Time* went into secondary schools throughout the country. This initiative was paired with Public Acts, the National's version of Works, which, through long relationships with communities, culminates in a pageant on a major stage. *Pericles* was the first version in 2018, followed by Woolery and Taub's *As You Like It*. In accordance with The Public's model, the pageants were performed on big stages: the Olivier Theatre and the Queen's Theatre. London's *Guardian*, echoing New York critics before, focused on the grandeur and the aesthetic of community gathering: "As our lovers come to the end of their story, the community gathers together once more. They sing of their fears for the future and then, in one booming voice, shout out: 'Still I will love.' The audience stands and cheers."[9]

How Public Works (and Public Acts) connects with what it means to be a "theater for all" is the most significant conversation that Works has restarted for the company. For Norris, that is complicated by his necessary need to work under the eye of the government that is paying for his company. He notes, "I walk into The Public and I go, this is the conversation that I want to be in. This is the conversation that I want to run. How do I turn the National foray and make it feel like this is where all of humanity is welcome and feel they've

---

[9]Miriam Gillinson, "*As You Like It* Review: Musical Take on Shakespeare Inspires and Thrills," *Guardian*, August 27, 2019.

got an ownership of it?" He says that at the National he lives in a far different political situation than Eustis does at The Public. Indeed, he notes, he has to be careful how far he can raise his head above the parapets. The bows and arrows of the British press always have their targets trained on him and ready to point out when a perceived liberal ethic goes too far. He laments, "Boogeymen [for the press] are generally subsidized arts organizations or the BBC."

Eustis does seem to have more luxury to wax poetic about the necessity of theater to humanity. Public Works is not about national identity, and he notes:

> [Public Works] is not a nationalist idea to demonstrate how great the United States is. It's an idea to demonstrate how powerful the idea of enfranchisement of the people is. ... The theater has thrived all over the world in moments of democratic enfranchisement, moments when the franchise expands suddenly, and more people are participating in the political system, the theater always prospers.
>
> *The Times of London*, which is not noted for its progressive politics—particularly since it's run by Rupert Murdoch—wrote a rave review of the show, and the critic said, "This was the first time I have seen the nation on stage at the National." At that point—that's not an American talking. That's not just an American idea ... without claiming that I have the authority to say this, I have the belief that these are human values that go far beyond the promises of this country.

That review was, indeed, an over-the-top rave, and it may be one time that Eustis and a Murdoch-employed reviewer are in lock step: "What is a national theater? What should it do? What should it look and sound like? The answer, as more than 200 amateur performers took to the Olivier stage to perform a joyous musical version of Shakespeare's *Pericles*, was defiantly this: inclusive, empowering, revitalizing, celebratory, multicultural, multilingual and downright fun."[10]

* * *

So, what happens when all of the theaters close, when Broadway shutters, when packed houses and hits like *Hamilton* and *The Lion King* feel like reminders of an era gone by? Classes and pageants could not be done for over a year and so Woolery and her team took the time to reassess its commitment to values. What does it mean for a wealthy, predominantly white organization to continue the good work of community organizing when so many of their constituents were hit so deeply by the pandemic? Zoom classes for communities that often don't have excellent access to Wi-Fi and whose programming budgets have been slashed caused great challenges.

---

[10]Chris Bennion, "Theater Review: *Pericles* at the Oliver," *The Times*, August 29, 2018.

The pandemic was a reminder, too, that Works still was a new initiative and perhaps needed some refocusing. While saying that the goal was to create longitudinal relationships between community and arts organizations, works needed to understand why that was so critical and if it was true to the mission. If it was there to highlight an "all of New York" approach to arts making and community collaboration, then why *Hercules*, in partnership with Disney? Why, then, were community members still seemingly the backdrop of the story while Broadway stars were the leads? Why, after a decade of work, was the initiative still just working with the original partners with only a couple of add-ons? That is not deepening.

The challenge of Public Works is that the brilliant idea, by 2019, had hit a bit of a plateau in which, ironically for an arts organization, it hadn't really sorted out what its *artistic* mission was. What sort of art was being created out of short retellings of Shakespeare on huge budgets? The pageant may have surpassed the dreams of Percy MacKaye and *Caliban of the Yellow Sands* in its display of celebration and massiveness. But in 2019, one might have asked: "Is this really full collaboration? What can come next?"

The pandemic may have offered a necessary reset, or stress test. Works had to pivot to the creation of videos and documentaries that expressed its values and featured its programming, the grassroots work alongside the pageant. The institution released a video early in the pandemic of members of the partner organizations, the Dallas, Seattle, and London offshoots and all of the national affiliates, joining in the now familiar Zoom boxes in a community rendition of the final song of *As You Like It*, "Still I Will Love." The song had already become the anthem of Public Works, and its singing, in the dark early days of the crisis, was a powerful reminder of the hope and light of the program: "On the heaviest day, on the bitterest night. Still, I will love. Still, I will love. When I'm tired and hungry and we're in a fight. ... Still, I will love. Still, I will love you."[11]

In the fall of 2020, Public Works released a documentary, *Under the Greenwood Tree*, about the making of *As You Like It*. Interviews with partner leaders, including with Woolery, Eustis, and Taub, were interspersed with songs and clips from past productions. Like so many efforts in 2020, while it was a beautifully produced work of art that celebrated joy, digital content was a melancholy reminder of loss in a world that turned its back on an art form that relied on shared space, shared time, and shared air. But as Woolery recognized, it was in exactly these sorts of difficult times that a program like Public Works needed to express its essentiality as a glue in a community. She said, "One of our community partners shared that city funding has been cut for summer programming. They already have their summer programming lined up

---

[11]Shaina Taub, *As You Like It*, 2017.

but now it's in limbo. Yet, funding for the police has not been reduced. Now, we are facing a summer with youth on the street with nothing to do and police in full force. It's a powder keg waiting to explode." Crisply edited video presentations eased some pain, but wouldn't solve the real problems that partner organizations faced.

That fall, Public Works embarked on the newly created Seed Project, a massive video installation along the façade of its Lafayette Street headquarters. The photographer Jennifer Young was sent out to take pictures of the city and of partner members, and those photos were used alongside quotations that completed the phrase, "Today I am planting a seed of—" in the creation of a Public Works photographic mural. The work alternated with the "Say Their Names" project, an installation by Garlia Cornelia Jones and Lucy Mackinnon that similarly used the façade of the building as a canvas for the names of 2,100 Black lives that had been lost at the hands of the police.

The use of the building was a poetic reminder of so many of the ways that Public Works and the Mobile Unit work to decenter *institutionality*. How does an artistic director put The Public back into The Public Theater? Since Eustis believes that Public Works is the greatest innovation of his tenure, the answer for him is completely literal. How to put The Public back in? *Actually* put the public in the plays and celebrate their image on the building.

* * *

While The New York Shakespeare Festival was founded as a mobile unit, roaming the parks of New York City in an old sanitation truck, it eventually disappeared. Michelle Hensley showed how it could come back. The renamed Public Theater at Astor Place, in an old library and home for displaced Jews, showed how a theater could be a sanctuary for its community. The gentrification of those neighborhoods and the massive expansion of programming and commercial successes that arose obscured that founding pillar. DeBessonet, Woolery, and Eustis showed how that could come back. And just as it was getting started, the pandemic and social unrest showed just how essential it actually was.

While the longterm changes to American theater are not fully known as this is written in 2022, it is clear that Mobile and Works represent the greatest artistic leap of the Eustis years. *Hamilton* and *Fun Home* will always be a prominent part of his biography, but in the worst days of 2020, in the winter of the darkest year in contemporary world history, the glorious infrastructures of The Public Theater were shuttered, and the grand old buildings became a canvas to project images of everyday members of the community, to tell their stories, to remember their lives and to dream of a future. On the heaviest day, on the bitterest night, *that* was the light.

And *that* is putting the public back into The Public.

INTERLUDE

Kwame Kwei-Armah

FIGURE 9.3 *Kwame Kwei-Armah. Courtesy* Washington Post.

The British artist Kwame Kwei-Armah is the current artistic director of London's Young Vic. Previously, he was the head of Baltimore Center Stage. He has directed several times at The Public, including The Public Works production of *Twelfth Night* (2016 and 2018) that he co-conceived with Shaina Taub. It was presented at the Delacorte and at the Young Vic. In November 2021, he discussed the current theater climate, his time at The Public, and the joy of directing a Public Works pageant. The interview is lightly edited for length.

Landis: What was it about the reputation that preceded The Public that made a young artist see that as a goal?

Kwei-Armah: I think I had just heard of all of the brilliant work that had been done there, and I'd read about all the brilliant work. And the Shakespeare in the Park thing just blew my mind. And so, the kinds of plays they were producing, and the reputation that the theater had, it read in Britain like the national theater of the US. And I knew that I just wanted to be there.

Landis: Having worked at The Public a lot, having been the artistic director of Baltimore Center Stage, has that viewpoint of The Public shifted at all? Do you see it as kind of a national theater?

Kwei-Armah: I do. It's about taste and adventure. And this is pre-*Hamilton*. Of course, its post *A Chorus Line*, but it's pre-*Hamilton*. It's the combination of Joe Papp and George C. Wolfe, and then Oskar. It's a combination of all of those things that makes you feel like this is the tastemaker. That the great artists wants to work there, they do work there. And that the taste of the artistic leadership is always worthy of looking at, at investigating and setting the trend.

Landis: When you say a tastemaker, what are some of the examples you think of at The Public, in which it moved the dial on American theater? Things that have changed because of what The Public is doing? …

Kwei-Armah: So, pre-*Hamilton*, my experience as an artistic director of a major original theater was that integrated casting hadn't quite penetrated the deepest parts of our audiences' minds. I have personal experiences and I directed Arthur Miller's adaptation of *Enemy of the People*. And I cast one actor Black, one actor white, not actually on purpose, just because they were the best actors that came into the room. And I went "great, I'm going to do that, and I know they're brothers." And it had some push back.

… That wasn't really done. Post-*Hamilton*, no one ever spoke about it again. One could do whatever you wanted to do with a cast that was Black, brown and white, in terms of integration. You could just do it, because that *Hamilton* experience had proven that American history can be turned through the lens of ethnicity, not only without it detracting, but with it adding, it was additive. And for my money in my time in American theater, that was the most revolutionary thing.

* * *

Landis: Are you seeing the same sort of energy and push back in the UK as we're seeing in the United States [relative to EDI etc.]?

Kwei-Armah: Oskar would argue with me and say that the United States is in a different place from the UK. I might argue and say I don't think that it is. I think we just express it slightly differently. I think the cultural lines are being redrawn everywhere. I think how one uses cultural tools to negotiate it may vary, but I think we're all under it. We're all under the microscope.

Gen Z and the millennials are of a mindset right now that everything should be burnt down in order to be rebuilt. And I'm of the opinion that some stuff needs to be burnt down, but you don't burn down the whole house at the same time. Because actually, what happens with most revolutions that we know is those who torch usually get burnt as well. The first round of revolutionary goes down with the revolution. We can look at Russia, or we could even look at the Muslim brotherhood in Egypt. We can see that revolutions turn very quickly.

And so, I think we're amid that revolution here. I happen to not really believe in revolution but in an accelerated *evolution*. But we are in the same spot I believe.

* * *

Landis: Could you say why the Mobile Unit grabbed your attention and how it influenced the way you programed in Baltimore?

Kwei-Armah: After doing Mobile a couple of times I then brought it to Baltimore. After taking it to Baltimore, I then came to London to the Young Vic and rode it out at the Young Vic. And basically, it's the premise that sometimes you don't have to bring the people to the castle, you have to take the castle to the people. And without asking them to return. ... everybody deserves access to theater. Everybody deserves what we call "high art." And sometimes you just got to bring it to the people, you got to bring high-quality work to the people. So, actually what they get to see are some of the best actors with beautiful directors doing wonderfully created, really good work. And so Mobile came first, I directed *Much Ado*, and then later I directed *Comedy of Errors*.

And going into the prisons and going on tour with Mobile, and seeing the work touch the audience in the way that it did, I mean, it was extraordinary. I'll give you an example: At one time we were at a prison, and it was a women's prison. And one of the inmates who was seeing the show, she took three programs, when we asked her why she took three programs she said, "Well, it's one for me, and one for each of my children. And I send the program to my children and then they read the play, and then we talk about it, and we talk about the show that I saw." I was like, "Yo, this is God's work." This is why we do what we do. To connect to people, art as a healer, art as a conduit, art as a catalyst. Mobile just taught me that. ...

Landis: Does Shakespeare provide too much of a monolithic version of theater history?

Kwei-Armah: You know, I personally believe it should be a mix diet … audience come in and go, "Oh, oh, they've given me Shakespeare, I don't understand Shakespeare." And then when they get to the end of it and it's done in the way that they do, they go, "Oh my god, I've understood Shakespeare and I really enjoyed Shakespeare." So, it's a win, win, win for me.

I think the idea of expanding it, it's just natural. It's like me wanting to create a canon of work that can go out, and new companies who wish to serve in this way can choose between the classic and the new plays. It's canon building for me. …

Landis: If people critique, and some do, that Mobile could be proselytizing what a theater company believes is important, Public Works is doing something a little bit different in its engaging with the community. Is that a fair way of putting it? And can you talk a little bit about how you became involved with Works?

Kwei-Armah: Yeah, again, I'll come at it from the rear, as it were. Stephanie Ybarra and Lear came down to see something of mine in Baltimore, and then she [Lear] was going to have a year off. And I was honored that she asked me to be the next person in. And we landed on *Twelfth Night*, and then we invited Shaina Taub to come in and play with that. And I had to say that it is one of the most magnificent experiences I've had in my life.

When we toured the five boroughs for casting—the idea that people came in, not only were they taught for a year before the audition, but people just came in and gave of themselves. They sang a song, they read some poetry. I mean, to see people want to be a part of a 250 [person] family was kind of moving. We had the most amazing rehearsal period where everybody, the professional actors and the ensemble, for want of a better term, that everybody gave of themselves a million percent.

And again, one of the things I wanted to do was to really push it to make it as slick a show as possible. But even just going to New York as I would do, to audition groups who would be in the community section of the play, was thrilling. You know, I won't stand for any criticism of it at all! Because you know again, all criticism is valid depending on where it is and how it's coming at you. But the beautiful thing about this program is that it wears its heart on its sleeve. It says, everyone deserves to be part of art. Not just take it in, but anyone can be a part of it. And that, that's magnificent to me. ...

Landis: From these sorts of nuts and bolts and structural standpoint, what is it like to direct 250 people on a stage in Central Park? That must be extraordinarily difficult?

Kwei-Armah: If I'm to be 100 percent honest, that was the last thing that I worried about. I worried far more about how we create the piece and shape the piece, so that everybody feels, or that most people feel, equitable. Prior to that, I had directed 500 people on a stage in Senegal at the opening ceremony at the festival of Black arts and culture.

So, actually I was not worried about that if that makes sense. I don't wish to sound cocky about it, but I wasn't worried. ... In my mind it is about creating shapes and creating the same shapes that you would create on a 14 x 14 map. People have got to be seen. The symmetry needs to be interesting. People need to know how to get on and off.

So, the logistics of that, the logistics of how you care for 200 people. How do you make them feel engaged, how you make them feel seen, how you make them want to give of themselves? I think that was the genius of the system that was created to support Public Works.

Landis: Would you articulate that a bit more, the strategies to help people be seen. Especially people who may have no experience. I imagine most don't have experience being on a major stage like that. How do you facilitate that desire to be fearless, I guess, if I could put it that way?

Kwei-Armah: I might approach this in two ways. The mechanism that Lear had created with the Public Works department was magnificent. Every member of their team and the extended team, when we went into production, really actually cared.

By the time everybody got into the rehearsal, they'd already been loved by the building, they'd already been fed by the building, and they were fed during rehearsals. They'd already been given, those who

	could not afford it, transportation, in order to get to the theater. They'd already been briefed about what it is and what would be expected of them. And so, then all a director has to do is come in and glue that together and say "hey, I love this, I love you, I love what we're about to do, let's do it."
Landis:	The potlucks. The getting together and eating. Can you say a bit about that, I don't fully understand how that works?
Kwei-Armah:	I mean, everybody just gathers and there's only one agenda, and that's let's eat together. And then let's celebrate what we did the last time, or celebrate what we're about to do. … People like something that says, "hey, I'm inviting you to come and eat with me." And it's wonderful because the atmosphere is almost party-like. People are so thrilled to be with other people and eating with other people, knowing that there is no agenda on one hand, but on the other hand the only agenda is to be *as one*.

* * *

Landis:	I think one of the things that comes up, especially as we think about Public Works, is that there was a robust infrastructure in place that Lear created. But when you went and took it to the Young Vic, presumably that infrastructure hadn't been built yet. …
Kwei-Armah:	Well, I was very fortunate that we have again, excuse the use of the word, but a very robust community department called Taking Part. They had produced work with choruses before from their community. So actually, for them we did have the infrastructure to kind of go out and find the people. And we talked through a little bit how we did it in New York and then we adapted it. And actually, it still is one of the highlights of my time at the Young Vic. To be able to open the theater, open my tenure with a community of fifty people on the stage.
Landis:	So, you think this model of Public Works, it's replicable outside of major theaters?
Kwei-Armah:	Facts, inside and out. Totally and utterly. It takes resource and it takes philosophy, but it absolutely can be repeated wherever one needs in the world, I believe. Because in essence, it's saying everybody deserves to be on the stage.

Landis: Kwame, the last thing I want to ask you, and thank you very much for these comments.

Kwei-Armah: No worries.

Landis: It's really illuminating. ... Is there anything else you want to say about Oskar, The Public Theater, and its importance in your career?

Kwei-Armah: I would say that Oskar has been among ... the greatest influences on my art. Both as a leader, and as an artist and as a director. It's hard to overstate how much he means to me. It's hard to overstate what a privilege it is to have access to that encyclopedic mind but even bigger heart. And that's very rare to find: someone with a heart the size of the Atlantic, and the mind that can scale Everest. It's very hard to find that in a being. And then to have access to that being. And to that gaze, that dramaturgical gaze that is almost second to none.

Hope

10

Rebirth

FIGURE 10.1 *Eustis on the bar at The Public lobby. Courtesy Nicholas Hunt.*

The Public Theater has a tradition at the beginning of the rehearsal process for every show. One morning is designated for a meet and greet in the lobby of 425. It's a lightly catered event, with cookies or bagels, some coffee and tea. After a bit of mingling, the staff gathers in a circle with the incoming production's team of directors, designers, and performers. Oskar Eustis stands on top of the café bar and talks about the upcoming production and why it is so essential for New York and America *right now*. The director will often say a few words, but the most important part of the thirty-minute ritual is when everyone in the room—marketers, producers, interns, directors, designers, technicians, *everyone*—is asked to introduce themselves and say what they do at The Public. It's more than organization-building, it is the symbolic encapsulation of "one public," an affirmation from the staff to the incoming artists that "we are all here for you."

It was with a sense of profound sadness that I entered 425 Lafayette in October 2021 and crossed that quiet lobby, waved to the masked staff member at the front desk, and dutifully walked into the Shiva Theater, a space that had been converted into a Covid testing center. I had an interview with Eustis a couple hours later and I needed to take my rapid test; there, in the room that once housed books, where Jewish immigrants took sanctuary in the Hebrew Immigrant Aid Society years, where George C. Wolfe staged *The Colored Museum,* in the exact spot that I watched Luis Alfaro's *Oedipus El Rey* four years before, where Jeanine and Lisa and Sam and Oskar and Mandy tweaked and tinkered with *Fun Home,* where *Tiny Beautiful Things* had an early performance, where Tarell Alvin McCraney's *The Brothers Size* performed after its Under the Radar debut. The formality of my occasion to be there was devastating. A nasal swab on those hallowed grounds? I rushed upstairs for my meeting as soon as I was cleared. As I passed by the poster that proclaimed, "We are one public" and "culture belongs to everyone," I took note of the silence and emptiness. It was heartbreaking.

But there was hope, too, and as I entered year seven of my oral history archive of the contemporary Public Theater, I allowed myself the moment to imagine the filled spaces, the busy conference room where staff talked about Aristotle and producers planned the next season. The stillness and loneliness of that day, for me, reinforced its opposite: The Public is a place of people, a bustling network of artists and idealists, coming and going and always challenging the conventions of how we make American theater.

As I waited for Oskar Eustis to finish a phone call, I sat in the empty adjoining office and saw something sitting on the desk that I had not noticed before: a little silver disk on a black stand, collecting some dust. I wandered over and picked it up: "American Theater Wing. Tony Award." For *A Chorus Line.* The Tony was a bolt of electricity in my hand and, even if briefly, this little symbol of the past revived the present and the hope for the future. I walked into Eustis's office and, as I had done so many times before, greeted him, sat in one of the big leather chairs, and tapped "record" on my phone.

***

The Public is an organization of many voices, of myriad perspectives, and a collection of some of the most brilliant minds and creative forces that the American theater has ever produced. The number of people considered in these pages, even if only a fraction of the creators that make The Public what it is, demonstrates that fact. But it is also instructive for a company that has only had four artistic leaders to look at leadership and how it focuses the route that the organization will take. Over the past decade or so studying The Public, and especially in the past three years, the centralizing theme about the Theater revolves around the question of "leadership" and is reflected in some of the thoughts that I posited in the introduction to this book: What will "leadership" in American theater look like in the near future and how has Eustis's career at The Public transformed the theater? Is The Public the de facto national theater? What are the founding principles that stay as we emerge into a new world? What happens next?

Over the years, I have asked Eustis, and people tied to him and the company, various versions of all of these questions. I asked him again in 2022 and his answers constitute the epilogue to this book.

Central to all of these queries is the *idea* of leadership and the *nature* of leadership in a tumultuous time. I italicized these terms consciously as it is clear that the words *idea* and *nature* contextualize the term very differently. The mission of The Public points to an idealized, socialist society, a roundtable of art creation that at its best reflects not only the people of its city but, at times, the country as a whole. Free tickets for all, cultural game changers like *Hamilton* and *Fun Home*, open facilities that invite The Public in without restrictions, festivals of art that celebrate international forms and techniques; ambassadors and politicians sitting cheek by jowl with regular New Yorkers and tourists at the Delacorte. All of that programming is "leadership" and shows a Public Theater that is, in Kwame Kwei-Armah's assessment, a company that is not only a "tastemaker" but perhaps the primary tastemaker of the American theater. With a focus on Public Works, the Mobile Unit, and a reinforced commitment to reaching beyond the cultural cathedrals of the Delacorte, 425, and Broadway, one can imagine that The Public will continue to lead by diversifying access and, hopefully, finding even more models of community building. In that way, The Public is a leader, maybe *the* leader. Belaboring that point is not necessary.

The *nature* of leadership at The Public is perhaps more convoluted and points to a question that is prevalent in theater companies, big and small, around the country. The question of a "megafauna," "great person" authority figure is something that historians in the past few decades have tried to resist when looking at governments and broad assessments of cultural history, lest the histories become inadvertently classicist, racist, ableist, or sexist. It is essential to be careful in that way. That noted, I have not avoided the visioning of The Public through the lens of a singular artistic director because to do that would actually create a false image of what The Public has been in its seventy-year history. Yes, it is a collaboration of extraordinary artists, whose passions and politics guide taste, but it's undeniably true that at least part of the socialist-leaning company's success is due to the presence of a powerful artistic director. This does not mean that it can't evolve into something else if changing theatrical landscapes dictate that as right and important, but to imply that it is something else is patently false.

The Public Theater was founded by the biggest theater carnival barker of the twentieth century; a man who *was* The Public Theater, so much so that a marketing campaign had to consciously decenter him after he died. Though Paula Scher's banners now define 425 with bold slogans and ideals, in vinyl lettering just above the central door, it still reads "The Joseph Papp Public Theater." The company was tightly associated with Joe Papp until his death in 1991, and beyond. When George C. Wolfe became the artistic leader, he came to the job as a New York celebrity, a Broadway director, and someone who very much wanted to continue his own artistic practice while producing the seasons at The Public. He insisted that he have the same title as Papp—not only the artistic director but also producer. He was the artistic center of many of the famous productions that came out of The Public Theater; the director of *Bring in 'da Noise, Bring in 'da Funk, On the Town, Elaine Stritch at Liberty, Topdog/Underdog, Caroline, or Change,* and *Mother Courage*. Wolfe is a superb director and writer and remained so over his tenure at The Public, even winning a Tony for *Noise/Funk* for his work as an *artist*. Though JoAnne Akalaitis did not have enough time to establish herself as the leader of The Public, her role as a director and creator at Mabou Mines makes her a celebrity of American theater history, as well.

The tenure of those two men, in addition to Akalaitis's entire body of work, are often on Oskar Eustis's mind, since his brand of leadership is different but pulls from all three. He says that he thinks of Papp every day relative to the mission of The Public and the sets of principles that have assured The Public a degree of success through boom and bust. Having a core set of beliefs has protected the company and, as suggested, even allowed for the types of controversies and slipups that actually propel the organization to a constant state of evolution. That's the Joe Papp Public Theater.

Akalaitis, Eustis thinks, is the "poster child" for radical theater and a mentor who showed young artists how to break out of boxes and notions of what theater should be. Perhaps even more leftist and political than Papp, she reinforced that classical theater should live side by side with experimental work. As an actress who became a director and then an artistic director, throughout her career she has pushed the bounds of theater, to ask questions about how form can guide content and influence a society. While she was not given the space to discover those areas of her leadership desires at The Public, one can imagine Akalaitis smiling at the programming of Under the

Radar or settling into a Richard Foreman extravaganza at The Public. That passion and radicalism is the JoAnne Akalaitis Public Theater.

Eustis thinks of George C. Wolfe for his focus on the mission of racial justice and the expansion of diversity that, while embedded from the founding, came to fruition under Wolfe's leadership. A Black, gay man guiding the company meant that, during his tenure, The Public could no longer just be seen as a white organization. That was a powerful and important statement for an American national theater, and must not and will not be lost in the scope of its history. Several artists of color have said to me that they are at the Theater—they are *in the theater generally*—because of George C. Wolfe. In addition, his passion for musical theater, as a producer, writer, and director on Broadway was, says Eustis, "the ultimate manifestation of success of what The Public did." The Wolfe years turned toward these issues and aesthetics, and his tenure trained the spotlight on The Public in new ways. While he was less interested in experimental theater and Shakespeare, his artistic acuity cast The Public in truly bright light. All of that was the George C. Wolfe Public Theater.

But this story has been about the "Era of Oskar Eustis" and while some resist the centralized leader model, the era here is defined by his tenure, by him. Eustis is the first to admit that, in a comparison between himself, Papp, and Wolfe, "I don't think I'm as great an artist as either of those guys—the specificity of their visions as artists was much stronger than mine. … And I think, like Joe, I'm not a *great* director. I like to think I'm *pretty* good, and I have fun." Eustis came to The Public because he was and is a visionary, a person committed to mission and goals, and one of the most eloquent speakers in the American theater. He was brought in as an "Artistic Director" in what he sees as the purest sense—a person who could look at the company, manage its output, and be certain that everything that they did would be mission centric. Unlike Papp, Akalaitis, and Wolfe, he came to the job not as a well-known New York persona; an artist, yes, but only seeing his artistry as secondary. His need was to elevate the American theater creator by providing a multiplicity of platforms of idea-making and development. Using his passion as a dramaturg, he would spend his effort as an institution builder; an institution that, he says, aspired to be radical at the center of culture. "I was trained in a Marxist tradition. And the beautiful thing for me about that tradition is that it puts absolutely no weight on the purity of your soul. … You are prone to influences that you wish weren't influencing you. It means you're participating in the capitalist system that I don't approve of. But the question isn't whether I approve of it. The question is can I have some influence over it?"

That's why he wanted to be at The Public Theater since he was in his youth. It was the greatest platform for new and exciting work, a place where he could change cultural conversations from the center. And in that approach to leadership, ironically, Oskar Eustis became a celebrity of American theater, something that he may well enjoy, but also vehemently resists. A Marxist contradiction that is mediated through the skill by which he handles the contradiction. Fame versus humility is the Eustisian dialectic.

And so, let us not lose sight of the reality of who Oskar Eustis is. Though he did not complete college, he is an extraordinary intellectual, eloquent in a way that no one in the American theater rivals, deeply committed to scholarship and the academy, a passionate person who weeps openly at the theater, a person who hugs freely, and quotes Marx obsessively. Everyone describes him as huge. He's not huge. He is perhaps larger than average, has lots of hair that he often runs his hands through as he talks, and wears unusual combinations of clothes that could be described as "sloppy/elegant." He quips and quotes from marvelous stories and intellectual theory, often based in dramatic literature and politics. One in particular is illustrative, and he has recounted it to me on a couple of occasions, always forgiving that he might be paraphrasing. In the Irish playwright George Bernard Shaw's *Man and Superman*, Eustis sees something he has always strived for. Shaw writes in the epistle: "This is the true joy in life, the being used for a purpose recognized by yourself as a mighty one; the being thoroughly worn out before you are thrown on the scrap heap; the being a force of Nature instead of a feverish, selfish little clod of ailments and grievances complaining that the world will not devote itself to making you happy."[1]

That principle, that need, and that hope for selfless dedication to core values is what has defined Oskar Eustis's Public Theater. And, as in the Shaw poetry, that includes a sense of a leading "force of nature" and the necessity of that force being used up and spent. In 2021–2—with a context of major highs, personal tragedy, glorious success, and painful realizations—when I sat with Eustis and tapped record on my phone, I could see that he was still very much a force of nature, but also exhausted and at least partially spent. The theater he was overseeing was careening toward an uncertain future in which no one could predict what would come next. He was grappling with the contradictions discussed in these pages: late-stage capitalistic forces built on white centrism intersecting with the ethical and mission-guided goals of radical inclusivity. A mighty purpose, indeed. And yet, as P. Carl reflected of American theater in this moment, "We find ourselves standing on the ledge of survival."

And so, to the question: *What comes next?*

Eustis sees it as critical that he shepherd The Public, and all of the great advancements that he has helped guide in his era, into a future that is more inclusive, more grassroots, and that proposes different conceptions of leadership. How that leadership comes to the fore is anyone's guess. As I have compiled this book, I have become aware of how many people are "former" Public Theater employees. No sooner can Eustis elevate an artist and administrator than they are snatched up and elevated at another

---

[1] George Bernard Shaw, *Man and Superman* (London: Penguin Books, [1903] 2004), p. 32.

organization. This is good, and reflects well on The Public. But it also has deeper implications about the nature of leadership in a changing society, and the national need that America has to be led by artists who have grown up in The Public model. It means that there will be lots of exits and rotations at the Pubic itself.

I spoke with several of those "former Public Theater artists" and what they see in this conundrum. Jesse Cameron Alick, now the associate artistic director of Vineyard Theater, said, "The pandemic created like a flower going to seed—and I mean this metaphor in a good way. The Public Theater is going to be totally fine. ... And now Oskar has to rebuild at the very end of his career, he has to start over again. What a thing, what a thing." Stephanie Ybarra, now the artistic director of Baltimore Center Stage, said, "I am watching my friend and my mentor continue to reach for something better. And I assume that at times he's going to trip over himself, as we all do. But I'm watching him reach."

One may then say that Eustis and his mentees, now spread out all over the country and world, can collectively see American theater into the future. It's a wildly impressive list: Ybarra at Baltimore, Alick at Vineyard, Maria Goyanes at Woolly Mammoth, Shanta Thake at Lincoln Center, Jacob Padrón at Long Wharf, Karen Ann Daniels at Folger, Kevin Moriarty at Dallas, Barry Edelstein at the Old Globe, Kwame Kwei-Armah at the Young Vic, and the list goes on. Each one necessarily, because of the nature of the job, is a leader in their community. Central leaders. Ybarra says, "Oskar has run this particular ball very far down the field. And he set up The Public and he has set up people like me to pick up the ball and keep running."

As the conversation shifts to the viability of co-leaders and even teams of leaders, some companies have even started shifting to that model. It remains to be seen how that, in turn, shifts the dialogue and growth of the form. A not-so-hidden concern comes with that decentering; just as people of color and people who have been marginalized have risen to the highest levels of artist leadership, having a conversation about decentering is complicated. *Now?!* It's a valid concern. If one of the core tenets of racial and social equality in the arts is dismantling the concentration of power, what happens when more and more of those people in power centers are people of color?

It seems that this question is unsettled, as is most everything in an industry beset by crisis. What feels clear, though, is that there is a need for a multiplicity of viewpoints, of collaboration and a *nature of leadership* in the future that guides toward something perhaps less national and more regional. Does it matter if that leadership is contained in one person in an organization, or three, or five? Is there space for the megafauna? Probably so. Is there space for a different model? Certainly. These conversations about leadership, while freshly being debated in the public sphere, underline a decades-long troubling of traditional models of how theater is made in the United States. What are the new ways of creating art, of opening access, of getting back to the roots of the form that all of its followers assert lives at the center of what it means to be a human being? In what ways are our capitalist models shutting out marginalized communities in favor of corporate revenue, Broadway profit, and survival? This is where the era of Oskar Eustis, a man famous for dramaturgy, has truly shone: It has refocused the attention on a "Theater Organization" in its society. He posits that a theater acts as an agora, a town square, where support is offered to artists and citizens to create and change their world. It is an active place that foregrounds race, gender, class, politics, and accessibility and then, in turn, invites criticism, even if painful. It's philosophical, for sure. But The Public Theater is a philosophical organization and always has been. It's a place where Aristotle and dramatic theory are discussed during lunch in the conference room.

* * *

Years ago, Eustis reminded me of the lessons of the Gilded Age, and the subsequent pageant movement that arose, a form of celebration that brought together community in the face of a system that was leaving the population behind. In this current moment of late-stage capitalism, of reckoning, of pandemic, Eustis, The Public, and theaters offering similar values face an existential challenge. Eustis, as is his wont, turns toward Marx, forgiving the slight paraphrase: "Men make history, but they do not make it in conditions of their own choosing."

Public Works, and the initiatives born from its ideals, perhaps offer an antidote to counter a system that often forces not-for-profit companies to contradict their missions. If this model flourishes and grows to meet its values, Oskar Eustis and his team will have furthered a way of working that was started decades ago on a flatbed truck in small parks around New York City, a model that survived the tumult and contradictory forces of capitalist impulses. In increasingly impossible times, with intersecting webs of pressures—from politics, to economics, to centralized leadership, to social justice, and mediatized rage—Eustis has hope. As theater stands on a ledge of survival, he sees a more just future, a theatrical landscape that can claim—even if the path is uncertain—that theater strives to be for all people, that art is radically inclusive, and that we can stand together as one public.

Epilogue: Oskar Eustis

January 2022

Landis: We are talking in 2022—what are the things as an artistic leader that are most on your mind in your day-to-day work right now?

Eustis: The first is, I'm trying to keep the business afloat. We are a small to medium-sized business facing the worst economic environment that the American theater has ever faced and trying to survive. And not just survive, but survive it with some strength intact as an organization.

That is really hard and is by no means guaranteed. Indeed, at this particular moment I've gotten more worried than I was in the last six months because it is clear that we are going to be sailing into year three of the pandemic as of March, and I think all bets are off in terms of the steadiness of the philanthropic community. ...

Then there's a second area that has more to do with the demand for racial justice and, even more broadly, the demand for equity that has swept across the field and certainly the country in the last two years. And that problem I define as almost theoretical, which is how can I devise a leadership structure for this theater that is more equitable, more inclusive, involves more diversity of voices involved in decision-making, but in no way compromises the brilliance, excellence, and at times improvisatory quality of artistic leadership?

If I'm going to have six people involved in decision-making as opposed to just me, how can I make sure that they can really be involved without killing impulses that are sometimes instinctive, sometimes require very fast movement? And so far, it seems to be working.

The third subject ... I'm still chewing on the long-term implications of Public Works. And where I am intellectually, is I am more and more interested in looking at theater not within the silos of profit and nonprofit and amateur and professional, but more looking at, what is the theater's role in America's life, and how can as many people as possible be given the opportunity to take the advantages and joys and riches that I think are there into their lives?

... I'm pretty excited about it and I'm looking forward to actively trying to work on what that means for the last part of my career, however long that may last.

Landis: One of the hallmarks, I think, of your time here has been the fact that there are people who have worked with you, who have worked in artistic positions at The Public are now running other institutions. And one of the great challenges: you've had many seconds-in-command, if I could put it that way, who get hired away very quickly. That must be a challenge.

Eustis: Yeah. And of course, it's a practical challenge. And in this particular time of crisis that practical challenge is increased, because of the loss of institutional memory, the loss of bandwidth is felt very acutely at this point. However, it in no way changes my mind that it's a sign of our success. ... That influence in certain ways is the most significant influence that we're having on the field as a whole, as there are people who are being raised in the culture and with the values of The Public Theater who are now taking those to posts around the country and trying to manifest those in other institutions. ...

What could be a more efficient way of changing the field? It's been stunning the last few years how much that's the case, to the point where I sometimes feel like it's extremely rare that somebody becomes an artistic director without having passed through here. But you know—in terms of the mission, it's nothing but good. We have to make sure the institution survives so we can keep doing it.

Landis: Knowing that you have more years that you want to make these changes and grow, could you look at your time at The Public and say, "what's the imprint of Oskar Eustis on The Public Theater?"—I know, I know you resist or are troubled by the singular artistic leader and what that means. I think you said megafauna once. But there is some truth to it.

If we talk about the Oskar Eustis era, what's your imprint?

Eustis: Well, you're going to see that more clearly than I do, Kevin. But let me tell you what I think about it. I think the fact that I'm a dramaturg, and therefore the heart of my artistic work is helping other people realize their visions, has affected the way this place works in a very positive way. I think I am the first artistic director who, for better or for worse, is not primarily focused on my own work on individual shows.

Embracing a number of different artists who are really writing the story of The Public Theater. What Jeanine Tesori and Lisa Kron and Tarell McCraney and Lin-Manuel, what they've been able to do in terms of their agency in creating what The Public Theater is, I think, has been fantastic. And that is something that I hope never goes away.

For me, it's part of the overall job of trying to institution-build and make sure that the institution is here forever and that the values of the institution are not located in any one person or any one job but rather diversified throughout the organization, from the board of directors to the box office, and therefore will have a life that is independent of the life of me, or of any artistic director.

So that feels like it's all part of the most important thing I'm doing in a way. The second thing, I think, is kind of a corollary of that, which is I feel like I very deliberately tried to set out to make all of the different missions of The Public cohere and come under one umbrella, so that hopefully we never have a situation where people question, "Why does a new play Festival do Shakespeare, why does the Shakespeare Festival do experimental work? Why do we have a cabaret at a home for new plays?" But hopefully I tried to elevate all of these, so the individual areas of focus were not only visible but are seen as a coherent whole, so that nobody's going to try to unravel that whole and turn us into a niche theater.

The breadth of our umbrella is at the essence of who we are. I've worked very hard to do that.

Landis: Looking back on your time at The Public, what are the things institutionally that you wish you could have a redo on?

Eustis: ... I did make some mistakes that I regret early on. You know, probably one of the very most painful things was what happened with John Guare's *Free Man of Color* and my relationship with John Guare. I had after years of work committed to doing a production of *Free Man of Color* in the fall of 2008 and I made that commitment in the winter of 2008.

What happened over the next few months is the economy tanked and I lost a million dollars in enhancement money that I thought I had in the bank. And I had to cancel the show, literally two, three months before it went into rehearsal. And it caused a terrible rift between John and I that's never been healed. We still don't—we're not on speaking terms, and it was tough with my relationship with George. It was a bad thing.

And the lesson I learned that when the artistic director of The Public says that The Public is going to do something, it has to mean exactly that. It can't be we're going to do our best to do something or we're going to try to do something or if nothing goes wrong—it has to mean we're going to do it.

The only other thing I will say is the learning of the last couple of years. My tradition, politically, took race very seriously, but perhaps did not center race as much ... I think, without being aware of it at all, that I was somewhat underestimating the necessity for a fierce grappling with racial equity in order to fulfill the mission of The Public. And you know, Marxist background, my class-based analysis tended to de-emphasize race.

And I still believe that, by the way, I believe that racism was invented to enforce capitalism, not the other way around. ... But nonetheless, race is so central to the American experience that I ... I think objectively I underestimated its importance until I was brought face to face with it in the last two years.

And I'm glad to have been brought face to face with it, but I am also aware that I needed to be.

Landis: I wonder if I could get to a couple specific moments that have brought great joy to you and pride for you at The Public, and similarly moments that have brought pain and discouragement. We can go in whatever order you want.

Eustis: Well, the moments of pride are—and joy are so many they're hard to number ... You could argue that maybe the happiest moment of my life was my fiftieth birthday, which was celebrated in Central Park with a performance of *Hair*, and I got up on stage and danced afterwards and the cast sang "Happy Birthday" to me. That was my fiftieth birthday. ... I mean just nothing was wrong. Everything was perfect. Partly because I loved *Hair* so much. ...

Public Works has been eye-opening, revelatory, totally—and there's much joy and so much revelation and learning that's been associated for me with the development of Public Works and so much I've learned from Lear and so much I've learned from the whole program ... I'm incredibly proud to have been part of that.

So that part's easy, just joy all there—because I believe in this so much, right? I'm an incredibly lucky guy who—I've got a job and the mission statement of the job and what I believe are bound together like, you know, Romulus and Remus. There's just no air between what I believe and what The Public's trying to do. So how fundamentally lucky is that? And it certainly produces an enormous amount of joy for me.

Pain. You know, the aforementioned dealings with John Guare was—and George Wolfe and the fallout from *Free Man of Color* was terribly painful and I will never forget that.

The degree of anger and distrust and disaffection in my staff when we first went through the response to the George Floyd crisis shocked me and really took me back and really hurt. And I am still struggling to learn from that, and only take from that what makes me better and not let it damage me or throw me off course. And that's still a daily struggle. But that first summer, that summer of 2020 was just a nightmare. ...

The experience around *Bloody Bloody Andrew Jackson* was so miserable that I just hope I never ever have to relive it. It revealed to me many of my own inadequacies of understanding, of management, of responsibility. I just was not—I didn't understand as much, nor was as responsible as I needed to be and should have been. And you know, honestly the fractured relationships, including with the board ... Again, I think I learned from them. I think the theater's grown from that and we're in a much better place now. But I could certainly have wished that that lesson-learning had been easier. ...

Obviously, Jack's death posed a huge challenge for me personally, but also professionally. You know, how was I going to be able to continue to work? How could I be effective? How could I put my professional life back together after a personal shattering? And again, that is a struggle that remains very much present for me as I go through. And there were many good consequences ... much of the work that was done in the last seven and a half years that I think is directly tie-able to my experience, and benefited from my experience if I could say so.

And there were also mistakes. I think one of the reactions I had to Jack's death was to turn more inward, to get more and more private, and to thus without knowing it, I both spent a lot more time in rehearsal starting in that summer of 2017, three years after he died. ... In general, I think I got a lot more private about how I was making decisions. ... My decision-making process grew more opaque, fewer people were involved in it. ...

I think part of what had gone wrong between me and the staff by the summer of 2020 was that I had become more removed from the staff.

Landis: If you would, would you say a bit more about the first part of that? That there were ways that processing Jack's death and the grief altered the art. ...

Eustis: Right. I mean you know, partly, in just a very simple way, there have been a lot more dead kids onstage at The Public, or lost kids on stage at The Public in the last seven years—not because I set out to do a series of shows about dead children but just because always part of what you're doing is choosing the things that resonate with you. And for example, *Tiny Beautiful Things* just took a high road to production because that one section, The Obliterated Place from the letter from the father, called "Living Dead Dad," is still the most powerful and moving letter and response to a letter than I've read on the subject. And I just couldn't wait to put that onstage because it felt so truthful to me.

Tarell's *Head of Passes* was probably the most dramatic part, where you know, Act Three, which was after the death of Phylicia's three children in rapid succession. And Part Two is a dialogue between her and God, in which God of course is silent, as is his wont. And we literally spent weeks going through that line by line, with me just directly saying "she wouldn't feel that right now. She'd feel this. This is too soon. This is—you can't feel that before"—you know, and I'd go through these dramaturgical sessions weeping the whole time. And we just all are sort of getting this. "OK, that's the condition of this dramaturgical session. We'll get on with it." ... And you know, I like to think that it had a very positive impact on that show, which I think is a masterpiece. ...

In a broader way, in which I hope dealing with this is making me a better person. And by better person, I mean, less confident that I know the answers to things, less assured of my own success, less cocky therefore, more humble. ...

What I have tried to do is say, I may have lost one of the deepest loves and connections that I could possibly have in this world but maybe I can partly replace with that a broader based, albeit shallower, set of connections with other people where I have more compassion, more empathy, for a larger group of people.

Landis: You know, I have a question actually that kind of dovetails, and it's about sort of optimism and forward thinking. You know, with that, with what you've gone through personally, what the theater's gone through, what we've all gone through in the last two years, are you in a place of optimism about the future of American theater?

Eustis: Yes. For two reasons. And the first is to quote a playwright you may have heard of, Tony Kushner. "Hope is not an emotion. It's a moral obligation." And I really believe that we actually have the obligation to be optimistic. We have the obligation to be hopeful. Because that is the only way that we can commit the actions that are required from us as ethical human beings ... I don't have the right to despair. I don't have the right to not be hopeful. I can feel unhopeful sometimes. But my moral obligation is to be optimistic.

And the second, I think there are reasons for optimism amid so many reasons for terrible pessimism, not the least of which, that as of right now the American theater is wider and more diverse and includes a greater cross segment of our continent's voices than at any time in American history.

And this, you know, latest push, since the summer of 2020, for equity, has had excesses, has made mistakes, has yet to prove itself, has, you know, damaged some people in ways that are just abhorrent. But it's also had successes. It's also started to change the field in ways that are really cool. And you know, some of what I'm defining now, Kevin, is that I need to figure out how we hang on to those achievements when the inevitable backlash comes.

Because it will come. There's just no question. And when it comes, we've got to make sure that all of the gains we've made don't get swept away in a Thermidor of regression but that we're able to hang on to some of the learnings and transformations that we've been making in the last two years. I think there's real reasons for optimism there. ...

Since the election of Donald Trump, what I can feel is that a huge section of this country and of this world is recognizing that there are more radical remedies that are needed to what is wrong with our system, that it's no longer a question of simply electing a president we like to change the system, but that we actually have to put socialism back on the table. We have to put universal healthcare back on the table.

And so, in the largest sense, we have to put the idea of an activist government that is there to aggressively level the playing field and aggressively improve the lives of all of its citizens, not simply be a caretaker and rules keeper for private property. I feel that in a way that I haven't felt since the 1960s. Now it's challenged by an equally—well, hopefully not equally strong, but by a very strong counter movement, which may win, and that's scary.

But the fact that we've got this kind of shift to the left I think is really, it's exciting. And I don't think it's meaningless. I think it carries a lot of meaning.

Landis: You know all the stories about the transition between Joe to JoAnne to George to you, and knowing that you've signed a contract that you have told me will be your last: When you think about the next artistic director for The Public Theater, what comes to mind? What sort of planning do you have, or do you hope that your board has?

Eustis: Well, I'm sort of in charge of it right now. ... Can I make this associate structure work and feel solid enough so that it could continue, mainly where there are a diversity of voices around the table when major artistic decisions are made by the artistic director? And that's a structure that so far is working for me; I think I can get it working better, but my hope is to get it sort of built in so that there never is simply a charismatic megafauna artistic director again, but there's always a sense of a team.

So, who knows if that'll succeed, but I'm going to try. ... By the time I step down, there should be ten to twelve people who know The Public and have really had experience and share its values and who the board already knows who could be serious candidates to replace me.

And you know, now that number probably stands at six. ... It might come a point where my successor is obvious, where, you know, just it's clear and then of course is how do I elegantly get out of the way?

Landis: We talked about the idea of The Public as a de facto national theater, which is thrown around in the press a lot. So, I'm going to just ask you a question I've asked before, is The Public a national theater?

Eustis: The Public's a national theater in the exact sense that we view our audience as national. We view our role as a national role. We obviously are very much a New York theater and proud to be a New York theater. Part of the New York community, responsive to our audience here on the ground in New York, in a very important way. Part of the mission is for us to try very consciously to pioneer directions, values, programs, shows, that we intend to have an influence far beyond the doors of this theater. And that, I think, we've been pretty successful at; at least I don't think there's any other American theater that's been more successful. I think we've done a pretty good job of serving as a direction finder for the field as a whole.

I don't think we'll ever be a national theater the way the National Theatre of Britain is—because it's really part of the

National Theatre's mandate to have the resources to share with the rest of the country and try to actually parcel out money and resources and opportunities to the whole country in a way that's not part of our job. I don't think it ever will be because the United States is never going to be as centralized culturally or any other way as in London.

I like our position and I'm not sure anybody should ever be more of a national theater. There could be other people doing the same thing. But I don't think there should be something more centralized or dominant than we are. And you know, the other thing I like, Kevin, is that because we don't have the kind of money that the National has, we have to lead by example.

If people are going to follow us, it's going to be because they're impressed by our work and our ideas, not because it's the royal road to riches to do what The Public Theater does. So, it means we're out there in the marketplace of aesthetics and the marketplaces of ideas and the marketplace with shows competing and having to demonstrate that this is actually worth doing. And again, we've been lucky. Intentional but also lucky at having achieved as much success as we've had.

Landis: Thank you, Oskar.
Eustis: Let me tell you one more regret I have.
Landis: OK.
Eustis: Everything isn't free. ...

NOTES AND SOURCES

As noted in the introduction, many of the stories and insight for this account of The Public come from the oral history archive that I have been collecting for The Public Theater over the course of the past decade. People who are directly quoted in this book are included in the list below, with the dates of their archival interviews. I have done many other interviews with people who work at The Public, off the record or on background. As such, those are not indicated in the list.

Reviews, scholarly journals, and books have been extensively used to provide further context and historical accuracy to the archival interviews. These sources are referenced in footnotes throughout the book.

Saheem Ali
Associate artistic director and resident director of The Public Theater in New York. He was the director of the 2021 production of *Merry Wives* in Central Park and *Fat Ham* in 2022 (December 29, 2020).

Jesse Cameron Alick
Former company dramaturg at The Public Theater and associate to Oskar Eustis. Alick is currently the associate artistic director of the Vineyard Theater in New York City (April 15, 2016 and November 24, 2021).

Alison Bechdel
Author of the graphic novels *Dykes to Watch Out For, Are You My Mother: A Comic Drama,* and *Fun Home: A Family Tragicomic,* the basis of the 2015 Tony Award-winning musical (November 17, 2021).

Justin Vivian Bond
Musician, singer, and monologist, Bond is a staple of Joe's Pub and cabaret clubs and concert halls around the world. They are also one half of the comedy and musical duo Kiki and Herb (December 17, 2017).

Beowulf Boritt
Set designer of the Central Park productions of *Much Ado About Nothing, Coriolanus,* and *Merry Wives.* He is the Tony-winning designer for *Act One* (January 4, 2022).

Allyn Burrows
Artistic director of Shakespeare and Co. in Lenox, Massachusetts (August 5, 2017).

David Byrne
The lead singer and guitarist for Talking Heads, Byrne wrote the music for *Here Lies Love* and *St. Joan* at The Public Theater. He is the recipient of an Academy Award, Tony Award, Grammy, and Golden Globe Award as well as a member of the Rock and Roll Hall of Fame (September 5, 2016).

P. Carl
A dramaturg, author, trans rights activist, and director. He was the founder of the online theater journal *HowlRound* and author of *Becoming a Man* (July 13, 2021).

Thomas Caruso
Director of *Southern Comfort* at The Public (September 8, 2020).

Chelsea Clinton
An author and global health activist, Clinton works for the Clinton Foundation and Clinton Global initiative. She is the daughter of President Bill Clinton and Secretary of State Hillary Clinton (November 2, 2018).

Steven Cohen
Former managing director of The Public Theater and associate of Joseph Papp (October 15, 2016 and January 21, 2022).

Karen Ann Daniels
Director of programming at the Folger Shakespeare Library and former director of the Mobile Unit at The Public (July 15, 2021 and September 7, 2021).

Gordon Davis
The longest serving member of the Board of The Public Theater. Davis is a lawyer, the founding Chair of Jazz at Lincoln Center, and the former parks commissioner for the City of New York under Ed Koch (April 7, 2017).

Lear deBessonet
Artistic Director of *Encores!* concert series. She is the founder and former director of Public Works. She directed *Romeo and Juliet*, *A Midsummer Night's Dream*, *Miss You Like Hell*, and *Hercules* at The Public (January 10, 2020).

Erika Dickerson-Despenza
Author of *Cullud Wattah*, the 2021 play about the Flint water crisis (February 3, 2022).

Jay Duckworth
Former head of the props department at The Public (May 6, 2016).

Barry Edelstein
Former head of the Shakespeare Initiative at The Public and is the current artistic director of the Old Globe in San Diego, California (April 25, 2016 and September 27, 2021).

Oskar Eustis
Fourth and current artistic director of The Public Theater in New York (February 23, 2016; June 1, 2016; June 20, 2016; August 11, 2016; January 13, 2017; May 17, 2017; June 18, 2017; July 21, 2017; November 10, 2017; April 12, 2019; May 31, 2019; May 12, 2020; August 31, 2021; November 5, 2021; and January 26, 2022).

Bridget Everett
A television and cabaret performer, Everett is a staple of the Joe's Pub repertoire (July 21, 2017).

Jesse Tyler Ferguson
Public Theater actor, known broadly for his television series *Modern Family* (July 15, 2016).

Michael Friedman
Musician and composer of *Bloody Bloody Andrew Jackson*, *Love's Labour's Lost*, and *The Fortress of Solitude* at The Public. He was the head of Public Forum, a lecture and discussion series (April 20, 2016).

Sam Gold
Tony Award-winning director of *Fun Home* and *Hamlet* at The Public (September 10, 2020).

Kristen Gongora
Senior development project manager at The Public (November 8, 2019 and January 12, 2020).

Michael Greif
Frequent director at The Public Theater and former artistic director of the La Jolla Playhouse. He directed *Rent*, *Next to Normal*, and *Dear Evan Hansen* on Broadway (June 25, 2019).

Heidi Griffiths
Codirector of casting at The Public (June 28, 2018).

Maria Goyanes
Former producer at The Public and current artistic director of Woolly Mammoth Theater in Washington, DC (June 9, 2016).

Mandy Hackett
Associate artistic director and director of Public Theater Productions (July 7, 2016; September 23, 2016; and June 15, 2017).

Shirley Brice Heath
Anthropologist and professor emerita of English, dramatic literature and linguistics at Stanford University (September 11, 2021).

Michelle Hensley
Founder and former artistic director of Ten Thousand Things Theater in Minneapolis (September 9, 2021).

David Henry Hwang
Playwright, screenwriter, and librettist. Hwang is a professor at Columbia and the author of *FOB*, *M. Butterfly*, *Golden Child*, *Yellowface*, and *Soft Power* (March 28, 2019).

Candis C. Jones
Director of *Cullud Wattah* at The Public and other prominent nonprofits in New York (January 25, 2022).

Ron C. Jones
Public Theater actor and principal actor in the Mobile Unit's 2012 *Richard III* (June 13, 2016).

Tommy Kail
Director of *Hamilton* and *Dry Powder* at The Public (August 25, 2020).

Andrew Kircher
Former director of the Devised Theater Initiative and associate for the Under the Radar Festival (September 23, 2016).

Chiara Klein
Current director of Producing and Artistic Planning at The Public (November 16, 2021).

Kevin Kline
Tony Award and Oscar-winning film and stage star. A staple of The Public stages, Kline performed in *Mother Courage*, *The Seagull*, *Measure for Measure*, *Much Ado About Nothing*, *Hamlet*, and *The Pirates of Penzance*, among others (May 5, 2016).

David Korins
Set designer for *Hamilton* and *Here Lies Love*, among others, at The Public Theater (November 27, 2021).

Lisa Kron
An actor and writer, Kron wrote and starred in *Well*. She wrote the stage production of *Fun Home*, for which she won the Tony Award (October 1, 2020).

Tony Kushner
The Pulitzer and Tony-winning playwright and screenwriter. Author of *A Bright Room Called Day*, *Caroline, or Change*, *The Intelligent Homosexual's Guide to Capitalism and Socialism with a Key to the Scriptures*, and *Mother Courage* (adaptation) at The Public (May 24, 2016).

Kwame Kwei-Armah
Artistic director of the Young Vic in London and the director of several plays at The Public, including The Public Works production of *Twelfth Night* (November 19, 2021).

Kenny Leon
Stage and screen director and actor. Director of *Much Ado About Nothing* at the Delacorte in 2019 (January 4, 2022).

Hamish Linklater
Actor in multiple productions at the Delacorte and at Lafayette (April 25, 2016).

Jose Llana
Public Theater actor. Originated the role of Ferdinand Marcos in *Here Lies Love* (November 8, 2021).

Arielle Tepper Madover
Chair of the Board of The Public Theater (November 4, 2016).

Jeremy McCarter
Former head of The Public Theater's Public Forum and author of *Hamilton: The Revolution* (June 13, 2016).

Ruthie Ann Miles
Tony Award-winning actor and originator of the role of Imelda Marcos in *Here Lies Love* (November 2, 2021).

Lin-Manuel Miranda
Composer, actor, and Tony Award winner. Author of the musicals *In the Heights* and *Hamilton*. Author of *Hamilton: The Revolution* (March 11, 2022).

Jack Moore
Director of new artists and dramaturgy pipeline at The Public (June 24, 2020 and January 11, 2022).

Kevin Moriarty
Artistic director of the Dallas Theater Center (August 11, 2017).

Richard Nelson
Playwright of multiple Public-produced plays including "The Apples" and "The Gabriels" cycles and *Illyria* (June 7, 2016 and November 18, 2021).

Rufus Norris
Artistic director of the National Theatre in London (December 17, 2019).

Lynn Nottage
Two-time winner of the Pulitzer Prize in playwriting. Author of *Sweat* and *Milma's Tail* at The Public Theater (March 27, 2019).

Jeanie O'Hare
Former director of New Work Development (July 5, 2017).

Gail Papp
Former developer of new plays and board member at The Public (August 3, 2017 and September 16, 2021).

Suzan-Lori Parks
Pulitzer Prize-winning writer in residence at The Public. Author of *Fucking A*, *America Play*, *Venus*, *Topdog/Underdog*, *Father Comes from the Wars 1,2,3*, and *White Noise*, among others (March 29, 2019).

Annie-B Parson
Director of Big Dance Theater and choreographer of *Here Lies Love* and *American Utopia* (November 13, 2021).

Diane Paulus
Tony-winning director of theater and opera. Paulus is the artistic director of the American Repertory Theater at Harvard, and was the director of the revival of *Hair* at the Delacorte and on Broadway (June 14, 2016).

Maryann Plunkett
Tony Award-winning actor and principal actor in Richard Nelson's "Rhinebeck Panorama" (April 30, 2018).

Samantha Power
Ambassador of the United States Agency for International Development and former United States ambassador to the United Nations (November 5, 2018).

Lily Rabe
Stage and screen actor. Played the role of Portia in *Merchant of Venice* among other performances at the Delacorte (April 26, 2016).

Toshi Reagon
Musician and performer at Joe's Pub (September 23, 2020).

Mark Russell
Founder and producer of Under the Radar Festival (June 3, 2016).

Jay O. Sanders
One of the most prolific performers in Shakespeare in the Park and a principal actor in Richard Nelson's "Rhinebeck Panorama" (June 15, 2016).

Paula Scher
A graphic designer and principal at Pentagram. Scher is the lead designer for The Public Theater brand (November 10, 2021).

James Shapiro
Author, Columbia University professor of English and comparative literature, and the Shakespeare scholar in residence at The Public (June 25, 2019).

NOTES AND SOURCES

Ruth Sternberg
Production executive at The Public (April 29, 2016 and July 15, 2021).

Daniel Sullivan
Tony winner and director of *The Visitor*, *King Lear*, *Comedy of Errors*, and *The Merchant of Venice*, among others at The Public (August 19, 2011).

Tony Taccone
Former artistic director of Berkeley Repertory Theater and the Eureka Theater (August 8, 2017).

Shaina Taub
A composer and actor, Taub wrote the adaptations for the Delacorte productions of *Twelfth Night* and *As You Like It* (May 31, 2019).

Paul Tazewell
Costume designer for *Hamilton*, *In the Heights*, *The Color Purple*, and *Caroline, or Change* (December 1, 2021).

Jeanine Tesori
Composer and two-time Tony winner. She was the composer of *Caroline, or Change*, *Mother Courage*, *Fun Home*, and *Soft Power* (July 20, 2016).

Shanta Thake
Former director of Joe's Pub, associate artistic director at The Public, and the current chief artistic officer at Lincoln Center for the Performing Arts (April 21, 2016 and November 13, 2020).

Jordan Thaler
Codirector of casting at The Public (June 28, 2018).

John Douglas Thompson
Actor in *Julius Caesar* and *Troilus and Cressida* at the Delacorte (July 1, 2017).

Rosemarie Tichler
Former artistic producer at The Public (January 13, 2017).

Alex Timbers
Director of *Joan of Arc*, *Here Lies Love*, and *Bloody Bloody Andrew Jackson* at The Public (May 28, 2016).

Jennifer Tipton
Lighting designer at Lafayette, Shakespeare in the Park, and theaters around the world (June 12, 2018).

Sam Waterston
Actor on stage and screen and the most prolific actor in the history of Shakespeare in the Park (January 25, 2017).

Kate Whoriskey
Director of *Sweat* and longtime collaborator with Lynn Nottage (January 14, 2022).

Danny Williams
Former Senior Director, Finance and Administration at The Public (November 3, 2021).

Patrick Willingham
Executive director of The Public Theater (July 21, 2016; June 25, 2018; and July 16, 2021).

Laurie Woolery
A director, educator, and playwright, Woolery is the current director of Public Works (April 12, 2019 and September 18, 2021).

Stephanie Ybarra
Artistic director of Baltimore Center Stage. Ybarra is the former head of the Mobile Unit at The Public (August 11, 2016; June 1, 2017; and August 20, 2021).

Chay Yew
Director of *Mojada*, *Oedipus El Rey*, and *Durango* at The Public. Yew was the artistic director of Victory Gardens Theater in Chicago (June 20, 2018).

INDEX

Note: Page numbers in *italics* refer to images.

Abraham, Arthur 107–8
Abramović, Marina 123
Abrams, Stacy 95–6
Ackerman, Robert Allan 117
acting classes 259–60
actors of color at The Public 60–2,
    117–18
  and all-Black *Much Ado* 93, 95
  and *Hamilton* 208
African Americans
  and *Cullud Wattah* 125–7
  experience and culture 4
  and inequality at The Public
    240
  and Shakespeare in the Park 62
  and Suzan-Lori Parks's plays 147–50,
    152
  see also Black, Indigenous & People
    of Color (BIPOC) Affinity Group;
    Black Lives Matter
"Afrosurreal Manifesto: Black is
    the New Black—a 21st century
    Manifesto" (Miller) 125
AIDS 37, 127, 160, 227
Ain't No Mo' (Cooper) 186
Akalaitis, JoAnne 3–4, *17*, 44, 123
  and artistic directorship of The Public
    28–30, 34, 62, 282–3
Aldridge, Tom 21
Alexander Hamilton (Chernow) 200
Ali, Saheem 54, 62, 112
Alick, Jessie Cameron 122, 240–2,
    243, 285
Almond, Todd 262
American Shakespeare 18, 54, 251
  and Delacorte Theater 20, 44–5

American soft power and the
    theater 58–60
Anderson, Jane 111
Angels in America (Kushner) 12, 31, 32,
    67, 114, 129
  HBO film version 68
Ansky, Shloyme 114
Anspacher, Florence Sutro 108
Anspacher Theater 133–4
antisemitism and *Merchant of Venice*
    77, 79, 80–1
Aquino, Ninoy 177
Aristophanes 55
Aristotle 12, 13, 14
Armitage, Karole 74
artistic directorship of The Public after
    Joseph Papp 28–33, 34, 294
  and diversity 62, 242–3
  see also Akalaitis, JoAnne; Eustis,
    Oskar; leadership and The Public;
    Wolfe, George C.
Astor, John Jacob 106, 139
Astor Place 104, *105*–7, 110
Astor Place Public Theater headquarters
    5, *11*, 20–1, *103*, *109*, 133–5, 158
  branding and marketing 137
  and diversity of programming 138–9
  and dramaturgy 130
  and free tickets 37
  history of 104–8
  renovation and restoration 109–10
As You Like It (Shakespeare) 267
Atlanta, Georgia, and *Much Ado* 94–6
Audio Abramović (Watts) 123
Avenue Q (Lopez and Marx) 181
Aziza, De'Adre 47

Bacchae, The (Euripides) 43–4, 45, 54
Baranski, Christine 54–5
Barnum, P.T. 106
Barthes, Roland 133
Beatty, John Lee 98
Bechdel, Alison 190, 191–2, 194, 195, 198
Bennett, Michael 22
Bergl, Emily 47
Bergman, Ingmar 147
Bioh, Jocelyn 54, 62
Black, Indigenous & People of Color (BIPOC) Affinity Group 239–42, 244
Black Lives Matter 93, 99–100, 240, 242
Blank, Jessica 239
Blankenbuehler, Andy 202
Bloody Bloody Andrew Jackson (Friedman and Timbers) 7, 171–2, 186, *221*, 226, 227, 291
  and contemporary politics 233
  development of 229–30
  Native American reaction to 230–2
Board of Rabbis and Papp's *Merchant* 79
Bond, Justin Vivian 159–62, *159*
Bondage (Hwang) 118
Bonney, Jo 153
Boritt, Beowulf 93–100, *93*
Brantley, Ben 43–4, 76, 183, 230
Bread and Puppet Theater 256
Brecht, Bertolt 13, 67, 113
  see also Mother Courage and Her Children (Brecht)
Brechtian theater 70, 150
Brecht-Schall, Barbara 69
Breitbart and *Julius Caesar* 88
Bright Room Called Day, A (Kushner) 113, 114
Bring in 'da Noise, Bring in 'da Funk (Wolfe, Waters, Mark, Duquesnay, and Gaines) 31
Broadway transfers 6, 138, 171, 186, 187
  and *Bloody Bloody Andrew Jackson* 227–8
  and *A Chorus Line* 22
  and *Fun Home* 190–1
  and *Hair* 76

and *Hamilton* 190–1, 201, 203–4, 213, 214
  and The Public's finances 172–3
Brook, Peter 132
Brooks, Danielle 93, 97
"Brush Up Your Shakespeare" (song) 55
Burrows, Allyn 86–7
Byrne, David 6, 173, 174–5, 178–9, 181, 182, 183–4, 185

cabaret 159–65
Caffall, Tyler 47
Caliban by the Yellow Sands (MacKaye) 258, 259, 267
Carl, P. 223, 234, 236, 238, 284
Caroline, or Change (Kushner and Tesori) 114–15, 116
Caruso, Tom 234, 237
Cascando (Beckett) 174
casting 111, 200, 235, 236–7, 247
Cavaglieri, Giorgio 24, 105, 108
Central Park 24
  and cultural value of the Delacorte 56–7, 60
  and *Julius Caesar* 82, 90
  and *Merchant of Venice* 81
  and modus operandi of productions 74
  and *Much Ado* 98
  and Papp/Moses admission fee dispute 19–20
  and Public Works pageant 7
  rules and restrictions 52
  and theatrical experience of Shakespeare in the Park 42–6
Cerveris, Michael 190
Chaudhuri, Una 46
Children's Aid Society 257, 260
choreography and *Here Lies Love* 178–80
Chorus Line, A (Hamlisch and Kleban) 1, 15, 24, 114, 133, 280
  and Lin-Manuel Miranda 211
  and The Public's finances 22–3, 135, 171, 224
cisgender actors and *Southern Comfort* 234–5
class and division in America 6, 59, 153
Classic Theater of Harlem 61
Clinton, Chelsea 35, 105

Close, Glenn 111, 186
Cogswell, Joseph 106
Cohen, Steven 16, 22, 26, 28–9, 31, 247–8
Collins, Dan 7
color-blind, race-blind, and race-conscious casting 60–1, 236, 247, 270
Comedy of Errors, The (Shakespeare) 46–8
Commentators, The (Stan's Cafe) 123
communist activities and sympathies, alleged 19–20, 27
Communist Party and Eustis family 35
community building and The Public 7, 8, 15, 257–63, 267, 268
  and Covid-19 266
  and Kwame Kwei-Armah 272–4
Condon, Larry 32
controversy and The Public 222–3, 226, 238–9
  see also Black, Indigenous & People of Color (BIPOC) Affinity Group; *Bloody Bloody Andrew Jackson* (Friedman and Timbers); *Julius Caesar* (Shakespeare); *Southern Comfort* (Collins)
Conversations in Tusculum (Nelson) 140–1
corporate sponsorship and The Public 86, 88–9, 91
Covid-19 4, 7, 64, 222, 239, 242
  and *Cullud Wattah* 126
  and the Mobile Unit 253
  and The Public's finances 225, 287
  and reopening of The Public 54
  and Shiva Theater 280
  and theater closures 266–7, 268
  and Zoom-based theater 5, 239
Cramer, Larry 25
Cullud Wattah (Dickerson-Despenza) 124–7, 193
Curious Incident of the Dog in the Nighttime, The (Stephens) 92, 265

Dallas Theater Center 264
Dalrymple, Dan 105–6
Daniels, Karen Ann 253

Davis, Gordon 24, 30
Davis, Kate 234
Davis, Paul 136
Dear Evan Hansen (Pasek and Paul) 92
Death and Life of Great American Cities (Jacobs) 57
deBessonet, Lear 7, 246, 256–63, 272
Delacorte, Valerie and George 42
Delacorte Theater 14, 20, 41, 42–52, 53
  and American soft power 58–60
  annual gala 2016 54–5
  and *Hair* 73–7
  and *Mother Courage* 71–2
  popularity with actors 65
  proposed renovation and expansion 55–6
Delsener, Ron 24
Delta Air Lines sponsorship and *Julius Caesar* 83, 91, 224
democracy 128
  and direct action 84
  and populism 232–3
Devised Theater Working Group 123–4
Devotees in the Garden of Love (Parks) 118
Dickerson-Despenza, Erika 125–7
disco and *Here Lies Love* 173–4, 176, 178, 179–80
Disney+ and *Hamilton* 23, 204, 207–8
Disney and *Hercules* 262, 267
diversity 16, 60–2, 241–3, 255
  and capitalism 286
  and commercial considerations 111–12
  George C. Wolfe's commitment to 30, 32–3
  and revolutionary change 271
Dixon, Brandon Victor 155–6
Domestic Workers United (DWU) 257, 260
Donkey Show, The (Paulus and Weiner) 73
Don Quixote (deBessonet) 256
dramaturgy
  definition 127–8
  and "The Gabriels" 141–4
  and *Hamilton* 206–7
  and *Here Lies Love* 176–8, 180
  and *Mother Courage* 68, 70

and Oskar Eustis 5, 12, 118, 124, 128–9, 215–17, 288–9, 292
practice of 129–30
and Suzan-Lori Parks 120, 148–51
and *Sweat* 154
see also workshopping process in dramaturgy and development
DreamYard 257
Duchin, Jason 90
Duckworth, Jay 204
Dybbuk, A, or Between Two Worlds (Ansky) 114
Dykes to Watch Out For (Bechdel) 191

Eads, Robert 234
East Village, New York 5, 104, 108, 110
Eclipsed (Gurira) 6, 186, 187
Edelhart, Taylor 235–6
Edelstein, Barry 247, 249, 251
egalitarianism *see* inclusivity and egalitarianism
Elevator Repair Service 123
elitism and The Public 90, 155, 156, 158, 248
and Shakespeare in the Park 60
Elizabeth I (Queen of England) 83
Elm, Steve 231
Emerging Writers Group 121–2
Enemy of the People, An (Ibsen) 270
Epstein, Helen 18 n.5, 29, 37
Ergo (Lind) 21
Eustis, Jack 37, 291–2
Eustis, Oskar 33, 34–6, 37–8, 279, 287–95
and artistic directorship of The Public 3, 34, 61–2, 64–5, 138, 186–7, 217–18, 242–4, 282–5
and *Bloody Bloody Andrew Jackson* 230, 231–2
and Bridget Everett 165
and Broadway 170, 171–2, 186, 208–9
and class divisions in America 153
and commercial considerations 136, 225
and commissioning 110–11
and Covid-19 239
and David Henry Hwang 118–19

and Delacorte Theater 55–6, 60
and Diane Paulus 73
and dramaturgy 5, 12, 118, 124, 128–9, 215–17, 288–9, 292
and Emerging Writers Group 122
and female representation 192–3
and George C. Wolfe 32, 67, 119, 137–8, 185–6, 283
and *Hamilton* 203, 211–12
and *Here Lies Love* 175–6, 180–1, 182, 184
and Jeanine Tesori 116
and JoAnne Akalaitis 30, 282
and Joseph Papp 2, 8, 15–16, 36–7, 114, 140, 252
and *Julius Caesar* 82–4, 86–8, 90, 92
and Kwame Kwei-Armah 275
and Lear deBessonet 256, 258
and Mark Russell 123
and *Merchant of Venice* 77, 78–9
and Michael Friedman 227, 235
and the Mobile Unit 248–9, 252
and *Mother Courage* 66, 68–9, 71–2
and Public Works 260–1, 265, 266
and Richard Nelson 139–41, 145
and *Southern Comfort* 235–6
and Suzan-Lori Parks 119–21, 148
and *Sweat* 155, 157
and Tony Kushner 114–15
and *White Noise* 152–3
Everett, Bridget 159, 162–5
Evita (Lloyd Webber) 176

Fat Ham (Ijames) 134, 244 n.17
Father Comes Home from the Wars (Parks) 5–6, 147–8, 149
Ferguson, Jesse Tyler 46–8, 72
financial and commercial difficulties of The Public 22, 27, 34 n.18, 287
and *A Free Man of Color* 289
and 425 Lafayette Street 108–9
and *Julius Caesar* 83, 86
and post-9/11 economic downturn 32
and sponsorship 88–9
financial success of The Public 4, 223
and Broadway transfers 171–2
and *A Chorus Line* 22–3
and *Hamilton* 23, 225
Floyd, George 93, 99, 240, 291

FOB (Hwang) 117–18
for colored girls who have considered suicide/when the rainbow is enuf (Shange) 25, 126
Ford Foundation 231, 232
Foreman, Richard 123
Fortress of Solitude, The (Friedman) 172, 227
Fortune Society 253, 257, 259–60
425 Lafayette Street theaters *see* Astor Place Public Theater headquarters
Fox News and *Julius Caesar* 86
freedom of speech 87
Free for All: Joe Papp, The Public, and the Greatest Story Ever Told (Turan) 2, 17, 36
Free Man of Color, A (Guare) 67, 289, 291
Free Shakespeare in the Park *see* Shakespeare in the Park
free ticket ethos 44, 49, 244, 248
  and diversity 60, 62
  and economic considerations 37, 57–8
Friedman, Michael 227
  and *Bloody Bloody Andrew Jackson* 176, 230, 232–3
  and *The Fortress of Solitude* 172
  and town hall for *Southern Comfort* 235
Fucking A (Parks) 151
funding, sponsorship, and donors 37, 57, 135–6, 223–5
  and Broadway transfers 171–2
  and 425 Lafayette Street 108
Fun Home (Tesori and Kron) 6, 21, 37, 116–17, *189*, 190, 209, 215
  workshopping and development 194–9

"Gabriels, The" cycle (Nelson) 5, 139–45, *139*, 153
Gatz (Elevator Repair Service) 123
gay marriage and *Hair* 76
gender and sexuality
  and cabaret 161, 163
  and filmmaking 191–2
  and *Fun Home* 190, 194
  and *Southern Comfort* 234, 237–8

geopolitics 64–5, 67
Gershwin Theater 49
Gersten, Bernard 18, 23, 25, 107
Girl from the North Country (McPherson and Dylan) 186
global financial crisis 64
  and *A Free Man of Color* 67, 289
  and *Merchant of Venice* 79, 81–2
Gold, Sam 111, 190, 194, 195, 197–8
Gongora, Kristen 57
Gordon, John 259–60
Green, Jesse 183
Greif, Michael 77, 114
Griffin, Kathy 84
Griffiths, Heidi 111, 181
Guare, John 289, 291
Guirgis, Stephen Adly 260
Gurira, Danai 62
Gyllenhaal, Jake 186
Gypsy (Sondheim, Styne and Laurents) 177

Hackett, Mandy 172–3, 184, 199
Hair (Ragni and Rado) 20, *63*, 72–7, 127, 186, 290
  and history of The Public 108
Hamburg Dramaturgy (Lessing) 127–8
Hamilton (Miranda) 1, 6, 8, 37–8, 127, 133, *200*, 216–17
  and actors of color 61
  advertising posters 137
  and Broadway 171
  and costume design 205–6
  and Disney+ film version 204, 207–8
  and Dixon's Pence-directed speech 155–6
  genesis of 211–12
  and immigration 15, 199
  and The Public's finances 23, 224, 225
  set design for 201–5, 206–7
  and Tony Awards 190
Hamilton Mix Tape 212
Hamlet (Shakespeare) 19, 45–6, 64, 111
  Naked Hamlet production 21
Harjo, Suzan Shown 231
Hathaway, Anne 51
Head of Passes (McCraney) 133, 292
Heath, Shirley Brice 257, 263, 264

Hebrew Immigrant Aid Society
    (HIAS) 107
Helen Hayes Theater 16, 49
Henry VI (Shakespeare) 18
Hensley, Michelle 248, 249, 268
Hercules (Menken, Zippel, Diaz, and
    Horn) 74, 262–3
Here Lies Love (Byrne and Fatboy
    Slim) 6, *169*, *180*
  and Alex Timbers 176
  and Broadway 184–5
  casting 181–2
  and choreography 178–81
  concept album 175
  critical reception of 183–4
  difficulties with concept 176–7
  and Imelda Marcos 173–4
  and transferability 171, 173, 183–4,
    187
*Historical Sketch of the Old Astor
    Library Building 1895, 1980,
    2002, An* (Dalrymple) 105–6
Hollander, Jack 21
Holmes, Rupert 25
House Un-American Activities
    Committee 19
Hudson, Ruben Santiago 78
Hwang, David Henry 112, 117–19
  and dramaturgy 129

Ijames, James 134, 244 n.17
immigration and naturalization
    ceremony in the Delacorte
    Theater 14–15
inclusivity and egalitarianism 1–2, 4,
    112, 238, 287
  and artists of color 236–7
  and BIPOC Affinity Group 240–1
  and casting *Southern Comfort*
    234–5
  and commercial considerations 6,
    15–16, 37
  and cultural value of the Delacorte
    56, 58–60
  and culture 7, 61
  and 425 Lafayette Street 110
  and George C. Wolfe 30–1
  and the Mobile Unit 252
  and Shakespeare 17

  and women 192–3
Ingraham, Laura 87
interviews and oral history of The
    Public 2–3, 4, 9
In the Heights (Miranda) 201
Iraq, war and occupation 67, 140–1
Isherwood, Charles 237

Jackson, Andrew 229, 231
Jacobs, Jane 57, 60
Jacobs-Jenkins, Branden 122
Janney, Allison 45
jazzercise classes 256, 259
Jensen, Erik 239
Joe's Pub 6, 49, 144–5, 159, 162–4
  and Diane Paulus 73
  founding of 31–2
Johnson, Jeh 14
Jones, Candis C. 125–6, 127, 193
Jones, Chris 228
Jones, Garlia Cornelia 268
Jones, James Earl 42, 78, 236
Jones, Ron C. 249
Jordan, Julia 192
Joseph Papp: An American Life
    (Epstein) 18 n.5, 37
Julia, Raúl 25
Julius Caesar (Shakespeare) 50, 85, 137
  and current political relevance 89–91
  and right-wing reaction 85–8
  and Trump 82–5, 92

Kail, Tommy 201, 202–3, 207, 208,
    212, 214
Kaufman, Moisés 66
Kiki and Herb cabaret act 160
Kimmelman, Michael 107
Kircher, Andrew 124
Kline, Kevin 16, 18–19, 28, 136
  and George C. Wolfe 31
  and *Mother Courage* 70
  and *The Pirates of Penzance* 25
Korins, David 6, 201–4, 207
Kron, Lisa 128–9, 192
  and *Fun Home* 194–5, 196, 198,
    199
  and Tony Awards 190, 193
Kushner, Tony 31, 32, 112, 113–14, 293
  and dramaturgy 129

INDEX

and Jeanine Tesori 116
and *Mother Courage* 67–71
Kwei-Armah, Kwame 243, 269–75,
  269, 281

Lampert, Jo 115
Lapine, James 28
Lark, The 125–6
Latin History for Morons
  (Leguizamo) 186
Leach, Wilfred 25
leadership and The Public 8, 27, 28–9,
  281–2, 288
  and BIPOC Affinity Group 240–1
  and egalitarian ethos 37, 112
  and Oskar Eustis 36, 243–4, 283–6
League of Professional Theatre
  Women 192
Lee, Ming Cho 14, 108
left-liberal socialist ethos 8, 16, 27, 78
  and audience for *Julius Caesar*
    84–5, 86
  and commercial considerations
    60, 135
  and diversity 60
  and free entry to Delacorte 57–8
  and *Mother Courage* 66–7
  and self-examination 222
Leon, Kenny 62, 93–100, 93
LeRoy, Warner 24
Lessing, Gotthold Ephraim 127–8
LGBTQ+
  and *Fun Home* 194, 199, 209
  and *Southern Comfort* 234
lighting design 43, 50, 143
  and *Hamilton* 202
Lincoln, Abraham 104
Lincoln Center 21
Lindsay, John 27
Linklater, Hamish 46, 78
Llana, Jose 179, 182, 183
Lloyd, Phillida 62
LuEsther Hall 6, 108, 134
  and *Here Lies Love* 170
Lukács, Georg 150
Lupton, Ellen 136

Mabou Mines 3, 123, 174, 282
Macbeth (Shakespeare) 66, 216

MacDermot, Galt 73–4
MacKaye, Percy 258, 259, 267
MacKinnon, Lucy 268
Madison Square Garden 107
Malcolm, Janet 129
Malone, Beth 197
Man and Superman (Shaw) 284
Mansour, Mona 122
Manus, Mara 32, 135
Marcos, Ferdinand 170, 173
Marcos, Imelda 170, 173–4, 176,
  179, 183
marketing and branding of The
  Public 136–8
Martinson Theater 108, 134
Marx, Bob 28–9
Marxist ethos 170, 184, 223, 243,
  283, 284
M. Butterfly (Hwang) 118
McCarter, Jeremy 211–12
McGregor, Patricia 253
McTeer, Janet 62
Mead, Rebecca 128
Measure for Measure (Shakespeare)
  18, 249
Mellman, Kenny 160
Melrose, Rob 87
Merchant of Venice, The (Shakespeare)
  14, 42, 77–82, 186
Merry Wives (Bioh) 54, 62
Mertz, LuEsther 23, 27, 135, 224
Midsummer Night's Dream, A
  (Shakespeare) 210–18, 254
  see also Donkey Show, The (Paulus
    and Weiner)
Miles, Ruthie Ann 178, 179, *180*,
  181, 183
Miller, D. Scot 125
Miranda, Lin-Manuel 19, 61, 200, 208,
  210–18, *210*
Mobile Unit 7, 8, 245, 246, 265
  Summer of Joy! program 253–5
  and *Sweat* 252–3
  and touring Shakespeare 249–
    52, 271–2
mobility model of theater and touring
  Shakespeare 247–8
Moore, Jack 122, 126
Moriarty, Kevin 264

Morisseau, Dominique 122
Moses, Robert 19–20, 230
Mother Courage and Her Children
  (Brecht) 14, 46, 65, 66–72
Motherfucker with the Hat, The
  (Guirgis) 260
Mother of the Maid (Anderson) 111
Much Ado About Nothing
  (Shakespeare) 62, 93–100
  and all-Black casting 95
  and ducks on stage 52, 98
musicals 111, 114–17
  and dramaturgy 128
  and Public Works Shakespeare
    pageants 262
  *see also Bloody Bloody Andrew
    Jackson* (Friedman and Timbers);
    Hair (Ragni and Rado); *Hamilton*
    (Miranda); *Here Lies Love* (Byrne
    and Fatboy Slim)
Music Lesson, The (Yamauchi) 118

Naked Hamlet 21
National Theatre, London 265–
  6, 294–5
National Theatre Story, The
  (Rosenthal) 8
Native Americans, racism and *Bloody
  Bloody* 229, 230–1, 232–3, 236
Native Theater Initiative 231, 232
Nelson, Richard 5, 139–45, 239,
  242
Neruda, Pablo 247
New Jerusalem (Jenkins) 117
Newman Theater 49, 108, *131*,
  132, 136
new writing, Public commitment to
  5–6, 23, 110–11, 112–13, 121–3
  and *Cullud Wattah* 126
  and *Hair* 20–1
  and Suzan-Lori Parks 119–20
  and Under the Radar 8
New York City
  and community engagement 257–60
  and cultural value of the
    Delacorte 56–7
  demographics of 61, 62
  and social value of Lafayette Street
    theatres 109–10

New York Daily News 79
New York Magazine profile of JoAnne
  Akalaitis 29, 30
New York Public Library 20, 107
New York Shakespeare Festival 18, 26,
  42, 246, 268
  and female representation 192
  and 425 Lafayette Street 107–8
  and Robert Moses 19–20
  see also Shakespeare in the Park
New York Times
  and *Caliban by the Yellow Sands* 258
  interview with Oskar Eustis 38
  on *Julius Caesar* 83, 87–8
  and resignation of George
    C. Wolfe 32–3
  review of *Bloody Bloody Andrew
    Jackson* 228
  review of *Hair* 76
  review of *The Bacchae* 43–4
Nichols, Mike 28, 68
9/11 terrorist attacks 64, 135
nonprofit model and commercial
  realities 171–2, 184, 185–6, 226
  and Broadway transfers 224–5
Norman, Marsha 192
Norris, Rufus 265–6
Nottage, Lynn 6, 153–8, 222
  see also Sweat (Nottage)

Obama, Barack 64, 191, 199
O'Hare, Jeanie 126
O'Neill Theater 117
On the Town (Bernstein, Comden, and
  Green) 171, 182
Oslo (Rogers) 194
Othello (Shakespeare) 69
O'Toole, Annette 237–8
outdoor theater 42, 43–8, 49–51

Pacino, Al 5, 14, 42, 77, 79–80, 81
Padrón, Jacob 127
pandemic *see* Covid-19
Papp, Anthony, death of 37
Papp, Gail 18, 28, 30, 31, 32, 33
  and female representation 192
Papp, Joseph 1, *17*
  and actors of color 60–1, 236
  and commercial considerations 135

and David Henry Hwang 118
ethos and influence of 13, 15–17, 24–5, 37, 185, 244, 282
and Gordon Davis 24
and his successors 3
and history of The Public 5, 17–18, 21–2, 26–30, 107–8, 246–7
and *Merchant of Venice* 78, 79
and New York Shakespeare Festival 42
and Robert Moses 19–20
and Tony Kushner 114
Parks, Suzan-Lori 5–6, 31, 112, 119–21, 146–53
Parson, Annie-B 178–81, 185
Passing Strange (Stew and Rodewald) 186, 201
Paulus, Diane 5, 73–7
Pence, Mike 155–6
Pericles (Shakespeare) 266
Peter and the Starcatcher (Elice) 176
Pirates of Penzance, The (Gilbert and Sullivan) 19, 25
Plenty (Hare) 133
Plunkett, Maryann 143
Poetics, The (Aristotle) 12, 13
political activism and protest 16–18, 19, 74
political and social divisions in America 4–5, 238–9, 244, 258, 293
and Black Lives Matter 99–100
and class 6, 153
and George Floyd murder 7
and *Julius Caesar* 85–7, 88, 90–1
and the Mobile Unit 254
and race 149, 152
and *Sweat* 154–7
see also LGBTQ+; Native Americans, racism and *Bloody Bloody*
political comment and satire 55
and *Bloody Bloody Andrew Jackson* 229
and *A Bright Room Called Day* 113
and cabaret 160–1, 163
and "The Gabriels" 144–5
and *Julius Caesar* 82–6, 90–1
Power, Samantha 58–9, 60, 187
presidential election 2016 5, 140, 144–5

Privacy (Graham and Rourke) 92, 133
Private Life of the Master Race, The (Brecht) 113
Psychoanalysis: The Impossible Profession (Malcolm) 129
Public Lab 124, 195–8, 199
Public Shakespeare Initiative 8
Public Works 7, 8, 256–64, 265–6, 267–8, 273–4, 286, 290
and national affiliates 264
Public Works Playbook, The (deBessonet and Woolery) 263
Pulitzer Prize 8, 119, 134, 153, 154, 194, 244 n.17

Rabe, Lily 42, 79–80
raccoons and the Delacorte 44, 45–6, 52, 98
racial inequalities, Black Lives Matter and Covid 240–3
racism 7, 125, 154, 238–9, 244
accusations of on social media 222
and *Bloody Bloody Andrew Jackson* 228, 229, 230–1
and capitalism 290
and George Floyd murder 240
and *New Jerusalem* "yellowface" protests 117
see also Black, Indigenous & People of Color (BIPOC) Affinity Group; Black Lives Matter
Radcliffe, Daniel 133
Rado, Jim 74
Rashad, Phylicia 133
Reading, Pennsylvania, and *Sweat* 154–5, 157
realism in *White Noise* 150–1
Reeve, Christopher 16
Rhinebeck, New York 139
Ricamora, Conrad 181, 182
Richard II (Shakespeare) 83
Richard III (Shakespeare) 18, 62, 249
Rigg, Adam 126
right-wing reaction to *Julius Caesar* 85–7, 88, 90
Rikers Island Prison 250–1
Romeo and Juliet (Shakespeare) 247, 250–1
Rubin, Ben 104

Russell, Arthur 174
Russell, Mark 122–4

Sanders, Jay O. 45, 51–2, 145
"Say Their Names" project 268
Scher, Paula 136–8
Schumann, Peter 256
Scott, George C. 42, 47, 78
Sea Wall/A Life (Stephens and Payne) 186
Seller, Jeffrey 201, 207, 214
Shakespeare and Company, and right-wing reaction to *Julius Caesar* 86–7
Shakespeare in a Divided America (Shapiro) 90
Shakespeare in the Park 5, 19–20, 37, 42, 48–9, 248–9
　as an American national tradition 91
　and *The Comedy of Errors* 46–8
　and contemporary issues 65, 66
　and free tickets and funding 57–8
　and non-Shakespearean plays 54
　see also New York Shakespeare Festival
Shakespeare's plays 64–5
　and diversity 62
　and founding of The Public Theater 17–18
　and Kwame Kwei-Armah 271–2
　and the Mobile Unit 7, 249–52
　see also plays by title
Shange, Ntozake 25
Shapiro, James 54, 83, 90
Shaw, George Bernard 284
Sheaffer, Laura 85–6
Sheik, Kacie 77
Sherman, Rebecca 47
Shiva Theater 108, 126, 134, 147, 280
slavery 232–3
　and *Father Comes Home from the Wars* 147–8
　and *White Noise* 149–50, 151, 153
social justice 15, 37, 74, 247
social media 64, 222
　and controversy 226
　and *Julius Caesar* 83, 87, 90, 91–2
Soft Power (Hwang and Tesori) 117, 118–19

Sontag, Susan 147
Southern Comfort (Collins) 7, 226
　and casting controversy 234–7
Stage Lives of Animals, The: Zoöesis and Performance (Chaudhuri) 46
Stan's Cafe 123
star actors in The Public's program 80, 111
star-making and The Public 18–19, 25, 65, 164
　and Joe's Pub 163
Steinem, Gloria 165
Sternberg, Ruth 49, 50
　and *Hair* 75–6
　and *Hamilton* 201
　and *Mother Courage* 71
Stoll, Corey 89
Streep, Meryl 5, 18, 28, 55, 136
　and *Mother Courage* 14, 65, 68–72
Stuhlbarg, Michael 46
Suffs (Taub) 193
Sullivan, Daniel 5, 46, 77, 79–81
Swados, Elizabeth 25
Sweat (Nottage) 6, 8, 91, 153–5, 157–8, 193–4
　and the Mobile Unit 252–3

Taccone, Tony 35, 67–8, 114, 186
Talking Heads 174, 178
Taming of the Shrew, The (Shakespeare) 45, 62
Taub, Shaina 262, 272
Taylor, Brianna 99
Tazewell, Paul 6, 205–6
Teenage Mutant Ninja Turtles 151
Tempest, The (Shakespeare) 45, 257–8, 259, 264
Ten Thousand Things theater company 248
Tesori, Jeanine 21, 46, 53, 112, 115–17
　and *Fun Home* 194–5, 196–7, 198, 199
　and *Mother Courage* 71
　and Tony Awards 190, 193
Thake, Shanta 112, 244
Thaler, Jordan 80, 111, 181, 237
theater experience 13, 59, 132–5
　and Delacorte Theater 42–6
　and *Here Lies Love* 178, 183

Theater of War (documentary film) (Walter) 72
Thompson, John Douglas 48, 51, 89
Threepenny Opera, The (Brecht and Weill) 113
tickets and revenue 223–4
  see also free ticket ethos
Timbers, Alex 7
  and *Bloody Bloody Andrew Jackson* 227, 229–30
  and *Here Lies Love* 175–6, 177–81, 184
Tiny Beautiful Things (Vardolos) 292
Tipton, Jennifer 43, 143
'Tis Pity She's a Whore (Ford) 30
Tony Awards
  and *Angels in America* 67
  and *Bloody Bloody Andrew Jackson* 228
  and *Caroline, or Change* 115
  and *A Chorus Line* 22, 280
  and Daniel Sullivan 77
  and female representation 193–4
  and *Fun Home* 117, 190–1
  and George C. Wolfe 3, 31, 185, 282
  and *Hair* 76
Topdog/Underdog (Parks) 151
Toro, Tom 53–4
transgender actors/identity and *Southern Comfort* 234–5, 236, 237
Travers, Peter 228
Travolta, John 25
Trelawny of the "Wells" (Pinero) 18
Trump, Donald 54–5, 64, 155, 191, 233, 293
  and Dixon's Pence-directed speech 156
  and *Julius Caesar* 82–6, 92
Turan, Kenneth 2, 36
Twelfth Night (Shakespeare) 50–1, 261, 262, 272
25 Years at The Public, A Love Story (Scher) 136
Two Gentlemen of Verona (Shakespeare) 23

Ukraine, Russian invasion of 58–9
Under the Greenwood Tree (documentary) 267
Under the Radar 8, 122–4

Vaughan, Gladys 78
Vauxhall Gardens 106
Vietnam War 73, 77
Violet (Tesori and Crawley) 116

Walken, Christopher 69–70
Walter, John 72
Wang, Meiyin 123
Watch Me Work 120–1
Waterston, Sam 17, 21, 36, 38, 247
Watts, Reggie 123
We are One Public fundraiser and BIPOC Affinity Group 240
weather and outdoor theater 47–8, 52
Weisz, Rachel 133
Well (Kron) 186
Werle, Donyale 227
"We See You, White American Theater" 244
White Noise (Parks) 5, *146*, 147, 148–53
white supremacy and the theater 238, 240, 244
Whoriskey, Kate 154, 155
Willingham, Patrick 22–3, 27, 135
Winter's Tale, The (Shakespeare) 77, 254
Wolfe, George C. 3–4, 17
  and artistic directorship of The Public 30–4, 62, 135, 282, 283
  and Broadway 171, 185–6
  and *Caroline, or Change* 114
  and David Henry Hwang 118
  and Jeanine Tesori 115, 116
  and Joe's Pub 159
  and *Mother Courage* 67–8, 70
  and *On the Town* 171, 182
  and Paula Scher 136–8
  and Suzan-Lori Parks 119
women in film and theater 191–3
Women of a Certain Age (Nelson) 144
Woolery, Laurie 7, 263, 266, 267–8
workshopping process in dramaturgy and development 111, 124, 147, 186, 211
  and *Cullud Wattah* 126–7
  and *Fun Home* 194–9
  and *Hamilton* 213
  and *Here Lies Love* 177–8, 181–2
Woyzeck (Büchner) 30

Yazzi, Rhiana 231
Ybarra, Stephanie 240, 251–2, 255, 285
Yellow Face (Hwang) 119
Yew, Chay 8
Young, Jennifer 268

Young Vic, London 269, 271, 274

Zaks, Jerry 28
Zinn, David 195
Zoom-based theater 5, 239